TOP 10

OF EVERYTHING

2005

TOP 10

OF EVERYTHING
2005
RUSSELL ASH

DK

Contents

LONDON, NEW YORK, MUNICH, MELBOURNE AND DELHI

A PENGUIN COMPANY

Senior Editor Becky Alexander
U.S. Editor Christine Heilmann
Senior Art Editor Mark Cavanagh
Production Controller Heather Hughes

Managing Editor Adèle Hayward
Managing Art Editor Karen Self
Category Publisher Stephanie Jackson

Produced for Dorling Kindersley by
The Bridgewater Book Company,
The Old Candlemakers, West Street,
Lewes, East Sussex BN7 2NZ

Editor Howard Spencer
Designer Lisa McCormick
Picture Research Rachael Swann

Author's Project Manager Aylla Macphail
Research Assistant Louise Reip

First American Edition 2004

Published in the United States by
DK Publishing, Inc.
375 Hudson Street
New York, New York 10014

2 4 6 8 10 9 7 5 3 1

Copyright © 2004 Dorling Kindersley Limited
Text copyright © 2004 Russell Ash

A Cataloging-in-Publication record for this book is
available from the Library of Congress

ISBN 07566 0519 9

Reproduction by Colourscan, Singapore
Printed and bound by GGP Media GmbH, Germany

See our complete catalogue at
www.dk.com

Contents

Introduction

SWEET SIXTEEN

THIS IS THE 16th annual edition of *The Top 10 of Everything*. During its lifetime, the world has undergone inexorable change, and I have monitored many of these developments, both important and trivial, by presenting a diverse range of lists that reflect everything from the growth of the Internet and the first films to make $1 billion to the higher-than-ever scores achieved in many sports, and the burgeoning of the DVD home entertainment format.

A WORLD OF LISTS

We are constantly bombarded with lists. Increasingly, newspapers and TV shows present rankings based on market research and polls, lists of safest cars, favorite songs, bestsellers, award-winners, crime rates, top schools, and so on. With the ever-faster pace of the Information Age, these and the lists in *The Top 10 of Everything* offer an overview of what might otherwise be a daunting mass of facts and figures.

LIST LIMITS

The *Top 10 of Everything* contains only definitive lists. Although there are some "bests," these are generally bestsellers (most film Top 10s, for example, are based on world box office income), and "worsts" (such events as crimes and disasters), so all can be quantified. This criterion imposes certain limitations: the top prices paid for works of art and collectibles are based on auction sales, and though even higher prices may occasionally have been paid privately for such things as paintings and rare cars, they are seldom made public. Certain sports seasons inconveniently fail to coincide with our deadline, and there are areas where one must treat data circumspectly: as work was in progress, press reports of an explosion in North Korea initially claimed over 3,000 dead; within days this had been revised to 161— no less tragic, but a graphic indicator of how divergent some figures can be.

INFORMATION SOURCES

My numerous sources include "official" and government departments, commercial and research organizations, and especially private individuals around the world who are specialists in everything from snakes to skyscrapers, and who have been generous enough to share with me the results of their research. My grateful thanks to them all.

KEEP IN CONTACT

Check out the book and contact me with any comments, corrections, or ideas for new lists via *The Top 10 of Everything* website:
http://www.top10ofeverything.com

Other Dorling Kindersley books by Russell Ash:
The Factastic Book of 1,001 Lists
The Factastic Book of Comparisons
Great Wonders of the World
The Top 10 of Sports (with Ian Morrison)
The Top 10 of Film

SPECIAL FEATURES

• Over 700 lists covering everything on Earth—and beyond

• Completely updated with many innovative lists, from the most expensive guitars to the oldest theaters and highest-earning film trilogies

• Top 10 lists that track changes over time, from the richest people in the world to the most common first names and the tallest buildings

• "The First To..." features reveal some of the individuals who were the first in an area of endeavor—including the first woman graduate, the first to sell a million records, and the first boxers to use gloves.

THE UNIVERSE
& THE EARTH

Stars & Galaxies

TOP 10 GALAXIES CLOSEST TO EARTH

	GALAXY	DISCOVERED	DIAMETER*	APPROX. DISTANCE*
1	Sagittarius Dwarf	1994	10	82
2	Large Magellanic Cloud	Prehist.	30	160
3	Small Magellanic Cloud	Prehist.	16	190
4	= Draco Dwarf	1954	3	205
	= Ursa Minor Dwarf	1954	2	205
6	Sculptor Dwarf	1937	3	254
7	Sextans Dwarf	1990	4	258
8	Carina Dwarf	1977	2	330
9	Fornax Dwarf	1938	6	450
10	Leo II	1950	3	660

* 1,000 light-years

Source: Peter Bond, Royal Astronomical Society

These, and other galaxies, are members of the so-called "Local Group," although with vast distances such as these, "local" is clearly a relative term.

TOP 10 STARS CLOSEST TO EARTH*

	STAR	LIGHT-YEARS	MILES (MILLIONS)	KM (MILLIONS)
1	Proxima Centauri	4.22	24,792,500	39,923,310
2	Alpha Centauri	4.39	25,791,250	41,531,595
3	Barnard's Star	5.94	34,897,500	56,195,370
4	Wolf 359	7.78	45,707,500	73,602,690
5	Lalande 21185	8.31	48,821,250	78,616,755
6	Sirius	8.60	50,525,000	81,360,300
7	Luyten 726-8	8.72	51,230,000	82,495,560
8	Ross 154	9.69	56,928,750	91,672,245
9	Ross 248	10.32	60,630,000	97,632,360
10	Epsilon Eridani	10.49	61,628,750	99,240,645

* Excluding the Sun

Source: Peter Bond, Royal Astronomical Society

A spaceship traveling at 25,000 mph (40,000 km/h)—which is faster than any human has yet reached in space—would take more than 113,200 years to reach Earth's closest stellar neighbor, Proxima Centauri. While the closest stars in this list lie just over four light-years away from Earth, others within the Milky Way lie at a distance of 2,500 light-years.

TOP 10 MOST COMMON ELEMENTS IN THE SUN

	ELEMENT	PARTS PER MILLION*
1	Hydrogen	750,000
2	Helium	230,000
3	Oxygen	9,000
4	Carbon	3,000
5	= Iron	1,000
	= Neon	1,000
	= Nitrogen	1,000
8	Silicon	900
9	Magnesium	700
10	Sulfur	400

* mg per kg

Helium was discovered in the Sun before it was detected on Earth, its name deriving from *helios*, the Greek word for Sun. More than 70 elements have been detected in the Sun, the most common of which correspond closely to those found in the universe as a whole, with some variations in ratios—including a greater proportion of the principal element, hydrogen. The atoms of hydrogen in the universe outnumber those of all the other elements combined.

THE 10 TYPES OF STARS

	TYPE	SPECTRUM	MAXIMUM SURFACE TEMPERATURE (°F)
1	W	Bright lines	144,000
2	O	Bright and dark lines	72,000
3	B	Bluish-white	45,000
4	A	White	18,000
5	F	White/slightly yellow	13,500
6	G	Yellowish	11,000
7	K	Orange	9,000
8	M	Orange-red	6,100
9	= C (formerly R and N)	Reddish	4,700
	= S	Red	4,700

Stars are classified by type according to their spectra, the colors in which they appear when viewed with a spectroscope. These vary according to the star's surface temperature. A letter is assigned to each—although there are some variations, Type C sometimes being divided into R and N. One mnemonic for remembering the sequence takes the initial letters of the words "Wow! O Be A Fine Girl Kiss Me Right Now Sweetie."

▶ **Bode's well**
Discovered in 1774 by German astronomer Johann Elert Bode (who also suggested the name of the planet Uranus), the classic spiral Bode's Galaxy (M81) can be seen with relatively small telescopes.

GALACTIC PIONEER

IT WAS NOT UNTIL 1923 that American astronomer Edwin Hubble used photographs taken by the 100-inch telescope at Mount Wilson Observatory to prove that the universe extends far beyond the Milky Way. He observed that the magnitude of the Cepheid variable star in the Andromeda Galaxy (M31) indicated that it was in an entirely separate galaxy, at a distance of 2.2 million light-years. The idea that our own galaxy is only one of many had been suggested by earlier observers, but Hubble was the first to demonstrate it as fact.

THE FIRST TO...

10

BRIGHTEST STARS*

AR	CONSTELLATION	DISTANCE#	APPARENT MAGNITUDE
ius	Canis Major	8.65	−1.46
nopus	Carina	313	−0.62
pha Centauri	Centaurus	4.35	−0.27
cturus	Boötes	36	−0.04
ga	Lyra	25	+0.03
pella	Auriga	42	+0.08
gel	Orion	773	+0.18
ocyon	Canis Minor	11.4	+0.38
chernar	Eridanus	144	+0.46
eta Centauri	Centaurus	525	+0.61

luding the Sun

n Earth in light-years

e: Peter Bond, Royal Astronomical Society

Top 10 is based on apparent visual magnitude as viewed from Earth—
wer the number, the brighter the star. At its brightest, the variable star
geuse would make the Top 10, but its average magnitude disqualifies it.

TOP 10 BRIGHTEST GALAXIES

	GALAXY NAME/NUMBER	DISTANCE*	APPARENT MAGNITUDE
1	Large Magellanic Cloud	0.17	0.91
2	Small Magellanic Cloud	0.21	2.70
3	Andromeda Galaxy (NGC 224, M31)	2.6	4.36
4	Triangulum Galaxy (NGC 598, M33)	2.8	6.27
5	Centaurus Galaxy (NGC 5128)	12.0	7.84
6	Bode's Galaxy (NGC 3031, M81)	12.0	7.89
7	Silver Coin Galaxy (NGC 253)	8.5	8.04
8	Southern Pinwheel Galaxy (NGC 5236, M83)	15.0	8.20
9	Pinwheel Galaxy (NGC 5457, M101)	24.0	8.31
10	Cigar Galaxy (NGC 55)	4.9	8.42

* From Earth in light-years

Messier (M) numbers are named after French astronomer Charles Messier
(1730–1817), who in 1781 compiled the first catalog of galaxies, nebulae, and
star clusters. From 1888, these were replaced by New General Catalog (NGC)
numbers. As well as the official names that have been assigned to them, galaxies
discovered prior to the change are identified by both M and NGC numbers.

Orbiting the Sun

TOP 10 LARGEST BODIES IN THE SOLAR SYSTEM

BODY	MAXIMUM DIAMETER (MILES)	(KM)
1 Sun	865,036	1,392,140
2 Jupiter	88,846	142,984
3 Saturn	74,898	120,536
4 Uranus	31,763	51,118
5 Neptune	30,778	49,532
6 Earth	7,926	12,756
7 Venus	7,520	12,103
8 Mars	4,222	6,794
9 Ganymede	3,274	5,269
10 Titan	3,200	5,150

Most of the planets are visible with the naked eye and have been observed since ancient times. The exceptions are Uranus, discovered on March 13, 1781 by British astronomer William Herschel; Neptune, found by German astronomer Johann Galle on September 23, 1846; and, outside the Top 10, Pluto, located using photographic techniques by American astronomer Clyde Tombaugh, who announced his discovery on March 13, 1930.

TOP 10 MOST MASSIVE BODIES IN THE SOLAR SYSTEM*

BODY	MASS#
1 Sun	332,830.000
2 Jupiter	317.828
3 Saturn	95.161
4 Neptune	17.148
5 Uranus	14.536
6 Earth	1.000
7 Venus	0.815
8 Mars	0.10745
9 Mercury	0.05527
10 Pluto	0.0022

* Excluding satellites

Compared with Earth = 1; the mass of Earth is approximately 81,000,000,000,000 tons

The mass of a body—the amount of material it contains—determines its gravitational attraction: Jupiter's high mass means that an object on it would weigh over 144,000 times as much as the same object on Pluto, which has a low mass.

TOP 10 MOST FREQUENTLY SEEN COMETS

COMET	YEARS BETWEEN APPEARANCES
1 Encke	3.302
2 Grigg-Skjellerup	4.908
3 Honda-Mrkós-Pajdusáková	5.210
4 Tempel 2	5.259
5 Neujmin 2	5.437
6 Brorsen	5.463
7 Tuttle-Giacobini-Kresák	5.489
8 Tempel-L. Swift	5.681
9 Tempel 1	5.982
10 Pons-Winnecke	6.125

The comets in the Top 10 and several others return with regularity (although with some notable variations), while others may not be seen again for many thousands of years. The most frequent visitor, Encke's Comet, is named after German astronomer Johann Franz Encke (1791–1865), who in 1818 calculated the period of its elliptical orbit. It is becoming extremely faint: comets often disappear through disintegration or changes in their orbits.

TOP 10 COMETS COMING CLOSEST TO EARTH

COMET	DATE*	(AU)#	DISTANCE (MILES)	(KM)
1 Comet of 1491	Feb. 20, 1491	0.0094	873,784	1,406,220
2 Lexell	July 1, 1770	0.0151	1,403,633	2,258,928
3 Tempel-Tuttle	Oct. 26, 1366	0.0229	2,128,688	3,425,791
4 IRAS-Araki-Alcock	May 11, 1983	0.0313	2,909,516	4,682,413
5 Halley	Apr. 10, 837	0.0334	3,104,724	4,996,569
6 Biela	Dec. 9, 1805	0.0366	3,402,182	5,475,282
7 Grischow	Feb. 8, 1743	0.0390	3,625,276	5,834,317
8 Pons-Winnecke	June 26, 1927	0.0394	3,662,458	5,894,156
9 Comet of 1014	Feb. 24, 1014	0.0407	3,783,301	6,088,633
10 La Hire	Apr. 20, 1702	0.0437	4,062,168	6,537,427

* Of closest approach to Earth

Astronomical Units: one AU = mean distance from Earth to the Sun (92,955,793 miles/149,597,870 km)

Since comets are composed of water ice and dust particles, the impact of a comet with Earth poses less potential danger than that of an asteroid, a large solid rock structure. One theory, however, suggests that it was just such a cometary collision 65 million years ago that wiped out the dinosaurs.

TOP 10 BODIES* FARTHEST FROM THE SUN

BODY	AVERAGE DISTANCE FROM THE SUN (MILES)	(KM)
1 Pluto	3,675,000,000	5,914,000,000
2 Neptune	2,794,000,000	4,497,000,000
3 Uranus	1,784,000,000	2,871,000,000
4 Chiron	1,740,000,000	2,800,000,000
5 Saturn	887,000,000	1,427,000,000
6 Jupiter	483,600,000	778,300,000
7 Mars	141,600,000	227,900,000
8 Earth	92,955,793	149,597,870
9 Venus	67,200,000	108,200,000
10 Mercury	36,000,000	57,900,000

* In the Solar System, excluding satellites and asteroids

Chiron, a "mystery object" that may be either a comet (Kowal-Meech-Belton) or an asteroid (Asteroid 2060), was discovered on November 1, 1977 by American astronomer Charles Kowal. It measures 124–186 miles (200–300 km) in diameter and orbits between Saturn and Uranus. "Planet X" (the name proposed by Percival Lowell; "Persephone" has also been suggested) is believed by some to orbit beyond Pluto, and would thus be the farthest planet from the Sun and Earth.

LARGEST
PLANETARY MOONS

MOON	PLANET	DIAMETER (MILES)	(KM)
Ganymede	Jupiter	3,274	5,269

Discovered by Galileo on January 11, 1610, Ganymede—one of Jupiter's 31 known satellites* and the largest moon in the solar system—is thought to have a surface of ice about 60 miles (100 km) thick. The 1979 *Voyager 1* and 2 space probes failed to detect evidence of an atmosphere. Launched in 1989, NASA's aptly named *Galileo* probe reached Ganymede in June 1996.

MOON	PLANET	DIAMETER (MILES)	(KM)
Titan	Saturn	3,200	5,150

Titan, the largest of Saturn's 30 confirmed moons, is actually larger than two of the planets in the solar system, Mercury and Pluto. It was discovered by Dutch astronomer Christiaan Huygens in 1655. We have no idea what its surface looks like because it has a dense atmosphere containing nitrogen, methane, and other gases that shroud its surface—not unlike that of Earth 4 billion years ago—but data sent back by *Voyager 1* during 1980 and recent radio telescope observations suggest that it may have ethane "oceans" and "continents" of ice or other solid matter. Recent research has suggested that gases were deposited there by impacting comets.

MOON	PLANET	DIAMETER (MILES)	(KM)
Callisto	Jupiter	2,983	4,800

Possessing a composition similar to Ganymede's, Callisto is heavily pitted with craters, perhaps more so than any other body in the Solar System.

MOON	PLANET	DIAMETER (MILES)	(KM)
Io	Jupiter	2,256	3,630

Most of what we know about Io was reported back by the 1979 *Voyager 1* probe, which revealed a crust of solid sulfur with massive volcanic eruptions in progress, hurling sulfurous material 185 miles (300 km) into space.

MOON	PLANET	DIAMETER (MILES)	(KM)
Moon	Earth	2,159	3,475

Our own satellite, a quarter of the size of Earth, is the fifth-largest moon in the Solar System and, to date, the only one to have been explored by humans.

MOON	PLANET	DIAMETER (MILES)	(KM)
Europa	Jupiter	1,950	3,138

Although Europa's ice-covered surface is apparently smooth and crater-free, it is covered with mysterious black lines, some of them 40 miles (65 km) wide and resembling canals.

MOON	PLANET	DIAMETER (MILES)	(KM)
7 Triton	Neptune	1,680	2,704

Discovered on October 10, 1846 by British brewer and amateur astronomer William Lassell, 17 days after German astronomer Johann Galle discovered Neptune itself, Triton is the only known satellite in the Solar System that revolves around its planet in the opposite direction of the planet's rotation. It is getting progressively closer to Neptune, and scientists think that in several million years the force of the planet's gravity may scatter it into a form like the rings of Saturn. Information sent back by *Voyager 2* in August 1989 revealed that Triton has an atmosphere composed largely of nitrogen and methane and a surface partly covered with nitrogen and methane ice glaciers. The ice layer shifts from one pole to the other and back again once every 165 years, the length of time it takes for Neptune to orbit the Sun.

MOON	PLANET	DIAMETER (MILES)	(KM)
8 Titania	Uranus	980	1,578

The largest of Uranus's seven moons, Titania was discovered by William Herschel (who had discovered the planet six years earlier) in 1787 and has a snowball-like surface of ice. Its size estimate was revised by data from *Voyager 2*.

MOON	PLANET	DIAMETER (MILES)	(KM)
9 Rhea	Saturn	949	1,528

Saturn's second-largest moon was discovered by 17th-century Italian-born French astronomer Jean-Dominique (formerly Giovanni) Cassini. *Voyager 1*, which flew past Rhea in November 1980, confirmed that its icy surface is pitted with craters, one of them 140 miles (225 km) in diameter.

MOON	PLANET	DIAMETER (MILES)	(KM)
10 Oberon	Uranus	946	1,523

Oberon was discovered by Herschel and given the name of the fairy-king husband of Queen Titania, both characters in Shakespeare's *A Midsummer Night's Dream*. Information from *Voyager 2* moved Oberon from 9th to 10th place in this list.

* *To May 2003*

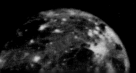

▶ **By Jupiter!**
Four of the largest moons in the Solar System, Io, Europa, Ganymede, and Callisto, are satellites of Jupiter, the largest planet.

Astronauts & Cosmonauts

 OLDEST ASTRONAUTS AND COSMONAUTS*

ASTRONAUT OR COSMONAUT[#]	BORN	LAST FLIGHT	AGE (YR)	(MTHS)	(DAYS)
1 John H. Glenn	July 18, 1921	Nov. 6, 1998	77	3	19
2 F. Story Musgrave	Aug. 19, 1935	Dec. 7, 1996	61	3	19
3 Dennis Tito	Aug. 8, 1940	May 6, 2001	60	8	21
4 Vance D. Brand	May 9, 1931	Dec. 11, 1990	59	7	2
5 Jean-Loup Chrétien (France)	Aug. 30, 1938	Oct. 6, 1997	59	1	7
6 Valey V. Ryumin (Russia)	Aug. 16, 1939	June 12, 1998	58	9	27
7 Karl G. Henize	Oct. 17, 1926	Aug. 6, 1985	58	9	20
8 Roger K. Crouch	Sept. 12, 1940	July 17, 1997	56	10	5
9 William E. Thornton	Apr. 14, 1929	May 6, 1985	56	0	22
10 Claude Nicollier (Switzerland)	Dec. 2, 1944	Dec. 28, 1999	55	0	26

* *Including payload specialists, etc.; to January 1, 2004*

[#] *US unless otherwise indicated*

John Glenn, who in 1962 was the first American astronaut to orbit Earth, reentered space on October 29, 1998 aboard Space Shuttle flight STS-95 *Discovery*, becoming the oldest astronaut of all time by a considerable margin.

 **LONGEST SPACEWALKS***

ASTRONAUTS[#]	SPACECRAFT	(DATE)	DURATION (HR:MIN)
1 James Voss, Susan Helms	STS-102/ISS[†]	Mar. 10–11, 2001	8:56
2 Thomas D. Akers, Richard J. Hieb, Pierre J. Thuot	STS-49	May 13, 1992	8:29
3 John M. Grunsfeld, Steven L. Smith	STS-103	Dec. 22, 1999	8:15
4 C. Michael Foale, Claude Nicollier	STS-103	Dec. 23, 1999	8:10
5 John M. Grunsfeld, Steven L. Smith	STS-103	Dec.24, 1999	8:08
6 Daniel T. Barry, Tamara E. Jernigan	STS-96/ISS	May 29, 1999	7:55
7 Jeffrey A. Hoffman, F. Story Musgrave	STS-61	Dec. 4, 1993	7:54
8 Steven S. Smith, Rex J. Walheim	STS 110/ISS	Apr. 11, 2002	7:48
9 Thomas D. Akers, Kathryn C. Thornton	STS-49	May 14, 1992	7:44
10 Takao Doi, Winston E. Scott	STS-87	Nov. 24, 1997	7:43

* *To January 1, 2004*

[#] *All US*

[†] *International Space Station*

YOUNGEST ASTRONAUTS AND COSMONAUTS*

ASTRONAUT OR COSMONAUT[#]	BORN	FIRST FLIGHT	AGE (YRS)	(MTHS)	(DAYS)
1 Gherman S. Titov	Sept. 11, 1935	Aug. 6, 1961	25	10	25
2 Valentina V. Tereshkova	Mar. 6, 1937	June 16, 1963	26	3	10
3 Boris B. Yegorov	Nov. 26, 1937	Oct. 15, 1964	26	10	19
4 Yuri A. Gagarin	Mar. 9, 1934	Apr. 12, 1961	27	1	3
5 Helen P. Sharman (UK)	May 30, 1963	May 18, 1991	27	11	19
6 Mark R. Shuttleworth (South Africa)	Sept. 18, 1973	Apr. 25, 2002	28	7	7
7 Dumitru D. Prunariu (Romania)	Sept. 27, 1952	May 14, 1981	28	7	24
8 Valery F. Bykovsky	Aug. 2, 1934	June 14, 1963	28	10	19
9 Salman Abdel Aziz Al-Saud (Saudi Arabia)	June 27, 1956	June 17, 1985	28	11	20
10 Vladimir Remek (Czechoslovakia)	Sept. 26, 1948	Mar. 2, 1978	29	5	6

* *To January 1, 2004*

[#] *All Soviet, unless otherwise stated*

LONGEST SPACE MISSIONS*

COSMONAUT[#]	MISSION DATES	DURATION (DAYS)	(HR)	(MIN)
1 Valeri V. Polyakov	Jan. 8, 1994–Mar. 22, 1995	437	17	59
2 Sergei V. Avdeyev	Aug. 13, 1998–Aug. 28, 1999	379	14	52
3 = Musa K. Manarov	Dec. 21, 1987–Dec. 21, 1988	365	22	39
= Vladimir G. Titov	Dec. 21, 1987–Dec. 21, 1988	365	22	39
5 Yuri V. Romanenko	Feb. 5–Dec. 5, 1987	326	11	38
6 Sergei K. Krikalyov	May 18, 1991–Mar. 25, 1992	311	20	1
7 Valeri V. Polyakov	Aug. 31, 1988–Apr. 27, 1989	240	22	35
8 = Oleg Y. Atkov	Feb. 8–Oct. 2, 1984	236	22	50
= Leonid D. Kizim	Feb. 8–Oct. 2, 1984	236	22	50
= Anatoli Y. Solovyov	Feb. 8–Oct. 2, 1984	236	22	50

* *To January 1, 2004*

[#] *All Soviet/Russian*

Thirteen Russians and one Kazakh have spent over 200 days on single missions. The longest by US astronauts are the Space Shuttle/International Space Station stays of Daniel W. Bursch and Carl E. Walz, who, with Russian cosmonaut Yuri I. Onufrienko, spent 195 days 19 hours 39 min 167 sec in space in 2001–2002.

▼ Men on the Moon

Apollo Lunar Module pilot Edwin "Buzz" Aldrin walks on the Moon, July 20, 1969. The *Eagle* module and astronaut Neil Armstrong, who took the photograph, are reflected on Aldrin's visor in this iconic image from the first Moon landing.

THE 10 FIRST MOONWALKERS

	ASTRONAUT	BORN	SPACECRAFT	TOTAL EVA* (HR:MIN)	MISSION DATES
1	Neil A. Armstrong	Aug. 5, 1930	*Apollo 11*	2:32	July 16–24, 1969
2	Edwin E. ("Buzz") Aldrin	Jan. 20, 1930	*Apollo 11*	2:15	July 16–24, 1969
3	Charles Conrad, Jr.	June 2, 1930	*Apollo 12*	7:45	Nov. 14–24, 1969
4	Alan L. Bean	Mar. 15, 1932	*Apollo 12*	7:45	Nov. 14–24, 1969
5	Alan B. Shepard	Nov. 18, 1923	*Apollo 14*	9:23	Jan. 31–Feb. 9, 1971
6	Edgar D. Mitchell	Sept. 17, 1930	*Apollo 14*	9:23	Jan. 31–Feb. 9, 1971
7	David R. Scott	June 6, 1932	*Apollo 15*	19:08	July 26–Aug. 7, 1971
8	James B. Irwin	Mar. 17, 1930	*Apollo 15*	18:35	July 26–Aug. 7, 1971
9	John W. Young	Sept. 24, 1930	*Apollo 16*	20:14	Apr. 16–27, 1972
10	Charles M. Duke, Jr.	Oct. 3, 1935	*Apollo 16*	20:14	Apr. 16–27, 1972

* Extra Vehicular Activity (i.e. time spent out of the lunar module on the Moon's surface)

Six US *Apollo* missions resulted in successful Moon landings (*Apollo 13*, April 11–17, 1970, was aborted after an oxygen tank exploded). During the last of these (*Apollo 17*; December 7–19, 1972), Eugene A. Cernan (b.March 14, 1934) and Harrison H. Schmitt (b.July 3, 1935) became the only other astronauts to date who have walked on the surface of the Moon, both spending a total of 22:04 in EVA.

Apollo 14 astronaut Alan B. Shepard made the first-ever golf shot on the Moon on February 6, 1971, using a 6-iron head attached to the handle of a rock-sample collector. The head is now in the US Golf Association Hall of Fame in New Jersey, but the balls still lie in a lunar bunker. These are not the only evidence of human visits: since there is no wind on the Moon, the astronauts' footprints will be visible for thousands of years. They also left the descent stages of six *Apollo* modules, three Lunar Rover electric vehicles worth $6 million each, and hundreds of other items they abandoned to reduce the weight of their craft when they took off, including cameras, scientific instruments, clothing, tools, and flags, as well as a memorial to deceased astronauts and cosmonauts. The 12 lunar astronauts collected 2,196 rock samples weighing a total of 841.6 lb (381.69 kg).

THE 10 FIRST PEOPLE TO ORBIT EARTH

	NAME	AGE	ORBITS	DURATION (HR:MIN)	SPACECRAFT/ COUNTRY OF ORIGIN	DATE
1	Yuri A. Gagarin	27	1	1:48	*Vostok I*/USSR	Apr. 12. 1961
2	Gherman S. Titov	25	17	25:18	*Vostok II*/USSR	Aug. 6–7, 1961
3	John H. Glenn	40	3	4:56	*Friendship 7*/US	Feb. 20, 1962
4	Malcolm S. Carpenter	37	3	4:56	*Aurora 7*/US	May 24, 1962
5	Andrian G. Nikolayev	32	64	94:22	*Vostok III*/USSR	Aug. 11–15, 1962
6	Pavel R. Popovich	31	48	70:57	*Vostok IV*/USSR	Aug. 12–15, 1962
7	Walter M. Schirra	39	6	9:13	*Sigma 7*/US	Oct. 3, 1962
8	Leroy G. Cooper	36	22	34:19	*Faith 7*/US	May 15–16, 1963
9	Valeri F. Bykovsky	28	81	119:6	*Vostok V*/USSR	June 14–19, 1963
10	Valentina V. Tereshkova	26	48	70:50	*Vostok VI*/USSR	June 16–19, 1963

No. 2 was the youngest-ever astronaut, at age 25 years 329 days. No. 10 was the first woman in space. Among early pioneering flights, neither Alan Shepard (May 5, 1961: *Freedom 7*) nor Gus Grissom (July 21, 1961: *Liberty Bell 7*) actually orbited, achieving altitudes of only 115 miles (185 km) and 118 miles (190 km), respectively, and neither flight lasted more than 15 minutes.

Chemical Elements

TOP 10 MOST COMMON ELEMENTS IN SEAWATER

ELEMENT	TONS PER CUBIC KM*
1 Oxygen[#]	944,681,600
2 Hydrogen[#]	118,829,300
3 Chlorine	21,902,900
4 Sodium	12,180,500
5 Magnesium	1,461,700
6 Sulfur	1,022,900
7 Calcium	465,200
8 Potassium	458,600
9 Bromine	74,200
10 Carbon	30,900

* 1 km3 = approx. ¼ mile3
# Combined as water

There are thought to be 5,000 million million tons of solids dissolved in the world's oceans—but sodium and chlorine (combined as sodium chloride, or common salt) are the only two that are extracted in substantial quantities.

TOP 10 MOST COMMON ELEMENTS IN EARTH'S CRUST

ELEMENT	PARTS PER MILLION*
1 Oxygen	461,000
2 Silicon	282,000
3 Aluminum	82,300
4 Iron	56,300
5 Calcium	41,500
6 Sodium	23,600
7 Magnesium	23,300
8 Potassium	20,900
9 Titanium	5,650
10 Hydrogen	1,400

* mg per kg

Source: *CRC Handbook of Chemistry and Physics* (77th ed.)

This is based on the average percentages of the elements in igneous rock. At an atomic level, out of every million atoms, some 200,000 are silicon, 63,000 aluminum, and 31,000 hydrogen.

EPONYMOUS ELEMENT

THE MINERAL SAMARKSITE was discovered in Russia in 1847 and named in honor of Vasilii Yefrafovich von Samarski-Bykhovets (1803–1870), chief of staff of the Russian Corps of Mining Engineers. In 1879 element number 62 was extracted from samarskite by French chemist Paul-Emile Lecoq de Boisbaudran. This was called samarium, the first element to be named after an individual. The most resistant element to demagnetization, it is used in the manufacture of personal stereos, lasers, and film studio lights.

THE FIRST TO...

▼ Water resource
Seawater contains a vast quantity of chemical elements, including up to two tons of gold in every cubic mile, but the costs of extracting them are greater than their value.

TOP 10 MOST COMMON ELEMENTS ON THE MOON

	ELEMENT	PERCENTAGE
1	Oxygen	40.0
2	Silicon	19.2
3	Iron	14.3
4	Calcium	8.0
5	Titanium	5.9
6	Aluminum	5.6
7	Magnesium	4.5
8	Sodium	0.33
9	Potassium	0.14
10	Chromium	0.002

This list is based on the analysis of the 45.8 lb (20.77 kg) of rock samples brought back to Earth by the crew of the 1969 *Apollo 11* lunar mission.

▶ **Moon rock**
Fragments brought back from the *Apollo 17* Taurus-Littrow landing site have enhanced our knowledge of the Moon's elemental makeup.

TOP 10 HEAVIEST ELEMENTS

	ELEMENT	DISCOVERER/ COUNTRY	YEAR DISCOVERED	DENSITY*
1	Osmium	Smithson Tennant, UK	1804	22.59
2	Iridium	Smithson Tennant	1804	22.56
3	Platinum	Julius Caesar Scaliger, Italy/France[#] Charles Wood, UK[†]	1557 1741	21.45
4	Rhenium	Walter K. Noddack *et al.*, Germany	1925	21.01
5	Neptunium	Edwin Mattison McMillan/ Philip H. Abelson, US	1940	20.47
6	Plutonium	Glenn Theodore Seaborg *et al.*, US	1940	20.26
7	Gold	—	Prehistoric	19.29
8	Tungsten	Juan José and Fausto de Elhuijar, Spain	1783	19.26
9	Uranium	Martin Heinrich Klaproth, Germany	1789	19.05
10	Tantalum	Anders Gustav Ekeberg, Sweden	1802	16.67

* *Grams per cm³ at 20°C*
[#] *Earliest reference to*
[†] *Discoverer*

The two heaviest elements, the metals osmium and iridium, were discovered at the same time by British chemist Smithson Tennant (1761–1815), who was also the first to prove that diamonds are made of carbon.

TOP 10 LIGHTEST ELEMENTS*

	ELEMENT	DISCOVERER/ COUNTRY	YEAR DISCOVERED	DENSITY[#]
1	Lithium	Johan August Arfvedson, Sweden	1817	0.533
2	Potassium	Humphry Davy, UK	1807	0.859
3	Sodium	Humphry Davy	1807	0.969
4	Calcium	Humphry Davy	1808	1.526
5	Rubidium	Robert Wilhelm Bunsen, Germany/ Gustav Kirchoff, Germany	1861	1.534
6	Magnesium	Humphry Davy	1808[†]	1.737
7	Phosphorus	Hennig Brandt, Germany	1669	1.825
8	Beryllium	Friedrich Wöhler, Germany/ Antoine-Alexandré Brutus Bussy, France	1828[∞]	1.846
9	Cesium	Robert Wilhelm Bunsen/ Gustav Kirchoff	1860	1.896
10	Sulfur	—	Prehistoric	2.070

* *Solids only*
[#] *Grams per cm³ at 20°C*
[†] *Recognized by Joseph Black, 1755, but not isolated*
[∞] *Recognized by Nicholas Vauquelin, 1797, but not isolated*

High & Mighty

HIGHEST MOUNTAINS IN NORTH AMERICA

	MOUNTAIN	LOCATION	HEIGHT* (FT)	(M)
1	McKinley	Alaska	20,320	6,194
2	Logan	Canada	19,545	5,959
3	Citlaltépetl (Orizaba)	Mexico	18,409	5,611
4	St. Elias	Alaska/Canada	18,008	5,489
5	Popocatépetl	Mexico	17,887	5,452
6	Foraker	Alaska	17,400	5,304
7	Ixtaccihuatl	Mexico	17,343	5,286
8	Lucania	Canada	17,147	5,226
9	King	Canada	16,971	5,173
10	Steele	Canada	16,644	5,073

* Height of principal peak; lower peaks of the same mountain are excluded

Mount McKinley (or Denali, in the local language) was spotted in 1794 by Captain James Vancouver, and in 1896 named after William McKinley, the then-president of the United States. It was first climbed in 1913 by a party of four, including the Rev. Hudson Stuck, Archdeacon of the Yukon. Today, over 600 people per year ascend its summit.

TOP 10 **COUNTRIES WITH THE HIGHEST ELEVATIONS***

	Country	Peak	Height (ft)	(m)
1	= China	Everest	29,035	8,850
	= Nepal	Everest	29,035	8,850
3	Pakistan	K2	28,238	8,607
4	India	Kangchenjunga	28,208	8,598
5	Bhutan	Khula Kangri	24,784	7,554
6	Tajikistan	Mt. Garmo (formerly Kommunizma)	24,590	7,495
7	Afghanistan	Noshaq	24,581	7,490
8	Kyrgystan	Pik Pobedy	24,406	7,439
9	Kazakhstan	Khan Tengri	22,949	6,995
10	Argentina	Cerro Aconcagua	22,834	6,960

* Based on the tallest peak in each country

While an elevation of more than 1,000 ft (305 m) is commonly regarded as a mountain, there is no international agreement. Using this criterion, almost every country in the world can claim to have at least one mountain. There are some 54 countries in the world with elevations of greater than 10,000 ft (3,048 m).

TOP 10 **HIGHEST MOUNTAINS IN EUROPE**

	MOUNTAIN	COUNTRY	HEIGHT* (FT)	(M)
1	Mont Blanc	France/Italy	15,771	4,807
2	Monte Rosa	Switzerland	15,203	4,634
3	Zumsteinspitze	Italy/Switzerland	14,970	4,564
4	Signalkuppe	Italy/Switzerland	14,941	4,555
5	Dom	Switzerland	14,911	4,545
6	Liskamm	Italy/Switzerland	14,853	4,527
7	Weisshorn	Switzerland	14,780	4,505
8	Täschorn	Switzerland	14,733	4,491
9	Matterhorn	Italy/Switzerland	14,688	4,477
10	Mont Maudit	France/Italy	14,649	4,466

* Height of principal peak; lower peaks of the same mountain are excluded

All 10 of Europe's highest mountains are in the Alps; there are, however, at least 15 mountains in the Caucasus (the mountain range that straddles Europe and Asia) that are taller than Mont Blanc. The highest of them, the west peak of Mt. Elbrus, measures 18,510 ft (5,642 m).

▶ **The top of the world**
Mount Everest was first recognized as the world's tallest mountain in 1856. Its height as computed at that time was accurate to within 0.001 percent of its current official height.

TOP 10 HIGHEST MOUNTAINS

	MOUNTAIN/LOCATION	FIRST ASCENT	TEAM NATIONALITY	HEIGHT* (FT)	(M)
1	Everest, Nepal/China	May 29, 1953	British/New Zealand	29,035	8,850
2	K2 (Chogori), Pakistan/China	July 31, 1954	Italian	28,238	8,607
3	Kangchenjunga, Nepal/India	May 25, 1955	British	28,208	8,598
4	Lhotse, Nepal/China	May 18, 1956	Swiss	27,923	8,511
5	Makalu I, Nepal/China	May 15, 1955	French	27,824	8,481
6	Lhotse Shar II, Nepal/China	May 12, 1970	Austrian	27,504	8,383
7	Dhaulagiri I, Nepal	May 13, 1960	Swiss/Austrian	26,810	8,172
8	Manaslu I (Kutang I), Nepal	May 9, 1956	Japanese	26,760	8,156
9	Cho Oyu, Nepal	Oct. 19, 1954	Austrian	26,750	8,153
10	Nanga Parbat (Diamir), Kashmir	July 3, 1953	German/Austrian	26,660	8,126

Height of principal peak; lower peaks of the same mountain are excluded

Dhaulagiri was once believed to be the world's tallest mountain, until Kangchenjunga was surveyed and declared to be even higher. However, when the results of the 19th-century Great Trigonometrical Survey of India were studied, it was realized that Everest (then called "Peak XV") was the tallest, its height being computed as 29,002 ft (8,840 m). The mountain's name was suggested in 1865, as a tribute to Sir George Everest, the Surveyor General of India who had led the Great Trigonometrical Survey. Errors in measurement were corrected in 1955, when it was adjusted to 29,029 ft (8,848 m). On April 20, 1993, using the latest measuring techniques, this was again revised to give a new figure of 29,028 ft (8,848 m). In November 1999 it was announced that an analysis of data beamed from sensors on Everest's summit to GPS (Global Positioning System) satellites had claimed a new height of 29,035 ft (8,850 m). This new height has been accepted and is the current "official" figure. The survey also indicated that Everest is growing higher and moving northeast at a rate of 2.4 in (6 cm) per year.

TOP 10 HIGHEST VOLCANOES

	VOLCANO/LOCATION	HEIGHT (FT)	(M)
1	Ojos del Salado, Argentina/Chile	22,595	6,887
2	Llullaillaco, Argentina/Chile	22,057	6,723
3	Tipas, Argentina	21,850	6,660
4	Cerro El Condor, Argentina	21,430	6,532
5	Coropuna, Peru	20,922	6,377
6	Parinacota, Chile	20,827	6,348
7	Chimborazo, Ecuador	20,702	6,310
8	Pular, Chile	20,449	6,233
9	Cerro Aucanquilcha, Chile	20,262	6,176
10	San Pedro, Chile	20,161	6,145

Of these volcanoes, only two have erupted in comparatively modern times: Llullaillaco in 1870 and San Pedro in 1960.

Oceans & Seas

SHALLOWEST OCEANS AND SEAS

SEA*/OCEAN	AVERAGE DEPTH (FT)	(M)
1 **Yellow Sea,** Pacific Ocean	121	36.8
2 **Baltic Sea,** Atlantic Ocean	180	54.8
3 **Hudson Bay,** Atlantic Ocean	305	92.9
4 **North Sea,** Atlantic Ocean	308	93.8
5 **Persian Gulf,** Indian Ocean	328	99.9
6 **East China Sea,** Indian Ocean	620	188.9
7 **Red Sea,** Indian Ocean	1,764	537.6
8 **Gulf of California,** Pacific Ocean	2,375	723.9
9 **Sea of Okhotsk,** Pacific Ocean	3,192	972.9
10 **Arctic Ocean**	3,407	1,038.4

* Excludes landlocked seas

The Yellow Sea, or Huang Hai, lies north of the China Sea between China and Korea. It has a maximum depth of 500 ft (152 m) and possesses few deep-water ports. Ice fields form during the winter in parts, while shifting sandbanks make it treacherous for shipping. Its name reflects the color of mineral deposits from the rivers that discharge into it, which would be dispersed in a deeper body of water. Eventually, it is likely that environmental changes will lead to its disappearance.

DEEPEST OCEANS AND SEAS

SEA/OCEAN	AVERAGE DEPTH (FT)	(M)
1 **Pacific Ocean**	12,925	3,939
2 **Indian Ocean**	12,598	3,840
3 **Atlantic Ocean**	11,730	3,575
4 **Caribbean Sea,** Atlantic Ocean	8,448	2,575
5 **Sea of Japan,** Pacific Ocean	5,468	1,666
6 **Gulf of Mexico,** Atlantic Ocean	5,297	1,614
7 **Mediterranean Sea,** Atlantic Ocean	4,926	1,501
8 **Bering Sea,** Pacific Ocean	4,893	1,491
9 **South China Sea,** Pacific Ocean	4,802	1,463
10 **Black Sea,** Atlantic Ocean	3,906	1,190

The deepest point in the deepest ocean is the Mariana Trench in the Pacific, given as 35,837 ft (10,924 m) in a recent survey, although the slightly lesser depth of 35,814 ft (10,916 m) was recorded on January 23, 1960 by Jacques Piccard (Switzerland) and Donald Walsh (US) in their 58-ft (17.7-m) bathyscaphe *Trieste* 2 during the deepest-ever ocean descent. Whichever is correct, it is close to 6.8 miles (11 km) down, or almost 29 times the height of the Empire State Building.

SMALLEST SEAS

SEA*/OCEAN	APPROXIMATE AREA (SQ MILES)	(SQ KM)
1 **Gulf of California,** Pacific Ocean	59,100	153,070
2 **Persian Gulf,** Indian Ocean	88,800	230,000
3 **Yellow Sea,** Pacific Ocean	113,500	293,960
4 **Baltic Sea,** Atlantic Ocean	147,500	382,000
5 **North Sea,** Atlantic Ocean	164,900	427,090
6 **Red Sea,** Indian Ocean	174,900	452,990
7 **Black Sea,** Atlantic Ocean	196,100	507,900
8 **Andaman Sea,** Indian Ocean	218,100	564,880
9 **East China Sea,** Pacific Ocean	256,600	664,590
10 **Hudson Bay,** Atlantic Ocean	281,900	730,120

* Excludes landlocked seas

The two smallest seas are both gulfs—meaning long bays that extend far inland. The Gulf of California stretches southeast from the mouth of the Colorado River, separating the Baja California peninsula from the Mexican mainland. It was once known as the Sea of Cortés, after the Spanish conquistador Hernan Cortés, who sent Francisco de Ulloa to explore it in 1540. The Persian Gulf is an arm of the Arabian Sea between Iran and Saudi Arabia.

LARGEST OCEANS AND SEAS

SEA/OCEAN	APPROXIMATE AREA (SQ MILES)	(SQ KM)
1 **Pacific Ocean**	64,186,300	166,241,750
2 **Atlantic Ocean**	33,420,000	86,557,400
3 **Indian Ocean**	28,350,500	73,427,450
4 **Arctic Ocean**	5,105,700	13,223,700
5 **South China Sea,** Pacific Ocean	1,148,500	2,974,600
6 **Caribbean Sea,** Atlantic Ocean	971,400	2,515,900
7 **Mediterranean Sea,** Atlantic Ocean	969,100	2,509,960
8 **Bering Sea,** Pacific Ocean	873,000	2,261,100
9 **Gulf of Mexico,** Atlantic Ocean	582,100	1,507,600
10 **Sea of Okhotsk,** Pacific Ocean	537,500	1,392,100

The geographical term "ocean" encompasses all the world's seawater, with the exception of such landlocked seas as the Caspian. A total of over 70 percent of the planet's surface is oceanic—the Pacific Ocean alone has an area over 25 percent greater than that of the land. Smaller divisions of certain oceans are separately identified as seas—including some that are partially landlocked. Wholly landlocked seas are considered alongside lakes, which in many instances are larger than those bearing the name "sea."

TOP 10 LARGEST ISLANDS

ISLAND/COUNTRY	AREA* (SQ MILES)	(SQ KM)
1 Greenland (Kalaatdlit Nunaat)	840,004	2,175,600
2 New Guinea	303,381	785,753
3 Borneo (Indonesia/Malaysia/Brunei)	288,869	748,168
4 Madagascar (Malagasy Republic)	226,917	587,713
5 Baffin Island (Canada)	194,574	503,944
6 Sumatra (Indonesia)	171,068	443,065
7 Great Britain	88,787	229,957
8 Honshu (Japan)	87,182	225,800
9 Victoria Island (Canada)	85,154	220,548
10 Ellesmere Island (Canada)	71,029	183,964

* Mainlands, including areas of inland water, but excluding offshore islands

Australia is regarded as a continental land mass rather than an island; otherwise, it would rank first, at 2,941,517 sq miles (7,618,493 sq km), or 11 times the size of Texas. The largest US island is Hawaii, which measures 4,037 sq miles (10,456 sq km), and the largest off the continental United States is Kodiak, Alaska, at 3,672 sq miles (9,510 sq km).

TOP 10 DEEPEST DEEP-SEA TRENCHES

TRENCH	DEEPEST POINT (FT)	(M)
1 Mariana	35,837	10,924
2 Tonga*	35,430	10,800
3 Philippine	34,436	10,497
4 Kermadec*	32,960	10,047
5 Bonin	32,786	9,994
6 New Britain	32,609	9,940
7 Kuril	31,985	9,750
8 Izu	31,805	9,695
9 Puerto Rico	28,229	8,605
10 Yap	27,973	8,527

* Some authorities consider these parts of the same feature

With the exception of the Puerto Rico (Atlantic), all the trenches in the Top 10 are in the Pacific. Each of the eight deepest would be deep enough to submerge Mount Everest, which is 29,035 ft (8,850 m) above sea level.

▼ A green and pleasant land
Reputedly so named to lure settlers there, Greenland is the world's largest and one of the most sparsely populated islands.

Rivers, Lakes & Waterfalls

TOP 10 HIGHEST WATERFALLS

Waterfall	River	Location	Total drop (ft)	(m)
1 Angel	Carrao	Venezuela	3,212	979*
2 Tugela	Tugela	South Africa	2,800	850
3 Utigård	Jostedal Glacier	Nesdale, Norway	2,625	800
4 Mongefossen	Monge	Mongebekk, Norway	2,540	774
5 Mutarazi	Mutarazi	Zimbabwe	2,499	762
6 Yosemite	Yosemite Creek	Yosemite National Park, California	2,425	739
7 Østre Mardøla Foss	Mardals	Eikisdal, Norway	2,152	656
8 Tyssestrengane	Tysso	Hardanger, Norway	2,120	646
9 Cuquenán	Arabopo	Venezuela	2,000	610
10 Sutherland	Arthur	South Island, New Zealand	1,904	580

* Longest single drop 2,648 ft (807 m)

TOP 10 COUNTRIES WITH THE GREATEST AREAS OF INLAND WATER

Country	Percent of total area	Water area (sq miles)	(sq km)
1 US*	4.88	292,125	756,600
2 Canada	7.60	291,573	755,170
3 India	9.56	121,391	314,400
4 China	2.82	104,460	270,550
5 Ethiopia	9.89	46,680	120,900
6 Colombia	8.80	38,691	100,210
7 Indonesia	4.88	35,908	93,000
8 Russia	0.47	30,657	79,400
9 Australia	0.90	26,610	68,920
10 Tanzania	6.25	22,799	59,050

* 50 states and District of Columbia

TOP 10 | LONGEST RIVERS

	River	Location	Length (miles)	(km)
1	Nile	Burundi, Dem. Rep. of Congo, Egypt, Eritrea, Ethiopia, Kenya, Rwanda, Sudan, Tanzania, Uganda	4,158	6,695
2	Amazon	Peru, Brazil	4,007	6,448
3	Chang Jiang (Yangtze)	China	3,964	6,378
4	Huang He (Yellow)	China	3,395	5,464
5	Amur	China, Russia	2,744	4,415
6	Lena	Russia	2,734	4,400
7	Congo	Angola, Dem. Rep. of Congo	2,718	4,373
8	Irtysh	China, Kazakhstan, Mongolia, Russia	2,640	4,248
9	Mackenzie	Canada	2,635	4,241
10	Mekong	Tibet, China, Myanmar, Thailand, Laos, Cambodia, Vietnam	2,600	4,183

The source of the Nile was discovered in 1858 when British explorer John Hanning Speke reached Lake Victoria Nyanza, in what is now Burundi. By following the Amazon from its source and up the Rio Pará, it is possible to sail for some 4,195 miles (6,750 km), but because experts do not regard this entire route as part of the Amazon basin, the Nile is still considered the world's longest river.

TOP 10 | GREATEST RIVERS*

	River	Outflow/sea	Average flow (cu m/sec)
1	Amazon	Brazil/South Atlantic	175,000
2	Zaïre	Angola–Congo/South Atlantic	39,000
3	Negro	Brazil/South Atlantic	35,000
4	Yangtze–Kiang	China/Yellow Sea	32,190
5	Orinoco	Venezuela/South Atlantic	25,200
6	Plata–Paraná–Grande	Uruguay/South Atlantic	22,900
7	Madeira–Mamoré–Grande	Brazil/South Atlantic	21,800
8	Brahmaputra	Bangladesh/Bay of Bengal	19,200
9	Yenisey–Angara–Selenga	Russia/Kara Sea	17,600
10	Lena–Kirenga	Russia/Arctic Ocean	16,600

* Based on rate of discharge at mouth

Rain falls on the Amazon basin on some 200 days a year, totaling over 80 in (200 cm). Fed by more than 1,000 tributaries, the river can reach a rate of almost 250,000 m3 per second in the rainiest month of June. A cubic meter (265 gallons) of water weighs over a ton, so every minute, on average, 10 million tons of water flows out—a discharge so great that it dilutes the salinity of the sea for over 100 miles (160 km) from the mouth.

TOP 10 | LARGEST LAKES

	Lake	Location	Approximate area (sq miles)	(sq km)
1	Caspian Sea	Azerbaijan/Iran/Kazakhstan/Russia/Turkmenistan	143,000	371,000
2	Michigan/Huron*	US/Canada	45,300	117,610
3	Superior	Canada/US	31,700	82,100
4	Victoria	Kenya/Tanzania/Uganda	26,828	69,500
5	Aral Sea	Kazakhstan/Uzbekistan	12,988	33,640
6	Tanganyika	Burundi/Tanzania/Dem. Rep. of Congo/Zambia	12,700	32,900
7	Baikal	Russia	12,162	31,500
8	Great Bear	Canada	12,096	31,328
9	Malawi (Nyasa)	Tanzania/Malawi/Mozambique	11,150	28,880
10	Great Slave	Canada	11,030	28,570

* Now considered as two lobes of the same lake

Lake Michigan/Huron is the world's largest freshwater lake. Lake Baikal (or Baykal) in Siberia, with a depth of as much as 1.02 miles (1.63 km) in parts, is the world's deepest. After two feeder rivers were diverted for irrigation, the area of the Aral Sea fell by so much between 1973 and 1989 that it dropped from 4th to 5th place.

TOP 10 | LAKES WITH THE GREATEST VOLUME OF WATER

	Lake	Location	Volume (Cu miles)	(cU km)
1	Caspian Sea	Azerbaijan/Iran/Kazakhstan/Russia/Turkmenistan	21,497	89,600
2	Baikal	Russia	5,517	22,995
3	Tanganyika	Burundi/Tanzania/Dem. Rep. of Congo/Zambia	4,391	18,304
4	Superior	Canada/US	2,921	12,174
5	Michigan/Huron*	US/Canada	2,642	8,449
6	Malawi (Nyasa)	Malawi/Mozambique/Tanzania	1,473	6,140
7	Victoria	Kenya/Tanzania/Uganda	604	2,518
8	Great Bear	Canada	542	2,258
9	Great Slave	Canada	425	1,771
10	Issyk	Kyrgyzstan	420	1,752

* Now considered as two lobes of the same lake

The Caspian Sea is the world's largest inland sea or lake, and receives more water than any other landlocked body of water—an average of 82 cu miles (340 km3) per annum, which is causing a steady rise in sea level. This environmental change, along with pollution and the overfishing of the Caspian's famed sturgeon population, is among many threats to its future.

World Weather

LOCATION/COUNTRY	HIGHEST TOTAL ANNUAL RAINFALL (IN)	(MM)
1 **Lloro,** Colombia	523.6	13,299.4
2 **Mawsynram,** India	467.4	11,872.0
3 **Mt. Waialeale,** Kauai, Hawaii, US	460.0	11,684.0
4 **Cherrapuni,** India	425.0	10,795.0
5 **Debundscha,** Cameroon	405.0	10,287.0
6 **Quibdo,** Colombia	354.0	8,991.6
7 **Bellenden Ker,** Queensland, Australia	340.0	8,636.0
8 **Andagoya,** Colombia	281.0	7,137.4
9 **Henderson Lake,** British Colombia, Canada	256.0	6,502.4
10 **Crkvica,** Bosnia	183.0	4,648.2

Puu Kukui, a mountain in Hawaii, holds the US record for the most rainfall in a single year, receiving 704.8 in (1,790 cm) in 1982.

LOCATION*	LOWEST TEMPERATURE (°F)	(°C)
1 **Vostok#,** Antarctica	−138.6	−89.2
2 **Plateau Station#,** Antarctica	−129.2	−84.0
3 **Oymyakon,** Russia	−96.0	−71.1
4 **Verkhoyansk,** Russia	−90.0	−67.7
5 **Northice#,** Greenland	−87.0	−66.0
6 **Eismitte#,** Greenland	−85.0	−64.9
7 **Snag,** Yukon, Canada	−81.4	−63.0
8 **Prospect Creek,** Alaska	−79.8	−62.1
9 **Fort Selkirk,** Yukon, Canada	−74.0	−58.9
10 **Rogers Pass,** Montana	−69.7	−56.5

* Maximum of two places per country listed

Present or former scientific research base

Source: Philip Eden

TOP 10 HOTTEST PLACES— EXTREMES

	LOCATION*	HIGHEST TEMPERATURE (°F)	(°C)
1	**Al'Azīzīyah**, Libya	136.4	58.0
2	**Greenland Ranch**, Death Valley, California	134.0	56.7
3	= **Ghudamis**, Libya	131.0	55.0
	= **Kebili**, Tunisia	131.0	55.0
5	**Tombouctou**, Mali	130.1	54.5
6	**Araouane**, Mali	130.0	54.4
7	**Tirat Tavi**, Israel	129.0	53.9
8	**Ahwāz**, Iran	128.3	53.5
9	**Agha Jārī**, Iran	128.0	53.3
10	**Wadi Halfa**, Sudan	127.0	52.8

* Maximum of two places per country listed

Source: Philip Eden

◀ **Rainy days**
Occasional rain is a fact of life in many of the world's cities, but few experience the intense downpours of the world's wettest places, where annual totals can exceed 20 feet!

TOP 10 WINDIEST PLACES IN THE U.S.

	LOCATION	MEAN WIND SPEED (MPH)	(KM/H)
1	**Mount Washington**, NH	35.1	56.5
2	**St. Paul Island**, AK	16.9	27.2
3	**Cold Bay**, AK	16.8	27.0
4	**Blue Hill**, MA	15.4	24.8
5	**Dodge City**, KS	13.9	22.4
6	**Amarillo**, TX	13.5	21.7
7	**Barter Island**, AK	13.2	21.2
8	**Rochester**, MN	13.1	21.1
9	= **Casper**, WY	12.9	20.8
	= **Cheyenne**, WY	12.9	20.8

Source: National Climatic Data Center

These are constantly updated mean figures kept by individual climatic data centers from the beginning of their records, the origins of which vary (some began collecting data over 100 years ago). Although famed since the 1880s as the "windy city," Chicago's reputation is unfounded: its average wind speed of 10.4 mph (16.7 km/h) is less than that of many American cities—both Boston and New York are windier.

TOP 10 HOTTEST PLACES IN THE U.S.

	LOCATION	MEAN TEMPERATURE (°F)	(°C)
1	**Key West***, FL	78.1	25.6
2	**Honolulu**, HI	77.5	25.3
3	**Miami**, FL	76.7	24.8
4	**Kahului**, HI	75.8	24.3
5	**Lihue**, HI	75.7	24.2
6	= **West Palm Beach**, FL	75.3	24.0
	= **Yuma**, AZ	75.3	24.0
8	**Fort Myers**, FL	74.9	23.8
9	**Hilo**, HI	73.9	23.3
10	**Brownsville**, TX	73.3	23.0

Source: National Climatic Data Center

Key West is notable for having a narrow range of year-round temperatures, rarely dipping below a January average of 70°F or topping 84°F in July and August. For comparison, the average for New York City is 54.1°F (12.3°C), Chicago 49.1°F (9.5°C), and Los Angeles 63.3°F (17.4°C).

TOP 10 SNOWIEST PLACES IN THE U.S.

	LOCATION	MEAN ANNUAL SNOWFALL (IN)	(MM)
1	**Valdez**, AK	326.0	8,280
2	**Mount Washington**, NH	260.6	6,619
3	**Blue Canyon**, CA	240.3	6,104
4	**Yakutat**, AK	195.3	4,961
5	**Marquette**, MI	141.0	3,581
6	**Sault Sainte Marie**, MI	117.4	2,982
7	**Syracuse**, NY	115.6	2,936
8	**Takeetna**, AK	115.4	2,931
9	**Caribou**, ME	111.6	2,835
10	**Mount Shasta**, CA	104.9	2,664

Source: National Climatic Data Center

Mount Washington, New Hampshire, appears in both this list and that of America's windiest places. Its extreme weather conditions and live webcam images from the summit can be viewed online by visitors to www.mountwashington.org.

Natural Disasters

WORST VOLCANIC ERUPTIONS

	LOCATION	DATE	ESTIMATED NUMBER KILLED

1 Tambora, Indonesia — Apr. 5–12, 1815 — 92,000
The cataclysmic eruption of Tambora on the island of Sumbawa killed about 10,000 islanders immediately, with a further 82,000 dying subsequently (38,000 on Sumbawa and 44,000 on neighboring Lombok) from disease and famine. An estimated 1.8 million tons of ash was expelled, which blocked out sunlight and affected the weather over large areas of the globe during the following year. One effect was to produce brilliant sunsets, depicted strikingly in paintings from the period, especially in the works of J.M.W. Turner.

2 Unsen, Japan — Apr. 1, 1793 — 53,000
During a period of intense volcanic activity in the area, the island of Unsen, or Unzen, completely disappeared, killing all its inhabitants.

3 Mont Pelée, Martinique — May 8, 1902 — 40,000
After lying dormant for centuries, Mont Pelée began to erupt in April 1902. Assured that there was no danger, the 30,000 residents of the main city, St. Pierre, stayed in their homes. At 7:30 am on May 8, the volcano burst apart and showered the port with molten lava, ash, and gas, destroying virtually all life and property.

4 Krakatoa, Sumatra/Java — Aug. 26–27, 1883 — 36,380
After a series of eruptions over the course of several days, the uninhabited island of Krakatoa exploded with what may have been the biggest bang ever heard by humans, audible up to 3,000 miles (4,800 km) away. Some sources put the fatalities as high as 200,000, most of them killed by subsequent tsunamis that reached 100 ft (30 m) high.

5 Nevado del Ruiz, Colombia — Nov. 13, 1985 — 22,940
The Andean volcano gave warning signs of erupting, but by the time it was decided to evacuate the local inhabitants, it was too late. The hot steam, rocks, and ash ejected from Nevado del Ruiz melted its ice cap, resulting in a mudslide that completely engulfed the town of Armero.

6 Mount Etna, Sicily — Mar. 11, 1669 — over 20,000
Europe's largest volcano (10,760 ft/3,280 m) has erupted frequently, but the worst instance occurred in 1669, when the lava flow engulfed the town of Catania, killing at least 20,000.

7 Laki, Iceland — Jan.–June 1783 — 20,000
Iceland is one the most volcanically active places on Earth, but since it is sparsely populated, eruptions seldom result in major loss of life. The worst exception was the events at the Laki volcanic ridge, culminating on June 11 with the largest lava flow ever recorded. It engulfed many villages in a river of lava up to 50 miles (80 km) long and 100 ft (30 m) deep.

8 Vesuvius, Italy — Aug. 24, AD 79 — 16–20,000
When the previously dormant Vesuvius erupted suddenly, the Roman city of Herculaneum was engulfed by a mudflow, while Pompeii was buried under a vast layer of pumice and volcanic ash. It was preserved in a near-perfect state and uncovered by archaeological excavations that began in 1738.

9 Vesuvius, Italy — Dec. 16–17, 1631 — up to 18,000
Although minor eruptions occurred at intervals after that of AD 79, the next major cataclysm was almost as disastrous, as lava and mudflows gushed down onto the surrounding towns, including Naples.

10 Mt. Etna, Sicily — 1169 — over 15,000
Many died in Catania cathedral, where they believed they were safe, and more were killed when a tsunami caused by the eruption hit the port of Messina.

COSTLIEST HURRICANES TO STRIKE THE U.S.

	HURRICANE	YEAR	DAMAGE ($)*
1	"Great Miami"	1926	83,814,000,000
2	Andrew	1992	38,362,000,000
3	North Texas	1900	30,856,000,000
4	North Texas	1915	26,144,000,000
5	Southwest Florida	1944	19,549,000,000
6	New England	1938	19,275,000,000
7	Southeast Florida/Lake Okeechobee	1928	15,991,000,000
8	Betsy	1965	14,413,000,000
9	Donna	1960	13,967,000,000
10	Camille	1969	12,711,000,000

* Adjusted to 1998 dollars

Source: *Atlantic Oceanographic and Meteorological Laboratory/National Oceanic and Atmospheric Administration*

▼ **After the storm**
The widespread destruction caused by Hurricane Andrew resulted in 725,000 insurance claims in the state of Florida alone, making it the costliest natural disaster of the post-war era.

THE 10 DEADLIEST TYPES OF DISASTERS*

	TYPE OF DISASTER	FREQUENCY (1993–2002)	REPORTED DEATHS (1993–2002)
1	Droughts and famines	263	275,522
2	Floods	1,075	93,561
3	Earthquakes	229	75,391
4	Transportation accidents	1,684	68,106
5	Wind storms	823	60,971
6	Extreme temperatures	135	12,549
7	Industrial accidents	410	10,932
8	Avalanches/landslides	187	9,488
9	Volcanoes	52	511
10	Forest/scrub fires	146	458

* Natural and human-made

Source: *EM-DAT, CRED, University of Louvain, Belgium*

At least one of the following criteria must be fulfilled for an event to be classified as a disaster by EM-DAT: (a) 10 or more people reported killed; (b) 100 people reported affected; (c) a call for international assistance; and/or (d) declaration of a state of emergency.

THE 10 WORST EARTHQUAKES

	LOCATION	DATE	ESTIMATED NUMBER KILLED
1	Near East/Mediterranean	May 20, 1202	1,100,000
2	Shenshi, China	Feb. 2, 1556	820,000
3	Calcutta, India	Oct. 11, 1737	300,000
4	Antioch, Syria	May 20, 526	250,000
5	Tang-shan, China	July 28, 1976	242,419
6	Nan-Shan, China	May 22, 1927	200,000
7	Yeddo, Japan	Dec. 30, 1703	190,000
8	Kansu, China	Dec. 16, 1920	180,000
9	Messina, Italy	Dec. 28, 1908	160,000
10	Tokyo/Yokohama, Japan	Sept. 1, 1923	142,807

In some cases there are discrepancies between the "official" death tolls and the estimates of other authorities: a figure of 750,000 is sometimes quoted for the Tang-shan earthquake of 1976, for example, and totals ranging from 58,000 to 250,000 for the Messina quake of 1908. In recent times, the Armenian earthquake of December 7, 1988, and the one that hit northwest Iran on June 21, 1990, led to the deaths of more than 55,000 (official estimate 28,854) and 50,000, respectively.

THE 10 WORST FLOODS

	LOCATION	DATE	ESTIMATED NUMBER KILLED
1	Huang He River, China	Aug. 1931	3,700,000
2	Huang He River, China	Spring 1887	1,500,000
3	Holland	Nov. 1, 1530	400,000
4	Kaifong, China	1642	300,000
5	Henan, China	Sept.–Nov. 1939	over 200,000
6	Bengal, India	1876	200,000
7	Yangtze River, China	Aug.–Sept. 1931	140,000
8	Holland	1646	110,000
9	North Vietnam	Aug. 30, 1971	over 100,000
10 =	Friesland, Holland	1228	100,000
=	Dort, Holland	Apr. 16, 1421	100,000
=	Canton, China	June 12, 1915	100,000
=	Yangtze River, China	Sept. 1911	100,000

Records of floods caused by China's Huang He, or Yellow River, date back to 2297 BC. Since then, it has flooded at least 1,500 times, resulting in millions of deaths and giving it the nickname "China's Sorrow." According to some accounts, the flood of 1887 may have resulted in as many as 6 million deaths, as more than 2,000 towns and villages were inundated. Even in the 1990s, almost 70 percent of the 1,026,700,000 people worldwide affected by floods were Chinese.

LIFE ON
EARTH

Rare & Many

ORDERS OF MAMMALS WITH THE MOST SPECIES

	ORDER	NO. OF SPECIES
1	Rodents	1,729
2	Bats	981
3	Insectivores	374
4	Carnivores	252
5	Marsupials	248
6	Even-toed ungulates (pigs, hippopotamuses, camels, deer, cattle, and antelopes)	194
7	Primates	193
8	Cetaceans (whales, dolphins, and porpoises)	92
9	Lagomorphs (rabbits, hares, and pikas)	66
10 =	Edentates (armadillos, sloths, and anteaters)	32
=	Seals	32
	Total (including those not in Top 10)	4,237

BORN TO BE WILD?

THE FIRST GORILLA born in captivity anywhere in the world was Colo, born on December 22, 1956 at Columbus [Ohio] Zoo. The offspring of Millie and Baron Macombo, who had been taken from the wild, Colo herself was successfully paired with Bongo, who was also born at the zoo. Colo celebrated her 47th birthday in 2003. Improvements in the rearing of great apes in zoos— Columbus Zoo alone has bred over 30 gorillas, including the children and grandchildren of Colo—mean that today few apes are taken from the wild.

THE FIRST TO...

◀ **Great ape**
Gorillas are the largest representatives of the primate order, which includes lemurs, monkeys, apes, and humans.

THE 10 | COUNTRIES WITH THE MOST THREATENED MAMMAL SPECIES

	COUNTRY	TOTAL NO. OF THREATENED MAMMAL SPECIES
1	Indonesia	147
2	India	86
3	China	81
4	Brazil	74
5	Mexico	72
6	Australia	63
7	Papua New Guinea	58
8	= Kenya	50
	= Madagascar	50
	= Malaysia	50
	= Philippines	50
	US	39

Source: 2003 IUCN Red List of Threatened Species

The IUCN Red List system classifies the degree of threat posed to wildlife on a sliding scale from Vulnerable (high risk of extinction in the wild) through Endangered (very high risk), to Critically Endangered (extremely high risk). The mammals numbered above belong to all of these categories.

THE 10 | COUNTRIES WITH THE MOST THREATENED REPTILE SPECIES

	COUNTRY	TOTAL NO. OF THREATENED REPTILE SPECIES
1	Australia	38
2	China	31
3	Indonesia	28
4	US	27
5	India	25
6	Vietnam	24
7	Brazil	22
8	Malaysia	21
9	= Bangladesh	20
	= Myanmar	20

Source: 2003 IUCN Red List of Threatened Species

The actual threats to endangered species of reptiles are many and varied, and include a range of both human activities and natural events, ranging from habitat loss and degradation, invasions by alien species, hunting, and accidental destruction to persecution, pollution, and natural disasters.

TOP 10 | MOST COMMON INSECTS*

	SPECIES/SCIENTIFIC NAME	APPROXIMATE NO. OF KNOWN SPECIES
1	Beetles (*Coleoptera*)	400,000
2	Butterflies and moths (*Lepidoptera*)	165,000
3	Ants, bees, and wasps (*Hymenoptera*)	140,000
4	True flies (*Diptera*)	120,000
5	Bugs (*Hemiptera*)	90,000
6	Crickets, grasshoppers, and locusts (*Orthoptera*)	20,000
7	Caddisflies (*Trichoptera*)	10,000
8	Lice (*Phthiraptera/Psocoptera*)	7,000
9	Dragonflies and damselflies (*Odonata*)	5,500
10	Lacewings (*Neuroptera*)	4,700

* By number of known species

This list includes only species that have been discovered and named: it is surmised that many thousands of species still await discovery. It takes no account of the absolute numbers of each species, which are truly colossal: there are at least one million insects for each of Earth's 6.3 billion humans, which together would weigh at least 12 times as much as the human race. Among the most common insects are ants, flies, beetles, and the little-known springtails, which inhabit moist topsoil the world over. The latter alone probably outweigh the entire human race.

TOP 10 | WILD MAMMALS WITH THE LARGEST LITTERS

	SPECIES/SCIENTIFIC NAME	AVERAGE LITTER
1	Common tenrec (*Tenrec ecaudatus*)	25
2	Virginia (common) opossum (*Didelphis virginiana*)	21
3	Southern (black-eared) opossum (*Didelphis marsupialis*)	10
4	= Ermine (*Mustela erminea*)	9
	= Prairie vole (*Microtus ochrogaster*)	9
	= Syrian (golden) hamster (*Mesocricetus auratus*)	9
7	African hunting dog (*Lycaon pictus*)	8.8
8	= Dhole (Indian wild dog) (*Cuon alpinus*)	8
	= Pygmy opossum (*Marmosa robinsoni*)	8
	= South American mouse opossum (*Gracilinanus agilis*)	8

The prairie vole probably holds the world record for most offspring produced in a season. It has up to 17 litters in rapid succession, bringing up to 150 young into the world. Rabbits, despite their reputation as fast breeders, fail to make the list with an average litter size of six. All the numbers in the list are averages: the tiny tenrec can produce as many as 31 in a single litter and instances of domestic pigs producing 30 or more piglets at one go are not uncommon. Despite these prodigious reproductive peaks, mammalian litter sizes appear minute when compared with those of other animal groups. Many fish, for instance, can lay more than 10,000 eggs at a time and many amphibians more than 1,000.

Fast & Slow

FASTEST BIRDS

	SPECIES/SCIENTIFIC NAME	MAXIMUM RECORDED SPEED (MPH)	(KM/H)
1	**Common eider** (*Somateria mollissima*)	47	76
2	**Bewick's swan** (*Cygnus columbianus*)	44	72
3 =	**Barnacle goose** (*Branta leucopsis*)	42	68
=	**Common crane** (*Grus grus*)	42	68
5	**Mallard** (*Anas platyrhynchos*)	40	65
6 =	**Red-throated loon** (*Gavia stellata*)	38	61
=	**Wood pigeon** (*Columba palumbus*)	38	61
8	**Oystercatcher** (*Haematopus ostralegus*)	36	58
9 =	**White-fronted goose** (*Anser albifrons*)	33	54
=	**Ring-necked pheasant** (*Phasianus colchichus*)	33	54

Source: *Chris Mead*

▼ Big cat nap

The seemingly leisurely lifestyle of the lion allows it to conserve energy to enable it to achieve bursts of speed when hunting.

FASTEST MAMMALS*

	SPECIES/SCIENTIFIC NAME	MAXIMUM RECORDED SPEED (MPH)	(KM/H)
1	**Cheetah** (*Acinonyx jubatus*)	71	114
2	**Pronghorn antelope** (*Antilocapra americana*)	57	95
3 =	**Blue wildebeest (brindled gnu)** (*Connochaetes taurinus*)	50	80
=	**Lion** (*Panthera leo*)	50	80
=	**Springbok** (*Antidorcas marsupialis*)	50	80
6 =	**Brown hare** (*Lepus capensis*)	48	77
=	**Red fox** (*Vulpes vulpes*)	48	77
8 =	**Grant's gazelle** (*Gazella granti*)	47	76
=	**Thomson's gazelle** (*Gazella thomsonii*)	47	76
10	**Horse** (*Equus caballus*)	45	72

* Of those species for which data available at time of collection

Along with its relatively slow rivals, the cheetah can deliver its astonishing maximum speed over only relatively short distances. For comparison, the human male hundred-meter record stands at 9.78 seconds, equivalent to a speed of 23 mph (37 km/h), so all the mammals in the Top 10, and several others, are capable of outrunning a person. If a human being ran the hundred meters at the cheetah's speed, the record would fall to 3 seconds.

SLEEPIEST MAMMALS

	SPECIES/SCIENTIFIC NAME	AVERAGE HOURS OF SLEEP PER DAY
1 =	**Lion** (*Panthera leo*)	20
=	**Three-toed sloth** (*Bradypus variegatus*)	20
3	**Little brown bat** (*Myotis lucifugus*)	19.9
4	**Big brown bat** (*Eptesicus fuscus*)	19.7
5 =	**Opossum** (*Didelphis virginiana*)	19.4
=	**Water opossum (yapok)** (*Chironectes minimus*)	19.4
7	**Giant armadillo** (*Priodontes maximus*)	18.1
8	**Koala** (*Phascolarctos cinereus*)	up to 18
9	**Nine-banded armadillo** (*Dasypus novemcinctus*)	17.4
10	**Southern owl monkey** (*Aotus azarai*)	17.0

The list excludes periods of hibernation, which can last up to several months among creatures such as the ground squirrel, marmot, and brown bear. At the other end of the scale comes the frantic shrew, which has to hunt and eat constantly or perish: it literally has no time for sleep.

▼ Designed for speed
The sprinters of the marine world, sailfish are capable of spurts of speed 13 times that of a champion human swimmer.

TOP 10 FASTEST FISH

	SPECIES/SCIENTIFIC NAME	MAXIMUM RECORDED SPEED (MPH)	(KM/H)
1	**Sailfish** (*Istiophorus platypterus*)	69	112
2	**Striped marlin** (*Tetrapturus audax*)	50	80
3	**Wahoo (peto, jack mackerel)** (*Acanthocybium solandri*)	48	77
4	**Southern bluefin tuna** (*Thunnus maccoyii*)	47	76
5	**Yellowfin tuna** (*Thunnus albacares*)	46	74
6	**Blue shark** (*Prionace glauca*)	43	69
7	= **Bonefish** (*Albula vulpes*)	40	64
	= **Swordfish** (*Xiphias gladius*)	40	64
9	**Tarpon (oxeye herring)** (*Megalops cyprinoides*)	35	56
10	**Tiger shark** (*Galeocerdo cuvier*)	33	53

Source: *Lucy T. Verma*

Flying fish are excluded: their top speed in the water is only 23 mph (37 km/h), but airborne they can reach 35 mph (56 km/h). Many sharks other than the two listed are contenders: the great white shark (of *Jaws* fame) can manage 30 mph (48 km/h) with ease. For smaller fish (up to salmon size), a handy formula for estimating top swimming speed is just over 10 times its own length in inches per second: thus a trout 6 in (15 cm) long swims at 63 in (160 cm) per second.

TOP 10 HIBERNATING MAMMALS WITH THE SLOWEST HEARTBEATS*

	SPECIES/SCIENTIFIC NAME	HEARTBEATS PER MINUTE NON-HIBERNATING	HIBERNATING
1	**Franklin's ground squirrel** (*Spermophilus franklinii*)	n/a	2–4
2	**Olympic marmot** (*Marmota olympus*)	130–140	4
3	**Syrian (golden) hamster** (*Mesocricetus auratus*)	500–600	6
4	**American black bear**# (*Ursus americanus*)	40–50	8
5	**European hedgehog** (*Erinaceus europaeus*)	190	20
6	**Garden dormouse** (*Eliomys quercinus*)	n/a	25
7	**Eastern pigmy possum (dormouse possum, possum mouse)** (*Cercartetus nanus*)	300–650	28–80
8	**Birch mouse** (*Sicista betulina*)	550–600	30
9	**Big brown bat** (*Eptesicus fuscus*)	450	34
10	**Edible dormouse** (*Myoxus glis*)	450	35

* *Of those species for which data are available; one species per genus listed*

\# *Not considered true hibernators by some experts—the heart rate drops but body temperature is not significantly lowered*

Big & Small

 **HEAVIEST TURTLES**

	SPECIES/SCIENTIFIC NAME	MAXIMUM WEIGHT (LB)	(KG)
1	**Pacific leatherback turtle*** (*Dermochelys coriacea*)	1,552	704.4
2	**Atlantic leatherback turtle*** (*Dermochelys coriacea*)	1,018	463.0
3	**Green sea turtle** (*Chelonia mydas*)	783	355.3
4	**Loggerhead turtle** (*Caretta caretta*)	568	257.8
5	**Alligator snapping turtle#** (*Macroclemys temmincki*)	220	100.0
6	**Flatback (sea) turtle** (*Natator depressus*)	171	78.2
7	**Hawksbill (sea) turtle** (*Eretmochelys imbricata*)	138	62.7
8	**Kemp's Ridley turtle** (*Lepidochelys kempi*)	133	60.5
9	**Olive Ridley turtle** (*Lepidochelys olivacea*)	110	49.9
10	**Common snapping turtle#** (*Chelydra serpentina*)	85	38.5

* One species, differing in size according to where they live

Freshwater species

Source: Lucy T. Verma

Prehistoric turtles such as *Stupendemys geographicus* may have weighed three times as much as the largest living species, but even these attain an impressive size, with shell lengths of exceptional specimens reaching 8 ft 5 in (2.56 m).

▶ **Turtleweight**
Several turtle species can attain weights four times that of a typical adult human.

SMALLEST PRIMATES

	SPECIES*/SCIENTIFIC NAME	WEIGHT# (OZ)	(G)
1	**Pygmy mouse lemur** (*Microcebus myoxinus*)	1.0	30
2	**Hairy-eared dwarf lemur** (*Allocebus trichotis*)	2.4–3.5	70–100
3	***Tarsius pumilus***	2.8–5.8	80–165
4	**Lesser bush baby** (*Galago moholi*)	4.9–8.1	140–230
5	**Greater dwarf lemur** (*Cheirogaleus major*)	6.2–21.1	177–600
6	**Buffy-headed marmoset** (*Callithrix flaviceps*)	8.1–15.9	230–453
7	**Cotton-top tamarin** (*Saguinus oedipus*)	9.1–13.4	260–380
8	**Golden potto** (*Arctocebus calabarensis*)	9.3–16.4	266–465
9	**Golden-rumped lion tamarin** (*Leontopithecus chrysopygus*)	10.5–24.6	300–700
10	***Callimico goeldii***	13.8–30.3	393–860

* Lightest species per genus

Weight ranges vary with gender; ranked by lightest

The pygmy mouse lemur weighs less than a golf ball and measures just 2.4 in (6.2 cm) long. Its diminutive size and nocturnal habits resulted in a lack of sightings for over a century, and it was believed to be extinct until it was rediscovered in western Madagascar in 1993.

TOP 10 LIGHTEST TERRESTRIAL MAMMALS

SPECIES*/SCIENTIFIC NAME	LENGTH# (IN)	(MM)	WEIGHT† (OZ)	(G)
1 **Pygmy shrew** (*Sorex hoyi*)	1.8–3.9	46–100	0.07–0.63	2.1–18
2 **Pygmy shrew** (*Suncus etruscus*)	1.4–1.9	35–48	0.22	2.5
3 **African pygmy mouse** (*Mus minutoides*)	1.8–3.2	45–82	0.09–0.42	2.5–12.0
4 **Desert shrew** (*Notiosorex crawfordi*)	1.9–2.7	48–69	0.1–0.17	3.0–5.0
5 **Forest musk shrew** (*Sylvisorex sp.*)	1.8–3.9	45–100	0.1–0.42	3.0–12.0
6 **White-toothed shrew** (*Crocidura suaveolens*)	1.6–3.9	40–100	0.1–0.46	3.0–13.0
7 **Asiatic shrew** (*Soriculus salenskii*)	1.7–3.9	44–99	0.17–0.21	5.0–6.0
8 **Delany's swamp mouse** (*Delanymys brooksi*)	1.9–2.5	50–63	0.18–0.23	5.2–6.5
9 **Birch mouse** (*Sicista sp.*)	1.9–3.5	50–90	0.21–0.49	6.0–14.0
10 **Pygmy mouse** (*Baiomys sp.*)	1.9–3.2	50–81	0.24–0.59	7.0–8.0

* Lightest species per genus

Some jerboas are smaller, but no weights have yet been recorded

† Ranked by lightest in range

TOP 10 HEAVIEST TERRESTRIAL MAMMALS

SPECIES*/SCIENTIFIC NAME	LENGTH (FT)	(M)	WEIGHT (LB)	(KG)
1 **African elephant** (*Loxodonta africana*)	24.6	7.5	16,534	7,500
2 **Hippopotamus** (*Hippopotamus amphibius*)	16.4	5.0	9,920	4,500
3 **White rhinoceros** (*Ceratotherium simum*)	13.7	4.2	7,937	3,600
4 **Giraffe** (*Giraffa camelopardalis*)	15.4	4.7	4,255	1,930
5 **American bison** (*Bison bison*)	11.4	3.5	2,205	1,000
6 **Moose** (*Alces alces*)	10.1	3.1	1,820	825
7 **Grizzly bear** (*Ursus arctos*)	9.8	3.0	1,720	780
8 **Arabian camel (dromedary)** (*Camelus dromedarius*)	11.3	3.45	1,521	690
9 **Siberian tiger** (*Pantheratigris altaica*)	10.8	3.3	793	360
10 **Gorilla** (*Gorilla gorilla gorilla*)	6.5	2.0	606	275

* Heaviest species per genus

The list excludes domesticated cattle and horses. It also avoids comparing close kin such as the African and Indian elephants, highlighting instead the sumo stars within distinctive large mammal groups such as the bears, deer, big cats, primates, and bovines (oxlike mammals).

Killer Creatures

TOP 10 LARGEST BIRDS OF PREY*

	SPECIES/SCIENTIFIC NAME	MAXIMUM LENGTH (IN)	(CM)
1	**Himalayan griffon vulture** (*Gyps himalayensis*)	59	150
2	**California condor** (*Gymnogyps californianus*)	53	134
3	**Andean condor** (*Vultur gryphus*)	51	130
4	= **Lammergeier** (*Gypaetus barbatus*)	45	115
	= **Lappet-faced vulture** (*Torgos tracheliotus*)	45	115
6	**Eurasian griffon vulture** (*Gyps fulvus*)	43	110
7	**European black vulture** (*Aegypus monachus*)	42	107
8	**Harpy eagle** (*Harpia harpyja*)	41	105
9	**Wedge-tailed eagle** (*Aquila audax*)	41	104
10	**Ruppell's griffon** (*Gyps rueppellii*)	40	101

By length; diurnal only, hence excluding owls

The entrants in this Top 10 all measure more than 39 in (1 m) from beak to tail; in all but the vultures, the female will be larger than the male. All these raptors, or aerial hunters, have remarkable eyesight and can spot their victims from great distances, but even if they kill animals heavier than themselves, they are generally unable to take wing with them: stories of eagles carrying off lambs and small children are usually fictitious.

THE 10 TYPES OF SHARKS THAT HAVE KILLED THE MOST HUMANS

	SPECIES/ SCIENTIFIC NAME	UNPROVOKED ATTACKS* (TOTAL)	(FATAL)[#]
1	**Great white** (*Carcharodon carcharias*)	205	58
2	**Tiger** (*Galeocerdo cuvier*)	82	20
3	**Bull** (*Carcharhinus leucas*)	64	17
4	**Requiem** (*Carcharhinus*[†])	33	8
5	**Blue** (*Prionace glauca*)	12	4
6	**Sand tiger** (*Carcharias taurus*)	29	2
7	**Shortfin mako** (*Isurus oxyrinchus*)	7	1
8	**Oceanic whitetip** (*Carcharhinus longimanus*)	5	1
9	**Dusky** (*Carcharhinus obscurus*)	3	1
10	= **Galapagos** (*Carcharhinus galapagensis*)	1	1
	= **Ganges** (*Carcharhinus gangeticus*)	1	1

1580–2003

[#] *Where fatalities are equal, entries are ranked by total attacks*

[†] *Species unspecified*

Source: *International Shark Attack File, Florida Museum of Natural History*

TOP 10 WIDEST-RANGING SOLITARY CARNIVORES*

	SPECIES/SCIENTIFIC NAME	MALE RANGE[#] (SQ KM)[†]
1	**Polar bear** (*Ursus maritimus*)	500–300,000
2	**Siberian tiger** (*Panthera tigris altaica*)	3,100–4,140
3	**Brown (grizzly) bear** (*Ursus arctos*)	293–3,029
4	**European lynx** (*Lynx lynx*)	275–450
5	**Mountain lion** (*Felis concolor*)	78–277
6	**Canadian lynx** (*Lynx canadensis*)	145–243
7	**Bobcat** (*Lynx rufus*)	13–201
8	**Jaguar** (*Panthera onca*)	3–200
9	**American black bear** (*Ursus americanus*)	109–115
10	**Tiger** (*Panthera tigris*)	60–100

* *Of those species for which data are available*

[#] *Ranked by the farthest in range*

[†] *1 km² = approx. ⅓ square mile*

The polar bear is the world's largest carnivore. There are an estimated 22,000 to 28,000 in the wild, and although they are not territorial, in their search for food, individual bears and females accompanied by cubs travel across a vast home range, covering an average of 5,500 miles (8,850 km) a year.

THE 10 | SNAKES WITH THE DEADLIEST BITES

	SPECIES/SCIENTIFIC NAME	ESTIMATED LETHAL DOSE FOR HUMANS (MG)	AVERAGE VENOM PER BITE (MG)	POTENTIAL HUMAN FATALITIES PER BITE
1	**Coastal taipan** (*Oxyuranus scutellatus*)	1	120	120
2	**Common krait** (*Bungarus caeruleus*)	0.5	42	84
3	**Philippine cobra** (*Naja naja philippinensis*)	2	120	60
4	= **King cobra** (*Ophiophagus hannah*)	20	1,000	50
	= **Russell's viper** (*Daboia russelli*)	3	150	50
6	**Black mamba** (*Dendroaspis polyepis*)	3	135	45
7	**Yellow-jawed tommygoff** (*Bothrops asper*)	25	1,000	40
8	= **Multibanded krait** (*Bungarus multicinctus*)	0.8	28	35
	= **Tiger snake** (*Notechis scutatus*)	1	35	35
10	**Jararacussu** (*Bothrops jarararcussu*)	25	800	32

Source: *Russell E. Gough*

In comparing the danger posed by poisonous snakes, this list takes account of such factors as venom strength—and hence its lethality—as well as the amount injected per bite (most snakes inject about 15 percent of their venom per bite).

▼ Big wings
One of the largest birds of prey, the Andean condor also has the greatest wing area of any bird, with some spanning more than 10 ft (3 m) from tip to tip.

THE 10 | DEADLIEST SPIDERS

	SPECIES/SCIENTIFIC NAME	RANGE
1	**Banana spider** (*Phonenutria nigriventer*)	Central and South America
2	**Sydney funnel web** (*Atrax robustus*)	Australia
3	**Wolf spider** (*Lycosa raptoria/erythrognatha*)	Central and South America
4	**Black widow** (*Latrodectus species*)	Widespread
5	**Brown recluse spider (violin spider)** (*Loxosceles reclusa*)	Widespread
6	**Slender sac spider** (*Cheiracanthium mildei*)	Widespread
7	**Tarantula** (*Eurypelma rubropilosum*)	Neotropics
8	**Tarantula** (*Acanthoscurria atrox*)	Neotropics
9	**Tarantula** (*Lasiodora klugi*)	Neotropics
10	**Tarantula** (*Pamphobeteus species*)	Neotropics

This list ranks spiders according to their "lethal potential"—their venom yield divided by their venom potency. The banana spider, for example, yields 6 mg of venom, with 1 mg the estimated lethal dose for a human. However, few spiders are capable of killing people—there were just 14 recorded deaths caused by black widows in the United States in the entire 19th century—since their venom yield is relatively low compared with that of the most dangerous snakes.

TOP 10 | HEAVIEST CARNIVORES

	SPECIES/SCIENTIFIC NAME	MAXIMUM LENGTH (FT)	(IN)	(M)	MAXIMUM WEIGHT (LB)	(KG)
1	**Southern elephant seal** (*Mirounga leonina*)	21	4	6.5	7,716	3,500
2	**Walrus** (*Odobenus rosmarus*)	12	6	3.8	2,646	1,200
3	**Steller's sea lion** (*Eumetopias jubatus*)	9	8	3.0	2,425	1,100
4	**Grizzly bear** (*Ursus arctos*)	9	8	3.0	1,720	780
5	**Polar bear** (*Ursus maritimus*)	8	6	2.6	1,323	600
6	**Tiger** (*Panthera tigris*)	9	2	2.8	661	300
7	**Lion** (*Panthera leo*)	6	3	1.9	551	250
8	**American black bear** (*Ursus americanus*)	6	0	1.8	500	227
9	**Giant panda** (*Ailuropoda melanoleuca*)	5	0	1.5	353	160
10	**Spectacled bear** (*Tremarctos ornatus*)	6	0	1.8	309	140

Of the 273 mammal species in the order *Carnivora* (meat-eaters), many (including bears) are in fact omnivorous, and around 40 specialize in eating fish or insects. All, however, share a common ancestry indicated by the butcher's-knife form of their canine teeth. Since the Top 10 would otherwise consist exclusively of seals and related marine carnivores, only three representatives have been included in order to allow the terrestrial heavyweight division to make an appearance.

THE 10 MOST COMMON ANIMAL PHOBIAS

	ANIMAL	MEDICAL TERM
1	Spiders	Arachnophobia
2	Snakes	Ophidiophobia, ophiophobia, ophiciophobia, herpetophobia, or snakephobia
3	Wasps	Spheksophobia
4	Birds (especially pigeons)	Ornithophobia
5	Mice	Musophobia or muriphobia
6	Fish	Ichthyophobia
7	Bees	Apiphobia or apiophobia
8	Dogs	Cynophobia or kynophobia
9	Caterpillars and other insects	Entomophobia
10	Cats	Ailurophobia, elurophobia, felinophbia, galeophobia, or gatophobia

Phobias directed at creatures that may bite or sting or carry disease, such as rabid dogs or rats during the Plague, are understandable. Such fears are so widespread that they have been exploited in movies including *Arachnophobia* (1990), *The Swarm* (1978), *Venom* (1982), and *The Birds* (1963).

▼ **Fear factor**
Snakes are the object of one of the most widespread animal phobias, prevalent even in countries where they are rare or unknown.

TOP 10 COUNTRIES WITH THE MOST CAPTIVE ELEPHANTS

	COUNTRY	ELEPHANTS*
1	US	622
2	Germany	265
3	UK	130
4	Italy	74
5	Sri Lanka	72
6	France	59
7	Spain	49
8	South Africa	46
9	= Canada	45
	= Netherlands	45

* *Total of known elephants in captivity in zoos, circuses, and private collections, 2001*

Source: *Absolut Elephant*

Of the 622 captive elephants in the US, 340 were in zoos, 241 in circuses, and 41 in private collections, including three at Michael Jackson's Neverland.

THE 10 LATEST GENESIS AWARDS FOR BEST FEATURE FILM

YEAR	FILM
2004	Legally Blonde 2
2003	Spirit: Stallion of the Cimarron
2002	Doctor Doolittle 2
2001	Chicken Run
2000	Instinct
1999	Mighty Joe Young
1998	Shiloh
1997	Fly Away Home
1996	Babe
1995	Black Beauty

Source: *The Ark Trust*

Since 1986 the Ark Trust, Inc., a US animal rights and welfare charity, has been presenting the Genesis Awards, including one for the best animal feature film that raises such issues.

TOP 10 PEARL-FISHING COUNTRIES

	COUNTRY	PEARLS MOTHER-OF-PEARL, SHELL (2001) (KG
1	Croatia	3,125,000
2	Philippines	2,433,000
3	Sri Lanka	498,000
4	Mexico	463,000
5	Tanzania	436,74:
6	Papua New Guinea	346,540
7	Australia	250,000
8	Russia	224,000
9	Palau	200,000
10	Fiji	160,000
	World total	10,275,350

Source: *Food and Agriculture Organization of the United Nations*

Two French overseas territories are excluded, not being independent states: French Polynesia (820,724 kg catch in 2001) and New Caledonia (342,700 kg).

TOP 10 INSECT AND SPIDER MOVIES

	FILM	CREATURE(S)	YEAR
1	A Bug's Life*	Various	1998
2	Antz*	Ants	1998
3	Arachnophobia	Spider	1990
4	The Fly	Housefly	1986
5	Mimic	Mutant insects	1997
6	James and the Giant Peach#	Various	1996
7	Microcosmos†	Insects	1996
8	The Fly II	Housefly	1989
9	Kingdom of the Spiders	Tarantulas	197:
10	The Swarm	Bees	1978

* *Animated*

\# *Part animated/part live action*

† *Documentary*

The creatures, which are central to the plots of these movies, range from the cute to the terrifying; many exploit widespread phobias relating to insects and spiders. Minor crawl-on roles, such as that of the genetically modified spider that turns Peter Parker into Spider-Man in the 2002 film, have been omitted.

Jaws of death
Although still a rare occurrence, shark attacks have increased in line with the popularity of diving and other water-based activities.

THE 10 PLACES WHERE SHARK ATTACKS ARE MOST COMMON

LOCATION	FATAL ATTACKS	LAST FATAL ATTACK	TOTAL ATTACKS*
1 US (excluding Hawaii)	38	2003	737
2 Australia	132	2003	282
3 South Africa	40	2003	199
4 Hawaii	14	1992	96
5 Brazil	19	2002	80
6 Papua New Guinea	26	2000	49
7 New Zealand	9	1968	44
8 Mexico	20	1997	35
9 Iran	8	1985	23
10 The Bahamas	1	1968	21

* Confirmed unprovoked attacks on humans, including non-fatal

Source: *International Shark Attack File/American Elasmobranch Society/Florida Museum of Natural History*

The International Shark Attack File monitors worldwide incidents, a total of more than 2,000 of which have been recorded since the 16th century. The 1990s had the highest attack total (514) of any decade, while 55 unprovoked attacks were recorded in 2003 alone. This upward trend is believed to reflect the increase in the numbers of people engaging in scuba diving and other aquatic activities, rather than any observed increase in the aggressive instincts of sharks.

TOP 10 SPECIES OF FISH MOST CAUGHT*

SPECIES	TOTAL CATCH (2001) (TONS)
1 Herring, sardines, and anchovies	22,554,013
2 Carp, barbels, and cyprinids	18,712,025
3 Cod, hake, and haddock	10,168,359
4 Tuna, bonito, and billfish	6,432,276
5 Oysters	4,857,706
6 Shrimp and prawns	4,653,641
7 Clams, cockles, and arkshell	4,318,825
8 Squid, cuttlefish, and octopuses	3,689,267
9 Salmon, trout, and smelt	2,946,495
10 Tilapia and cichlids	2,279,779
World total	143,529,200

* Including shellfish and mollusks

Source: *Food and Agriculture Organization of the United Nations*

The world's total fishing catch comprises 101,805,100 tons caught in the wild, and 41,723,977 tons from fish farms—equivalent to 45.4 lb (20.6 kg) for each person on the planet, although not all fish caught is for human consumption. The trade is worth $55.9 billion a year, with Thailand and China the leading countries, each exporting around $4 billion worth.

Dogs & Cats

TOP 10 DOG NAMES IN THE U.S.

	NAME
1	Max
2	Buddy
3	Molly
4	Bailey
5	Maggie
6	Lucy
7	Jake
8	Rocky
9	Sadie
10	Lucky

Source: *American Pet Classics*

▼ Top dog
Popular as a hunting dog since the early 19th century, the Labrador retriever heads the list of leading dog breeds by a considerable margin.

TOP 10 DOG BREEDS IN THE U.S.

	BREED	NO. REGISTERED BY AMERICAN KENNEL CLUB, INC. (2003)
1	Labrador retriever	144,934
2	Golden retriever	52,530
3	Beagle	45,033
4	German shepherd	43,950
5	Dachshund	39,473
6	Yorkshire terrier	38,256
7	Boxer	34,136
8	Poodle	32,176
9	Shih tzu	26,935
10	Chihuahua	24,930

Source: *The American Kennel Club*

The Labrador retriever tops the list for the thirteenth consecutive year. This breed is also No. 1 in the UK.

TOP 10 PET DOG POPULATIONS

	COUNTRY	ESTIMATED DOG POPULATION (2002)
1	United States	61,080,000
2	Brazil	30,051,000
3	China	22,908,000
4	Japan	9,650,000
5	Russia	9,600,000
6	South Africa	9,100,000
7	France	8,150,000
8	Italy	7,600,000
9	Poland	7,520,000
10	Thailand	6,900,000

Source: *Euromonitor*

Dog ownership in the US has become increasingly humanized: not only are dogs given human names and often considered as "one of the family," but a huge industry has grown up to cater to their nutrition and welfare to a standard that rivals that of many people. In second-place Brazil, dogs make up almost 43 percent of the total pet population and account for 77 percent of pet food sales.

TOP 10 PET CAT POPULATIONS

	COUNTRY	ESTIMATED CAT POPULATION (2002)
1	United States	76,430,000
2	China	53,100,000
3	Russia	12,700,000
4	Brazil	12,466,000
5	France	9,600,000
6	Italy	9,400,000
7	UK	7,700,000
8	Ukraine	7,350,000
9	Japan	7,300,000
10	Germany	7,000,000

Source: *Euromonitor*

Estimates of the number of domestic cats in the 20 leading countries total more than 221 million, with the greatest increases experienced in Brazil, where the cat population grew by 28.4 percent, from 9,709,000 in 1998 to 12,466,000 in 2002.

▶ **Persian puss**
Foremost among all US cat breeds, the Persian has been bred in Europe since the 16th century.

PUT ON A CAT SHOW

THE FIRST TO...

BRITISH ARTIST HARRISON WEIR devised the first-ever cat show and provided illustrations of the entrants for the *Illustrated London News*. The show was held at the Crystal Palace, London, on July 13, 1871, when some 160 cats were exhibited. Cat shows became hugely popular, having among their followers Queen Victoria, who owned Persian cats. In the US, one of the first shows took place at Bunnell's Museum on Broadway in New York City in 1881, but the first major national event was held in 1895 at Madison Square Garden—and included wild cats and ocelots.

TOP 10 CAT BREEDS IN THE U.S.

	BREED	NO. REGISTERED*
1	Persian	20,431
2	Maine coon	4,385
3	Exotic	2,720
4	Siamese	1,921
5	Abyssinian	1,417
6	Birman	1,057
7	Oriental	952
8	American shorthair	874
9	Tonkinese	864
10	Burmese	772

* *Year ending December 31, 2003*
Source: *Cat Fanciers' Association*

TOP 10 CAT NAMES IN THE U.S.

	NAME
1	Tiger
2	Smokey
3	Tigger
4	Max
5	Oreo
6	Kitty
7	Shadow
8	Princess
9	Oliver
10	Sam

Source: *American Pet Classics*

Farm Facts

FRUIT CROPS

	CROP	PRODUCTION (2003) (METRIC TONS)
1	Tomatoes	110,513,591
2	Watermelons	83,199,791
3	Bananas	68,279,192
4	Oranges	62,170,503
5	Grapes	62,150,308
6	Apples	57,938,065
7	Coconuts	50,227,217
8	Plantains	32,796,160
9	Mangoes	26,196,090
10	Cantaloupes and other melons	21,750,512

Source: *Food and Agriculture Organization of the United Nations*

TYPES OF LIVESTOCK

	ANIMAL	WORLD STOCKS (2003)
1	Chickens	16,381,477,000
2	Cattle	1,368,054,950
3	Ducks	1,107,445,000
4	Sheep	1,028,594,330
5	Pigs	952,899,660
6	Goats	764,510,558
7	Rabbits	530,066,000
8	Turkeys	257,133,000
9	Geese	247,122,000
10	Buffaloes	170,458,495

Source: *Food and Agriculture Organization of the United Nations*

CATTLE COUNTRIES

	COUNTRY	CATTLE (2003)
1	India	226,100,000
2	Brazil	176,500,000
3	China	108,251,500
4	US	96,106,000
5	Argentina	50,869,000
6	Sudan	38,325,000
7	Ethiopia	35,500,000
8	Mexico	30,800,000
9	Australia	27,215,000
10	Russia	26,524,540
	World total	1,368,054,950

Source: *Food and Agriculture Organization of the United Nations*

Since the 1960s, growing and increasingly wealthy populations have raised the demand for milk and meat, prompting an increase in the number of cattle: the world total has risen by over 30 percent since 1961, while that of China has more than doubled.

VEGETABLE CROPS

	CROP*	PRODUCTION (2003 (METRIC TONS)		CROP*	PRODUCTION (2003) (METRIC TONS)
1	Sugar cane	1,350,293,120	6	Cabbages	62,013,881
2	Potatoes	311,416,329	7	Onions (dry)	52,068,053
3	Sugar beets	238,281,136	8	Yams	39,581,313
4	Soybeans	189,523,638	9	Cucumbers and gherkins	37,607,067
5	Sweet potatoes	136,656,488	10	Eggplants	28,913,000

* Excluding cereals

Source: *Food and Agriculture Organization of the United Nations*

TOP 10 | MILK-PRODUCING COUNTRIES

COUNTRY	PRODUCTION* (2003) (METRIC TONS)
1 US	78,155,000
2 India	36,500,000
3 Russia	32,800,000
4 Germany	28,012,000
5 France	24,800,000
6 Brazil	23,315,000
7 UK	15,054,000
8 New Zealand	14,200,000
9 Ukraine	13,600,000
10 China	13,333,250
World total	507,384,506

* Fresh cow's milk

Source: *Food and Agricultural Organization of the United Nations*

TOP 10 | COUNTRIES WHERE SHEEP MOST OUTNUMBER PEOPLE

COUNTRY	SHEEP (2003)	HUMAN POPULATION (2003)	SHEEP PER PERSON (2003)
1 New Zealand	44,700,000	3,951, 307	11.31
2 Australia	98,200,000	19,731,984	4.98
3 Mongolia	11,797,000	2,712,315	4.35
4 Uruguay	11,000,000	3,413,329	3.22
5 Mauritania	8,700,000	2,912,584	2.99
6 Iceland	470,000	280,798	1.67
7 Turkmenistan	6,000,000	4,775,544	1.27
8 = Ireland	4,828,500	3,924,023	1.23
= Namibia	2,370,000	1,927,447	1.23
= Sudan	47,000,000	38,114,160	1.23
US	6,350,000	290,342,554	0.02
World total	1,028,594,330	6,302,486,693	0.16

Source: *Food and Agricultural Organization of the United Nations*

The estimated total world sheep population in 2003 was 1,028,594,330—a global average of one sheep for every 6.08 people (or 0.16 sheep per person)—but, as this Top 10 shows, there are a number of countries where the tables are turned, and sheep far outnumber humans.

▼ **The cows come home**
First introduced by pioneer settlers in 1624, cattle ranching in the United States became one of the nation's major industries.

Tree Tops

TOP 10 COUNTRIES WITH THE LARGEST AREAS OF FOREST

COUNTRY	AREA (2000) (SQ MILES)	(SQ KM)
1 Russia	3,287,243	8,513,920
2 Brazil	2,100,359	5,439,905
3 Canada	944,294	2,445,710
4 US	872,564	2,259,930
5 China	631,200	1,634,800
6 Australia	596,678	1,545,390
7 Dem. Rep. of Congo	522,037	1,352,070
8 Indonesia	405,353	1,049,860
9 Angola	269,329	697,560
10 Peru	251,796	652,150
World total	14,888,715	38,561,590

Source: *Food and Agriculture Organization of the United Nations*, State of the World's Forests, 2003

TOP 10 COUNTRIES WITH THE LARGEST AREAS OF TROPICAL FOREST

COUNTRY	AREA (SQ MILES)	(SQ KM)
1 Brazil	1,163,222	3,012,730
2 Dem. Rep. of Congo	521,512	1,350,710
3 Indonesia	343,029	887,440
4 Peru	292,032	756,360
5 Bolivia	265,012	686,380
6 Venezuela	214,730	556,150
7 Columbia	205,352	531,860
8 Mexico	176,700	457,650
9 India	171,622	444,500
10 Angola	145,035	375,640
World total	5,434,964	14,076,490

Source: *Food and Agriculture Organization of the United Nations*, State of the World's Forests, 2003

TOP 10 POLLINATORS IN TROPICAL FORESTS*

POLLINATOR	PERCENTAGE OF POLLINATION SYSTEMS
1 Bee	50.6
2 Other insects	15.1
3 Beetle	9.2
4 Bird	8.4
5 Moth	5.6
6 Bat	2.6
7 Butterfly	2.3
8 Wind	2.1
9 Large wasp	1.0
10 Fly	0.5

* *Based on pollination systems in Costa Rican and Malaysian tropical forests*

TOP 10 LARGEST NATIONAL FORESTS IN THE U.S.

	FOREST	LOCATION	AREA (SQ MILES)	(SQ KM)
1	Tongass National Forest	Sitka, Alaska	25,913	67,114
2	Chugach National Forest	Anchorage, Alaska	8,433	21,841
3	Toiyabe National Forest	Sparks, Nevada	5,051	13,082
4	Tonto National Forest	Phoenix, Arizona	4,489	11,626
5	Gila National Forest	Silver City, New Mexico	4,232	10,961
6	Boise National Forest	Boise, Idaho	4,145	10,736
7	Humboldt National Forest	Elko, Nevada	3,878	10,044
8	Challis National Forest	Challis, Idaho	3,851	9,974
9	Shoshone National Forest	Cody, Wyoming	3,808	9,863
10	Flathead National Forest	Kalispell, Montana	3,682	9,536

Source: *Land Areas of the National Forest System*

This list's No. 1 is actually larger than all 10 of the smallest states and the District of Columbia put together. Even the much smaller No. 2 is larger than Connecticut, while the two at the bottom of the list cover an area similar to that of Delaware and Rhode Island combined.

TOP 10 TIMBER-PRODUCING COUNTRIES

	COUNTRY	(ROUNDWOOD PRODUCTION 2002) (CU FT)	(CU M)
1	United States	16,874,095,560	477,821,131
2	India	11,280,142,920	319,418,047
3	China	10,061,441,040	284,908,256
4	Brazil	8,386,070,966	237,467,063
5	Canada	7,074,446,865	200,326,008
6	Russia	6,247,165,123	176,900,000
7	Indonesia	4,098,346,982	116,052,252
8	Ethiopia	3,272,248,564	92,659,752
9	Nigeria	2,453,745,484	69,482,328
10	Sweden	2,383,740,225	67,500,000
	World total	119,379,720,200	3,380,456,910

Source: *Food and Agriculture Organization of the United Nations*

WORLD'S TALLEST TREE

IT'S A FACT

UNTIL RECENTLY, a coast redwood at Montgomery State Reserve near Ukiah, California, at 367 ft 6 in (112.01 m), was considered the record-holder, but it has been overtaken by a recent discovery, the so-called "Stratosphere Giant" redwood of 386 ft (117.8 m) in the Rockefeller Forest, Humboldt Redwoods State Park, California. Its location is kept secret to protect it from tourists. Australia once claimed a 492-ft (150-m) eucalyptus tree in Watts River, Victoria, but the tallest surviving example, in the Styx Forest, Tasmania, is 300 ft 6 in (91.6 m).

TOP 10 TALLEST TREES IN THE U.S.*

	TREE	LOCATION	HEIGHT (FT)	(M)
1	Coast redwood	Humboldt Redwoods State Park, CA	386	117.8
2	Douglas fir	Coos Bay BLM District, OR	329	100.3
3	Sitka spruce	Prairie Creek Redwood State Park, CA	317	96.7
4	Giant sequoia	Redwood Mountain Grove, CA	316	96.3
5	Noble fir	Mount St. Helens National Monument, WA	295	89.9
6	Sugar pine	Yosemite National Park, CA	268	81.7
7	Grand fir	Glacier Peak Wilderness, WA	267	81.4
8	Ponderosa pine	Siskiyou National Forest, OR	258	78.6
9	Western hemlock	Prairie Creek Redwood State Park, CA	256	78.0
10	Red fir	Sequoia National Park, CA	252	76.8

* By species (tallest known example of each of the 10 tallest species)

Source: *Robert Van Pelt, American Forests*

◀ **Tree Line**
Olympic National Park in Washington contains 987 sq miles (2,557 sq km) of forest, including the only rainforest in the northern hemisphere.

THE HUMAN
WORLD

Human Body & Health

HEALTHIEST COUNTRIES

	COUNTRY	HEALTHY LIFE EXPECTANCY AT BIRTH*
1	Japan	75.0
2	San Marino	73.4
3	Sweden	73.3
4	Switzerland	73.2
5	Monaco	72.9
6	Iceland	72.8
7	Italy	72.7
8	= Australia	72.6
	= Spain	72.6
10	= Canada	72.0
	= France	72.0
	= Norway	72.0
	US	69.3

* *Average number of years expected to be spent in good health*

Source: *World Health Organization,* World Health Report 2003

▶ **Long life**
Diet and other factors have allowed Japanese healthy life expectancy to top the world league table.

THE 10 **MOST COMMON ALLERGENS***

FOOD		ENVIRONMENTAL
Nuts	1	House dust mite
Shellfish/seafood	2	Grass pollens
Milk	3	Tree pollens
Wheat	4	Cats
Eggs	5	Dogs
Fresh fruit (apples, oranges, strawberries, etc.)	6	Horses
Fresh vegetables (potatoes, cucumbers, etc.)	7	Molds (*Aspergillus fumigatus, Alternaria cladosporium,* etc.)
Cheese	8	Birch pollen
Yeast	9	Weed pollen
Soy protein	10	Wasp/bee venom

* *Substances that cause allergies*

Source: *Dr Chris Corrigan, Consultant Allergist, The Allergy Clinic, Guy's Hospital, London*

THE 10 **MOST COMMON PHOBIAS**

	OBJECT OF PHOBIA	MEDICAL TERM
1	Open spaces	Agoraphobia, cenophobia, or kenophobia
2	Driving	No medical term, can be a symptom of agoraphobia
3	Vomiting	Emetophobia or emitophobia
4	Confined spaces	Claustrophobia, cleisiophobia, cleithrophobia, or clithrophobia
5	Insects	Entemophobia
6	Illness	Nosemophobia
7	Animals	Zoophobia
8	Flying	Aerophobia or aviatophobia
9	Blushing	Erythrophobia
10	Heights	Acrophobia, altophobia, hypsophobia, or hypsiphobia

Source: *National Phobics Society*

TOP 10 LONGEST BONES IN THE HUMAN BODY

	BONE	AVERAGE LENGTH (IN)	(CM)
1	Femur (thighbone–upper leg)	19.88	50.50
2	Tibia (shinbone–inner lower leg)	16.94	43.03
3	Fibula (outer lower leg)	15.94	40.50
4	Humerus (upper arm)	14.35	36.46
5	Ulna (inner lower arm)	11.10	28.20
6	Radius (outer lower arm)	10.40	26.42
7	7th rib	9.45	24.00
8	8th rib	9.06	23.00
9	Innominate bone (hipbone–half pelvis)	7.28	18.50
10	Sternum (breastbone)	6.69	17.00

These are average dimensions of the bones of an adult male measured from their extremities (ribs are curved, and the pelvis measurement is taken diagonally). The same bones in the female skeleton are usually 6 to 13 percent smaller, with the exception of the sternum, which is virtually identical.

THE 10 MOST COMMON HOSPITAL EMERGENCY ROOM CASES

	CASE	VISITS (2002)
1	Stomach and abdominal pain, cramps, and spasms	7,152,000
2	Chest pain and related symptoms	5,637,000
3	Fever	5,310,000
4	Cough	3,016,000
5	Shortness of breath	2,943,000
6	Headache, pain in head	2,844,000
7	Back symptoms	2,713,000
8	Throat symptoms	2,483,000
9	Vomiting	2,422,000
10	Pain, unspecific	2,176,000
	Total visits (including those not in Top 10)	*110,155,000*

Source: *National Ambulatory Medical Care Survey/Center for Disease Control/National Center for Health Statistics*

TOP 10 LARGEST HUMAN ORGANS

	ORGAN		AVERAGE WEIGHT (OZ)	(G)
1	Skin		384.0	10,886
2	Liver		55.0	1,560
3	Brain	male	49.7	1,408
		female	44.6	1,263
4	Lungs	total	38.5	1,090
		right	20.5	580
		left	18.0	510
5	Heart	male	11.1	315
		female	9.3	265
6	Kidneys	total	10.2	290
		right	4.9	140
		left	5.3	150
7	Spleen		6.0	170
8	Pancreas		3.5	98
9	Thyroid		1.2	35
10	Prostate	male only	0.7	20

This list is based on average immediate postmortem weights, as recorded by St. Bartholomew's Hospital, London, UK, and other sources over a 10-year span.

THE 10 LEAST HEALTHY COUNTRIES

	COUNTRY	HEALTHY LIFE EXPECTANCY AT BIRTH*
1	Sierra Leone	28.6
2	Lesotho	31.4
3	Angola	33.4
4	Zimbabwe	33.6
5	Swaziland	34.2
6	= Malawi	34.9
	= Zambia	34.9
8	Burundi	35.1
9	Liberia	35.3
10	= Afghanistan	35.5
	= Niger	35.5

* *Average number of years expected to be spent in good health*

Source: *World Health Organization,* World Health Report 2003

HALE (Health Adjusted Life Expectancy) differs from life expectancy in that an adjustment is made for years spent in ill health as a result of poor diet, disease, lack of healthcare, and other factors. It is the method used by the World Health Organization, and graphically illustrates the contrast between Western and developing countries.

TOP 10 COUNTRIES THAT SPEND THE MOST ON HEALTHCARE

	COUNTRY	HEALTH SPENDING PER CAPITA (1997–2000) ($)
1	US	4,499
2	Switzerland	3,573
3	Japan	2,908
4	Norway	2,832
5	Denmark	2,512
6	Germany	2,422
7	Sweden	2,179
8	Canada	2,058
9	France	2,057
10	Belgium	1,936

Source: *World Bank,* World Development Indicators 2003

It is estimated that an average expenditure of $12 per capita per annum is required to provide the minimum of preventive and essential health services, but the spending of many low-income countries falls well short of this figure. Ethiopia, for example, spends only $4 per capita on healthcare.

Births & Life Spans

COUNTRIES WITH THE MOST BIRTHS

COUNTRY	EST. BIRTHS (2005)
1 India	24,111,501
2 China	16,759,417
3 Nigeria	5,303,493
4 Indonesia	5,011,279
5 Pakistan	4,381,029
6 Bangladesh	4,331,032
7 US	4,181,681
8 Brazil	3,132,278
9 Dem. Rep. of Congo	2,666,572
10 Ethiopia	2,665,717
World	*129,217,147*

Source: *US Census Bureau, International Data Base*

▼ **Youth full**
The high birth rate in many African countries increasingly contrasts with the single-figure and declining rates found in western Europe.

COUNTRIES WITH THE HIGHEST LIFE EXPECTANCY

COUNTRY	EST. LIFE EXPECTANCY AT BIRTH (2005)
1 Andorra	83.5
2 San Marino	81.6
3 Japan	81.2
4 Singapore	80.7
5 = Australia	80.4
= Sweden	80.4
= Switzerland	80.4
8 Hong Kong	80.2
9 = Canada	80.1
= Iceland	80.1
World	*64.3*
US	*77.7*

Source: *US Census Bureau, International Data Base*

COUNTRIES WITH THE HIGHEST BIRTH RATES

COUNTRY	EST. BIRTH RATE (LIVE BIRTHS PER 1,000, 2005)
1 Niger	48.3
2 Mali	46.8
3 Uganda	46.1
4 Chad	46.0
5 Somalia	45.6
6 Angola	44.6
7 Dem. Rep. of Congo	44.4
8 = Burkina Faso	44.2
= Liberia	44.2
10 Malawi	44.0
World	*20.0*
US	*14.1*

Source: *US Census Bureau, International Data Base*

The countries with the highest birth rates are among the poorest countries in the world. In these countries, people often have large families so that the children can earn income for the family when they are older.

TOP 10 | COUNTRIES WITH THE LOWEST INFANT MORTALITY

	COUNTRY	EST. DEATH RATE PER 1,000 LIVE BIRTHS (2005)
1	Sweden	2.8
2	Japan	3.3
3	= Iceland	3.5
	= Singapore	3.5
5	Finland	3.6
6	Norway	3.7
7	Czech Republic	3.9
8	Andorra	4.0
9	Germany	4.2
10	= France	4.3
	= Slovenia	4.3
	US	6.5

Source: *US Census Bureau, International Data Base*

The low mortality and small family sizes of these countries reflect the major medical advances of the 20th century: previously, large numbers of babies died before reaching their first birthday.

THE 10 | COUNTRIES WITH THE HIGHEST INFANT MORTALITY

	COUNTRY	EST. DEATH RATE PER 1,000 LIVE BIRTHS (2005)
1	Angola	191.2
2	Sierra Leone	143.6
3	Afghanistan	137.9
4	Mozambique	136.4
5	Liberia	128.9
6	Niger	121.7
7	Mali	116.8
8	Somalia	116.7
9	Tajikistan	110.8
10	Guinea-Bissau	107.2
	World	*49.0*

Source: *US Census Bureau, International Data Base*

Deaths as a ratio of live births is a commonly employed measure of a country's medical and social conditions. In sharp contrast to the single-digit mortality rates of many Western countries, these figures represent the most disadvantaged people.

THE 10 | COUNTRIES WITH THE LOWEST BIRTH RATES

	COUNTRY	EST. BIRTH RATE (LIVE BIRTHS PER 1,000, 2005)
1	Germany	8.3
2	Austria	8.8
3	Italy	8.9
4	Andorra	9.0
5	= Czech Republic	9.1
	= Slovenia	9.1
7	Latvia	9.2
8	Japan	9.5
9	= Bulgaria	9.7
	= Greece	9.7

Source: *US Census Bureau, International Data Base*

Improvements in birth control, the cost of raising children, and the deliberate decision of many to limit the size of their families are among a range of reasons why the birth rate in many countries has steadily declined in modern times: in 2003, the US birth rate was reported as having fallen to the lowest ever recorded, at 13.9 per 1,000. If counted as an independent country, the Vatican, with a birth rate of zero, would head this list.

INFANT MORTALITY

IT'S A FACT

IN THE PAST 100 YEARS, worldwide infant mortality rates have been driven down by progressive improvements in health care and nutrition. One hundred years ago, the US average was 157 deaths per 1,000 children and the figure was as high as 212 in Italy. The large families typical of that era were partly insurance against this level of risk. In the same period, Scandinavian countries were among the first to achieve levels below 100 deaths per 1,000— Sweden with a rate of 91 and Norway 81. The rates in many developing countries today are thus comparable to those of Western countries 100 years ago.

THE 10 | COUNTRIES WITH THE FEWEST BIRTHS ATTENDED BY SKILLED HEALTH PERSONNEL

	COUNTRY	PERCENTAGE OF ATTENDED BIRTHS*
1	Equatorial Guinea	5
2	Ethiopia	10
3	Bangladesh	13
4	Bhutan	15
5	Chad	16
6	Burundi	19
7	Pakistan	20
8	= Eritrea	21
	= Laos	21
10	Yemen	22

* In those countries/latest year for which data available

Source: *UNICEF*

THE 10 | COUNTRIES WITH THE LOWEST LIFE EXPECTANCY

	COUNTRY	EST. LIFE EXPECTANCY AT BIRTH (2005)
1	Botswana	29.4
2	Zambia	35.1
3	Swaziland	35.6
4	Mozambique	36.0
5	Angola	36.6
6	= Lesotho	36.7
	= Zimbabwe	36.7
8	Malawi	37.0
9	Namibia	38.3
10	Rwanda	39.0

Source: *US Census Bureau, International Data Base*

Matters of Life & Death

WORST EPIDEMICS AND PANDEMICS

	EPIDEMIC OR PANDEMIC	LOCATION	DATE	ESTIMATED NO. KILLED
1	Black Death	Europe/Asia	1347–1380s	75,000,000
2	AIDS	Worldwide	1981–	21,800,000
3	Influenza	Worldwide	1918–20	21,640,000
4	Bubonic plague	India	1896–1948	12,000,000
5	Typhus	Eastern Europe	1914–15	3,000,000
6	= "Plague of Justinian"	Europe/Asia	541–90	millions*
	= Cholera	Worldwide	1846–60	millions*
	= Cholera	Europe	1826–37	millions*
	= Cholera	Worldwide	1893–94	millions*
10	Smallpox	Mexico	1530–45	>1,000,000

* *No precise figures available*

Diseases that spread throughout populations are considered epidemics when more than 400 people out of every 100,000 are affected, while pandemics are those that sweep across wide geographical areas, such as the influenza pandemic that followed World War I, killing more people than died during the conflict.

MOST COMMON CAUSES OF DEATH BY INFECTIOUS AND PARASITIC DISEASES

	CAUSE	APPROXIMATE NO. OF DEATHS (2002)
1	Lower respiratory infection	3,766,000
2	HIV/AIDS	2,821,000
3	Diarrheal diseases	1,767,000
4	Tuberculosis	1,605,000
5	Malaria	1,222,000
6	Measles	760,000
7	Whooping cough (pertussis)	301,000
8	Neonatal tetanus	292,000
9	Meningitis	173,000
10	Syphilis	157,000

Source: *World Health Organization*, World Health Report 2003

In 2002, infectious and parasitic diseases accounted for some 11,122,000 of the 57,027,000 deaths worldwide, or 19.5 percent of the total. Certain childhood diseases, including measles and whooping cough, showed an increase in this year.

▼ **The scourge of AIDS**
South Africa is the hardest hit of all countries affected by the AIDS pandemic. It has been estimated that by 2008, some 500,000 people will die there every year, and average life expectancy will fall from 60 to 40.

COUNTRIES WITH THE MOST CASES OF AIDS

	COUNTRY	DEATHS	ESTIMATED NO. OF CASES
1	South Africa	360,000	5,000,000
2	India	N/A	3,970,000
3	Nigeria	170,000	3,500,000
4	Kenya	190,000	2,500,000
5	Zimbabwe	200,000	2,300,000
6	Ethiopia	160,000	2,100,000
7	Tanzania	140,000	1,500,000
8	Dem. Rep. of Congo	120,000	1,300,000
9	Zambia	120,000	1,200,000
10	Mozambique	60,000	1,100,000
	World total	*3,000,000*	*40,000,000*
	US	*15,000*	*900,000*

Source: *UNAIDS*, Report on the Global HIV/AIDS Epidemic, July 2002

First identified in 1981, AIDS has killed nearly 22 million and affected the social and economic fabric of many African countries by orphaning children, decimating labour forces, and stretching medical resources to their limit.

COUNTRIES WITH THE MOST CREMATIONS

	COUNTRY	PERCENTAGE OF DEATHS	NO. OF CREMATIONS*
1	China	50.60	4,152,000
2	Japan	99.53	1,028,615
3	US	37.78	676,890
4	UK	71.89	437,124
5	Germany	40.10	338,469
6	France	20.38	109,950
7	Canada	48.50	108,436
8	Czech Republic	77.05	83,406
9	Netherlands	49.51	70,951
10	Sweden	67.84	63,273

* In latest year for which data available

Source: *The Cremation Society of Great Britain*

Cremation is least practiced in traditionally Roman Catholic countries, such as Italy (6.91 percent) and the Republic of Ireland (6.41 percent). A shortage of land for burials and cultural factors have led to cremation being the dominant means of disposal of the dead in Japan. A typical funeral in Japan costs about 2.3 million yen—approximately $20,500.

COUNTRIES WITH THE MOST DEATHS FROM HEART DISEASE

	COUNTRY	DEATH RATE PER 100,000*
1	Ukraine	935.8
2	Bulgaria	887.8
3	Russia	746.6
4	Latvia	734.7
5	Estonia	715.6
6	Romania	701.6
7	Hungary	687.1
8	Moldova	632.0
9	Croatia	609.6
10	Czech Republic	566.5
	US	*349.3*

* In those countries' latest year for which data available

Source: *United Nations*

High risk factors including diet and smoking have contributed to the former Soviet states having rates of coronary heart disease that are seven or eight times greater than those of France and Italy.

COUNTRIES WITH THE LOWEST DEATH RATES

	COUNTRY	ESTIMATED DEATH RATE (DEATHS PER 1,000, 2005)
1	Kuwait	2.4
2	Jordan	2.6
3	Brunei	3.4
4	Libya	3.5
5	Oman	3.9
6	Solomon Islands	4.0
7	Bahrain	4.1
8	= Costa Rica	4.3
	= United Arab Emirates	4.3
10	Guam	4.4
	World average	*8.8*
	US	*8.2*

Source: *US Census Bureau, International Data Base*

Crude death rate is derived by dividing the total number of deaths in a given year by the total population and multiplying by 1,000. These tend to mean that countries with young populations have low death rates and older populations, high rates.

COUNTRIES WITH THE HIGHEST DEATH RATES

	COUNTRY	ESTIMATED DEATH RATE (DEATHS PER 1,000, 2005)
1	Botswana	36.5
2	Angola	25.9
3	Swaziland	25.3
4	Lesotho	25.0
5	Mozambique	24.9
6	Zimbabwe	24.7
7	Zambia	24.4
8	Malawi	23.4
9	Namibia	23.1
10	South Africa	23.0

Source: *US Census Bureau, International Data Base*

All 10 of the countries with the highest death rates are in Africa, with all but Niger and Rwanda located between 10° and 30° south.

Accidents & Fires

 MOST ACCIDENT-PRONE COUNTRIES

	COUNTRY	ACCIDENT DEATH RATE PER 100,000*
1	Estonia	102.8
2	Latvia	101.4
3	Russia	100.2
4	Ukraine	83.0
5	Lithuania	75.2
6	Hungary	58.6
7	Moldova	56.7
8	= Finland	52.8
	= France	52.8
10	Belarus	51.7
	US	36.2

In those countries/latest year for which data available

Source: *UN Demographic Yearbook*

MOST COMMON TYPES OF INJURIES IN THE U.S.

	TYPE OF INJURY	NO. OF EMERGENCY DEPARTMENT VISITS (2001)
1	Falls	7,762
2	Struck against by objects or persons	4,382
3	Motor vehicle accidents	4,370
4	Cutting or piercing	2,974
5	Overexertion and strenuous movements	1,699
6	Natural/environmental	1,496
7	Adverse effects of medical treatment	1,445
8	Assault	1,387
9	Poisoning	720
10	Burns	502

Source: *National Center for Health Statistics*

MOST COMMON CAUSES OF ACCIDENTAL DEATH IN THE U.S.

	CAUSE	TOTAL*	PERCENTAGE OF ALL ACCIDENTAL DEATHS*
1	Motor vehicle	42,271	42.1
2	Fall	14,992	14.9
3	Poisoning	14,053	14.0
4	Suffocation	4,941	4.9
5	Burning	3,370	3.4
6	Drowning	3,179	3.2
7	Transportation (excluding motor vehicles)	2,799	2.8
8	Natural/environmental	1,387	1.4
9	Pedestrian	1,236	1.2
10	Striking by/against object	890	0.9
	Total unintentional and adverse event-related deaths	*100,441*	*100*

Figures (2001) exclude deaths of those under one year old

Source: *National Center for Injury Prevention and Control*

Accidents or unintentional injuries are ranked fifth among the leading causes of death in the US. Definitive statistics for 2002 have not yet been issued, but provisional figures itemized 813 deaths resulting from the accidental discharge of firearms, making this cause a close runner-up to the Top 10.

TOP 10 | PRODUCTS MOST OFTEN INVOLVED IN ACCIDENTS IN THE U.S.

	PRODUCT GROUP*	ESTIMATED NO. OF INJURIES (2002)
1	Stairs, ramps, landings, and floors	2,028,968
2	Beds, mattresses, and pillows	515,666
3	Chairs, sofas, and sofa beds	438,173
4	Doors and panels (non-glass)	345,000
5	Tables	307,843
6	Bathroom structures and fixtures	301,375
7	Cans and other containers	262,909
8	Desks, cabinets, shelves, and racks	254,699
9	Ladders and stools	210,833
10	Toys	204,563

* Excluding sports and recreational equipment

Source: US Consumer Product Safety Commission/NEISS (National Electronic Injury Surveillance System)

These figures are based on a survey of injuries caused by some 15,000 types of products, based on a sample of 99 US hospitals. Just under 10 percent of the accidents in the stairs category were either fatal or required hospitalization.

THE 10 | WORST SINGLE-BUILDING FIRES

	LOCATION/DATE	BUILDING/ STRUCTURE	NO. KILLED
1	**London,** UK, July 11, 1212	London Bridge	3,000*
2	**Santiago,** Chile, Dec. 8, 1863	Church of La Compañía	2,500#
3	**Canton,** China, May 25, 1845	Theater	1,670
4	**Shanghai,** China, June 1871	Theater	900
5	**Vienna,** Austria, Dec. 8, 1881	Ring Theater	640–850
6	**St. Petersburg,** Russia, Feb. 14, 1836	Lehmann Circus	800
7	**Antoung,** China, Feb. 13, 1937	Movie theater	658
8	**Chicago,** Illinois, Dec. 30, 1903	Iroquois Theater	602
9	**Mandi Dabwali,** India, Dec. 23, 1995	School tent	over 500
10	**Boston,** MA, Nov. 28, 1942	Cocoanut Grove Night Club	491

* Burned, crushed, and drowned in ensuing panic; the year is somtimes given as 1213

Precise figure uncertain

◀ **An accident waiting to happen**
Although statistically included with other surfaces in the home, stairs are implicated in a high proportion of domestic accidents in US homes.

Marriage & Divorce

THE 10 COUNTRIES WITH THE LOWEST DIVORCE RATES

	COUNTRY	DIVORCE RATE PER 1,000*
1	Guatemala	0.12
2	Libya	0.25
3	Mongolia	0.34
4 =	Armenia	0.35
=	Georgia	0.35
6	Chile	0.42
7	Jamaica	0.44
8	Italy	0.47
9	Turkey	0.49
10	Macedonia	0.52

In those countries/latest year for which data available

Source: *United Nations*

THE 10 COUNTRIES WITH THE HIGHEST DIVORCE RATES

	COUNTRY	DIVORCE RATE PER 1,000*
1	Belarus	4.71
2	US	4.19
3	Russia	3.66
4	Estonia	3.09
5	Ukraine	3.59
6	Aruba	3.40
7	Cuba	3.39
8	Lithuania	3.08
9	Switzerland	2.91
10	Finland	2.72

In those countries/latest year for which data available

Source: *United Nations*

THE 10 COUNTRIES WHERE WOMEN MARRY THE YOUNGEST

	COUNTRY	AVERAGE AGE AT FIRST MARRIAGE
1	Dem. Rep. of Congo	16.6
2 =	Afghanistan	17.8
=	São Tomé and Principe	17.8
4	Niger	17.6
5 =	Chad	18.0
=	Mozambique	18.0
7	Bangladesh	18.1
8	Uganda	18.2
9 =	Congo	18.4
=	Mali	18.4

Source: *United Nations*

Child bride
Traditionally, Afghan brides are among the youngest in the world. The average age of women marrying is half that of those in other countries including Sweden and most Caribbean islands.

COUNTRIES WITH THE HIGHEST MARRIAGE RATE

	COUNTRY	MARRIAGES PER 1,000 PER ANNUM*
1	Barbados	13.1
2	Liechtenstein	12.8
3	Cyprus	12.3
4	Seychelles	11.5
5	Jamaica	10.4
6	Ethiopia	10.2
7	Fiji	10.1
8	Bangladesh	9.5
9	Sri Lanka	9.3
10	Iran	8.4
	US	8.2

* In those countries/latest year for which data available

Source: *United Nations*

The highest figures are actually recorded in places that are not independent countries. Gibraltar, for example, has a marriage rate of 24.9 per 1,000.

COUNTRIES WITH THE LOWEST MARRIAGE RATE

	COUNTRY	MARRIAGES PER 1,000 PER ANNUM*
1	United Arab Emirates	2.5
2	Georgia	2.9
3	= Peru	3.2
	= Saudi Arabia	3.2
5	St. Lucia	3.3
6	= Andorra	3.4
	= Qatar	3.4
8	= South Africa	3.5
	= Tajikistan	3.5
10	Panama	3.7

* In those countries/latest year for which data available

Source: *United Nations*

Marriage rates around the world vary according to a range of religious and cultural factors. These vary from high costs of traditional dowry payments to a shift away from marriage as an institution in Scandinavian countries.

COUNTRIES WITH THE MOST MARRIAGES

	COUNTRY	MARRIAGES PER ANNUM*
1	US	2,329,000
2	Bangladesh	1,181,000
3	Russia	911,162
4	Japan	798,140
5	Mexico	743,856
6	Brazil	731,920
7	Ethiopia	630,290
8	Iran	511,277
9	Egypt	503,651
10	Turkey	485,035

* In those countries/latest year for which data available

Source: *United Nations*

This list, based on United Nations statistics, regrettably excludes certain large countries such as India, Indonesia, and Pakistan, which fail to provide accurate data.

MARRIAGE RATES

IT'S A FACT

TODAY THERE ARE BARELY 10 countries in the world with double-figure marriage rates (those with more than 10 marriages annually for every 1,000 of the population). In contrast, 100 years ago only a handful of countries, including Ireland, Uruguay, and Japan, had marriage rates of less than 10 per 1,000, while the rate of 18 or more recorded in Russia and parts of Germany was not uncommon. The institution of marriage has declined to such an extent in certain countries that the rate is less than one-third of that at the beginning of the 20th century; Sweden's rate has plummeted from 11.9 to 3.5.

OVERSEAS HONEYMOON DESTINATIONS FOR U.S. COUPLES

	DESTINATION
1	Jamaica
2	Tahiti
3	Bermuda
4	St. Lucia
5	Italy
6	Aruba
7	US Virgin Islands
8	Australia
9	France
10	The Bahamas

Source: Modern Bride

MOST COMMON GROUNDS FOR DIVORCE ON U.S. STATE STATUTE BOOKS

	GROUNDS
1	Irretrievable breakdown
2	Separation
3	Desertion/abandonment
4	Adultery
5	Cruelty
6	Insanity
7	Addiction
8	Felony
9	= Impotency
	= Imprisonment
	= Incompatability of temperament

Source: *Relate National Marriage Guidance*

Names of the Decades 1900s–1990s

FIRST NAMES OF THE 1900s IN THE U.S.

BOYS		GIRLS
John	1	Mary
William	2	Helen
James	3	Margaret
George	4	Anna
Joseph	5	Ruth
Charles	6	Elizabeth
Robert	7	Dorothy
Frank	8	Marie
Edward	9	Mildred
Henry	10	Alice

FIRST NAMES OF THE 1910s IN THE U.S.

BOYS		GIRLS
John	1	Mary
William	2	Helen
James	3	Dorothy
Robert	4	Margaret
Joseph	5	Ruth
George	6	Mildred
Charles	7	Anna
Edward	8	Elizabeth
Frank	9	Frances
Walter	10	Marie

FIRST NAMES OF THE 1920s IN THE U.S.

BOYS		GIRLS
Robert	1	Mary
John	2	Dorothy
James	3	Helen
William	4	Betty
Charles	5	Margaret
George	6	Ruth
Joseph	7	Virginia
Richard	8	Doris
Edward	9	Mildred
Donald	10	Elizabeth

FIRST NAMES OF THE 1960s IN THE U.S.

BOYS		GIRLS
Michael	1	Lisa
David	2	Mary
John	3	Karen
James	4	Susan
Robert	5	Kimberly
Mark	6	Patricia
William	7	Linda
Richard	8	Donna
Thomas	9	Michelle
Jeffrey	10	Cynthia

FIRST NAMES OF THE 1970s IN THE U.S.

BOYS		GIRLS
Michael	1	Jennifer
Christopher	2	Amy
Jason	3	Melissa
David	4	Michelle
James	5	Kimberly
John	6	Lisa
Robert	7	Angela
Brian	8	Heather
William	9	Stephanie
Matthew	10	Jessica

All the lists on these pages are based on a five percent sample of US Social Security applications made for babies born in the decade under review. The largest number surveyed was in the baby-booming 1950s, when the total sample comprised 1,059,301 males and 1,002,464 females.

TOP 10 FIRST NAMES OF THE 1930s IN THE U.S.

BOYS		GIRLS
Robert	1	Mary
James	2	Betty
John	3	Barbara
William	4	Shirley
Richard	5	Patricia
Charles	6	Dorothy
Donald	7	Joan
George	8	Margaret
Thomas	9	Nancy
Joseph	10	Helen

TOP 10 FIRST NAMES OF THE 1940s IN THE U.S.

BOYS		GIRLS
John	1	Mary
Robert	2	Linda
John	3	Barbara
William	4	Patricia
Richard	5	Carol
David	6	Sandra
Charles	7	Nancy
Thomas	8	Judith
Michael	9	Sharon
Ronald	10	Susan

TOP 10 FIRST NAMES OF THE 1950s IN THE U.S.

BOYS		GIRLS
Michael	1	Mary
James	2	Linda
Robert	3	Patricia
John	4	Susan
David	5	Deborah
William	6	Barbara
Richard	7	Debra
Thomas	8	Karen
Mark	9	Nancy
Charles	10	Donna

TOP 10 FIRST NAMES OF THE 1980s IN THE U.S.

BOYS		GIRLS
Michael	1	Jessica
Christopher	2	Jennifer
Matthew	3	Amanda
Joshua	4	Ashley
David	5	Sarah
Daniel	6	Stephanie
James	7	Melissa
Robert	8	Nicole
John	9	Elizabeth
Joseph	10	Heather

TOP 10 FIRST NAMES OF THE 1990s IN THE U.S.

BOYS		GIRLS
Michael	1	Ashley
Christopher	2	Jessica
Matthew	3	Emily
Joshua	4	Sarah
Jacob	5	Samantha
Andrew	6	Brittany
Daniel	7	Amanda
Nicholas	8	Elizabeth
Tyler	9	Taylor
Joseph	10	Megan

◄ **Naming baby**
The choosing of names for babies has taxed generations of parents, with the top choices across the decades combining the traditional and the fashionable.

THE TOP 10 FIRST FEMALE PRIME MINISTERS AND PRESIDENTS

PRIME MINISTER/PRESIDENT	COUNTRY	FIRST PERIOD IN OFFICE
Sirimavo Bandaranaike (PM)	Ceylon	July 1960–Mar. 1965
Indira Gandhi (PM)	India	Jan. 1966–Mar .1977
Golda Meir (PM)	Israel	Mar. 1969–June 1974
Maria Estela Perón (President)	Argentina	July 1974–Mar. 1976
Elisabeth Domitien (PM)	Central African Republic	Jan. 1975–Apr. 1976
Margaret Thatcher (PM)	UK	May 1979–Nov. 1990
Dr. Maria Lurdes Pintasilgo (PM)	Portugal	Aug. 1979–Jan. 1980
Mary Eugenia Charles (PM)	Dominica	July 1980–June 1995
Vigdís Finnbogadóttir (President)	Iceland	Aug. 1980–Aug. 1996
Gro Harlem Brundtland (PM)	Norway	Feb.–Oct. 1981

Sirimavo Bandaranaike of Ceylon (now Sri Lanka) became the world's first female prime minister on July 21, 1960. Margaret Thatcher became Britain's first on May 4, 1979. The first 10 were followed by Corazón Aquino, who became president of the Philippines in 1986, and Benazir Bhutto, who was prime minister of Pakistan between 1988 and 1990.

THE TOP 10 ROYALS IN LINE FOR THE BRITISH THRONE

ROYAL

HRH The Prince of Wales (Prince Charles Philip Arthur George)
b. Nov. 14, 1948; *then his elder son:*

HRH Prince William of Wales (Prince William Arthur Philip Louis)
b. June 21, 1982; *then his younger brother:*

HRH Prince Henry of Wales (Prince Henry Charles Albert David)
b. Sept. 15, 1984; *then his uncle:*

HRH The Duke of York (Prince Andrew Albert Christian Edward)
b. Feb. 19, 1960; *then his elder daughter:*

HRH Princess Beatrice of York (Princess Beatrice Elizabeth Mary)
b. Aug. 8, 1988; *then her younger sister:*

HRH Princess Eugenie of York (Princess Eugenie Victoria Helena)
b. Mar. 23, 1990; *then her uncle:*

HRH Prince Edward (Prince Edward Antony Richard Louis)
b. Mar. 10, 1964; *then his daughter:*

Lady Louise Alice Elizabeth Mary Mountbatten Windsor
b. Nov. 8, 2003; *then her aunt:*

HRH The Princess Royal (Princess Anne Elizabeth Alice Louise)
b. Aug. 15, 1950; *then her son:*

Master Peter Mark Andrew Phillips
b. Nov. 15, 1977

The birth of Lady Louise Windsor to the Count and Countess of Wessex in November 2003 means that Princess Anne's daughter, Zara Phillips, has now fallen out of the Top 10.

TOP 10 LONGEST-SERVING PRESIDENTS TODAY

	PRESIDENT	COUNTRY	TOOK OFFICE
1	General Gnassingbé Eyadéma	Togo	Apr. 14, 1967
2	El Hadj Omar Bongo	Gabon	Dec. 2, 1967
3	Colonel Mu'ammar Gadhafi	Libya	Sept. 1, 1969*
4	Zayid ibn Sultan al-Nuhayyan	United Arab Emirates	Dec. 2, 1971
5	Fidel Castro	Cuba	Nov. 2, 1976
6	France-Albert René	Seychelles	June 5, 1977
7	Ali Abdullah Saleh	Yemen	July 17, 1978
8	Maumoon Abdul Gayoom	Maldives	Nov. 11, 1978
9	Teodoro Obiang Nguema Mbasogo	Equatorial Guinea	Aug. 3, 1979
10	José Eduardo Dos Santos	Angola	Sept. 21, 1979

* *Since a reorganization in 1979, Colonel Gadhafi has held no formal position, but continues to rule under the ceremonial title of "Leader of the Revolution"*

All the presidents in this list have been in power for more than 20 years, some for over 30. Fidel Castro was prime minister of Cuba from February 1959 and effectively ruled as dictator from then, but he was not technically president until the Cuban constitution was revised in 1976.

TOP 10 LONGEST-REIGNING LIVING MONARCHS*

	MONARCH	COUNTRY	DATE OF BIRTH	ACCESSION
1	Bhumibol Adulyadej	Thailand	Dec. 5, 1927	June 9, 1946
2	Prince Rainier III	Monaco	May 31, 1923	May 9, 1949
3	Elizabeth II	UK	Apr. 21, 1926	Feb. 6, 1952
4	Malietoa Tanumafili II	Samoa	Jan. 4, 1913	Jan. 1, 1962#
5	Taufa'ahau Tupou IV	Tonga	July 4, 1918	Dec. 16 1965†
6	Haji Hassanal Bolkiah	Brunei	July 15, 1946	Oct. 5, 1967
7	Sayyid Qaboos ibn Said al-Said	Oman	Nov. 18, 1942	July 23, 1970
8	Margrethe II	Denmark	Apr. 16, 1940	Jan. 14, 1972
9	Jigme Singye Wangchuk	Bhutan	Nov. 11, 1955	July 24, 1972
10	Carl XVI Gustaf	Sweden	Apr. 30, 1946	Sept. 19, 1973

* *Including hereditary rulers of principalities, dukedoms, etc.*

\# *Sole ruler since April 15, 1963*

† *Full sovereignty from June 5, 1970, when British protectorate ended*

There are 28 countries that have emperors, kings, queens, princes, dukes, sultans, or other hereditary rulers as their heads of state. This list formerly included Birendra Bir Bikram Shah Dev, King of Nepal since January 31, 1972. On June 1, 2001, he was shot dead by his own son, Crown Prince Dipendra, who then committed suicide. Any further deaths, coups, or abdications will elevate, in order, Juan Carlos I of Spain, who ascended to the throne on the death of General Franco and the restoration of the monarchy on November 22, 1975, Shaikh Jabir al-Ahmad al-Jabir al-Sabah, Amir of Kuwait (December 31, 1977), and Queen Beatrix of the Netherlands (April 30, 1980).

TOP 10 LONGEST-REIGNING MONARCHS

	MONARCH	COUNTRY	REIGN	AGE AT ACCESSION	YEARS REIGNED
1	King Louis XIV	France	1643–1715	5	72
2	King John II	Liechtenstein	1858–1929	18	71
3	Emperor Franz-Josef	Austria-Hungary	1848–1916	18	67
4	Queen Victoria	UK	1837–1901	18	63
5	Emperor Hirohito	Japan	1926–89	25	62
6	Emperor K'ang Hsi	China	1661–1722	8	61
7	King Sobhuza II*	Swaziland	Dec. 22, 1921–Aug. 21, 1982	22	60
8	Emperor Ch'ien Lung	China	Oct. 18, 1735–Feb. 9, 1796	25	60
9	King Christian IV	Denmark	Apr. 4, 1588–Feb. 21, 1648	11	59
10	King George III	UK	Oct. 26, 1760–Jan. 29, 1820	22	59

* Paramount chief until 1967, when Great Britain recognized him as king with the granting of internal self-government

King Harald I of Norway is said to have ruled for 70 years from 870–940, and the even longer reigns of 95 years and 94 years are credited respectively to King Mihti of Arakan (Myanmar, as known today) around 1279–1374, and Pharaoh Phiops (Pepi) II of Egypt around 2269–2175 BC, but there is inadequate historical evidence to substantiate any of these claims.

TOP 10 LONGEST-REIGNING QUEENS

	QUEEN*	REIGN COUNTRY	REIGN	YEARS
1	Victoria	UK	1837–1901	63
2	Wilhelmina	Netherlands	1890–1948	58
3	Elizabeth II	UK	1952–	52
4	Wu Chao	China	655–705	50
5	Salote Tubou	Tonga	1918–65	47
6	Elizabeth I	England	1558–1603	44
7	Maria Theresa	Hungary	1740–80	40
8	Maria I	Portugal	1777–1816	39
9	Joanna I	Italy	1343–81	38
10	Suiko Tenno	Japan	592–628	36

* Queens and empresses who ruled in their own right, not as consorts of kings or emperors

◀ **Sun King**
By ascending the French throne as a child and living a then exceptional 77 years, Louis XIV broke all records for the longest substantiated reign.

US Presidents

TOP 10 | OLDEST PRESIDENTS

	PRESIDENT	AGE ON TAKING OFFICE (YEARS)	(DAYS)
1	Ronald W. Reagan	69	349
2	William H. Harrison	68	23
3	James Buchanan	65	315
4	George H.W. Bush	64	223
5	Zachary Taylor	64	100
6	Dwight D. Eisenhower	62	98
7	Andrew Jackson	61	354
8	John Adams	61	125
9	Gerald R. Ford	61	26
10	Harry Truman	60	339

Born on February 6, 1911, Ronald Reagan was 77 years 349 days old when he completed his second term on January 20, 1989. In 2001, Reagan also topped the list of longest-lived former presidents by outliving John Adams, who died on July 4, 1826, at the age of 90 years 247 days. Herbert Hoover is the only other nonagenarian ex-president, dying in 1964 at age 90 years 71 days, but at 31 years 231 days, his was the longest life-span after leaving office.

TOP 10 | SHORTEST-SERVING PRESIDENTS

	PRESIDENT	PERIOD IN OFFICE (YEARS)	(DAYS)
1	William H. Harrison*	—	32
2	James A. Garfield*	—	199
3	Zachary Taylor*	1	127
4	Warren G. Harding*	2	151
5	Gerald R. Ford	2	166
6	Millard Fillmore	2	236
7	John F. Kennedy*	2	306
8	Chester A. Arthur	3	166
9	Andrew Johnson	3	323
10	John Tyler	3	332

* Died in office

Ninth and second-oldest president William Harrison caught pneumonia while delivering an inaugural address in the rain on March 4, 1831. The longest on record, its 8,578 words took him 1 hour 45 minutes to deliver. He was ill throughout his record shortest term in office, and became the first president to die in office and the first to die in the White House. Outside these 10, all other presidents have served either one or two full four-year terms—three in the case of Franklin D. Roosevelt.

TOP 10 | YOUNGEST PRESIDENTS

	PRESIDENT	AGE ON TAKING OFFICE (YEARS)	(DAYS)
1	Theodore Roosevelt	42	322
2	John F. Kennedy	43	236
3	William J. Clinton	46	149
4	Ulysses S. Grant	46	311
5	Grover Cleveland	47	351
6	Franklin Pierce	48	101
7	James A. Garfield	49	105
8	James K. Polk	49	122
9	Millard Fillmore	50	184
10	John Tyler	51	8

Vice-President Theodore Roosevelt became president following the assassination of William McKinley. John F. Kennedy was the youngest president to be elected. The Constitution insists that a president must be at least 35 years old on taking office. George W. Bush was 54 years 6 months 14 days old when he took office in 2001. Despite his appearance in this list, Polk holds the record for the shortest life-span after leaving office: he ended his four-year term on March 3, 1849, and died 103 days later at the age of 53 years 225 days.

TOP 10 | PRESIDENTS WITH THE MOST ELECTORAL COLLEGE VOTES

	PRESIDENT	YEAR	VOTES
1	Ronald W. Reagan	1984	525
2	Franklin D. Roosevelt	1936	523
3	Richard M. Nixon	1972	520
4	Ronald W. Reagan	1980	489
5	Lyndon B. Johnson	1964	486
6	Franklin D. Roosevelt	1932	472
7	Dwight D. Eisenhower	1956	457
8	Franklin D. Roosevelt	1940	449
9	Herbert C. Hoover	1928	444
10	Dwight D. Eisenhower	1952	442
	George W. Bush	*2000*	*271*

Each political party in each state is allocated a number of electors equal to the number of its senators (two per state) plus the number of its representatives. Voters vote for the electors, who comprise the Electoral College, which in turn votes for the presidential and vice-presidential candidates.

TOP 10 | PRESIDENTS WITH THE MOST POPULAR VOTES

	PRESIDENT	YEAR	VOTES
1	Ronald W. Reagan	1984	54,281,858
2	George W. Bush	2000	50,459,211
3	George H.W. Bush	1988	48,881,221
4	William J. Clinton	1996	47,401,185
5	Richard M. Nixon	1972	47,165,234
6	William J. Clinton	1992	44,908,254
7	Ronald W. Reagan	1980	43,899,248
8	Lyndon B. Johnson	1964	43,126,506
9	Jimmy Carter	1976	40,828,929
10	Dwight D. Eisenhower	1956	35,585,316

Despite population increases and the enfranchisement of 18- to 21-year-olds in 1972, this Top 10 shows that it is not the most recent presidential elections that have attracted the greatest number of popular votes for the winning candidate. Also, many presidents have won with less than 50 percent of the total popular vote: in 1824, John Quincy Adams achieved only 108,740 votes—30.5 percent of the total; and in 1860, Abraham Lincoln had 1,865,593—39.8 percent.

MOST POPULAR PRESIDENTS

	PRESIDENT	SURVEY DATE	APPROVAL RATING (%)
1	George W. Bush	Sept. 21–22, 2001	90
2	George H.W. Bush	Feb. 28, 1991	89
3	Harry S. Truman	May–June 1945	87
4	Franklin D. Roosevelt	Jan. 1942	84
5	John F. Kennedy	Apr. 28, 1961	83
6	Dwight D. Eisenhower	Dec. 14, 1956	79
7	Lyndon B. Johnson	Dec. 5, 1963	78
8	Jimmy Carter	Mar. 18, 1977	75
9	Gerald R. Ford	Aug. 16, 1974	71
10	William J. Clinton	Jan. 30–Feb. 1, 1998	69

Source: *The Gallup Organization*

The Gallup Organization began surveying approval and disapproval ratings of presidents in October 1938. Since then, the only president to not make the Top 10 is Richard M. Nixon, whose highest approval rating was 67 percent on two occasions: November 12, 1969, and January 26, 1973.

LEAST POPULAR PRESIDENTS

	PRESIDENT	SURVEY DATE	DISAPPROVAL RATING (%)
1	Richard M. Nixon	Aug. 2, 1974	66
2	Harry S. Truman	Jan. 1952	62
3	George H.W. Bush	July 31, 1992	60
4	Jimmy Carter	June 29, 1979	59
5	Ronald W. Reagan	Jan. 28, 1983	56
6	William J. Clinton	Sept. 6–7, 1994	54
7	Lyndon B. Johnson	Mar. 10, 1968; Aug. 7, 1968	52
8 =	Franklin D. Roosevelt	Nov. 1938	46
=	Gerald R. Ford	Apr. 18, 1975; Nov. 21, 1975; Dec. 12, 1975	46
10	George W. Bush	Sept. 7–10, 2001	39

Source: *The Gallup Organization*

The one president to not make the Top 10 is John F. Kennedy, whose highest disapproval rating was 30 percent on November 8, 1963, the last survey compiled before his assassination.

Human Achievements

THE 10 | FIRST MOUNTAINEERS TO CLIMB MOUNT EVEREST

	MOUNTAINEER/COUNTRY OF ORIGIN	DATE
1	**Edmund Hillary,** New Zealand	May 29, 1953
2	**Tenzing Norgay,** Nepal	May 29, 1953
3	**Jürg Marmet,** Switzerland	May 23, 1956
4	**Ernst Schmied,** Switzerland	May 23, 1956
5	**Hans-Rudolf von Gunten,** Switzerland	May 23, 1956
6	**Adolf Reist,** Switzerland	May 24, 1956
7	**Wang Fu-chou,** China	May 24, 1960
8	**Chu Ying-hua,** China	May 25, 1960
9	**Konbu,** Tibet	May 25, 1960
10 =	**Nawang Gombu,** India	May 1, 1963
=	**James Whittaker,** US	May 1, 1963

Nawang Gombu and James Whittaker are 10th equal because, neither wishing to deny the other the privilege of being first, they ascended the last steps to the summit side by side.

▶ **On top of the world**
Edmund Hillary (b. 1919) and Sherpa Tenzing Norgay (1914–86) celebrate their conquest of Everest.

THE 10 | FIRST PEOPLE TO GO OVER NIAGARA FALLS AND SURVIVE

	NAME	METHOD	DATE
1	**Annie Edson Taylor**	Wooden barrel	Oct. 24, 1901
2	**Bobby Leach**	Steel barrel	July 25, 1911
3	**Jean Lussier**	Steel and rubber ball equipped with oxygen cylinders	July 4, 1928
4	**William Fitzgerald** (a.k.a. Nathan Boya)	Steel and rubber ball equipped with oxygen cylinders	July 15, 1961
5	**Karel Soucek**	Barrel	July 3, 1984
6	**Steven Trotter**	Barrel	Aug. 18, 1985
7	**Dave Mundy**	Barrel	Oct. 5, 1985
8 =	**Peter de Bernardi**	Metal container	Sept. 28, 1989
=	**Jeffrey Petkovich**	Metal container	Sept. 28, 1989
10	**Dave Mundy**	Diving bell	Sept. 26, 1993

Source: *Niagara Falls Museum*

Captain Matthew Webb, the first person to swim the English Channel, was killed on July 24, 1883, attempting to swim the rapids beneath Niagara Falls. Having survived the Falls, Bobby Leach (1842–1920) went on a world lecture tour: while in New Zealand, he slipped on some orange peel and died of his injuries.

ASCEND EVEREST

AS EARLY AS THE MID-19TH CENTURY, it was realized that Mount Everest was the world's highest peak, but it was 100 years before it was successfully climbed. No attempts were made until the 1920s. In 1922 the second expedition reached a height of 27,297 ft (8,320 m). Although a member of the third expedition attained 28,150 ft (8,580 m), two members of the party vanished. Over subsequent years, many expeditions tried and failed. The first successful ascent, that of Hillary and Tenzing, was achieved on May 29, 1953.

THE 10 FIRST CROSS-CHANNEL SWIMMERS

	SWIMMER	COUNTRY	TIME (HR:MIN)	DATE
1	Matthew Webb	UK	21:45	Aug. 24–25, 1875
2	Thomas Burgess	UK	22:35	Sept. 5–6, 1911
3	Henry Sullivan	US	26:50	Aug. 5–6, 1923
4	Enrico Tiraboschi	Italy	16:33	Aug. 12, 1923
5	Charles Toth	US	16:58	Sept. 8–9, 1923
6	Gertrude Ederle	US	14:39	Aug. 6, 1926
7	Millie Corson	US	15:29	Aug. 27–28, 1926
8	Arnst Wierkotter	Germany	12:40	Aug. 30, 1926
9	Edward Temme	UK	14:29	Aug. 5, 1927
10	Mercedes Gleitze	UK	15:15	Oct. 7, 1927

The first three crossings were from England to France, the rest from France to England. Gertrude Ederle was the first woman to swim the Channel—but it was not until September 11, 1951 that American swimmer Florence Chadwick became the first woman to swim from England to France.

THE 10 FIRST PEOPLE TO REACH THE SOUTH POLE

	NAME/COUNTRY	DATE
1	= Roald Amundsen,* Norway	Dec. 14, 1911
	= Olav Olavsen Bjaaland, Norway	Dec. 14, 1911
	= Helmer Julius Hanssen, Norway	Dec. 14, 1911
	= Helge Sverre Hassel, Norway	Dec. 14, 1911
	= Oscar Wisting, Norway	Dec. 14, 1911
6	= Robert Falcon Scott,* UK	Jan. 17, 1912
	= Henry Robertson Bowers, UK	Jan. 17, 1912
	= Edgar Evans, UK	Jan. 17, 1912
	= Lawrence Edward Grace Oates, UK	Jan. 17, 1912
	= Edward Adrian Wilson, UK	Jan. 17, 1912

* Expedition leader

Just 33 days separate the first two expeditions to reach the South Pole. Scott's British Antarctic Expedition was organized with its avowed goal "to reach the South Pole and to secure for the British Empire the honor of this achievement." Meanwhile, Norwegian explorer Roald Amundsen also set out on an expedition to the Pole. When Scott eventually reached his goal, he discovered that the Norwegians had beaten them. Demoralized, Scott's team began the arduous return journey, but plagued by illness, hunger, bad weather, and exhaustion, the entire expedition died just as Amundsen's triumph was being reported to the world.

THE 10 FIRST PEOPLE TO REACH THE NORTH POLE

	NAME/COUNTRY OR NATIONALITY	DATE
1	= Robert Edwin Peary, US	Apr. 6, 1909
	= Matthew Alexander Henson, US	Apr. 6, 1909
	= Ooqueah, Inuit	Apr. 6, 1909
	= Ootah, Inuit	Apr. 6, 1909
	= Egingwah, Inuit	Apr. 6, 1909
	= Seegloo, Inuit	Apr. 6, 1909
7	= Pavel Afanaseyevich Geordiyenko, USSR	Apr. 23, 1948
	= Mikhail Yemel'yenovich Ostrekin, USSR	Apr. 23, 1948
	= Pavel Kononovich Sen'ko, USSR	Apr. 23, 1948
	= Mikhail Mikhaylovich Somov, USSR	Apr. 23, 1948

There remains some doubt as to the validity of Peary's team's claim to have reached the North Pole overland in 1909. The first undisputed "conquest," that of the 1948 Soviet team, was achieved by landing in an aircraft. The first team known to have attained the Pole overland was led by Ralph S. Plaisted (US), along with Walter Pederson, Gerald Pitzel, and Jean Luc Bombardier, who arrived on April 18, 1968.

Criminal Records

THE 10 COUNTRIES WITH THE HIGHEST REPORTED CRIME RATES

	COUNTRY	RATE PER 100,000 (2002*)
1	Finland	14,525.74
2	Sweden	13,350.27
3	Guyana	12,933.18
4	New Zealand	12,586.64
5	England and Wales	11,326.60
6	Grenada	10,177.89
7	Norway	9,822.91
8	Denmark	9,005.77
9	Belgium	8,597.66
10	Canada	8,572.50
	US	4,160.51

* Or latest year for which data available

Source: *Interpol*

An appearance in this list does not necessarily mark these as the most crime-ridden countries, since the rate of reporting relates closely to factors such as confidence in local law enforcement authorities.

THE 10 COUNTRIES WITH THE HIGHEST PRISON POPULATION RATE

	COUNTRY	PRISONERS PER 100,000*
1	US	701
2	Russia	606
3	Kazakhstan	522
4	Turkmenistan	489
5	= Belarus	459
	= Belize	459
7	Suriname	437
8	Dominica	420
9	Ukraine	415
10	Maldives	414

* Most figures relate to dates between 1999–2003

Source: *UK Home Office*, World Prison Population List (5th ed.)

▼ **Cell multiplication**
In recent years, prison inmate numbers have risen in many countries, putting pressure on often old and inadequate jails.

TOP 10 COUNTRIES WITH THE LOWEST REPORTED CRIME RATES

	COUNTRY	RATE PER 100,000 (2002*)
1	Georgia	9.00
2	Burkina Faso	9.30
3	Mali	10.03
4	Syria	42.26
5	Cambodia	47.97
6	Yemen	63.22
7	Indonesia	63.48
8	Myanmar	64.54
9	Angola	71.52
10	Cameroon	78.17

* Or latest year for which data available

Source: *Interpol*

It should be noted that for propaganda purposes, many countries do not publish accurate figures, while in certain countries crime is so common and law enforcement so inefficient or corrupt that countless incidents are unreported.

THE 10 COUNTRIES WITH THE MOST PRISONERS

COUNTRY	PRISONERS*
1 US	2,033,331
2 China	1,512,194#
3 Russia	864,590
4 India	304,893
5 Brazil	284,989
6 Thailand	258,076
7 Ukraine	198,858
8 South Africa	180,952
9 Iran	163,526
10 Mexico	154,765

* Most figures relate to dates between 1999-2003

Sentenced prisoners only

Source: UK Home Office, World Prison Population List (5th ed.)

THE 10 MOST COMMON OFFENSES FOR WHICH PEOPLE ARE IMPRISONED IN THE U.S.

TYPE OF OFFENSE	NO. OF PRISONERS*	PERCENTAGE OF PRISON POPULATION
1 Drug offenses	85,209	54.8
2 Weapons, explosives, and arson	17,311	11.2
3 Immigration offenses	16,369	10.5
4 Robbery	10,284	6.6
5 Burglary, larceny, and property offenses	7,138	4.6
6 Extortion, fraud, and bribery	7,046	4.5
7 Homicide, aggravated assault, and kidnapping	5,170	3.3
8 Sex offenses	1,584	1.0
9 Banking and insurance, counterfeit, and embezzlement offenses	1,046	0.7
10 Courts or corrections offenses (e.g. obstructing justice)	743	0.5

* As of August 31, 2003

Source: Department of Justice, Federal Bureau of Prisons

THE 10 U.S. STATES WITH THE HIGHEST CRIME RATES

STATE	CRIMES PER 100,000 (1999)
1 Arizona	6,386.3
2 Hawaii	6,043.7
3 Florida	5,420.6
4 South Carolina	5,297.3
5 Texas	5,189.6
6 Washington	5,106.8
7 Louisiana	5,098.1
8 New Mexico	5,077.8
9 Tennessee	5,018.9
10 Oregon	4,868.4

Source: FBI Uniform Crime Reports

Murder By Numbers

MOST PROLIFIC SERIAL KILLERS*

MURDERER/COUNTRY/CRIMES	VICTIMS
1 Behram (India)	931

Behram (or Buhram) was the leader of the Thugee cult in India, which is thought to have been responsible for the deaths of up to 2 million people. At his trial, Behram was found guilty of personally committing 931 murders between 1790 and 1830, mostly by ritual strangulation with the cult's traditional cloth, known as a ruhmal. From the end of his reign of terror onward, the British in India mounted a campaign against Thugee, and the cult was eventually suppressed.

2 Countess Erszébet Báthory (Hungary)	up to 650

In the period up to 1610 in Hungary, Báthory (1560–1614), known as "Countess Dracula"—the title of a 1970 horror movie about her life and crimes—was alleged to have murdered between 300 and 650 girls (her personal list of 610 victims was described at her trial) in the belief that drinking their blood would prevent her from aging. She was eventually arrested in 1611, tried, and found guilty. She died on August 21, 1614 walled up in her own castle in Csejthe.

3 Pedro Alonso López (Colombia)	300

Captured in 1980, López, nicknamed the "Monster of the Andes," led police to 53 graves, but probably murdered at least 300 in Colombia, Ecuador, and Peru. He was sentenced to life imprisonment.

4 Harold Shipman (UK)	215

In January 2000, Shipman, a physician, was found guilty of the murder of 15 women patients; the official enquiry into his crimes put the figure at 215, with 45 possible further cases, but some authorities believe that the total could be as high as 400. Shipman hanged himself in his prison cell on January 13, 2004.

5 Henry Lee Lucas (US)	200

Lucas (1936–2001) admitted in 1983 to 360 murders, many committed with his partner-in-crime Ottis Toole. He died while on Death Row in Huntsville Prison in Texas.

6 Gilles de Rais (France)	up to 200

A fabulously wealthy French aristocrat, Gilles de Laval, Baron de Rais (1404–40), a one-time supporter of Joan of Arc, allegedly committed murders as sacrifices during black magic rituals. He was accused of having kidnapped and killed between 60 and 200 children, although these figures may have been fabricated by his political enemies. Charged with a catalog of crimes that included "the conjuration of demons," he was tried, tortured, and found guilty. He was strangled and his body burned in Nantes on October 25, 1440.

7 Hu Wanlin (China)	196

Hu Wanlin, who posed as a doctor specializing in ancient Chinese medicine, was sentenced on October 1, 2000, to 15 years' imprisonment for three deaths, but authorities believe he was responsible for considerably more: an estimated 20 in Taiyuan, 146 in Shanxi, and 30 in Shangqui.

8 Luis Alfredo Garavito (Colombia)	189

Garavito confessed in 1999 to a spate of murders. On May 28, 2000, he was sentenced to a total of 835 years' imprisonment.

MURDERER/COUNTRY/CRIMES	VICTIMS
9 Hermann Webster Mudgett (US)	up to 150

Also known as "H. H. Holmes," Mudgett (1860–96), a former doctor, may have lured 150 women to his "castle" on 63rd Street in Chicago, which he operated as a hotel. The building contained a warren of secret passages and windowless, soundproof cells with gas valves. It was equipped for torturing, murdering, and dissecting victims and disposing of their bodies in furnaces or an acid bath. Arrested in 1894 and found guilty of the murder of an ex-partner, Benjamin F. Pitezel, Mudgett confessed to killing 27, but may have killed up to 150 times (some authorities calculated that the remains of 200 victims were found at his home). Mudgett, regarded as the first US mass murderer, was hanged at Moyamensing Prison, Philadelphia, on May 7, 1896.

10 Jack Kevorkian (US)	130

In 1999, Kevorkian, a doctor who admitted to assisting in 130 suicides since 1990, was convicted of second-degree murder. His appeal against his 10- to 25-year prison sentence was rejected on November 21, 2001.

* Includes only individual murderers; excludes murders by bandits, those carried out by terrorist groups, political and military atrocities, and gangland slayings.

Because of the secrecy surrounding the horrific crimes of serial killers, and the time spans involved, it is almost impossible to calculate the precise numbers of their victims. The numbers of murders attributed to the criminals listed should therefore be taken as "best estimates" based on the most reliable evidence available. Such is the magnitude of the crimes of some of the serial killers, however, that some of the figures may be underestimates.

MOST COMMON MURDER WEAPONS AND METHODS IN THE U.S.

WEAPON OR METHOD	VICTIMS (2002)
1 Handguns	7,176
2 Knives or cutting instruments	1,767
3 "Personal weapons" (hands, feet, fists, etc.)	933
4 Blunt objects (hammers, clubs, etc.)	666
5 Rifles	480
6 Shotguns	476
7 Strangulation	143
8 Fire	104
9 Asphyxiation	103
10 Narcotics	48
Total	*14,054*

Source: *FBI Uniform Crime Reports*

The proportion of killings involving firearms has gone down compared with the early 20th century: in 1920, for example, 4,178 out of a total of 5,815 murders were committed with firearms or explosives.

► **Shoot to kill**
The use of firearms in murders varies around the world. In the United States, they are the most commonly used weapon, while the strict prohibition on guns in the UK means they are only rarely used.

 WORST YEARS FOR GUN MURDERS IN THE U.S.

	YEAR	VICTIMS
1	1993	16,136
2	1992	15,489
3	1994	15,463
4	1991	14,373
5	1995	13,790
6	1980	13,650
7	1990	13,035
8	1981	12,523
9	1974	12,474
10	1975	12,061

During the Prohibition era, gangland gun killings increased the total from 4,178 in 1920 to 7,863 by Prohibition's 1933 repeal. Thereafter the total steadily declined to a post-war low of 3,807 in 1955, before climbing again. Gun murders first exceeded 10,000 in 1969, but dropped below this figure in 1998.

COUNTRIES WITH THE HIGHEST MURDER RATES

	COUNTRY	REPORTED MURDERS PER 100,000 POPULATION (2002*)
1	Honduras	154.02
2	South Africa	114.84
3	Colombia	69.98
4	Lesotho	50.41
5	Rwanda	45.08
6	Jamaica	43.71
7	El Salvador	34.33
8	Venezuela	33.20
9	Bolivia	31.98
10	Namibia	26.32
	US	5.61

* Or latest year for which data available

Source: *Interpol*

COUNTRIES WITH THE LOWEST MURDER RATES

	COUNTRY	REPORTED MURDERS PER 100,000 POPULATION (2002*)
1	= Burkina Faso	0.38
	= Cameroon	0.38
3	Senegal	0.63
4	= Gambia	0.71
	= Mali	0.71
	= Saudi Arabia	0.71
7	Mauritania	0.76
8	Indonesia	0.80
9	Oman	0.91
10	Hong Kong	1.03

* Or latest year for which data available

Source: *Interpol*

Erratic recording and the desire by some countries to downplay their lack of security may explain some of of the low published figures.

Capital Punishment

THE 10 COUNTRIES WITH THE MOST EXECUTIONS

	COUNTRY	EXECUTIONS* (2002)
1	China	126
2	US	71
3	Iran	69
4	Saudi Arabia	47
5	Singapore	18
6	Jordan	13
7	Vietnam	12
8	Thailand	6
9	Kuwait	5
10	Pakistan	4

* Verifiable reported executions

Some 112 countries have abolished the death penalty in law or in practice, while 83 retain it. Of the latter, a small group of countries executes the most prisoners. According to Amnesty International, in 2002 a total of 1,562 people were executed in 31 countries.

THE 10 FIRST COUNTRIES TO ABOLISH CAPITAL PUNISHMENT

	COUNTRY	ABOLISHED
1	Russia	1826
2	Venezuela	1863
3	Portugal	1867
4	= Brazil	1882
	= Costa Rica	1882
6	Ecuador	1897
7	Panama	1903
8	Norway	1905
9	Uruguay	1907
10	Colombia	1910

Some countries listed abolished capital punishment in peacetime only, or for all crimes except treason. One US state, Michigan, abolished the death penalty for every offense except treason in 1846.

THE 10 STATES WITH THE MOST EXECUTIONS 1976–2004

	STATE	EXECUTIONS*
1	Texas	321
2	Virginia	90
3	Oklahoma	73
4	Missouri	61
5	Florida	58
6	Georgia	34
7	North Carolina	31
8	South Carolina	29
9	Alabama	28
10	Louisiana	27

* To Mar. 30, 2004

Source: *Death Penalty Information Center*

A total of 906 people have been executed since 1976, when the death penalty was reintroduced after a 10-year moratorium. During this period, six states have not carried out any executions.

▲ **Death chamber**
From 1976 to April 2004, a total of 321 executions were carried out in Huntsville, Texas, the most of any state and almost four times as many as in Virginia, which recorded the second-highest figure.

STATES WITH THE MOST PRISONERS ON DEATH ROW

	STATE	PRISONERS UNDER DEATH SENTENCE*
1	California	634
2	Texas	458
3	Florida	381
4	Pennsylvania	237
5	North Carolina	213
6	Ohio	205
7	Alabama	196
8	Arizona	128
9	Georgia	114
10	Oklahoma	106

* As of January 1, 2004

Source: *NAACP Legal Defense Fund*

STATES WITH THE MOST WOMEN SENTENCED TO DEATH

	STATE	WOMEN SENTENCED TO DEATH*
1	= California	16
	= North Carolina	16
3	= Florida	15
	= Texas	15
5	Ohio	10
6	Alabama	9
7	= Illinois	7
	= Mississippi	7
	= Oklahoma	7
10	= Georgia	6
	= Pennsylvania	6

* As of June 30, 2003

Source: *Victor L. Streib, Ohio Northern University*

YEARS WITH MOST EXECUTIONS IN THE U.S.

	YEAR	EXECUTIONS*
1	1935	199
2	1936	195
3	1938	190
4	1934	168
5	= 1933	160
	= 1939	160
7	1930	155
8	= 1931	153
	= 1947	153
10	= 1937	147
	= 1942	147

* All offenses, 1930–2003

Source: *Department of Justice/Death Penalty Information Center*

FIRST U.S. EXECUTIONS BY LETHAL INJECTION

	NAME	VICTIM(S)	EXECUTED
1	Charles Brooks	David Gregory	Dec. 7, 1982
2	James Autry	Shirley Drouet/ Joe Broussard	Mar. 14, 1984
3	Ronald O'Bryan	Timothy O'Bryan	Mar. 31, 1984
4	Thomas Barefoot	Carl LeVin	Oct. 30, 1984
5	Dovle Skillem	Patrick Randel	Jan. 16, 1985
6	Stephen Morin	Carrie Marie Smith/ Jann Bruce/Sheila Whalen	Mar. 13, 1985
7	Jesse de la Rosa	Masaoud Ghazali	May 15, 1985
8	Charles Milton	Menaree Denton	June 25, 1985
9	Henry M. Porter	Henry Mailloux	July 9, 1985
10	Charles Rumbaugh	Michael Fiorello	Sept. 11, 1985

Source: *Death Penalty Information Center/Amnesty International*

Execution by lethal injection was first proposed in the late 1880s, but electrocution was introduced in preference. Oklahoma was the first state to legalize the method, but it was not used there until 1990, and all of the above were executed in Texas (where, curiously, Death Row inmates with the first name of Charles figure prominently). The only woman to be so executed is 52-year-old Velma Barfield, on November 2, 1984, at Central Prison, Raleigh, NC. Lethal injection is now the most commonly used form of execution in the United States.

LAST PEOPLE EXECUTED FOR WITCHCRAFT IN AMERICA

	NAME	RESIDENCE	EXECUTED
1	= Martha Cory	Salem	Sept. 22, 1692
	= Mary Easty	Topsfield	Sept. 22, 1692
	= Alice Parker	Salem	Sept. 22, 1692
	= Mary Parker	Andover	Sept. 22, 1692
	= Ann Pudeator	Salem	Sept. 22, 1692
	= Wilmot Reed	Marblehead	Sept. 22, 1692
	= Margaret Scott	Rowley	Sept. 22, 1692
	= Samuel Wardwell	Andover	Sept. 22, 1692
9	Giles Cory	Salem	Sept. 19, 1692
10	= George Jacobs	Salem	Aug. 19, 1692
	= Martha Carrier	Andover	Aug. 19, 1692
	= Rev. George Burroughs	Wells, Maine	Aug. 19, 1692
	= John Proctor	Salem	Aug. 19, 1692
	= John Willard	Salem	Aug. 19, 1692

A number of trials for witchcraft took place in Colonial America. The first to be executed for the crime was Alse Young, hanged in Hartford, Connecticut, on May 26, 1647. From then until 1688, a total of about 20 "witches" were hanged in New England. Then, in 1692, the most famous witch trial of all, that in Salem, Massachusetts, took place, and 20 people were found guilty. Of them, 19 were hanged, and 80-year-old Giles Cory became the last person to be pressed to death.

World Wars

LARGEST ARMED FORCES OF WORLD WAR I

COUNTRY	PERSONNEL*
1 Russia	12,000,000
2 Germany	11,000,000
3 British Empire	8,904,467
4 France	8,410,000
5 Austria-Hungary	7,800,000
6 Italy	5,615,000
7 US	4,355,000
8 Turkey	2,850,000
9 Bulgaria	1,200,000
10 Japan	800,000

* Total at peak strength

Russia's armed forces were relatively small in relation to the country's population—some six percent, compared with 17 percent in Germany. In total, more than 65 million combatants were involved in fighting some of the costliest battles, in terms of numbers killed, that the world has ever known.

COUNTRIES SUFFERING THE GREATEST MILITARY LOSSES IN WORLD WAR I

COUNTRY	NO. KILLED
1 Germany	1,773,700
2 Russia	1,700,000
3 France	1,357,800
4 Austria-Hungary	1,200,000
5 British Empire*	908,371
6 Italy	650,000
7 Romania	335,706
8 Turkey	325,000
9 US	116,516
10 Bulgaria	87,500

* Including Australia, Canada, India, New Zealand, South Africa, etc.

Romania had the highest military death rate, at 45 percent of its total mobilized forces; Germany's was 16 percent, Austria-Hungary's and Russia's 15 percent, and the British Empire's 10 percent.

COUNTRIES WITH THE MOST PRISONERS OF WAR CAPTURED IN WORLD WAR I

COUNTRY	NO. CAPTURED
1 Russia	2,500,000
2 Austria-Hungary	2,200,000
3 Germany	1,152,800
4 Italy	600,000
5 France	537,000
6 Turkey	250,000
7 British Empire	191,652
8 Serbia	152,958
9 Romania	80,000
10 Belgium	34,659

▼ War graves
The vast extent of many European World War I war cemeteries is a tangible reminder of the military casualties sustained by the participants.

LARGEST ARMED FORCES OF WORLD WAR II

	COUNTRY	PERSONNEL*
1	USSR	12,500,000
2	US	12,364,000
3	Germany	10,000,000
4	Japan	6,095,000
5	France	5,700,000
6	UK	4,683,000
7	Italy	4,500,000
8	China	3,800,000
9	India	2,150,000
10	Poland	1,000,000

Total at peak strength

Allowing for deaths and casualties, the total number of forces mobilized during the course of the war is, of course, greater than the peak strength figures: that of the USSR, for example, has been put as high as 20,000,000; the United States, 16,354,000; Germany, 17,900,000; Japan, 9,100,000; and the UK, 5,896,000.

COUNTRIES SUFFERING THE GREATEST MILITARY LOSSES IN WORLD WAR II

	COUNTRY	NO. KILLED
1	USSR	13,600,000*
2	Germany	3,300,000
3	China	1,324,516
4	Japan	1,140,429
5	British Empire[†]	357,116
6	Romania	350,000
7	Poland	320,000
8	Yugoslavia	305,000
9	US	292,131
10	Italy	279,800
	Total	21,268,992

* Total, of which 7,800,000 were battlefield deaths, 2,500,000 were those who died later of wounds received in battle and disease, and, of the 5,800,000 who were taken prisoner, as many as 3,300,000 who died in captivity.

† Including Australia, Canada, India, New Zealand, etc.

COUNTRIES SUFFERING THE GREATEST MERCHANT SHIPPING LOSSES IN WORLD WAR II

	COUNTRY	VESSELS SUNK NO.	TONNAGE
1	UK	4,786	21,194,000
2	Japan	2,346	8,618,109
3	Germany	1,595	7,064,600
4	US	578	3,524,983
5	Norway	427	1,728,531
6	Netherlands	286	1,195,204
7	Italy	467	1,155,080
8	Greece	262	883,200
9	Panama	107	542,772
10	Sweden	204	481,864

During 1939–45, Allied losses in the Atlantic alone totaled 3,843 ships (16,899,147 tons). June 1942 was the worst period of the war, with 131 vessels (652,487 tons) lost in the Atlantic and a further 42 vessels (181,709 tons) elsewhere.

Modern Military

TOP 10 COUNTRIES WITH THE HIGHEST MILITARY/CIVILIAN RATIO

	COUNTRY	RATIO* (2003)
1	North Korea	489
2	Israel	266
3	Qatar	203
4	Jordan	193
5	Syria	188
6	United Arab Emirates	177
7	Iraq	162#
8	Bahrain	155
9	Oman	153
10	Taiwan	130
	US	49

* Military personnel per 10,000 population

\# Prior to the 2003 conflict

TOP 10 COUNTRIES WITH THE HIGHEST PER CAPITA DEFENSE EXPENDITURE

	COUNTRY	EXPENDITURE PER CAPITA (2002) ($)
1	Qatar	3,115
2	Israel	1,572
3	Kuwait	1,536
4	US	1,203
5	Singapore	1,072
6	Saudi Arabia	1,038
7	United Arab Emirates	982
8	Oman	846
9	Norway	796
10	Brunei	783

▶ **Strength in numbers**
Except for border conflicts, China's gigantic military force—almost twice as large as that of the US—has not yet been tested in combat.

TOP 10 COUNTRIES WITH THE LARGEST DEFENSE BUDGETS

	COUNTRY	BUDGET ($)
1	US	376,200,000,000
2	Japan	41,400,000,000
3	UK	41,300,000,000
4	France	34,900,000,000
5	Germany	27,400,000,000
6	China	22,400,000,000
7	Italy	22,300,000,000
8	Saudi Arabia	18,400,000,000
9	India	15,600,000,000
10	South Korea	14,800,000,000

The so-called "peace dividend"—the savings made as a consequence of the end of the Cold War between the West and the former Soviet Union—was short-lived. In response to the threats of international terrorism and "rogue states," such as Iraq, the budgets of the United States and her allies have increased to record levels.

TOP 10 COUNTRIES WITH THE SMALLEST DEFENSE BUDGETS

	COUNTRY*	BUDGET ($)
1	Gambia	3,400,000
2 =	Antigua and Barbuda	4,000,000
=	Guinea-Bissau	4,000,000
4	Equatorial Guinea	4,500,000
5	Guyana	5,400,000
6	Mauritius	7,200,000
7	Surinam	8,500,000
8	Cape Verde	9,000,000
9	Seychelles	12,000,000
10 =	Barbados	13,000,000
=	Malawi	13,000,000

* Includes only those countries that declare defense budgets

If their defense expenditure is expressed as a proportion of their gross domestic product, several of these countries' spending is actually on a par with many larger and wealthier nations.

THE FIRST TO...

FIRST AIR FORCE

THE WORLD'S FIRST—and smallest—air force was the Aeronautical Division of the US Army Signal Corps, set up under Captain Charles de Forest Chandler on August 1, 1907 to "have charge of all matters pertaining to military ballooning, air machines and all kindred subjects." Initially, the force comprised only Chandler and two enlisted men with just two balloons, but in 1909 it acquired its first military aircraft, a Wright Flyer. Chandler went on to achieve another first on May 7, 1912, becoming the first to fly a plane with a machine gun.

COUNTRIES WITH THE SMALLEST ARMED FORCES*

COUNTRY	ESTIMATED TOTAL ACTIVE FORCES#
1 Antigua and Barbuda	170
2 Seychelles	450
3 Barbados	610
4 Gambia	800
5 Bahamas	860
6 Luxembourg	900
7 Belize	1,050
8 Cape Verde	1,200
9 Equatorial Guinea	1,320
10 Guyana	1,600

* Includes only those countries that declare a defense budget

In latest year for which data available

A number of small countries maintain military forces for ceremonial purposes, national prestige, or reasons other than national defense, and would be unable to resist an invasion. Luxembourg's army continues a long military tradition, however, and took an active part in peacekeeping operations in former Yugoslavia.

COUNTRIES WITH THE LARGEST ARMED FORCES

COUNTRY	ESTIMATED ACTIVE FORCES* ARMY	NAVY	AIR	TOTAL
1 China	1,700,000	250,000	400,000	2,250,000
2 US	485,000	400,000	367,600	1,427,000#
3 India	1,100,000	55,000	170,000	1,325,000
4 North Korea	950,000	46,000	86,000	1,082,000
5 Russia	321,000	155,000	184,600	960,600[†]
6 South Korea	560,000	63,000	63,000	686,000
7 Pakistan	550,000	25,000	45,000	620,000
8 Iran	350,000	18,000	52,000	540,000∞
9 Turkey	402,000	52,750	60,100	514,850
10 Vietnam	412,000	42,000	30,000	484,000

* In latest year for which data available

Includes 174,400 Marine Corps

† Includes Strategic Deterrent Forces, Paramilitary, National Guard, etc.

∞ Includes 120,000 Revolutionary Guards

In addition to the active forces listed here, many countries have substantial reserves on standby; South Korea's has been estimated at some 4.5 million, Vietnam's at 3–4 million, and China's at 500–600,000. Russia's former total of 3 million has steadily dwindled as a result of both the end of the Cold War and the economic problems faced by the post-Soviet military establishment.

World Religions

TOP 10 | LARGEST MUSLIM POPULATIONS

	COUNTRY	MUSLIM POPULATION (2004)
1	Pakistan	150,850,000
2	India	132,480,000
3	Bangladesh	128,700,000
4	Indonesia	120,670,000*
5	Turkey	70,250,000
6	Iran	66,890,000
7	Egypt	61,900,000
8	Nigeria	53,500,000
9	Algeria	31,300,000
10	Morocco	30,560,000

* An additional 46 million people are considered Muslims by the Indonesian government but are more properly categorized as New Religionists (Islamicized syncretistic religions)

Source: *World Christian Database, www.worldchristiandatabase.org, October 2003*

TOP 10 | LARGEST BUDDHIST POPULATIONS

	COUNTRY	BUDDHIST POPULATION (2004)
1	China	110,000,000
2	Japan	70,560,000
3	Thailand	52,580,000
4	Vietnam	40,490,000
5	Myanmar	36,730,000
6	Sri Lanka	13,150,000
7	Cambodia	12,450,000
8	India	7,460,000
9	South Korea	7,350,000
10	Taiwan	4,820,000

Source: *World Christian Database, www.worldchristiandatabase.org, October 2003*

◄ **Path of enlightenment**
Founded in India over 2,500 years ago, Buddhism spread throughout East Asia and beyond to become one of the world's foremost religions.

TOP 10 LARGEST HINDU POPULATIONS

	COUNTRY	HINDU POPULATION (2004)
1	India	801,360,000
2	Nepal	19,030,000
3	Bangladesh	18,500,000
4	Indonesia	7,550,000
5	Sri Lanka	2,170,000
6	Pakistan	2,050,000
7	Malaysia	1,830,000
8	US	1,130,000
9	South Africa	1,080,000
10	Myanmar	1,000,000

Source: *World Christian Database,*
www.worldchristiandatabase.org, October 2003

Hindus constitute some 75 percent of the population of India and 70 percent of that of Nepal, but only 13 percent of that of Bangladesh and as little as three percent of Indonesia's.

TOP 10 LARGEST JEWISH POPULATIONS

	COUNTRY	JEWISH POPULATION (2004)
1	US	5,795,000
2	Israel	5,096,000
3	France	599,000
4	Argentina	490,000
5	Canada	420,000
6	Palestine	400,000
7	Brazil	379,000
8	UK	312,000
9	Germany	225,000
10	Russia	210,000

Source: *World Christian Encyclopedia*

The Diaspora—or scattering—of Jewish people has been in progress for nearly 2,000 years, and as a result, Jewish communities are found in virtually every country in the world. The worldwide Jewish population is now estimated to exceed 13 million.

TOP 10 LONGEST-SERVING POPES

	POPE	PERIOD IN OFFICE	YRS*
1	Pius IX	June 16, 1846–Feb. 7, 1878	31
2	Leo XIII	Feb. 20, 1878–July 20, 1903	25
3	John Paul II	Oct. 16, 1978–#	25
4	Peter	between c.32–c.64	c.25
5	Pius VI	Feb. 15, 1775–Aug. 29, 1799	24
6	Adrian I	Feb. 1, 772–Dec. 25, 795	23
7	Pius VII	Mar. 14, 1800–Aug. 20, 1823	23
8	Alexander III	Sept. 7, 1159–Aug. 30, 1181	21
9	Sylvester	Jan. 31, 314–Dec. 31, 335	21
10	Leo I	Sept. 29, 440–Nov. 10, 461	21

* *Equal entries are separated by months*

\# *Still in office; duration as of Oct. 16, 2003*

Although St. Peter is regarded as the first pope, some authorities doubt the historical accuracy of his reign. If he is omitted as unhistorical, Nos. 4–10 all move up one place and 10th becomes Clement XI (Sept. 23, 1700–Mar. 19, 1721, a reign of 20 years).

TOP 10 LARGEST CHRISTIAN POPULATIONS

	COUNTRY	CHRISTIAN POPULATION (2004)
1	US	246,543,000
2	Brazil	164,122,000
3	China	106,902,000
4	Mexico	101,541,000
5	Russia	85,234,000
6	Philippines	73,862,000
7	India	68,125,000
8	Germany	62,557,000
9	Nigeria	59,148,000
10	Dem. Rep. of Congo	55,340,000

Source: *World Christian Database*
www.worldchristiandatabase.org, October 2003

The Christian populations of these 10 countries make up 45 percent of the world total. Although Christian communities are found in almost every country in the world, it is difficult to put a precise figure on nominal membership (a declared religious persuasion) rather than active participation (regular attendance at a place of worship).

TOP 10 RELIGIONS IN THE U.S.

	RELIGION	FOLLOWERS (2001)
1	Christianity	159,030,000
2	Judaism	2,831,000
3	Islam	1,104,000
4	Buddhism	1,082,000
5	Hinduism	766,000
6	Unitarianism/Universalism	629,000
7	Paganism	140,000
8	Wicca	134,000
9	Spiritualism	116,000
10	Native American religions	103,000

Source: *American Religious Identity Survey (ARIS) 2001*

These figures are based on the results of a random digit-dialed telephone survey of 50,281 US households from February to June 2001. The disparities between this and the US figures included in some of the global lists (estimated from other sources) make clear the difficulties involved in the collection of these types of statistical data.

TOP 10 RELIGIOUS BELIEFS

	RELIGION	FOLLOWERS (2004)
1	Christianity	2,090,763,000
2	Islam	1,271,884,000
3	Hinduism	841,078,000
4	Agnosticism	774,800,000
5	Chinese folk religions	400,600,000
6	Buddhism	376,574,000
7	Ethnic religions	242,882,000
8	Atheism	149,564,000
9	New religions	106,937,000
10	Sikhism	24,402,000

Source: *David B. Barrett & Todd M. Johnson,* International Bulletin of Missionary Research, January 2004

These authoritative estimates imply that almost one-third of the world's population are nominally (self-declared), if not practicing, Christians, and one-fifth are followers of Islam. Most of the major religions are sectarian: some 17 percent of Christians are Roman Catholic, while 83 percent of Muslims are Sunni and 16 percent Shiite.

Town & Country

Countries of the World

SMALLEST COUNTRIES

COUNTRY	AREA (SQ MILES)	(SQ KM)
1 Vatican City	0.2	0.44
2 Monaco	0.7	2
3 Nauru	8	21
4 Tuvalu	10	26
5 San Marino	23	60
6 Liechtenstein	62	161
7 Marshall Islands	70	181
8 Maldives	115	300
9 Malta	124	321
10 Grenada	130	339

Source: *US Census Bureau, International Data Base*

The "country" status of the Vatican is questionable, since its government and other features are intricately linked with those of Italy. Formerly part of the Papal States, it became part of unified Italy in the 19th century. Its identity as an independent state was enshrined in the Lateran Treaty of February 11, 1929.

LARGEST COUNTRIES

COUNTRY	% OF WORLD TOTAL	AREA (SQ MILES)	(SQ KM)
1 Russia	13.0	6,592,850	17,075,400
2 Canada	7.6	3,855,103	9,984,670
3 China	7.1	3,600,948	9,326,411
4 US	6.9	3,539,245	9,166,601
5 Brazil	6.4	3,265,077	8,456,511
6 Australia	5.8	2,941,300	7,617,931
7 India	2.2	1,148,148	2,973,190
8 Argentina	2.1	1,056,642	2,736,690
9 Kazakhstan	2.1	1,049,155	2,717,300
10 Algeria	1.8	919,595	2,381,741
World total	100.0	50,580,568	131,003,055

Source: *US Census Bureau, International Data Base/ Statistics Canada*

COUNTRIES WITH THE LONGEST BORDERS

COUNTRY	TOTAL BORDER LENGTH (MILES)	(KM)
1 China	13,761	22,147
2 Russia	12,403	19,961
3 Brazil	9,129	14,691
4 India	8,763	14,103
5 US	7,611	12,248
6 Dem. Rep. of Congo	6,676	10,744
7 Argentina	6,006	9,665
8 Canada	5,526	8,893
9 Mongolia	5,071	8,162
10 Sudan	4,776	7,687

This list represents the total length of borders, compiled by adding together the lengths of individual land borders. The wholly European country with the longest total borders is Germany, at 2,248 miles (3,618 km). The total length of the world's land boundaries is thought to be approximately 156,262 miles (251,480 km), with shared boundaries counted only once.

▼ Shore thing

The coast of mainland Canada comprises 35,889 miles (57,759 km) of its total coastline length, the balance being the total coastline lengths of its 52,455 offshore islands.

COUNTRIES WITH THE LONGEST COASTLINES

COUNTRY	TOTAL COASTLINE LENGTH (MILES)	(KM)
1 Canada	125,566	202,080
2 Indonesia	33,999	54,716
3 Russia	23,396	37,653
4 Philippines	22,559	36,289
5 Japan	18,486	29,751
6 Australia	16,007	25,760
7 Norway	13,624	21,925
8 US	12,380	19,924
9 New Zealand	9,404	15,134
10 China	9,010	14,500

With all its islands, the coastline of Canada is more than six times as long as the distance around the Earth at the Equator (24,902 miles/40,076 km).

TOP 10 LARGEST LANDLOCKED COUNTRIES

COUNTRY/NEIGHBORS	AREA (SQ MILES)	(SQ KM)
1 **Kazakhstan,** China, Kyrgyzstan, Russia, Turkmenistan, Uzbekistan	1,049,156	2,717,300
2 **Mongolia,** China, Russia	604,250	1,565,000
3 **Niger,** Algeria, Benin, Burkina Faso, Chad, Libya, Mali, Nigeria	489,075	1,266,699
4 **Chad,** Cameroon, Central African Republic, Libya, Niger, Nigeria, Sudan	486,180	1,259,201
5 **Mali,** Algeria, Burkina Faso, Côte d'Ivoire, Guinea, Mauritania, Niger, Senegal	471,044	1,219,999
6 **Ethiopia,** Djibouti, Eritrea, Kenya, Somalia, Sudan	432,312	1,119,683
7 **Bolivia,** Argentina, Brazil, Chile, Paraguay, Peru	418,685	1,084,389
8 **Zambia,** Angola, Dem. Rep. of Congo, Malawi, Mozambique, Namibia, Tanzania, Zimbabwe	285,993	740,719
9 **Afghanistan,** China, Iran, Pakistan, Tajikistan, Turkmenistan, Uzbekistan	250,001	647,500
10 **Central African Republic,** Cameroon, Chad, Congo, Dem. Rep. of Congo, Sudan	240,534	622,980

Source: *US Census Bureau, International Data Base*

There are 42 landlocked countries in the world. Kazakhstan and Turkmenistan both have coasts on the Caspian Sea—which is itself landlocked.

TOP 10 SMALLEST LANDLOCKED COUNTRIES

COUNTRY/NEIGHBORS	AREA (SQ MILES)	(SQ KM)
1 **Vatican City,** Italy	0.2	0.44
2 **San Marino,** Italy	23	60
3 **Liechtenstein,** Austria, Switzerland	62	161
4 **Andorra,** France, Spain	174	451
5 **Luxembourg,** Belgium, France, Germany	998	2,585
6 **Swaziland,** Mozambique, South Africa	6,641	17,200
7 **Rwanda,** Burundi, Dem. Rep. of Congo, Tanzania, Uganda	9,633	24,949
8 **Burundi,** Dem. Rep. of Congo, Rwanda, Tanzania	9,903	25,649
9 **Macedonia,** Albania, Bulgaria, Greece, Yugoslavia	9,928	25,713
10 **Armenia,** Azerbaijan, Georgia, Iran, Turkey	11,506	29,800

Source: *US Census Bureau, International Data Base*

Landlocked countries—those lacking direct access to the sea—often suffer through having to rely on their neighbors for trade routes. In times of conflict this makes them especially vulnerable to blockades. Two countries in the world are actually doubly landlocked—completely surrounded by other landlocked countries. They are Liechtenstein, which is surrounded by Austria and Switzerland, and Uzbekistan, surrounded by Afghanistan, Kazakhstan, Kyrgyzstan, Tajikistan, and Turkmenistan.

TOP 10 COUNTRIES WITH THE MOST NEIGHBORS

COUNTRY/NEIGHBORS	NO. OF NEIGHBORS
1 = **China,** Afghanistan, Bhutan, India, Kazakhstan, Kyrgyzstan, Laos, Mongolia, Myanmar, Nepal, North Korea, Pakistan, Russia, Tajikistan, Vietnam	14
= **Russia,** Azerbaijan, Belarus, China, Estonia, Finland, Georgia, Kazakhstan, Latvia, Lithuania, Mongolia, North Korea, Norway, Poland, Ukraine	14
3 **Brazil,** Argentina, Bolivia, Colombia, French Guiana, Guyana, Paraguay, Peru, Suriname, Uruguay, Venezuela	10
4 = **Dem. Rep. of Congo,** Angola, Burundi, Central African Republic, Congo, Rwanda, Sudan, Tanzania, Uganda, Zambia	9
= **Germany,** Austria, Belgium, Czech Republic, Denmark, France, Luxembourg, Netherlands, Poland, Switzerland	9
= **Sudan,** Central African Republic, Chad, Dem. Rep. of Congo, Egypt, Eritrea, Ethiopia, Kenya, Libya, Uganda	9
7 = **Austria,** Czech Republic, Germany, Hungary, Italy, Liechtenstein, Slovakia, Slovenia, Switzerland	8
= **France,** Andorra, Belgium, Germany, Italy, Luxembourg, Monaco, Spain, Switzerland	8
= **Turkey,** Armenia, Azerbaijan, Bulgaria, Georgia, Greece, Iran, Iraq, Syria	8
10 = **Mali,** Algeria, Burkina Faso, Côte d'Ivoire, Guinea, Mauritania, Niger, Senegal	7
= **Niger,** Algeria, Benin, Burkina Faso, Chad, Libya, Mali, Nigeria	7
= **Saudi Arabia,** Iraq, Jordan, Kuwait, Oman, Qatar, United Arab Emirates, Yemen	7
= **Tanzania,** Burundi, Kenya, Malawi, Mozambique, Rwanda, Uganda, Zambia	7
= **Ukraine,** Belarus, Hungary, Moldova, Poland, Romania, Russia, Slovakia	7
= **Zambia,** Angola, Dem. Rep. of Congo, Malawi, Mozambique, Namibia, Tanzania, Zimbabwe	7

It should be noted that some countries have more than one discontinous border with the same country; this has been counted only once.

Country Populations

TOP10 MOST POPULATED COUNTRIES

COUNTRY	POPULATION (2005 EST.)
1 China	1,302,207,986
2 India	1,080,264,388
3 US	295,734,134
4 Indonesia	241,973,879
5 Brazil	186,112,794
6 Pakistan	156,689,148
7 Bangladesh	144,319,628
8 Russia	143,736,793
9 Nigeria	140,601,615
10 Japan	127,417,244
World total	6,448,780,202

Source: *US Census Bureau, International Data Base*

TOP10 LEAST POPULATED COUNTRIES

COUNTRY	POPULATION (2005 EST.)
1 Tuvalu	11,636
2 Nauru	13,048
3 Palau	20,303
4 San Marino	28,880
5 Monaco	32,409
6 Liechtenstein	33,317
7 St. Kitts and Nevis	38,958
8 Marshall Islands	59,071
9 Antigua and Barbuda	68,722
10 Dominica	69,029

Source: *US Census Bureau, International Data Base*

TOP10 LEAST POPULATED COUNTRIES, 2050

COUNTRY	POPULATION (2050 EST.)
1 Tuvalu	20,018
2 Nauru	22,696
3 Palau	26,300
4 Monaco	32,964
5 San Marino	35,335
6 Liechtenstein	35,776
7 St. Kitts and Nevis	52,348
8 Andorra	69,129
9 Antigua and Barbuda	69,259
10 Aruba	69,990

Source: *US Census Bureau, International Data Base*

TOP 10 MOST POPULATED COUNTRIES, 2050

	COUNTRY	POPULATION (2050 EST.)
1	India	1,601,004,572
2	China	1,417,630,630
3	US	420,080,587
4	Indonesia	336,247,428
5	Nigeria	307,420,055
6	Bangladesh	279,955,405
7	Pakistan	267,813,495
8	Brazil	228,426,737
9	Dem. Rep. of Congo	181,260,098
10	Mexico	147,907,650
	World total	*9,084,495,405*

Source: *US Census Bureau, International Data Base*

◀ Population explosion
In 1999, India became only the second country after China with a population of over one billion. If the present rate of increase is maintained, India's population will overtake that of China around 2045.

TOP 10 LEAST DENSELY POPULATED COUNTRIES

	COUNTRY	AREA (SQ MI)	POPULATION (2005 EST.)	POPULATION PER SQ MILE
1	Mongolia	604,247	2,791,272	4.61
2	Namibia	317,872	1,975,848	6.22
3	Australia	2,941,283	20,090,437	6.76
4	Botswana	226,011	1,545,285	6.84
5	Iceland	38,707	283,443	7.02
6	Surinam	62,344	438,144	7.07
7	Mauritania	397,837	3,086,859	7.74
8	Libya	679,358	5,765,563	8.50
9	Canada	3,560,217	32,805,041	9.22
10	Guyana	76,004	710,662	9.35
	US	*3,539,224*	*295,734,134*	*83.81*

Source: *US Census Bureau, International Data Base*

These sparsely populated countries generally present environmental disadvantages that make human habitation challenging: some contain large tracts of mountain, desert, or dense forest, or have extreme climates.

TOP 10 COUNTRIES WITH THE YOUNGEST POPULATIONS

	COUNTRY	PERCENTAGE UNDER 15 (2005 EST.)
1	Uganda	50.3
2	Dem. Rep. of Congo	48.1
3	Chad	47.9
4	São Tomé and Príncipe	47.6
5	Niger	47.3
6	Mali	47.1
7	Malawi	46.9
8	= Benin	46.5
	= Yemen	46.5
10	Burkina Faso	46.0
	World average	*27.8*
	US	*20.6*

Source: *US Census Bureau, International Data Base*

Countries with high proportions of their population under the age of 15 are usually characterized by high birth rates and high death rates. If regions without country status were included from this list, the Gaza Strip would be at No. 2, with almost one in two people (48.5 percent) under age 15.

TOP 10 COUNTRIES WITH THE OLDEST POPULATIONS

	COUNTRY	PERCENTAGE OVER 65 (2005 EST.)
1	Monaco	22.4
2	Japan	19.5
3	Italy	19.4
4	Germany	18.9
5	Greece	18.8
6	Spain	17.6
7	= Belgium	17.4
	= Sweden	17.4
9	Bulgaria	17.2
10	San Marino	16.9
	World average	*7.3*
	US	*12.4*

Source: *US Census Bureau, International Data Base*

Nine of the 10 countries with the oldest populations are in Europe, implying that this region has lower death rates and a higher life expectancy than the rest of the world. On average, one in every 6.3 people in Europe is over the age of 65 (15.9 percent). In contrast, the lowest percentages of old people are found in Africa, where the average is only one in every 30 people (3.3 percent).

World Cities

THE 10 | FIRST CITIES WITH POPULATIONS OF MORE THAN A MILLION

	CITY	COUNTRY
1	Rome	Italy
2	Alexandria	Egypt
3	Angkor	Cambodia
4	Hangchow	China
5	London	England
6	Paris	France
7	Peking	China
8	Canton	China
9	Berlin	Germany
10	New York	US

Rome's population is thought to have exceeded 1 million some time in the 2nd century BC, and Alexandria soon after. Angkor and Hangchow had both reached this figure by about AD 900 and 1200, respectively, but all three afterward declined (Angkor was completely abandoned in the 15th century). No other city attained 1 million until London in the early years of the 19th century. The next cities to pass the million mark did so between about 1850 and the late 1870s.

TOP 10 | LARGEST NON-CAPITAL CITIES

	CITY/COUNTRY	CAPITAL	POPULATION (2003 EST.)
1	New York City (including Newark and Paterson, NJ), US	Washington, DC	21,750,000
2	São Paulo (including Guarulhos), Brazil	Brasília	20,200,000
3	Mumbai (including Kalyan, Thane, and Ulhasnagar), India	Delhi	18,800,000
4	Los Angeles (including Riverside and Anaheim), US	Washington, DC	17,450,000
5	Osaka (including Kobe and Kyoto), Japan	Tokyo	16,700,000
6	Calcutta* (including Haora), India	Delhi	14,950,000
7	Karachi,* Pakistan	Islamabad	13,100,000
8	Shanghai, China	Beijing	12,500,000
9	Rio de Janeiro* (including Nova Iguaçu and São Gonçalo), Brazil	Brasília	12,150,000
10	Istanbul,* Turkey	Ankara	10,900,000

Former capital

Source: *Th. Brinkhoff*: The Principal Agglomerations of the World, *http://www.citypopulation.de, Sept. 16, 2003*

TOP 10 | FASTEST-GROWING CITIES

	CITY/COUNTRY	AVERAGE ANNUAL POPULATION GROWTH RATE* (PERCENTAGE, 2000–05)
1	Ansan, South Korea	9.15
2	Toluca, Mexico	6.15
3	Sana'a, Yemen	5.83
4	Niamey, Niger	5.70
5	Songnam, South Korea	5.47
6	P'ohang, South Korea	5.43
7	Rajshahi, Bangladesh	5.29
8	Kabul, Afghanistan	5.10
9	= Antananarivo, Madagascar	5.05
	= Campo Grande, Brazil	5.05
	Norfolk/Virginia Beach/Newport News, VA	*1.73*

* *Of urban agglomerations with 750,000 inhabitants or more*

Source: *United Nations Population Division*, World Urbanization Report: The 2001 Revision

▶ **Capital gain**
Including the adjacent areas of Ecatepec, Nezahualcóyotl, and Naucalpan, Mexico City has undergone phenomenal growth from its 1950 population of 3 million.

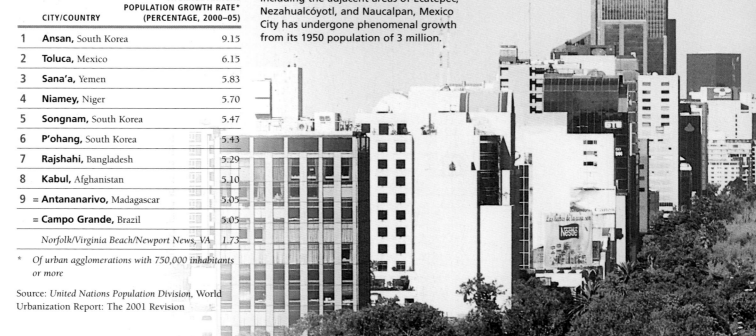

TOP 10 LARGEST CAPITAL CITIES

	CITY/COUNTRY	POPULATION (2003 EST.)
1	**Tokyo** (including Yokohama and Kawasaki), Japan	33,750,000
2	**Mexico City,** (including Ecatepec, Nezahualcóyotl, and Naucalpan), Mexico	21,850,000
3	**Seoul** (including Bucheon, Goyang, Incheon, Seongnam, and Suweon), South Korea	21,700,000
4	**Delhi** (including Faridabad and Ghaziabad), India	18,100,000
5	**Jakarta** (including Bekasi, Bogor, Depok, and Tangerang), Indonesia	16,300,000
6	**Cairo** (including Al-Jizah and Shubra al-Khaymah), Egypt	15,600,000
7	**Moscow,** Russia	15,350,000
8	**Manila** (including Kalookan and Quezon City), Philippines	14,000,000
9	**Buenos Aires** (including San Justo and La Plata), Argentina	13,900,000
10	**Dhaka,** Bangladesh	12,050,000

Source: *Th. Brinkhoff*: The Principal Agglomerations of the World, *http://www.citypopulation.de, Sept. 16, 2003*

TOP 10 LARGEST CITIES IN THE U.S.

	CITY/STATE	POPULATION (2003)*
1	**New York** (including Newark and Paterson, NJ), New York	21,750,000
2	**Los Angeles** (including Riverside and Anaheim), California	17,450,000
3	**Chicago,** Illinois	9,650,000
4	**Washington, DC** (including Baltimore, MD), Dist. of Columbia	7,900,000
5	**San Francisco** (including Oakland and San Jose), California	7,250,000
6	**Philadelphia,** Pennsylvania	5,950,000
7	**Detroit** (including Windsor, ON, Canada), Michigan	5,750,000
8	= **Boston,** Massachusetts	5,700,000
	= **Dallas** (including Fort Worth), Texas	5,700,000
10	**Miami** (including Fort Lauderdale), Florida	5,400,000

* Of urban agglomeration

Source: *Th. Brinkhoff*: The Principal Agglomerations of the World, *http://www.citypopulation.de, Sept. 16, 2003*

TOP 10 COUNTRIES WITH THE MOST MILLION-PLUS CITIES

	COUNTRY	CITIES WITH POPULATIONS OF OVER 1 MILLION
1	**US**	51
2	**China***	45
3	**India**	40
4	**Brazil**	19
5	= **Japan**	14
	= **Russia**	14
7	**Germany**	11
8	= **Indonesia**	8
	= **Pakistan**	8
	= **UK**	8

* Includes Hong Kong

Source: *Th. Brinkhoff*: The Principal Agglomerations of the World, *http://www.citypopulation.de, Sept. 16, 2003*

There are some 418 cities in the world with populations of more than a million. These cities are found in 100 different countries, but many of these countries contain only one city of a million-plus (in most instances, their capitals). This list thus covers an elite group with more than eight apiece.

US States

MOST POPULOUS STATES

STATE	POPULATION (1900)	POPULATION (2000)
1 California	1,485,053	33,871,648
2 Texas	3,048,710	20,851,820
3 New York	7,268,894	18,976,457
4 Florida	528,542	15,982,378
5 Illinois	4,821,550	12,419,293
6 Pennsylvania	6,302,115	12,281,054
7 Ohio	4,157,545	11,353,140
8 Michigan	2,420,982	9,938,444
9 New Jersey	1,883,669	8,414,350
10 Georgia	2,216,231	8,186,453

Source: *US Census Bureau*

The total population of the United States according to the 1900 Census was 76,212,168, compared to the preliminary results of the April 1, 2000 Census, which put the total at 281,421,906. Some states have grown faster than others: Florida's population is now more than 30 times its 1900 figure.

LEAST POPULOUS STATES

STATE	POPULATION (2000)
1 Wyoming	493,782
2 Vermont	608,827
3 Alaska	626,932
4 North Dakota	642,200
5 South Dakota	754,844
6 Delaware	783,600
7 Montana	902,195
8 Rhode Island	1,048,319
9 Hawaii	1,211,537
10 New Hampshire	1,235,786
District of Columbia	572,059

Source: *US Census Bureau*

With a high proportion of its area devoted to agriculture and almost half its land federally owned, Wyoming is likely to maintain its low population density.

MOST DENSELY POPULATED STATES

STATE	POPULATION* PER (SQ MILE)	POPULATION* PER (SQ KM)
1 New Jersey	1,134.2	437.9
2 Rhode Island	1,003.2	387.3
3 Massachusetts	810.0	312.7
4 Connecticut	702.9	271.4
5 Maryland	541.8	209.2
6 New York	401.8	155.1
7 Delaware	400.8	154.7
8 Florida	296.3	114.4
9 Ohio	277.2	107.0
10 Pennsylvania	274.0	105.8

* Of land area as of 2000

Source: *US Census Bureau*

Population densities have increased dramatically over the past 200 years: that of New Jersey, for example, was 250.7 per square mile (96.8 per sq km) in 1900, and just 28.1 per square mile (10.8 per sq km) in 1800.

STATES WITH THE MOST FOREIGN-BORN RESIDENTS

STATE	FOREIGN-BORN RESIDENTS*
1 California	8,864,255
2 New York	3,868,133
3 Texas	2,899,642
4 Florida	2,670,828
5 Illinois	1,529,058
6 New Jersey	1,476,327
7 Massachusetts	772,983
8 Arizona	656,183
9 Washington	614,457
10 Georgia	577,273
Total of all states	*31,107,889*

* Based on 2000 Census

Source: *US Census Bureau*

At the time of the 2000 Census, California had the greatest proportion of foreign-born residents of any state—26.2 percent, compared with 11.1 percent for the United States as a whole.

▶ **California dreaming**
The 1849 gold rush and the mild Pacific coast climate led to the growth of San Francisco and to California's becoming the most populous states.

TOP 10 LEAST DENSELY POPULATED STATES

STATE	POPULATION* PER (SQ MILE)	(SQ KM)
1 Alaska	1.1	0.4
2 Wyoming	5.1	1.9
3 Montana	6.2	2.4
4 North Dakota	9.3	3.6
5 South Dakota	10.0	3.8
6 New Mexico	15.0	5.8
7 Idaho	15.6	6.0
8 Nevada	18.2	7.0
9 Nebraska	22.3	8.6
10 Utah	27.2	10.5

Of land area as of 2000

Source: *US Census Bureau*

TOP 10 SMALLEST STATES

STATE	LAND AREA (SQ MILES)	(SQ KM)
1 Rhode Island	1,045	2,706
2 Delaware	1,955	5,063
3 Connecticut	4,845	12,548
4 Hawaii	6,423	16,635
5 New Jersey	7,419	19,215
6 Massachusetts	7,838	20,300
7 New Hampshire	8,969	23,229
8 Vermont	9,249	23,955
9 Maryland	9,775	25,317
10 West Virginia	24,087	62,385

Smallest state Rhode Island has the longest official name: "State of Rhode Island and Providence Plantations". A total of 546 Rhode Islands—which also includes some 500 sq miles (1,295 sq km) of inland water—could be fitted into the land area of largest state Alaska.

TOP 10 LARGEST STATES

STATE	LAND AREA* (SQ MILES)	(SQ KM)
1 Alaska	571,951	1,481,347
2 Texas	261,797	678,051
3 California	155,959	403,933
4 Montana	145,552	376,979
5 New Mexico	121,356	314,309
6 Arizona	113,635	294,312
7 Nevada	109,826	284,448
8 Colorado	103,718	268,627
9 Wyoming	97,100	251,489
10 Oregon	95,997	248,631

Excluding water

The admission of Alaska to the Union on January 3 and Hawaii on August 20, 1959, increased the land area of the United States by almost 20 percent, bringing it to its present 3,540,999 square miles (9,171,146 sq km).

Place Names

COUNTRIES WITH THE LONGEST OFFICIAL NAMES

	OFFICIAL NAME*	COMMON ENGLISH NAME	LETTERS
1	al-Jamahīrīyah al-'Arabīyah al-Lībīyah ash-Sha'bīyah al-Ishtirākīyah al-Uẓma	Libya	65
2	al-Jumhūrīyah al-Jazā' irīyah ad-Dīmuqrāṭīyah ash-Sha'bīyah	Algeria	51
3	United Kingdom of Great Britain and Northern Ireland	Great Britain	45
4	Śri Lanka Prajatantrika Samajavadi Janarajaya	Sri Lanka	41
5	República Democrática de São Tomé e Príncipe	São Tomé and Príncipe	38
6 =	al-Jumhūrīyah al-Islāmīyah al-Mūrītanīyah	Mauritania	36
=	Federation of Saint Christopher and Nevis	Saint Kitts and Nevis	36
8	Federal Democratic Republic of Ethiopia	Ethiopia	35
9 =	al-Mamlakah al-Urdunnīyah al-Hāshimīyah	Jordan	34
=	Sathalanalat Paxathipatai Paxaxôn Lao	Laos	34

* Some official names have been transliterated from languages that do not use the Roman alphabet; their length may vary according to the method used

There is clearly no connection between the length of names and the longevity of the nation-states that bear them, for since this list was first published in 1991, three countries have ceased to exist: Socijalisticka Federativna Republika Jugoslavija (Yugoslavia, 45 letters), Soyuz Sovetskikh Sotsialisticheskikh Respublik (USSR, 43), and Ceskoslovenská Socialistická Republika (Czechoslovakia, 36). Uruguay's official name of La República Oriental del Uruguay is sometimes given in full as the 38-letter La República de la Banda Oriental del Uruguay, which would place it in 6th position.

▶ **The long and the short of it**
A bustling market in Libya. The country's short and commonly used name appeared in Egyptian hieroglyphics 4,000 years ago. Its modern official name, adopted on March 8, 1977, translates as "The Great Socialist People's Libyan Arab Jamahiriya."

LONGEST PLACE NAMES*

	NAME	LETTERS
1	**Krung thep mahanakhon amon rattanakosin mahinthara ayuthaya mahadilok phop noppharat ratchathani burirom udomratchaniwet mahasathan amon piman awatan sathit sakkathattiya witsanukam prasit**	168

When the poetic name of Bangkok, capital of Thailand, is used, it is usually abbreviated to "Krung Thep" (city of angels).

2	**Taumatawhakatangihangakoauauotamateaturipukakapiki-maungahoronukupokaiwhenuakitanatahu**	85

This is the longer version (the other has a mere 83 letters) of the Maori name of a hill in New Zealand. It translates as "The place where Tamatea, the man with the big knees, who slid, climbed and swallowed mountains, known as land-eater, played on the flute to his loved one."

3	**Gorsafawddacha'idraigodanheddogleddollônpenrhynareurdraethceredigion**	67

A name contrived by the Fairbourne Steam Railway, Gwynedd, North Wales, for publicity purposes and in order to outdo its rival, No. 4. It means "The Mawddach station and its dragon teeth at the Northern Penrhyn Road on the golden beach of Cardigan Bay."

4	**Llanfairpwllgwyngyllgogerychwyrndrobwllllantysiliogogogoch**	58

This is the place in Gwynedd famed especially for the length of its railway tickets. It means "St. Mary's Church in the hollow of the white hazel near to the rapid whirlpool of the church of St. Tysilio near the Red Cave." Questions have been raised about its authenticity, since its official name comprises only the first 20 letters, and the full name appears to have been invented as a hoax in the 19th century by a local tailor.

5	**El Pueblo de Nuestra Señora la Reina de los Ángeles de la Porciúncula**	57

The site of a Franciscan mission and the full Spanish name of Los Angeles; it means "the town of Our Lady the Queen of the Angels of the Little Portion." Nowadays it is customarily known by its initial letters, "LA," making it also one of the shortest-named cities in the world.

6	**Chargoggagoggmanchaugagoggchaubunagungamaug**	43

Loosely translated, the Indian name of this lake near Webster, Massachusetts, means "You fish on your side, I'll fish on mine, and no one fishes in the middle." It is said to be pronounced "Char-gogg-a-gogg (pause) man-chaugg-a-gog (pause) chau-bun-a-gung-a-maug." It is, however, an invented extension of its real name (Chaubunagungamaug, or "boundary fishing place"), devised in the 1920s by Larry Daly, the editor of the Webster *Times*.

7	= **Lower North Branch Little Southwest Miramichi**	40

Canada's longest place name—a short river in New Brunswick.

	= **Villa Real de la Santa Fé de San Francisco de Asis**	40

The full Spanish name of Santa Fe, New Mexico, translates as "Royal city of the holy faith of St. Francis of Assisi."

9	**Te Whakatakanga-o-te-ngarehu-o-te-ahi-a-Tamatea**	38

The Maori name of Hammer Springs, New Zealand; like the second name in this list, it refers to a legend of Tamatea, explaining how the springs were warmed by "the falling of the cinders of the fire of Tamatea." Its name is variously written either hyphenated or as a single word.

10	**Meallan Liath Coire Mhic Dhubhghaill**	32

The longest multiple name in Scotland, a place near Aultanrynie, Highland, alternatively spelled Meallan Liath Coire Mhic Dhughaill (30 letters).

* Including single-word, hyphenated, and multiple names

MOST COMMON CITY NAMES IN THE U.S.

	NAME	OCCURRENCES*
1	Fairview	66
2	Midway	52
3	Oak Grove	44
4	= Franklin	40
	= Riverside	40
6	Centerville	39
7	Mount Pleasant	38
8	Georgetown	37
9	Salem	36
10	Greenwood	34

* Incorporated city status only

By the mid-19th century, when there were already 31 American cities named Salem, attempts were made to alter that of Salem, Oregon, to "Chemeketa", a local Indian name, but the change was overruled and it remains the name of the state's capital city.

MOST COMMON PLACE NAMES IN THE U.S.

	NAME	OCCURRENCES
1	Fairview	287
2	Midway	252
3	Riverside	180
4	Oak Grove	179
5	Five Points	155
6	Oakland	149
7	Greenwood	145
8	= Bethel	141
	= Franklin	141
10	Pleasant Hill	140

Source: *US Geological Survey*

As a place name, rather than a city name, Fairview figures even more prominently, especially in certain states—there are 29 in Tennessee alone. It is also the 7th most common cemetery name in the US, with no fewer than 55 examples.

Tallest Buildings 1900–2005

TOP 10 — TALLEST HABITABLE BUILDINGS IN 1900

	BUILDING*/LOCATION#/ YEAR COMPLETED	STORIES	HEIGHT (FT)	(M)
1	Park Row Building, 1899	30	391	119.2
2	Manhattan Life Insurance Building,† 1894	18	348	106.1
3	Bank of Tokyo, 1896	26	338	103.0
4	St. Paul Building,† 1898	26	315	96.0
5	World Building,∞ 1890 spire	20	309 / 349	94.2 / 106.4
6	Masonic Temple,◊ Chicago, IL, 1892	21	302	92.1
7	Central Tower, San Francisco, CA, 1898	21	299	91.1
8	Park Place Tower, 1895	23	292	89.0
9	Home Life Insurance Building, 1894	16	279	85.0
10	Gillender Building,† 1897	19	272	82.9

* Excluding low-rise habitable buildings with adjoining tower (such as various US city halls)
# All in New York City unless otherwise specified
† Demolished 1910
∞ Demolished 1955
◊ Demolished 1939

TOP 10 — TALLEST HABITABLE BUILDINGS IN 1910

	BUILDING*/LOCATION#/ YEAR COMPLETED	STORIES	HEIGHT (FT)	(M)
1	Metropolitan Life Tower, 1909	50	700	213.4
2	Singer Building,† 1908	47	612	186.6
3	City Investing Building,† 1908	33	486	148.1
4	Park Row Building, 1899	30	391	119.2
5	Hanover National Bank,∞ 1903	22	385	117.4
6	Liberty Tower, 1910	33	384	117.0
7	One Times Square, 1905	25	364	111.0
8	Manhattan Life Insurance Building,◊ 1894	18	348	106.1
9	Oliver Building, Pittsburgh, PA, 1910	25	347	105.8
10	Land Title & Trust Building Annex, Philadelphia, PA, 1902	23	345	105.2

* Excluding low-rise habitable buildings with adjoining tower (such as various US city halls)
# All in New York City unless otherwise specified
† Demolished 1968
∞ Demolished 1931
◊ Demolished 1964

TOP 10 — TALLEST HABITABLE BUILDINGS IN 1920

	BUILDING*/LOCATION#/ YEAR COMPLETED	STORIES	HEIGHT (FT)	(M)
1	Woolworth Building, 1913	57	792	241.4
2	Metropolitan Life Tower, 1909	50	700	213.4
3	Singer Building,† 1908	47	612	186.5
4	Municipal Building, 1914 spire	34	580 / 600	176.8 / 182.9
5	= Bankers Trust Building, 1912	37	538	164.0
	= Equitable Building, 1915	39	538	164.0
7	Travelers Tower, Hartford, CT, 1919	24	527	160.6
8	Custom House Tower, Boston, MA, 1915	32	496	151.2
9	PNC Tower, Cincinnati, OH, 1913	31	495	150.9
10	City Investing Building,† 1908	33	486	148.1

* Excluding low-rise habitable buildings with adjoining tower (such as various US city halls)
# All in New York City unless otherwise specified
† Demolished 1968

TOP 10 — TALLEST HABITABLE BUILDINGS IN 1960

	BUILDING/LOCATION*/ YEAR COMPLETED	STORIES	HEIGHT (FT)	(M)
1	Empire State Building, 1931 spire	102	1,250 / 1,472	381.0 / 448.7
2	Chrysler Building, 1929 spire	77	925 / 1,046	281.9 / 318.8
3	40 Wall Street, 1929 spire	71	866 / 927	264.0 / 282.4
4	GE Bulding, 1933	69	850	259.1
5	American International Building, 1932 spire	67	826 / 952	251.8 / 290.2
6	1 Chase Manhattan Plaza, 1960	60	813	247.8
7	Woolworth Building, 1913	57	792	241.4
8	20 Exchange Place, 1931 spire	57	741 / 748	225.8 / 228.0
9	Terminal Tower, Cleveland, OH, 1930 spire	52	708 / 771	215.8 / 235.0
10	Metropolitan Life Tower, 1909	50	700	213.4

* All in New York City unless otherwise specified

TOP 10 — TALLEST HABITABLE BUILDINGS IN 1970

	BUILDING/LOCATION*/ YEAR COMPLETED	STORIES	HEIGHT (FT)	(M)
1	Empire State Building, 1931 spire	102	1,250 / 1,472	381.0 / 448.7
2	John Hancock Center, Chicago, IL, 1968 spire	100	1,127 / 1,500	343.5 / 427.2
3	Chrysler Building, 1929 spire	77	925 / 1,046	281.9 / 318.8
4	40 Wall Street, 1929 spire	71	866 / 927	264.0 / 282.4
5	= Bank One Plaza, Chicago, IL, 1969	60	850	259.1
	= GE Building, 1933	69	850	259.1
7	US Steel Tower, Pittsburgh, PA, 1970	64	840	256.0
8	American International Building, 1932 spire	67	826 / 952	251.8 / 290.2
9	1 Chase Manhattan Plaza, 1960	60	813	247.8
10	Met Life (formerly PanAmerican) Building, 1963	58	808	246.3

* All in New York City unless otherwise specified

TOP 10 — TALLEST HABITABLE BUILDINGS IN 1980

	BUILDING/LOCATION*/ YEAR COMPLETED	STORIES	HEIGHT (FT)	(M)
1	Sears Tower, Chicago, IL, 1974 spire	108	1,450 / 1,730	442.0 / 527.3
2	1 World Trade Center,# 1972 spire	110	1,368 / 1,727	417.0 / 526.4
3	2 World Trade Center,# 1973 spire	110	1,363 / 1,727	415.4 / 526.4
4	Empire State Building, 1931 spire	102	1,250 / 1,472	381.0 / 448.7
5	Aon Center, Chicago, IL, 1973	83	1,136	346.3
6	John Hancock Center, Chicago, IL, 1968 spire	100	1,127 / 1,500	343.5 / 427.2
7	First Canadian Place, Toronto, Canada, 1975 spire	72	978 / 1,165	298.1 / 355.1
8	Chrysler Building, 1929 spire	77	925 / 1,046	281.9 / 318.8
9	Citigroup Center, 1977	59	915	278.9
10	40 Wall Street, 1929 spire	71	866 / 927	264.0 / 282.4

* All in New York City unless otherwise specified
# Destroyed by 9/11 terrorist attacks

TOP 10 | TALLEST HABITABLE BUILDINGS IN 1930

BUILDING/LOCATION*/ YEAR COMPLETED	STORIES	HEIGHT (FT)	(M)
1 **Chrysler Building**, 1929	77	925	281.9
spire		1,046	318.8
2 **40 Wall Street**, 1929	71	866	264.0
spire		927	282.6
3 **Woolworth Building**, 1913	57	792	241.4
4 **Terminal Tower**, Cleveland, OH, 1930	52	708	215.8
spire		771	235.0
5 **Metropolitan Life Tower**, 1909	50	700	213.4
6 **Lincoln Building**, 1930	53	673	205.1
7 **Chanin Building**, 1930	56	649	197.8
spire		680	207.3
8 **Mercantile Building**, 1929	48	620	189.0
9 **New York Life Building**, 1928	40	615	187.5
spire		665	202.7
10 **Singer Building**,# 1908	47	612	186.5

* All in New York City unless otherwise specified
# Demolished 1968

TOP 10 | TALLEST HABITABLE BUILDINGS IN 1940/1950

BUILDING/LOCATION*/ YEAR COMPLETED	STORIES	HEIGHT (FT)	(M)
1 **Empire State Building**, 1931	102	1,250	381.0
spire		1,472	448.7
2 **Chrysler Building**, 1929	77	925	281.9
spire		1,046	318.8
3 **40 Wall Street**, 1929	71	866	264.0
spire		927	282.4
4 **GE Building**, 1933	69	850	259.1
5 **American International Building**, 1932	66	826	251.8
spire		952	290.2
6 **Woolworth Building**, 1913	57	792	241.4
7 **20 Exchange Place**, 1931	57	741	225.9
spire		748	228.0
8 **Terminal Tower**, Cleveland, OH, 1930	52	708	215.8
spire		771	235.0
9 **Metropolitan Life Tower**, 1909	50	700	213.4
10 **500 Fifth Avenue**, 1931	60	697	212.5

* All in New York City unless otherwise specified

It interesting to note that the world's Top 10 buildings in 1950 were identical to those in 1940. As this list shows, although several skyscrapers were built during the Depression, economic concerns followed by World War II put further building on hold, with no rivals to any of these structures appearing until the 1960s.

TOP 10 | TALLEST HABITABLE BUILDINGS IN 1990

BUILDING/LOCATION/ YEAR COMPLETED	STORIES	HEIGHT (FT)	(M)
1 **Sears Tower**, Chicago, IL, 1974	108	1,450	442.0
spire		1,730	527.3
2 **1 World Trade Center**,* New York City, 1972	110	1,368	417.0
spire		1,727	526.4
3 **2 World Trade Center**,* New York City, 1973	110	1,363	415.4
spire		1,727	526.4
4 **Empire State Building**, New York City, 1931	102	1,250	381.0
spire		1,472	448.7
5 **Aon Center**, Chicago, IL, 1973	83	1,136	346.3
6 **John Hancock Center**, Chicago, IL, 1968	100	1,127	343.5
spire		1,500	427.2
7 **Library Tower**, Los Angeles, CA, 1990	73	1,018	310.3
8 **JPMorganChase Tower**, Houston, TX, 1982	75	1,002	305.4
9 **Bank of China Tower**, Hong Kong, 1989	71	1,001	305.1
spires		1,205	367.3
10 **First Canadian Place**, Toronto, Canada, 1975	72	978	298.1
spire		1,165	355.1

* Destroyed by 9/11 terrorist attacks

TOP 10 | TALLEST HABITABLE BUILDINGS IN 2000

BUILDING/LOCATION/ YEAR COMPLETED	STORIES	HEIGHT (FT)	(M)
1 **Petronas Towers**, Kuala Lumpur, Malaysia, 1998	88	1,483	452.0
2 **Sears Tower**, Chicago, IL, 1974	108	1,450	442.0
spire		1,730	527.3
3 **1 World Trade Center**,* New York City, 1972	110	1,368	417.0
spire		1,727	526.4
4 **2 World Trade Center**,* New York City, 1973	110	1,363	415.4
spire		1,727	526.4
5 **Jin Mao Building**, Shanghai, China, 1998	88	1,255	382.5
spire		1,380	420.6
6 **Empire State Building**, New York City, 1931	102	1,250	381.0
spire		1,472	448.7
7 **Tuntex 85 Sky Tower**, Kao-hsiung, Taiwan, 1997	85	1,140	347.5
spire		1,240	378.0
8 **Aon Center**, Chicago, IL, 1973	83	1,136	346.3
9 **John Hancock Center**, Chicago, IL, 1968	100	1,127	343.5
spire		1,500	427.2
10 **Ryogyong Hotel**,# Pyongyang, North Korea, 1992	105	1,083	330.1

* Destroyed by 9/11 terrorist attacks
# Not completed or occupied

TOP 10 | TALLEST HABITABLE BUILDINGS IN 2005

BUILDING/LOCATION/ YEAR COMPLETED	STORIES	HEIGHT (FT)	(M)
1 **Petronas Towers**, Kuala Lumpur, Malaysia, 1998	88	1,483	452.0
2 **Taipei 101**, Taipei, Taiwan, 2004	101	1,470	448.1
spire		1,667	508.1
3 **Sears Tower**, Chicago, IL, 1974	108	1,450	442.0
spire		1,730	527.3
4 **2 International Finance Centre**, Hong Kong, China, 2003	90	1,335	406.9
spire		1,364	415.8
5 **Jin Mao Building**, Shanghai, China, 1998	88	1,255	382.5
spire		1,380	420.6
6 **Empire State Building**, New York City, 1931	102	1,250	381.0
spire		1,472	448.7
7 **Tuntex 85 Sky Tower**, Kao-hsiung, Taiwan, 1997	85	1,140	347.5
spire		1,240	378.0
8 **Aon Center**, Chicago, IL, 1973	83	1,136	346.3
9 **John Hancock Center**, Chicago, IL, 1968	100	1,127	343.5
spire		1,500	427.2
10 = **China World Trade Center**, Beijing, China, 2005	80	1,083	330.1
= **Ryogyong Hotel**,* Pyongyang, North Korea, 1992	105	1,083	330.1

* Not completed or occupied

Bridges & Tunnels

TOP 10 LONGEST ROAD TUNNELS

	TUNNEL/LOCATION	YEAR COMPLETED	LENGTH (FT)	(M)
1	**Laerdal,** Norway	2000	80,413	24,510
2	**Zhongnanshan,** China	U/C 2007*	59,186	18,040
3	**St. Gotthard,** Switzerland	1980	55,505	16,918
4	**Arlberg,** Austria	1978	45,850	13,972
5	**Hsuehshan,** Taiwan	U/C 2005*	42,323	12,900
6	**Fréjus,** France/Italy	1980	42,306	12,895
7	**Mont-Blanc,** France/Italy	1965	38,094	11,611
8	**Gudvangen,** Norway	1991	37,493	11,428
9	**Folgefonn,** Norway	2001	36,417	11,100
10	**Kan-Etsu II** (southbound), Japan	1990	36,122	11,010

* Under construction; scheduled completion date

Numbers 1, 3, 4, and 7 have all held the record as "world's longest road tunnel." Previous record-holders include the 19,206 ft (5,854 m) Grand San Bernardo (Italy/Switzerland; 1964), the 16,841 ft (5,133 m) Alfonso XIII or Viella (Spain; 1948), the 10,620 ft (3,237 m) Queensway (Mersey) Tunnel (connecting Liverpool and Birkenhead, UK; 1934), and the 10,453 ft (3,186 m) Col de Tende (France/Italy; 1882), originally built as a rail tunnel and converted in 1928.

TOP 10 LONGEST RAIL TUNNELS

	TUNNEL/LOCATION	YEAR COMPLETED	LENGTH (FT)	(M)
1	**AlpTransit Gotthard,** Switzerland	U/C 2010*	187,244	57,072
2	**Seikan,** Japan	1988	176,673	53,850
3	**Channel Tunnel,** France/England	1994	165,518	50,450
4	**Moscow Metro** (Medvedkovo/ Belyaevo section), Russia	1979	127,625	38,900
5	**Guadarrama,** Spain	U/C 2007*	97,100	28,377
6	**London Underground** (East Finchley/ Morden, Northern Line), UK	1939	91,339	27,840
7	**Hakkouda,** Japan	U/C 2013*	86,795	26,455
8	**Iwate,** Japan	U/C 2013*	84,678	25,810
9	**Iiyama,** Japan	U/C 2013*	72,917	22,225
10	**Dai-Shimizu,** Japan	1982	72,904	22,221

* Under construction; scheduled completion date

The world's longest rail tunnel, the Gotthard AlpTransit, Switzerland, was proposed as early as 1947, before finally being given the go-ahead in 1998 after a referendum of the Swiss electorate. When completed, trains will travel through it at 155 mph (250 km/h).

TOP 10 LONGEST SUSPENSION BRIDGES

	BRIDGE/LOCATION	YEAR COMPLETED	LENGTH OF MAIN SPAN (FT)	(M)
1	**Akashi-Kaikyo,** Kobe-Naruto, Japan	1998	6,532	1,991
2	**Izmit Bay,** Turkey	U/C*	5,472	1,668
3	**Great Belt,** Denmark	1997	5,328	1,624
4	**Humber Estuary,** UK	1980	4,626	1,410
5	**Jiangyin,** China	1998	4,544	1,385
6	**Tsing Ma,** Hong Kong, China	1997	4,518	1,377
7	**Verrazano Narrows,** New York	1964	4,260	1,298
8	**Golden Gate,** San Francisco, CA	1937	4,200	1,280
9	**Höga Kusten** (High Coast), Veda, Sweden	1997	3,970	1,210
10	**Mackinac Straits,** Michigan	1957	3,800	1,158

* Under construction

Work will begin in 2004–5 on the Messina Strait Bridge between Sicily and Calabria, Italy; it will take 5–6 years and cost roughly $6 billion. It will have by far the longest center span of any bridge, at 10,827 ft (3,300 m), although at 12,828 ft (3,910 m), Japan's Akashi-Kaikyo bridge, completed in 1998 and with a main span of 6,529 ft (1,990 m), is the world's longest overall.

TOP 10 LONGEST UNDERWATER TUNNELS

	TUNNEL/LOCATION	YEAR COMPLETED	LENGTH (FT)	(M)
1	**Seikan,** Japan	1988	176,673	53,850
2	**Channel Tunnel,** France/UK	1994	165,518	50,450
3	**Dai-Shimizu,** Japan	1982	72,904	22,221
4	**Shin-Kanmon,** Japan	1975	61,286	18,680
5	**Tokyo Bay Aqualine Expressway,*** Japan	1997	31,440	9,583
6	**Great Belt Fixed Link** (Eastern Tunnel), Denmark	1997	26,325	8,024
7	**Bømlafjord,*** Norway	2000	25,988	7,921
8	**Eiksund,*** Norway	U/C 2006[†]	25,581	7,797
9	**Oslofjord,*** Norway	2000	23,819	7,260
10	**Severn,** UK	1886	22,992	7,008

* *Road; others rail*

[†] *Under construction; scheduled completion date*

The Seikan tunnel connects the Japanese islands of Honshu and Hokkaido, and runs 330 ft (100 m) below the seabed for 14.4 miles (23.3 km) of its length. It is bored through strata that presented such enormous engineering problems that it took 24 years to complete. The long-awaited Channel Tunnel (pilot borings were undertaken more than 100 years ago) was finally opened to the public in 1994. Its overall length is shorter than the Seikan tunnel, but the undersea portion is longer at 23.6 miles (38.0 km).

TOP 10 LONGEST BRIDGES IN THE U.S.

	BRIDGE/LOCATION	YEAR COMPLETED	LENGTH OF MAIN SPAN (FT)	(M)
1	**Verrazano Narrows,** New York	1964	4,260	1,298
2	**Golden Gate,** San Francisco, CA	1937	4,200	1,280
3	**Mackinac Straits,** Michigan	1957	3,800	1,158
4	**George Washington,** New York	1931/62*	3,500	1,067
5	**Tacoma Narrows II,** Washington	1950	2,800	853
6	**Transbay#,** San Francisco, CA	1936	2,310	704
7	**Bronx-Whitestone,** New York	1939	2,300	701
8	**Delaware Memorial#,** Wilmington, DE	1951/68	2,150	655
9	**Walt Whitman,** Philadelphia, PA	1957	2,000	610
10	**Ambassador,** Detroit, MI	1929	1,850	564

* *Lower deck added*

Twin spans

All are suspension bridges. The United States also has the two longest steel arch bridges in the world, the New River Gorge Bridge, Fayetteville, WV (1977: 1,700 ft/518 m), and the Kill van Kull, Bayonne, NJ (1931: 1,652 ft/504 m).

TOP 10 LONGEST ROAD AND RAIL TUNNELS IN THE U.S.*

	TUNNEL/LOCATION	TYPE	YEAR COMPLETED	LENGTH (MILES)	(KM)
1	**Cascade,** Washington	Rail	1929	7.79	12.54
2	**Flathead,** Montana	Rail	1970	7.78	12.48
3	**Moffat,** Colorado	Rail	1928	6.21	10.00
4	**Hoosac,** Massachusetts	Rail	1875	4.70	7.56
5	**BART Transbay Tubes,** San Francisco, CA	Rail	1974	3.60	5.79
6	**Brooklyn-Battery,** New York	Road	1950	1.73	2.78
7	**E. Johnson Memorial,** Colorado	Road	1979	1.70	2.74
8	**Eisenhower Memorial#,** Colorado	Road	1973	1.69	2.72
9	**Holland Tunnel,** New York	Road	1927	1.62	2.61
10	**Lincoln Tunnel I,** New York	Road	1937	1.56	2.51

* *Excluding subways*

The highest-elevation highway tunnel in the world

◄ **Longest bridge so far**
The longest, tallest, and most expensive bridge in the world, Japan's Akashi-Kaikyo, measures 12,828 ft (3,910 m) overall. It was built to withstand winds of up to 180 mph (290 km/h) and earthquakes of up to 8.5 on the Richter scale.

CULTURE & LEARNING

Word for Word

TOP 10 — MOST WIDELY SPOKEN LANGUAGES

	LANGUAGE	APPROX. NO. OF SPEAKERS*
1	Chinese (Mandarin)	874,000,000
2	Hindustani*	426,000,000
3	Spanish	358,000,000
4	English	341,000,000
5	Bengali	207,000,000
6	Arabic#	206,000,000
7	Portuguese	176,000,000
8	Russian	167,000,000
9	Japanese	125,000,000
10	German (standard)	100,000,000

* Hindi and Urdu are essentially the same language, Hindustani. As the official language of Pakistan it is written in modified Arabic script and called Urdu. As the official language of India it is written in the Devanagari script and called Hindi.

Includes 16 variants of the Arabic language

TOP 10 — LANGUAGES OFFICIALLY SPOKEN IN THE MOST COUNTRIES

	LANGUAGE	COUNTRIES
1	English	57
2	French	33
3	Arabic	23
4	Spanish	21
5	Portuguese	7
6	= Dutch	5
	= German	5
8	= Chinese (Mandarin)	3
	= Danish	3
	= Italian	3
	= Malay	3

There are many countries in the world with more than one official language—both English and French are recognized officially in Canada, for example. English is used in numerous countries as the lingua franca, the common language that enables people who speak mutually unintelligible languages to communicate with each other.

TOP 10 — COUNTRIES WITH THE MOST ENGLISH LANGUAGE SPEAKERS

	COUNTRY	APPROX. NO. OF SPEAKERS*
1	US	215,424,000
2	UK	58,190,000
3	Canada	20,000,000
4	Australia	14,987,000
5	Ireland	3,750,000
6	= New Zealand	3,700,000
	= South Africa	3,700,000
8	Jamaica#	2,600,000
9	Trinidad and Tobago#	1,145,000
10	Guyana#	650,000

* People for whom English is their mother tongue

Includes English Creole

The Top 10 represents the countries with the greatest numbers of inhabitants who speak English as their mother tongue. The world total is probably in excess of 500 million, in addition to which there are perhaps 1 billion who speak English as a second language.

COUNTRIES WITH THE MOST FRENCH LANGUAGE SPEAKERS

	COUNTRY	APPROX. NO. OF SPEAKERS*
1	France	55,100,000
2	Canada	7,158,000
3	Haiti#	6,868,000
4	Belgium†	3,350,000
5	US∞	2,250,000
6	Switzerland	1,380,000
7	Mauritius∞	878,000
8	Réunion#	660,000
9	Guadeloupe∞	407,000
10	Martinique∞	372,000

* People for whom French is their mother tongue

French Creole

† Walloon French

∞ French/French Creole

COUNTRIES WITH THE MOST SPANISH LANGUAGE SPEAKERS

	COUNTRY	APPROX. NO. OF SPEAKERS*
1	Mexico	91,080,000
2	Colombia	41,880,000
3	Argentina	35,860,000
4	Spain	29,860,000#
5	Venezuela	23,310,000
6	US	20,720,000
7	Peru	20,470,000
8	Chile	13,640,000
9	Ecuador	11,760,000
10	Dominican Republic	8,270,000

* People for whom Spanish is their mother tongue

Castilian Spanish

LANGUAGES IN THE WORLD 50 YEARS AGO

	LANGUAGE	APPROX. NO. OF SPEAKERS*
1	Chinese	400,000,000
2	English	200,000,000
3	Russian	140,000,000
4 =	Japanese	100,000,000
=	Western Hindi	100,000,000
6	German	80,000,000
7 =	French	70,000,000
=	Spanish	70,000,000
9	Portuguese	60,000,000
10 =	Bengali	50,000,000
=	Italian	50,000,000

* Mother tongue

A WORLD LANGUAGE

BEFORE ENGLISH gained its pre-eminence as a world language, various artificial languages were proposed to enable international communication. The first to gain a following was Volapük ("World's Speech"), invented by Johann Martin Schleyer (1831–1912), a German priest, in 1879. Volapük clubs were formed all over Europe and America and it had some 100,000 speakers at its peak. It was eclipsed by Esperanto, a much simpler artificial language devised in 1887 by Polish oculist L.L. Zamenhof (1859–1917).

THE FIRST TO...

◀ **Big talk**
Some two-thirds of China's 1.3 billion inhabitants, along with millions more in other countries, speak Mandarin, the official version of Chinese.

COUNTRIES WITH THE MOST GERMAN LANGUAGE SPEAKERS

	COUNTRY	APPROX. NO. OF SPEAKERS*
1	Germany	75,060,000
2	Austria	7,444,000
3	Switzerland	4,570,000
4	US	1,850,000
5	Brazil	910,000
6	Poland	500,000
7	Canada	486,000
8	Kazakhstan	460,000
9	Russia	350,000
10	Italy	310,000

* People for whom German is their mother tongue

As well as these countries, which have historical connections with Germany or contain high numbers of German immigrants or expatriates, several other countries have German speakers, including Denmark, Slovakia, and Luxembourg. Liechtenstein's population of just 33,436 supports a German-language newspaper, *Liechtensteiner Vaterland*.

COUNTRIES WITH THE MOST ARABIC LANGUAGE SPEAKERS

	COUNTRY	APPROX. NO. OF SPEAKERS*
1	Egypt	65,080,000
2	Algeria	26,280,000
3	Saudi Arabia	20,920,000
4	Morocco	18,730,000
5	Iraq	17,490,000
6	Yemen	17,400,000
7	Sudan	17,320,000
8	Syria	14,680,000
9	Tunisia#	6,710,000
10	Libya	4,910,000

* People for whom Arabic is their mother tongue

Another 2,520,000 people speak Arabic-French and 300,000 speak Arabic-English

Written or classical Arabic has changed little since the 7th century, but spoken Arabic varies from country to country. Along with Chinese, English, French, Russian, and Spanish, Arabic is one of the official languages used by the United Nations.

Out of School

TOP 10 COUNTRIES WITH THE MOST STUDENTS IN HIGHER EDUCATION

	COUNTRY	HIGHER EDUCATION STUDENTS*
1	United States	14,350,000
2	India	5,007,000
3	Russia	3,597,900
4	China	3,174,000
5	Japan	3,136,834
6	Indonesia	2,703,886
7	France	2,083,129
8	Philippines	2,022,106
9	Brazil	1,948,200
10	UK	1,820,849

* In latest year for which data available

Source: UNESCO

TOP 10 COUNTRIES SPENDING THE MOST ON EDUCATION

	COUNTRY	PUBLIC EXPENDITURE AS PERCENTAGE OF GNP* (2000/01#)
1	Zimbabwe	11.1
2	Yemen	10.6
3	Saudi Arabia	9.3
4	Cuba	8.7
5	Denmark	8.3
6	Botswana	8.1
7 =	Lesotho	7.9
=	Namibia	7.9
=	Seychelles	7.9
=	Sweden	7.9
	US	4.9

* Gross National Product

Or latest year available; in countries for which data available

Source: UNESCO

TOP 10 LARGEST UNIVERSITIES

	UNIVERSITY/COUNTRY	STUDENTS
1	Kameshwara Singh Darbhanga Sanskrit, India	515,000
2	Calcutta, India	300,000
3	Paris, France	279,978
4	Mexico, Mexico	269,000
5	Bombay, India	262,350
6	Chhatrapati Shahuji Maharaj University, India	220,000
7	Utkal, India	200,000
8	Rome, Italy	189,000
9	Buenos Aires, Argentina	183,397
10	Guadalajara, Mexico	180,776

With 594,227 students, the Indira Gandhi National Open University in India is the world's largest distance-learning establishment.

TOP 10 COUNTRIES WITH THE MOST ELEMENTARY SCHOOL PUPILS

	COUNTRY	ELEMENTARY SCHOOL PUPILS*
1	China	139,954,000
2	India	110,390,406
3	Brazil	35,838,372
4	Indonesia	29,236,283
5	US	24,045,967
6	Nigeria	16,190,947
7	Pakistan	15,532,000
8	Mexico	14,650,521
9	Philippines	12,159,495
10	Bangladesh	11,939,949

* In latest year for which data available

Source: UNESCO

This Top 10 reflects the relative proportion of elementary school-age children—thus, Brazil, despite having a smaller population than the US, ranks higher. Despite having populations greater than both Mexico and the Philippines, Russia and Japan, with older population structures, do not feature at all.

TOP 10 COUNTRIES WITH THE MOST HIGH SCHOOL PUPILS

	COUNTRY	PERCENTAGE FEMALE	HIGH SCHOOL PUPILS*
1	China	45	71,883,000
2	India	38	68,872,393
3	US	49	21,473,692
4	Indonesia	46	14,209,974
5	Russia	50	13,732,000
6	Japan	49	9,878,568
7	Iran	46	8,776,792
8	Germany	48	8,382,335
9	Mexico	49	7,914,165
10	UK	52	6,548,786

* In latest year for which data available

Source: UNESCO

The number of high school pupils as a proportion of total population varies from 8 percent in the United States to 11 in the UK and 14 in Germany. The figures are surprisingly high in some Asian countries, such as China (6), India (7), and Iran (14), reflecting both these countries' emphasis on education and their large populations of school-age children.

A WOMAN GRADUATES

THE FIRST TO...

VENICE-BORN Elena Lucrezia Piscopia Cornaro (1646–84) started studying Latin and Greek at age 7, later mastering a total of seven languages. In addition to languages, she studied mathematics, philosophy, and theology. Although she was not allowed to attend lectures with men and had to work privately, on June 25, 1678 she was awarded a degree by the University of Padua, thus becoming the first woman in the world to be so recognized. She was one of only three female graduates before the 19th century.

▶ **Prime numbers**
Although elementary school education is compulsory in India, many children are employed in rural activities or family businesses and fail to enroll or complete their schooling.

TOP 10 LARGEST UNIVERSITIES IN THE U.S.

UNIVERSITY*/LOCATION	ENROLMENTS (1998–99)
1 University of Texas at Austin	50,616
2 Ohio State University, Columbus	48,477
3 University of Minnesota, Minneapolis	46,597
4 Arizona State University, Tempe	45,693
5 University of Florida, Gainesville	45,114
6 Texas A&M University, College Station	44,618
7 Michigan State University, East Lansing	44,227
8 University of Wisconsin, Madison	41,552
9 Penn State, University Park	40,828
10 University of Illinois at Urbana-Champaign	38,759

Four-year colleges only

Source: *Peterson's*, Annual Survey of Undergraduate Institutions, 2001–02

The first institution to top 50,000 enrollments, the University of Texas originated in 1839 when the Congress of the Republic of Texas allocated "50 leagues" (231,400 acres) of land, but it was not formally established until 1883.

TOP 10 COUNTRIES WITH THE LONGEST SCHOOL ATTENDANCE

COUNTRY	AVERAGE YEARS IN EDUCATION*		
	GIRLS	BOYS	OVERALL
1 Norway	17.60	16.29	16.94
2 Finland	17.24	16.19	16.71
3 Australia	16.81	16.41	16.60
4 UK	16.82	15.96	16.38
5 Sweden	16.96	15.13	16.02
6 Netherlands	15.76	16.04	15.91
7 Belgium	15.99	15.67	15.83
8 Iceland	16.53	15.08	15.81
9 Denmark	16.01	15.16	15.58
10 France	15.66	15.17	15.41

In latest year/countries for which data available

Source: *UNESCO*

The United States is excluded from UNESCO data, but other sources rate its total average length of school attendance at 15.2 years. The world average is thought to be 11.97, but there are a number of developing countries where few children spend more than seven years in full-time education.

By the Book

TOP 10 | MOST EXPENSIVE BOOKS AND MANUSCRIPTS

BOOK OR MANUSCRIPT/SALE/DETAILS	PRICE ($)*
1 The Codex Hammer (formerly Codex Leicester) Christie's, New York, Nov. 11, 1994 This is one of Leonardo da Vinci's notebooks, which includes many scientific drawings and diagrams. It was purchased by Bill Gates, the billionaire founder of Microsoft.	28,800,000
2 The Rothschild Prayerbook, *c.* 1505 Christie's, London, UK, July 8, 1999 This holds the world record price for an illuminated manuscript.	12,557,220 (£7,800,000)
3 The Gospels of Henry the Lion, *c.* 1173–75 Sotheby's, London, UK, Dec. 6, 1983 At the time of its sale, it became the most expensive manuscript, book, or work of art other than a painting ever sold.	10,841,000 (£7,400,000)
4 John James Audubon's The Birds of America, 1827–38 Christie's, New York, March 10, 2000 The record for any natural history book. Further copies of the same book, a collection of more than 400 large, hand-colored engravings, have also fetched high prices: Sotheby's, London, June 21, 1990 (£1,600,000/ $2,756,800); Christie's, New York, April 24, 1992 ($2,120,000); Christie's, New York, October 29, 1993 ($2,700,000).	8,000,000

BOOK OR MANUSCRIPT/SALE/DETAILS	PRICE ($)*
5 The Canterbury Tales, Geoffrey Chaucer, *c.* 1476–77 Christie's, London, UK, July 8, 1998 Printed by William Caxton, and purchased by Sir Paul Getty. In 1776, the same volume had changed hands for just £6.	7,570,941 (£4,621,500)
6 Comedies, Histories, and Tragedies, The First Folio of William Shakespeare, 1623 Christie's, New York, Oct. 8, 2001 The auction record for a 17th-century book.	6,166,000
7 The Gutenberg Bible, 1455 Christie's, New York, Oct. 22, 1987 One of the first books ever printed.	5,390,000
8 The Northumberland Bestiary, *c.* 1250–60 Sotheby's, London, UK, Nov. 29, 1990	5,049,000 (£2,700,000)
9 The Burdett Psalter and Hours, *c.* 1282–86 Sotheby's, London, UK, June 23, 1998	4,517,640 (£2,500,000)
10 The Cornaro Missal, *c.* 1503, Christie's, London, UK, July 8, 1999 The world record price for an Italian manuscript.	4,185,740 (£2,600,000)

* Includes buyer's premium

TOP 10 MASS MARKET PAPERBACK BESTSELLERS, 2003

TITLE/AUTHOR	SALES
1 **Dr. Atkins' New Diet Revolution,** Robert C. Atkins	4,220,000
2 **The King of Torts,** John Grisham	3,700,000
3 **Seabiscuit,** Laura Hillenbrand	2,666,012
4 **Key of Light,** Nora Roberts	2,500,000
5 **Key of Knowledge,** Nora Roberts	2,400,000
6 **Key of Valor,** Nora Roberts	2,300,000
7 **Three Fates,** Nora Roberts	2,000,000
8 **Angels and Demons: A Novel,** Dan Brown	1,900,000
9 **Red Rabbit,** Tom Clancy	1,800,000
10 **The Beach House,** James Patterson and Peter De Jonge	1,773,180

Source: Publishers Weekly

◀ **High Flier**
Having sold for £380 ($1,800) in 1909 and $352,000 in 1977, Audubon's *The Birds of America* soared to a new record in 2000 when the ruler of Qatar paid over $8 million for the magnificent book.

TOP 10 BESTSELLING BOOKS

BOOK/AUTHOR/DATE FIRST PUBLISHED	APPROX. SALES
1 **The Bible,** *c.* 1451–55	over 6,000,000,000*
2 **Quotations from the Works of Mao Tse-Tung,** 1966	900,000,000
3 **The Lord of the Rings,** J.R.R. Tolkien, 1954–55	over 100,000,000
4 **American Spelling Book,** Noah Webster, 1783	up to 100,000,000
5 **The Guinness Book of Records (now Guinness World Records),** 1955	over 95,000,000*#
6 **World Almanac,** 1868	over 80,000,000#
7 **The McGuffey Readers,** William Holmes McGuffey, 1836	60,000,000
8 **The Common Sense Book of Baby and Child Care,** Benjamin Spock, 1946	over 50,000,000
9 **A Message to Garcia,** Elbert Hubbard, 1899	up to 40,000,000
10 = **In His Steps: "What Would Jesus Do?",** Rev. Charles Monroe Sheldon, 1896	over 30,000,000
= **Valley of the Dolls,** Jacqueline Susann, 1966	over 30,000,000

* *Including translations*

Aggregate sales of annual publication

It is extremely difficult to establish precise sales even of contemporary books, and virtually impossible to do so with books published long ago. Variant editions, translations, and pirated copies all affect the global picture, and few publishers or authors are willing to expose their royalty statements to public scrutiny. As a result, this Top 10 list offers no more than the "best guess" at the great bestsellers of the past, and it may well be that there are other books with a valid claim to a place in it: Margaret Mitchell's *Gone with the Wind* (1936) and Harper Lee's *To Kill a Mockingbird* (1960), for example, may each have sold around 30 million copies.

TOP 10 HARDBACK FICTION TITLES IN THE U.S., 2003

TITLE/AUTHOR	SALES
1 **The Da Vinci Code,** Dan Brown	5,724,750
2 **The Five People You Meet in Heaven,** Mitch Albom	2,901,259
3 **The King of Torts,** John Grisham	2,323,000
4 **Bleachers,** John Grisham	1,621,750
5 **Armageddon: The Cosmic Battle of the Ages,** Tim F. LaHaye and Jerry B. Jenkins	1,620,480
6 **The Teeth of the Tiger,** Tom Clancy	1,400,863
7 **The Big Bad Wolf: A Novel,** James Patterson	1,093,891
8 **Blow Fly: A Scarpetta Novel,** Patricia Cornwell	1,024,496
9 **The Lovely Bones: A Novel,** Alice Sebold	902,891
10 **The Wedding,** Nicholas Sparks	801,086

Source: Publishers Weekly

Following the success of his previous bestseller *Angels and Demons*, Dan Brown's thriller *The Da Vinci Code* debuted at No. 1. It is being filmed by Ron Howard, who directed Oscar-winning *A Beautiful Mind*, with a 2005 release slated.

TOP 10 FICTION TITLES IN THE U.S. 50 YEARS AGO

TITLE	AUTHOR
1 **Marjorie Morningstar**	Herman Wouk
2 **Auntie Mame**	Patrick Dennis
3 **Andersonville**	MacKinlay Kantor
4 **Bonjour Tristesse**	Françoise Sagan
5 **The Man in the Gray Flannel Suit**	Sloan Wilson
6 **Something of Value**	Robert Ruark
7 **Not as a Stranger**	Morton Thompson
8 **No Time for Sergeants**	Mac Hyman
9 **The Tontine**	Thomas B. Costain
10 **Ten North Frederick**	John O'Hara

Source: Publishers Weekly

Marjorie Morningstar, the bestselling novel of 1955, sold 191,349 copies, while the 10th title on the list, *Ten North Frederick,* sold 65,900 copies—but within only a month of its Thanksgiving Day publication.

Libraries & Borrowing

TOP 10 OLDEST NATIONAL LIBRARIES

	LIBRARY/LOCATION	FOUNDED
1	**Národní Knihovně České Republiky** (National Library of the Czech Republic), Prague, Czech Republic	1366
2	**Österreichische Nationalbibliothek** (National Library of Austria), Vienna, Austria	1368
3	**Biblioteca Nazionale Marciana** (St. Mark's Library), Venice, Italy	1468
4	**Bibliothèque Nationale de France,** (National Library of France), Paris, France	1480
5	**National Library of Malta,** Valetta, Malta	1555
6	**Bayericsche Staatsbibliothek** (Bavarian State Library), Munich, Germany	1558
7	**Bibliothèque Royale Albert 1er** (National Library of Belgium), Brussels, Belgium	1559
8	**Nacionalna i Sveučilišna Knjiznica** (Zagreb National and University Library), Zagreb, Croatia	1606
9	**Helsingin Yliopiston Kirjasto** (National Library of Finland), Helsinki, Finland	1640
10	**Kongeligie Bibliotek** (National Library of Denmark), Copenhagen, Denmark	1653

What may claim to be the world's first national library was that in Alexandria, Egypt, founded in about 307 BC by King Ptolemy I Soter. It assembled the world's largest collection of scrolls, which was partially destroyed during Julius Caesar's invasion of 47 BC, and totally destroyed by Arab invaders in AD 642, an event that is considered one of the greatest losses ever to world scholarship. Among national libraries in the English-speaking world, Scotland's dates from 1682 (thus predating the British Library, originally part of the British Museum, established in 1753). The United States Library of Congress was founded in 1800.

▼ Shelf life
Dating from 1366, when Charles IV donated a collection of manuscripts to Prague University, the Czech National Library is considered the most venerable of all national libraries.

THE 10 FIRST PUBLIC LIBRARIES IN THE U.S.

	LIBRARY/LOCATION	FOUNDED
1	**Peterboro Public Library,** Peterboro, NH	1833
2	**New Orleans Public Library,** New Orleans, LA	1843
3	**Boston Public Library,** Boston, MA	1852
4	**Public Library of Cincinnati and Hamilton County,** Cincinnati, OH	1853
5	**Springfield City Library,** Springfield, MA	1857
6	**Worcester Public Library,** Worcester, MA	1859
7	**Multnomah County Library,** Portland, OR	1864
8 =	**Detroit Public Library,** Detroit, MI	1865
=	**St. Louis Public Library,** St. Louis, MO	1865
10	**Atlanta-Fulton Public Library,** Atlanta, GA	1867

Source: *Public Library Association*

TOP 10 LARGEST UNIVERSITY LIBRARIES IN THE U.S.

	LIBRARY	BOOKS HELD
1	Harvard University	13,143,330
2	Yale University	10,500,544
3	University of California, Berkeley	8,946,754
4	University of Illinois at Urbana-Champaign	8,840,000
5	Stanford University	7,700,000
6	University of California, Los Angeles	7,401,780
7	University of Michigan, Ann Arbor	7,200,000
8	Columbia University	7,000,000
9	University of Texas at Austin	6,835,983
10	Indiana University, Bloomington	6,177,219

TOP 10 LARGEST PUBLIC LIBRARIES IN THE U.S.

	LIBRARY/BRANCHES	LOCATION	FOUNDED	BOOKS HELD[#]
1	Boston Public Library (25)	Boston, MA	1852	14,612,532
2	Chicago Public Library (79)	Chicago, IL	1872	10,943,765
3	Public Library of Cincinnati and Hamilton County (41)	Cincinnati, OH	1853	9,829,015
4	Queens Borough Public Library (62)	Jamaica, NY	1896	9,151,020
5	County of Los Angeles Public Library (85)	Los Angeles, CA	1872	8,796,269
6	Detroit Public Library (23)	Detroit, MI	1865	7,314,712
7	New York Public Library (The Branch Libraries) (85)	New York, NY	1895*	6,647,603
8	Carnegie Library of Pittsburgh (19)	Pittsburgh, PA	1895	6,303,408
9	Free Library of Philadelphia (52)	Philadelphia, PA	1891	6,219,231
10	Brooklyn Public Library (58)	Brooklyn, NY	1896	6,049,372

* Astor Library founded 1848; consolidated with Lenox Library and Tilden Trust to form New York Public Library, 1895

[#] Lending library and reference library holdings available for loan

Source: American Library Association

Boston Public Library was founded as the first major free municipal library in the United States, and opened to the public in a former schoolhouse on March 20, 1854. It moved to the present Copley Square building in 1895. An architectural masterpiece, it is adorned with murals by some of the leading artists of the era, including French painter Puvis de Chavannes and Americans Edwin Austin Abbey and John Singer Sargent.

TOP 10 LARGEST LIBRARIES

	LIBRARY	LOCATION	FOUNDED	BOOKS
1	Library of Congress	Washington, DC	1800	29,000,000
2	National Library of China	Beijing, China	1909	22,000,000
3	Library of the Russian Academy of Sciences	St. Petersburg, Russia	1714	20,000,000
4	National Library of Canada	Ottawa, Canada	1953	18,800,000
5	Deutsche Bibliothek*	Frankfurt, Germany	1990	18,557,445
6	British Library[#]	London, UK	1753	16,000,000
7	Institute for Scientific Information on Social Sciences of the Russian Academy of Science	Moscow, Russia	1969	13,500,000
8	Harvard University Library	Cambridge, MA	1638	13,143,330
9	Vernadsky National Scientific Library of Ukraine	Kiev, Ukraine	1919	13,000,000
10	New York Public Library[†]	New York, NY	1895	11,300,000

* Formed in 1990 through the unification of the Deutsche Bibliothek, Frankfurt (founded 1947), and the Deutsche Bucherei, Leipzig

[#] Founded as part of the British Museum, 1753; became an independent body in 1973

[†] Astor Library founded 1848, consolidated with Lenox Library and Tilden Trust to form New York Public Library, 1895

Press Power

TOP 10 | DAILY NEWSPAPERS

	NEWSPAPER	COUNTRY	AVERAGE DAILY CIRCULATION
1	Yomiuri Shimbun	Japan	14,246,000
2	Asahi Shimbun	Japan	12,326,000
3	Mainichi Shimbun	Japan	5,635,000
4	Nihon Keizai Shimbun	Japan	4,737,000
5	Chunichi Shimbun	Japan	4,571,000
6	Bild-Zeitung	Germany	4,220,000
7	The Sun	UK	3,461,000
8	Sankei Shimbun	Japan	2,665,000
9	USA Today	US	2,603,000
10	Canako Xiaoxi (Beijing)	China	2,530,000

Source: *World Association of Newspapers*, World Press Trends 2003,
www.wan-press.org

Yomiuri Shimbun was founded in 1874 in emulation of the Western press. The name *Yomiuri*, "selling by reading," refers to the Japanese practice of vendors reading aloud from news-sheets in the era before movable type.

TOP 10 | ENGLISH-LANGUAGE DAILY NEWSPAPERS

	NEWSPAPER	COUNTRY	AVERAGE DAILY CIRCULATION
1	The Sun	UK	3,461,000
2	USA Today	US	2,603,000
3	Daily Mail	UK	2,411,000
4	The Times of India	India	2,131,000
5	The Mirror	UK	2,117,000
6	The Wall Street Journal	US	1,821,000
7	The New York Times	US	1,673,000
8	Los Angeles Times	US	1,396,000
9	The Washington Post	US	1,049,000
10	Chicago Tribune	US	1,016,000

Source: *World Association of Newspapers*, World Press Trends 2003,
www.wan-press.org

The world's bestselling English language dailies represent both long-established publications and relative newcomers: the UK *Daily Herald*, the first paper ever to sell two million copies, was launched in 1911, became *The Sun* in 1964, and was relaunched as a tabloid in 1969. The *Daily Mail* started in 1896, absorbing the *News Chronicle* in 1960 and *Daily Sketch* in 1971. *USA Today*, launched in 1982, was one of the first newspapers to use computers and to transmit editions for simultaneous publication around the world. *The Times of India* began in 1838 as *The Bombay Times and Journal of Commerce*, changing to its present name in 1861. It is thought to have the highest readership (as distinct from sale) of any English-language newspaper, at some 4.42 million daily.

TOP 10 | OLDEST NEWSPAPERS IN THE U.S.

	NEWSPAPER	YEAR ESTABLISHED
1	The Hartford Courant, Hartford, CT	1764
2 =	Poughkeepsie Journal, Poughkeepsie, NY	1785
=	The Augusta Chronicle, Augusta, GA	1785
=	The Register Star, Hudson, NY	1785
5 =	Pittsburgh Post–Gazette, Pittsburgh, PA	1786
=	Daily Hampshire Gazette, Northampton, MA	1786
7	The Berkshire Eagle, Pittsfield, MA	1789
8	Norwich Bulletin, Norwich, CT	1791
9	The Recorder, Greenfield, MA	1792
10	Intelligencer Journal, Lancaster, PA	1794

Source: Editor & Publisher Year Book

Among even older newspapers that are no longer extant is the *Boston News-Letter*, first published in 1704 by New England postmaster John Campbell. It measured just 7.5 x 12 in (19 x 30.5 cm)and had a circulation of 300 copies.

TOP 10 | LONGEST RUNNING MAGAZINES IN THE U.S.

	MAGAZINE	FIRST PUBLISHED
1	Scientific American	1845
2	Town & Country	1846
3	Harper's*	1850
4	The Moravian	1856
5	The Atlantic Monthly	1857
6	Armed Forces Journal#	1863
7	The Nation	1865
8	American Naturalist	1867
9	Harper's Bazaar	1867
10	Animals†	1868

* *Originally* Harper's New Monthly Magazine

Originally Army and Navy Journal

† *Originally* Our Dumb Animals

Source: *Magazine Publishers of America*

The longest continuously published American magazine, *Scientific American*, the brainchild of Rufus Porter, was first published on August 28, 1845. Originally a four-page newspaper, it included features on both science and technology and nonscientific topics, including religion and poetry. Soon afterward, Porter sold it for $800 to 22-year-old Orson Desaix Munn and his 19-year-old friend Alfred Ely Beach, whose father published the New York *Sun*. They focused the magazine on science and established it as the world's most popular scientific journal.

TOP 10 LONGEST-RUNNING COMIC STRIPS IN THE U.S.

	STRIP	FIRST PUBLISHED
1	Katzenjammer Kids	1897
2	Gasoline Alley	1918
3	Barney Google and Snuffy Smith	1919
4	Tarzan	1929
5	Blondie	1930
6	Dick Tracy	1931
7	Alley Oop	1933
8	The Phantom	1936
9	Prince Valiant	1937
10	Nancy	1938

©2004 Gemstone Publishing, Inc. All rights reserved.

TOP 10 MAGAZINES IN THE U.S.

	MAGAZINE/ISSUES PER YEAR	AVERAGE PAID CIRCULATION, (2002)
1	AARP Bulletin (10)	21,622,237
2	AARP The Magazine* (6)	21,035,278
3	Reader's Digest (12)	11,067,522
4	TV Guide (52)	9,018,212
5	Better Homes and Gardens (12)	7,608,913
6	National Geographic Magazine (12)	6,644,167
7	Good Housekeeping (12)	4,679,941
8	Family Circle (17)	4,615,536
9	Woman's Day (17)	4,166,097
10	Time (54)	4,104,284

* Modern Maturity and My Generation combined in 2003 as AARP The Magazine

Source: Magazine Publishers of America

▶ Hot off the press
Competition from television, the Internet, and other media has done little to assuage the world's passion for newspapers.

Fine Art

MOST EXPENSIVE PAINTINGS

PAINTING/ARTIST/SALE	PRICE ($)
1 Portrait du Dr. Gachet, Vincent Van Gogh (Dutch; 1853–90), Christie's, New York, May 15, 1990 Both this painting and the one in No. 2 position were bought by Ryoei Saito, chairman of Daishowa Paper Manufacturing.	75,000,000
2 Au Moulin de la Galette, Pierre-Auguste Renoir (French; 1841–1919), Sotheby's, New York, May 17, 1990	71,000,000
3 Massacre of the Innocents, Sir Peter Paul Rubens (Flemish; 1577–1640), Sotheby's, London, July 10, 2002	68,400,000 (£45,000,000)
4 Portrait de l'Artiste Sans Barbe, Vincent Van Gogh, Christie's, New York, Nov. 19, 1998	65,000,000
5 Rideau, Cruchon et Compotier, Paul Cézanne , (French; 1839–1906), Sotheby's, New York, May 10, 1999	55,000,000
6 Les Noces de Pierrette, Pablo Picasso (Spanish; 1881–1973), Binoche et Godeau, Paris, Nov. 30, 1989 This painting was sold by financier Fredrik Roos and bought by Tomonori Tsurumaki, a property developer.	51,671,920 (F.Fr315,000,000)

PAINTING/ARTIST/SALE	PRICE ($)
7 Femme aux Bras Croises, Pablo Picasso, Christie's Rockefeller, New York, Nov. 8, 2000	50,000,000
8 Irises, Vincent Van Gogh, Sotheby's, New York, Nov. 11, 1987 After much speculation, its mystery purchaser was eventually confirmed as Australian businessman Alan Bond. However, as he was unable to pay for it in full, its former status as the world's most expensive work of art has been disputed.	49,000,000
9 Femme Assise Dans un Jardin, Pablo Picasso, Sotheby's, New York, Nov. 10, 1999	45,000,000
10 Le Rêve, Pablo Picasso, Christie's, New York, Nov. 10, 1997 Victor and Sally Ganz had paid $7,000 for this painting in 1941.	44,000,000

The subsequent history of Van Gogh's *Portrait du Dr. Gachet* is shrouded in mystery: Although the owner, Ryoei Saito, claimed that he would have it burned in his coffin to avoid paying taxes, it is rumored that after his death in 1996 it was re-purchased by Christie's, though its current whereabouts are unknown.

MOST EXPENSIVE AMERICAN PAINTINGS

PAINTING/ARTIST/SALE	PRICE ($)
1 **Polo Crowd,** George Bellows (1882–1925), Sotheby's, New York, Dec. 1, 1999	25,000,000
2 **Interchange,** Willem de Kooning* (1904–97), Sotheby's, New York, Nov. 8, 1989	18,800,000
3 **Orange Marilyn,** Andy Warhol (1928–87), Sotheby's, New York, May 14, 1998	15,750,000
4 **False Start,** Jasper Johns (b. 1930), Sotheby's, New York, Nov. 10, 1988	15,500,000
5 **White and Black on Wine,** Mark Rothko (1903–1970), Christie's Rockefeller, New York, May 14, 2003	14,600,000
6 **Woman,** Willem de Kooning, Christie's, New York, Nov. 20, 1996	14,200,000
7 **Yellow over Purple,** Mark Rothko, Sotheby's, New York, May 17, 2000	13,000,000
8 **Orestes,** Willem de Kooning, Sotheby's, New York, Nov. 12, 2002	12,000,000
9 **Two Flags,** Jasper Johns, Sotheby's, New York, Nov. 8, 1989	11,000,000
10 **Number 8,** Jackson Pollock (1925–56), Sotheby's, New York, May 2, 1989	10,500,000

* Dutch-born, naturalized US citizen

Though perhaps less well known than some of the other artists in the Top 10, George Wesley Bellows, a member of the so-called Ashcan School of American painting, rocketed to the top of this list when Microsoft chairman Bill Gates purchased *Polo Crowd*. Gates is reputed to have paid even more—$36 million—for Winslow Homer's *Lost on the Grand Banks*, the highest price paid for an American work in a private sale.

◀ **Record Rubens**
Massacre of the Innocents, a previously neglected painting by Rubens, broke the record for an Old Master when purchased by Canadian collector David Thomson for 10 times its pre-sale estimate.

ARTISTS WITH THE MOST WORKS SOLD FOR MORE THAN ONE MILLION DOLLARS

ARTIST	TOTAL VALUE OF WORKS SOLD ($)	NO. OF WORKS SOLD FOR OVER $1 MILLION
1 **Pablo Picasso** (Spanish; 1881–1973)	1,508,757,408	334
2 **Claude Monet** (French; 1840–1926)	1,104,865,017	249
3 **Pierre Auguste Renoir** (French; 1841–1919)	712,824,343	219
4 **Edgar Degas** (French; 1834–1917)	410,550,803	118
5 **Henri Matisse** (French; 1869–1954)	375,520,390	98
6 **Paul Cézanne** (French; 1839–1906)	541,195,573	92
7 **Camille Pissaro** (French; 1830–1903)	170,554,194	90
8 **Marc Chagall** (Russian; 1887–1985)	173,544,194	79
9 **Andy Warhol** (American; 1928–87)	191,751,857	74
10 **Amedeo Modigliani** (Italian; 1884–1920)	326,013,301	69

MOST EXPENSIVE PAINTINGS BY WOMEN ARTISTS

PAINTING/ARTIST/SALE	PRICE ($)
1 **Calla Lilies with Red Anemone,** Georgia O'Keeffe (American; 1887–1986), Christie's Rockefeller, New York, May 23, 2001	5,600,000
2 **The Conversation,** Mary Cassatt (American; 1844–1926), Christie's, New York, May 11, 1988	4,100,000
3 **Cache-cache,** Berthe Morisot (French; 1841–1895), Sotheby's, New York, Nov. 9, 2000	4,000,000
4 **Marche au Minho,** Sonia Delaunay (French/Russian; 1885–1979), Laurence Calmels, Paris, June 14, 2002	3,887,013 (€4,100,000)
5 = **Black Cross with Stars and Blue,** Georgia O'Keeffe, Christie's Rockefeller, New York, May 23, 2001	3,700,000
= **In the Box,** Mary Cassatt, Christie's, New York, May 23, 1996	3,700,000
7 = **Cache-cache,** Berthe Morisot, Sotheby's, New York, May 10, 1999	3,500,000
= **Mother, Sara and the Baby,** Mary Cassatt, Christie's, New York, May 10, 1989	3,500,000
9 **From the Plains,** Georgia O'Keeffe, Sotheby's, New York, Dec. 3, 1997	3,300,000
10 **Après le Dejeuner,** Berthe Morisot, Christie's, New York, May 14, 1997	3,250,000

The Top 10 reflects the status of three artists in particular: 20th-century painter Georgia O'Keeffe, whose work focused on natural forms, such as flowers and shells, and Berthe Morisot and Mary Cassatt, whose portraits and intimate domestic scenes are among the most revered works by women of the Impressionist movement.

Art on Show

TOP 10 | BEST-ATTENDED ART EXHIBITIONS IN NEW YORK, 2003

	EXHIBITION/VENUE	DATES	ATTENDANCE TOTAL	ATTENDANCE DAILY
1	**Leonardo da Vinci, Master Draftsman,** Metropolitan Museum of Art	Jan. 22–Mar. 30	401,004	6,863
2	**Thomas Struth,** Metropolitan Museum of Art	Feb. 4–Mar. 30	273,793	5,790
3	**Manet/Velázquez: The French Taste for Spanish Painting,** Metropolitan Museum of Art	Feb. 25–June 29	553,622	5,160
4	**Matisse Picasso,** Museum of Modern Art, Queens	Feb. 13–May 19	342,223	4,970
5	**Picasso to Pollock: Classics of Modern Art,** Solomon R. Guggenheim Museum	July 4–Sept. 28	247,586	3,314
6	**Matthew Barney: The Cremaster Cycle,** Solomon R. Guggenheim Museum	Feb. 21–June 11	300,206	3,151
7	**Goddess,** Metropolitan Museum of Art	May 1–Aug. 3	227,974	2,795
8	**Roy Lichtenstein on the Roof,** Metropolitan Museum of Art	May 1–Nov. 2	332,295	2,082
9	**Art of the First Cities,** Metropolitan Museum of Art	May 8–Aug. 17	174,113	1,988
10	**Ansel Adams at 100,** Museum of Modern Art, Queens	July 11–Nov. 3	144,033	1,732

Source: The Art Newspaper

TOP 10 | BEST-ATTENDED ART EXHIBITIONS, 2003

	EXHIBITION/VENUE/CITY	DATES	ATTENDANCE* TOTAL	ATTENDANCE* DAILY
1	**Leonardo da Vinci, Master Draftsman,** Metropolitan Museum of Art, New York	Jan. 22–Mar. 30	401,004	6,863
2	**Thomas Struth,** Metropolitan Museum of Art, New York	Feb. 4–Mar. 30	273,793	5,790
3	**Peter the Great,** State Hermitage, St. Petersburg	June 2–Aug. 31	450,000	5,759
4	**Leonardo da Vinci: Drawings and Manuscripts,** Musée du Louvre, Paris	May 8–July 14	322,000	5,511
5	**Manet/Velázquez: The French Taste for Spanish Painting,** Metropolitan Museum of Art, New York	Mar. 4–June 29	553,622	5,160
6	**Matisse Picasso,** Museum of Modern Art, Queens, New York	Feb. 13–May 19	342,223	4,970
7	**Nicolas de Staël,** Centre Georges Pompidou, Paris	Mar. 12–June 30	431,492	4,576
8	**Titian,** Museo del Prado, Madrid	June 10–Sept. 7	361,522	4,519
9	**Albrecht Dürer,** Albertina, Vienna	Sept. 5–Dec. 8	427,000	4,495
10	**Vincent's Choice,** Van Gogh Museum, Amsterdam	Feb. 14–June 15	527,685	4,325

* *Approximate totals provided by museums*

Source: The Art Newspaper

▶ **The genius of Leonardo**
Two of the most popular exhibitions of 2003 provided an opportunity to view drawings by Leonardo da Vinci that are rarely shown publicly.

TOP 10 TALLEST FREE-STANDING STATUES

STATUE/LOCATION	HEIGHT (FT)	(M)
1 **Chief Crazy Horse,** Thunderhead Mountain, South Dakota Started in 1948 by Polish American sculptor Korczak Ziolkowski and continued after his death in 1982 by his widow and eight of his children, this gigantic equestrian statue remains unfinished.	563	172
2 **Buddha,** Tokyo, Japan Unveiled in 1993, this statue weighs 1,000 tons.	394	120
3 **The Indian Rope Trick,** Riddersberg Säteri, Jönköping, Sweden Sculptor Calle Örnemark's 144-ton wooden sculpture depicts a long "rope" held by a fakir, while another figure ascends.	337	103
4 **Motherland,** 1967, Volgograd, Russia This concrete statue of a woman with a raised sword commemorates the Soviet victory at the Battle of Stalingrad (1942–43).	270	82
5 **Kannon,** Sanukimachi, Tokyo Bay, Japan This statue of the goddess of mercy was unveiled in 1961.	184	56
6 **Statue of Liberty,** New York City Designed by Auguste Bartholdi and presented to the US by the people of France, the statue was shipped in sections to Liberty (formerly Bedloes) Island, where it was unveiled on October 28, 1886.	151	46
7 **Christ,** Rio de Janeiro, Brazil This figure of Christ was unveiled in 1931.	125	38
8 **Tian Tan (Temple of Heaven) Buddha,** Po Lin Monastery, Hong Kong After 20 years' work this was unveiled on December 29, 1993.	112	34
9 **Quantum Cloud,** Greenwich, London, UK This gigantic steel human figure with steel struts was created in 1999 by Antony Gormley.	95	29
10 **Kim Il-Sung,** Pyongyang, North Korea Claimed to be the world's largest one-piece bronze statue, it was erected to mark the North Korean leader's 60th birthday in 1972.	75	23

TOP 10 BEST-ATTENDED EXHIBITIONS AT THE METROPOLITAN MUSEUM OF ART, NEW YORK

EXHIBITION	YEARS	ATTENDANCE
1 **The Treasures of Tutankhamun**	1978–79	1,226,467
2 **Mona Lisa**	1963	1,007,521
3 **The Vatican Collection: The Papacy and Art**	1983	896,743
4 **Glory of Russian Costume**	1976–77	835,862
5 **Origins of Impressionism**	1994–95	794,108
6 **Romantic and Glamorous Hollywood**	1974–75	788,665
7 **The Horses of San Marco**	1980	742,221
8 **Man and the Horse**	1984–85	726,523
9 **Masterpiece of Fifty Centuries**	1979–81	690,471
10 **Seurat**	1991–92	642,408

Collectibles

 ## MOST EXPENSIVE ITEMS OF POP MEMORABILIA

ITEM*/SALE	PRICE ($)#
1 **John Lennon's 1965 Rolls-Royce Phantom V touring limousine,** Sotheby's, New York, June 29, 1985 Finished in psychedelic paintwork.	2,299,000
2 **John Lennon's Steinway Model Z upright piano,** Fleetwood-Owen online auction, Hard Rock Café, London and New York, Oct. 17, 2000 Teak veneered, complete with cigarette burns. The piano Lennon played at Woodstock in 1969 and on which he composed *Imagine*. It was purchased by George Michael.	1,450,000
3 **John Lennon's handwritten lyrics for *Nowhere Man* (1965),** Christie's, New York, Nov. 18, 2003	455,500
4 **Bernie Taupin's handwritten lyrics for the rewritten *Candle in the Wind*,** Christie's, Los Angeles, Feb. 11, 1998 Played by Sir Elton John at the funeral of Diana, Princess of Wales, sold to Diana's brother Earl Spencer. The sale, part of a charity auction, established a world record for pop lyrics.	400,000
5 **Paul McCartney's handwritten lyrics for *Getting Better* (1967),** Sotheby's, London, Sept. 14, 1995	249,380 (£161,000)
6 **John Lennon's 1970 Mercedes-Benz 600 Pullman four-door limousine,** Christie's, London, Apr. 27, 1989	232,169 (£137,500)
7 **John Lennon's 1965 Ferrari 330 GT 2+2 two door coupe, right-hand drive,** Fleetwood-Owen online auction, Hard Rock Cafe, London and New York, Oct. 17, 2000	188,304
8 **Mal Evan's notebook, compiled 1967–68, which includes a draft by Paul McCartney of the lyrics for *Hey Jude*,** Sotheby's, London, Sept. 15, 1998	187,110 (£111,500)
9 **Elvis Presley's 1963 Rolls-Royce Phantom V touring limousine,** Sotheby's, London, Aug. 28, 1986	163,240 (£110,000)
10 **Charlie Parker's Grafton saxophone,** Christie's, London, Sept. 8, 1994	144,925 (£93,500)

* Excluding guitars

 # Including 10 percent buyer's premium, where appropriate

MOST EXPENSIVE GUITARS SOLD AT AUCTION

GUITAR/SALE	PRICE ($)*
1 **Jerry Garcia's "Tiger" guitar,** Guernsey's at Studio 54, New York, May 9, 2002	957,500
2 **Jerry Garcia's "Wolf" guitar,** Guernsey's at Studio 54, New York, May 9, 2002	789,500
3 **Eric Clapton's "Brownie" guitar,** Christie's, New York, June 24, 1999 Clapton used the 1956 sunburst Fender Stratocaster, one of his favorite electric guitars, to record the whole *Layla* album.	497,500
4 **George Harrison's first guitar,** a Spanish-style Egmond "Firewood", Cooper Owen/Hard Rock Café, London, Nov. 21, 2003	470,470 (£276,000)
5 **George Harrison's rosewood Telecaster Odyssey,** Los Angeles, Sept. 13, 2003	434,750

 ## MOST VALUABLE AMERICAN COMICS

COMIC	VALUE ($)*
1 **Action Comics No. 1** Published in June 1938, the first issue of *Action Comics* marked the original appearance of Superman.	400,000
2 **Detective Comics No. 27** Issued in May 1939, it is prized as the first comic book to feature Batman.	350,000
3 **Marvel Comics No. 1** The Human Torch and other heroes were first introduced in the issue dated October 1939.	300,000
4 **Superman No. 1** The first comic book devoted to Superman, reprinting the original *Action Comics* story, was published in summer 1939.	240,000
5 **All American Comics No. 16** The Green Lantern made his debut in the issue dated July 1940.	135,000
6 = **Batman No. 1** Published in spring 1940, this was the first comic book devoted to Batman.	115,000
= **Captain America Comics No. 1** Published in March 1941, this was the original comic in which Captain America appeared.	115,000
8 **Flash Comics No. 1** Dated January 1940, and featuring The Flash, it is rare because it was produced in small numbers for promotional purposes, and was unique as issue #2 was retitled *Whiz Comics*.	92,000
9 **Whiz Comics No. 1** Published in February 1940—and confusingly numbered "2"— it was the first comic book to feature Captain Marvel.	80,000
10 **More Fun Comics No. 52** The Spectre made his debut in the issue dated February 1940.	78,000

* For example in "Near Mint" condition

Source: The Overstreet Comic Book Price Guide, No. 33, 2003. ©2003 Gemstone Publishing, Inc. All rights reserved

GUITAR/SALE	PRICE ($)*
6 **Acoustic guitar owned by David Bowie, Paul McCartney, and George Michael** Christie's, London, May 18, 1994	331,122 (£220,000)
7 **Jimi Hendrix's Fender Stratocaster electric guitar,** Sotheby's, London, Apr. 25, 1990	323,522 (£198,000)
8 **John Lennon's Gallotone Champion,** Sotheby's/Hard Rock Café, London, Sept. 14, 1999	249,800 (£155,600)
9 **Buddy Holly's Gibson acoustic guitar (c. 1945), in a tooled leather case made by Holly,** Sotheby's, New York, June 23, 1990	242,000
10 **Eric Clapton's 1954 Fender Stratocaster** Christie's, New York, June 24, 1999	190,000

* Including buyer's premium, where appropriate

MOST EXPENSIVE PHOTOGRAPHS

PHOTOGRAPH*/PHOTOGRAPHER/SALE	PRICE ($)
1 **Athenes, Temple de Jupiter Olympien Pris de l'Est** (19th century), Joseph Philibert Girault de Prangey (French; 19th century), Christie's, London, May 20, 2003	710,000 (£500,000)
2 **Noire et Blanche** (1926), Man Ray (American; 1890–1976), Christie's, New York, Oct. 4, 1998	607,500
3 **Karnac, Pylone, Pris de l'Ouest** (19th century), Joseph Philibert Girault de Prangey, Christie's, London, May 20, 2003	567,000 (£350,000)
4 **Mullein, Maine** (1927), Paul Strand (American; 1890–1976), Phillips, New York, Apr. 15, 2002	550,000 (£384,615)
5 **Untitled V** Andreas Gursky (German; b.1955), Christie's, London, Feb. 6, 2002 0	549,900 (£390,000)
6 **Paris, Montparnasse** (1993), Andreas Gursky Christie's Rockefeller, New York, Nov. 15, 2001	540,000
7 **Light Trap for Henry Moore No. 1** (1967), Bruce Nauman (American; b.1941), Sotheby's, New York, May 17, 2000	480,000

PHOTOGRAPH*/PHOTOGRAPHER/SALE	PRICE ($)
8 **Rome, Colonne Trajane** (19th century), Joseph Philibert Girault de Prangey, Christie's, London, May 20, 2003	453,600 (£280,000)
9 **Chicago, Board of Trade** (1997), Andreas Gursky, Sotheby's, New York, Nov. 12, 2003	420,000
10 **Klitschko** (1999), Andreas Gursky, Phillips, New York, May 15, 2003	410,000

* Single prints only

Coincidentally, a close runner-up to those in the Top 10 is a portrait of Georgia O'Keeffe, the artist who herself heads the list of the most expensive paintings by women artists. *Georgia O'Keeffe: A Portrait—Hands with Thimble* (1930), by her husband, the photographer Alfred Stieglitz (American; 1864–1946), was sold at Christie's, New York, on October 8, 1993 for $398,500. The top price paid for a collection of photographs was $710,000 (£500,000) for the *Craven Memorial Album*—an album of photographs taken by William Craven, the 2nd Earl of Craven (British; 1809–66). The album was bought on May 12, 2001 at Bearne's, Exeter, England. At the same auction, *The North American Indian* (1907–30), a 20-volume set of photographs by Edward S. Curtis (American; 1868–1952), was purchased for $624,800 (£440,000).

▼ Black and White
The most expensive photograph sold in the 20th century, surrealist Man Ray's *Noire et Blanche*, a portrait of model Kiki de Montparnasse with an African mask, was taken in 1926.

MUSIC & MUSICIANS

Record Firsts

FIRST MILLION-SELLING ROCK 'N' ROLL SINGLES IN THE U.S.

	TITLE	ARTIST OR GROUP	YEAR
1	Rock Around the Clock	Bill Haley & His Comets	1954
2	Shake, Rattle and Roll	Bill Haley & His Comets	1954
3	Maybellene	Chuck Berry	1955
4	Ain't That a Shame	Fats Domino	1955
5	Ain't That a Shame	Pat Boone	1955
6	Seventeen	Boyd Bennett	1955
7	I Hear You Knocking	Gale Storm	1955
8	See You Later Alligator	Bill Haley & His Comets	1955
9	Tutti Frutti	Little Richard	1955
10	Heartbreak Hotel	Elvis Presley	1956

"Rock Around the Clock" and "Shake, Rattle and Roll" were both recorded on the same day: April 12, 1954. The first, which topped the US chart for seven weeks, is considered to be the disc that launched the rock era, selling all over the world and receiving a further impetus when it was featured in the 1955 film *Blackboard Jungle*. With innumerable cover versions in many languages, one authoritative estimate put the global sales of "Rock Around the Clock" at over 100 million.

FIRST FEMALE SINGERS TO HAVE A U.S. NO. 1 HIT DURING THE ROCK ERA

	ARTIST	TITLE	DATE AT NO. 1
1	Joan Weber	Let Me Go Lover	Jan. 1, 1955
2	Georgia Gibbs	Dance with Henry (Wallflower)	May 14, 1955
3	Kay Starr	Rock and Roll Waltz	Feb. 18, 1956
4	Gogi Grant	The Wayward Wind	June 16, 1956
5	Debbie Reynolds	Tammy	Aug. 19, 1957
6	Connie Francis	Everybody's Somebody's Fool	June 27, 1960
7	Brenda Lee	I'm Sorry	July 18, 1960
8	Shelley Fabares	Johnny Angel	Apr. 7, 1962
9	Little Eva	The Loco-motion	Aug. 25, 1962
10	Little Peggy March	I Will Follow Him	Apr. 27, 1963

Source: *Music Information Database*

Joan Weber's "Let Me Go Lover" was adapted from an anti-rum temperance song called "Let Me Go, Devil." The head of Columbia Records persuaded the producers of a TV crime program to include the song in the background of the show, as a result of which it became an instant hit, the 18-year-old artist's sole No. 1 record, and her only million-seller.

ALBUMS IN THE FIRST U.S. ALBUMS TOP 10

	TITLE	ARTIST OR GROUP
1	Al Jolson (Volume III)	Al Jolson
2	A Presentation of Progressive Jazz	Stan Kenton
3	Emperor's Waltz	Bing Crosby
4	Songs of Our Times	Carmen Cavallaro
5	Wizard at the Organ	Ken Griffin
6	Glenn Miller Masterpieces	Glenn Miller
7	Busy Fingers	Three Suns
8	Songs of Our Times	B. Grant Orchestra
9	Glenn Miller	Glenn Miller
10	Theme Songs	Various artists

Source: Billboard

This was the first albums Top 10 compiled by *Billboard* magazine, for its issue dated September 3, 1948. The presence of two collections by big band master Glenn Miller was a posthumous achievement, Miller himself having been killed four years earlier in a mysterious flying accident. The release of the 1954 film *The Glenn Miller Story* and accompanying album triggered a further revival—paradoxically in the year that also saw the birth of rock 'n' roll.

SINGLES IN THE FIRST U.S. TOP 10

	TITLE	ARTIST(S)
1	I'll Never Smile Again	Tommy Dorsey
2	The Breeze and I	Jimmy Dorsey
3	Imagination	Glenn Miller
4	Playmates	Kay Kyser
5	Fools Rush In	Glenn Miller
6	Where Was I	Charlie Barnet
7	Pennsylvania 6-5000	Glenn Miller
8	Imagination	Tommy Dorsey
9	Sierra Sue	Bing Crosby
10	Make-Believe Island	Mitchell Ayres

Source: Billboard

This was the first "Best Sellers In Store" chart compiled by *Billboard* magazine, for its issue dated July 20, 1940. Since the 7-inch 45-rpm single was still the best part of a decade in the future, all these would have been 10-inch 78-rpm disks. Note the almost total domination of big-name bands more than a half century ago—and spare a thought for Mitchell Ayres, who crept in at the bottom of this very first chart, and then never had a hit again.

FIRST GOLD ALBUMS IN THE U.S.

	TITLE	ARTIST	CERTIFICATION DATE
1	Oklahoma!	Soundtrack	July 8, 1958
2	Hymns	Tennessee Ernie Ford	Feb. 20, 1959
3	Johnny's Greatest Hits	Johnny Mathis	June 1, 1959
4 =	Sing Along with Mitch	Mitch Miller	Nov. 16, 1959
=	The Music Man	Original Cast	Nov. 16, 1959
6	South Pacific	Soundtrack	Dec. 18, 1959
7	Peter Gunn	Henry Mancini	Dec. 31, 1959
8	The Student Prince	Mario Lanza	Jan. 19, 1960
9	Pat's Great Hits	Pat Boone	Feb. 12, 1960
10 =	Elvis	Elvis Presley	Feb. 17, 1960
=	60 Years of Music	Various Artists	Feb. 17, 1960

Source: *RIAA*

The original stage cast album of *Oklahoma!* had been a million-seller in 1943, when—for the first time ever, and before the invention of the Long Playing album—an entire Broadway musical was released on a set of 78-rpm discs. The soundtrack of the 1955 film musical was still selling steadily when gold albums were launched three years later, and stayed in the US charts for five years.

FIRST BEATLES SINGLES TO CHART IN THE U.S.

	TITLE	WEEK OF ENTRY
1	A Hard Day's Night	Jan. 18, 1964
2	She Loves You	Jan. 25, 1964
3	Please Please Me	Feb. 1, 1964
4	I Saw Her Standing There	Feb. 8, 1964
5	My Bonnie	Feb. 15, 1964
6	From Me to You	Mar. 7, 1964
7	Twist and Shout	Mar. 14, 1964
8	Roll Over Beethoven	Mar. 21, 1964
9 =	All My Loving	Mar. 28, 1964
=	Can't Buy Me Love	Mar. 28, 1964
=	Do You Want to Know a Secret	Mar. 28, 1964

Source: *Popular Music Database*

▼ **Beatlemania**
The Beatles first charted in the US more than a year after their first UK appearances, with their 1964 US TV and concert debuts firmly establishing their transatlantic status.

Female Solo Singers

SINGLES BY FEMALE SOLO SINGERS IN THE U.S.

	TITLE/SINGER	YEAR
1	I Will Always Love You, Whitney Houston	1992
2	How Do I Live, LeAnn Rimes	1997
3	Fantasy, Mariah Carey	1995
4	Vogue, Madonna	1990
5	Mr. Big Stuff, Jean Knight	1971
6	You Were Meant for Me/ Foolish Games, Jewel	1996
7	You Light up My Life, Debby Boone	1977
8	The Power of Love, Celine Dion	1993
9	Believe, Cher	1999
10	Physical, Olivia Newton-John	1981

Source: *Popular Music Database*

Among this list of platinum sellers, it is fitting that Whitney Houston's multi-platinum success, from the original soundtrack of *The Bodyguard*, was also written by a woman – Dolly Parton.

FEMALE SOLO SINGERS IN THE U.S.

	SINGER	TOTAL CHART HITS
1	Aretha Franklin	76
2	= Connie Francis	56
	= Dionne Warwick	56
4	Brenda Lee	55
5	Madonna	50
6	= Patti Page	41
	= Diana Ross	41
	= Barbra Streisand	41
9	Olivia Newton-John	40
10	Whitney Houston	37

Source: *Music Information Database*

SELL A MILLION

AMERICAN BLUES SINGER BESSIE SMITH was the first female solo singer to achieve a million-selling disc in the pre-chart era. *Down Hearted Blues*, recorded on February 15, 1923 and the first song that she cut, sold at least 800,000 copies at 75 cents in its first year. It went on to sell a total of over two million, making it Columbia Records' first major hit. She later became one of the most successful singers of her generation, and one of the most prolific, recording some 160 songs for the Columbia label.

THE FIRST TO...

TOP 10 | YOUNGEST FEMALE SOLO SINGERS TO HAVE A NO. 1 SINGLE IN THE U.S.

	SINGER/TITLE	YEAR	AGE (YRS)	(MTHS)	(DAYS)
1	**Little Peggy March,** I Will Follow Him	1963	15	1	20
2	**Brenda Lee,** I'm Sorry	1960	15	7	7
3	**Tiffany,** I Think We're Alone Now	1987	16	1	5
4	**Lesley Gore,** It's My Party	1963	17	0	30
5	**Little Eva,** The Loco-Motion	1962	17	1	27
6	**Britney Spears,** ...Baby One More Time	1999	17	1	29
7	**Monica,** The First Night	1998	17	11	9
8	**Shelley Fabares,** Johnny Angel	1962	18	2	19
9	**Debbie Gibson,** Foolish Beat	1988	18	6	4
10	**Christina Aguilera,** Genie in a Bottle	1999	18	7	13

Source: *Music Information Database*

While Britney Spears and other teen singers have a place in this list, it is notable that half the girls in the Top 10 scored their No. 1 hits in the 1960s: Little Peggy March's "I Will Follow Him" was a translation of a French hit song, "Chariot." March's real name was Margaret Annemarie Battivio, her stage name deriving from her diminutive height (4 ft 10 in) and birth month.

TOP 10 | OLDEST FEMALE SOLO SINGERS TO HAVE A NO. 1 SINGLE IN THE U.S.

	SINGER/TITLE	YEAR	AGE (YRS)	(MTHS)	(DAYS)
1	**Cher,** Believe	1999	52	9	15
2	**Tina Turner,** What's Love Got to Do With It	1984	45	9	5
3	**Aretha Franklin,** I Knew You Were Waiting (for Me)	1987	45	0	24
4	**Bette Midler,** The Wind Beneath My Wings	1989	44	8	24
5	**Madonna,** Music	2000	42	1	0
6	**Kim Carnes,** Bette Davis' Eyes	1981	35	9	26
7	**Dolly Parton,** 9 to 5	1981	35	1	2
8	**Janet Jackson,** All for You	2001	34	10	28
9	**Georgia Gibbs,** Dance with Me Henry	1955	34	8	18
10	**Deniece Williams,** Let's Hear It for the Boy	1985	33	11	23

Source: *Music Information Database*

In contrast with the male counterpart to this list, whose entrants are 46 or older, it is telling that "old" here refers to veterans over age 33. The earliest entry, that of Georgia Gibbs, was the last of three million-selling singles by an artist who had established her singing career with bands in the pre-War era.

TOP 10 | FEMALE SINGERS WITH THE LONGEST GAPS BETWEEN NO. 1 HIT SINGLES IN THE U.S.

	SINGER	PERIOD	GAP (YRS)	(MTHS)	(DAYS)
1	**Cher**	Mar. 23, 1974–Mar. 19, 1999	24	11	27
2	**Aretha Franklin**	July 1, 1967–Apr. 11, 1987	19	11	10
3	**Madonna**	Apr. 15, 1995–Sept. 9, 2000	5	4	25
4	**Jennifer Warnes**	Nov. 27, 1982–Nov. 21, 1987	4	11	25
5	**Diana Ross**	July 10, 1976–Aug. 30, 1980	4	1	20
6	**Janet Jackson**	Dec. 25, 1993–Jan. 24, 1998	4	0	30
7	**Olivia Newton-John**	Mar. 15, 1975–June 3, 1978	3	2	19
8	**Barbra Streisand**	Feb. 9, 1974–Feb. 26, 1977	3	0	17
9	**Janet Jackson**	Oct. 25, 1986–Sept. 30, 1989	2	11	5
10	**Whitney Houston**	Feb. 26, 1993–Nov. 18, 1995	2	8	23

Source: *Music Information Database*

◄ **Whip hand**
By the time of her 1992 *Erotica* release, Madonna had already achieved more than half her total tally of chart hits in a career spanning just eight years.

TOP 10 | ALBUMS BY FEMALE SOLO SINGERS IN THE U.S.

	TITLE/SINGER	YEAR
1	**Come on Over,** Shania Twain	1997
2	**The Bodyguard** (Soundtrack), Whitney Houston	1992
3	**Jagged Little Pill,** Alanis Morissette	1995
4	= **...Baby One More Time,** Britney Spears	1999
	= **Whitney Houston,** Whitney Houston	1985
6	**The Woman in Me,** Shania Twain	1995
7	= **Pieces of You,** Jewel	1997
	= **Falling into You,** Celine Dion	1996
9	= **Let's Talk About Love,** Celine Dion	1997
	= **Like a Virgin,** Madonna	1984
	= **Music Box,** Mariah Carey	1993
	= **Tapestry,** Carole King	1971
	= **The Immaculate Collection,** Madonna	1990
	= **Up!,** Shania Twain	2003

Source: *Music Information Database*

Male Solo Singers

 MALE SINGERS WITH THE LONGEST GAPS BETWEEN NO. 1 HIT SINGLES IN THE U.S.

SINGER	PERIOD	GAP (YRS)	(MTHS)	(DAYS)
1 Paul Anka	Aug. 15, 1959–Aug. 17, 1974	15	0	2
2 Rod Stewart	Mar. 10, 1979–Jan. 15, 1994	14	10	5
3 George Harrison	July 7, 1973–Jan. 9, 1988	14	6	2
4 Neil Sedaka	Aug. 25, 1962–Jan. 25, 1975	12	5	0
5 Herb Alpert	July 20, 1968–Oct. 13, 1979	11	2	23
6 Stevie Wonder	Aug. 31, 1963–Jan. 20, 1973	9	4	20
7 Elton John	Sept. 4, 1976–Jan. 11, 1986	9	4	7
8 Dean Martin	Feb. 18, 1956–Aug. 8, 1964	8	5	21
9 David Bowie	Oct. 3, 1975–May 14, 1983	7	7	11
10 Elvis Presley	May 5, 1962–Oct. 25, 1969	7	5	20

Source: *Music Information Database*

MALE SOLO SINGERS IN THE U.S.

	SINGER	TOTAL CHART HITS
1	Elvis Presley	151
2	James Brown	94
3	Ray Charles	76
4	Elton John	69
5	Frank Sinatra	67
6	Fats Domino	66
7	Stevie Wonder	63
8	= Pat Boone	60
9	= Nat "King" Cole	60
10	Marvin Gaye	57

Source: *Music Information Database*

In January 2004, the RIAA confirmed Elvis Presley as the bestselling solo artist in US history: in addition to his record tally of chart singles, his overall album sales were reappraised as totaling 117.5 million.

▶ **You wear it well**
After hitting US No. 1 in 1979 with "Da Ya Think I'm Sexy," Rod Stewart had to wait until 1994 to return to the top slot with "All for Love" (shared with Bryan Adams and Sting)—which also earned him a place among the oldest singers with a US No. 1.

TOP 10 OLDEST MALE SOLO SINGERS TO HAVE A NO. 1 SINGLE IN THE U.S.

	SINGER/TITLE	YEAR	AGE* (YRS)	(MTHS)	(DAYS)
1	**Louis Armstrong,** Hello Dolly!	1964	63	9	5
2	**Lawrence Welk,** Calcutta	1961	57	11	14
3	**Morris Stoloff,** Moonglow and Theme from Picnic	1956	57	10	8
4	**Lorne Greene,** Ringo	1964	50	9	23
5	**Elton John,** Candle in the Wind (1997)/ Something About the Way You Look Tonight ‡	1997	50	9	21
6	**Frank Sinatra,** Strangers in the Night	1967	50	6	28
7	**Rod Stewart,** All for Love	1994	49	0	12
8	**Dean Martin,** Everybody Loves Somebody	1964	47	2	8
9	**Sammy Davis Jr.,** The Candy Man	1972	46	6	16
10	**Meat Loaf,** I'd Do Anything for Love (But I Won't do That)	1993	46	2	7

*During last week of No. 1 US single
Duet with Nancy Sinatra
‡ Duet with Jennifer Warnes
Source: Music Information Database

TOP 10 YOUNGEST MALE SOLO SINGERS TO HAVE A NO. 1 SINGLE IN THE U.S.

	SINGER/TITLE	YEAR	AGE* (YRS)	(MTHS)	(DAYS)
1	**Stevie Wonder,** Fingertips	1963	13	2	28
2	**Donny Osmond,** Go Away Little Girl	1971	13	9	2
3	**Michael Jackson,** Ben	1972	14	1	15
4	**Laurie London,** He's Got the Whole World in His Hands	1958	14	3	0
5	**Paul Anka,** Diana	1957	16	1	16
6	**Brian Hyland,** Itsy Bitsy Teenie Weenie Yellow Polkadot Bikini	1960	16	9	1
7	**Shaun Cassidy,** Da Doo Ron Ron	1977	17	9	19
8	**Bobby Vee,** Take Good Care of My Baby	1961	18	4	24
9	**Usher,** Nice & Slow	1998	19	4	0
10	**Andy Gibb,** I Just Want to be Your Everything	1977	19	4	25

*During first week of debut No. 1 US single
Source: Music Information Database

If group members were eligible for the list, all three Hanson brothers would be in the Top 10. Isaac was 16 years and 6 months, Taylor 14 years and 2 months, and Zachary 11 years and 7 months when "Mmmbop" topped the charts in 1997.

TOP 10 SINGLES BY MALE SOLO SINGERS IN THE U.S.

	TITLE/SINGER	YEAR
1	**Candle in the Wind (1997)/Something About the Way You Look Tonight,** Elton John	1997
2	**White Christmas,** Bing Crosby	1942
3	**Hound Dog/Don't Be Cruel,** Elvis Presley	1956
4	**Gangsta's Paradise,** Coolio featuring L.V.	1995
5	**(Everything I Do) I Do It For You,** Bryan Adams	1991
6	**Love Me Tender/Any Way You Want Me,** Elvis Presley	1956
7	**All Shook Up,** Elvis Presley	1957
8	**Jailhouse Rock,** Elvis Presley	1957
9	**Heartbreak Hotel/I Was The One,** Elvis Presley	1956
10	**Baby Got Back,** Sir Mix-A-Lot	1992

Source: Music Information Database

TOP 10 ALBUMS BY MALE SOLO SINGERS IN THE U.S.

	TITLE/SINGER	YEAR	SALES
1	**Thriller,** Michael Jackson	1982	26,000,000
2 =	**No Fences,** Garth Brooks	1990	16,000,000
=	**Greatest Hits,** Elton John	1974	16,000,000
4	**Born in the USA,** Bruce Springsteen	1984	15,000,000
5 =	**Ropin' the Wind,** Garth Brooks	1991	14,000,000
=	**Bat Out of Hell,** Meat Loaf	1977	14,000,000
7 =	**No Jacket Required,** Phil Collins	1985	12,000,000
=	**Breathless,** Kenny G	1992	12,000,000
=	**Greatest Hits,** Kenny Rogers	1980	12,000,000
10 =	**Devil Without a Cause,** Kid Rock	1999	11,000,000
=	**James Taylor's Greatest Hits,** James Taylor	1976	11,000,000

Source: RIAA

Within two years of its release, Michael Jackson's Thriller album had sold a record total of 20 million copies, but it continued to sell into its second and third decades, being certified for record sales of 26 million copies in 2000. The album's total world sales run to more than 50 million.

Groups & Duos

TOP 10 SINGLES BY DUOS IN THE U.S.

	TITLE/DUO	YEAR
1	**Whoomp! (There It Is)**, Tag Team	1993
2	**Jump,** Kris Kross	1992
3	**Unchained Melody,** Righteous Brothers	1965/1990
4	**Rump Shaker,** Wreckx-N-Effect	1992
5	**Déjà Vu (Uptown Baby),** Lord Tariq & Peter Gunz	1997
6	**Wake Me Up Before You Go Go,** Wham!	1984
7	**Reunited,** Peaches & Herb	1979
8	**Careless Whisper,** Wham!	1984
9	**Summertime,** DJ Jazzy Jeff & the Fresh Prince	1991
10	**Ain't No Stoppin' Us Now,** McFadden & Whitehead	1979

Source: *Music Information Database*

Less than a year after its release, Tag Team's "Whoomp! (There It Is)" was certified with sales of 4 million copies. "Unchained Melody" by the Righteous Brothers (Bill Medley and Bobby Hatfield) made a surprise return to the charts after featuring in the soundtrack of the 1990 film *Ghost*, providing it with the platinum status that did not even exist when it was first released.

TOP 10 SINGLES BY GROUPS IN THE U.S.

	TITLE/GROUP	YEAR
1	**We Are the World,** USA For Africa	1985
2	**Hey Jude,** The Beatles	1968
3	**Macarena,** Los Del Rio	1995
4	**Rump Shaker,** Wreckx-N-Effect	1992
5	**Eye of the Tiger,** Survivor	1982
6	**I Wanna Sex You Up,** Color Me Badd	1991
7	**O.P.P.,** Naughty By Nature	1991
8	**Tha Crossroads,** Bone Thugs-N-Harmony	1996
9	**Let It Be,** The Beatles	1970
10	**Get Back,** The Beatles with Billy Preston	1969

Source: *Music Information Database*

TOP 10 ALBUMS BY GROUPS IN THE U.S.

	TITLE/GROUP	YEAR
1	**Their Greatest Hits, 1971–1975,** The Eagles	1976
2	**Led Zeppelin IV** (untitled), Led Zeppelin	1971
3	**Rumours,** Fleetwood Mac	1977
4	**Back in Black,** AC/DC	1980
5	**Boston,** Boston	1976
6	**Hotel California,** The Eagles	1977
7	**Cracked Rear View,** Hootie & the Blowfish	1995
8	**Dark Side of the Moon,** Pink Floyd	1973
9	**Appetite For Destruction,** Guns N' Roses	1987
10	**Supernatural,** Santana	1999

Source: *Music Information Database*

This list has changed considerably in recent times, with official sales figures being updated in the US on several perennially big-selling albums—most notably those by the recently resurrected Eagles, whose *Greatest Hits* and *Hotel California* collections are now certified as having sold in excess of 28 million and 16 million copies, respectively.

TOP 10 FEMALE GROUPS IN THE U.S.

	GROUP	TOTAL CHART HITS
1	**The Supremes**	45
2	**The McGuire Sisters**	29
3	**The Pointer Sisters**	27
4	**The Shirelles**	26
5	**Martha & the Vandellas**	23
6	**The Fontane Sisters**	18
7	**TLC**	15
8	= **En Vogue**	14
	= **SWV**	14
10	= **Expose**	12
	= **Salt 'N Pepa**	12

Source: *Music Information Database*

Coincidentally, two groups in this list—the McGuire Sisters and the Fontane Sisters (real name Rosse)—each consisted of three sisters. Both groups achieved their chart hits in the 1950s. The McGuires' 1955 version of "Sincerely" was a million-seller, remaining at US No. 1 for 10 weeks. The Fontanes reached No. 1 in 1954 with "Hearts of Stone."

TOP 10 GROUPS IN THE U.S.

	GROUP	TOTAL CHART HITS
1	The Beatles	73
2	The Beach Boys	60
3	The Rolling Stones	57
4	The Temptations	55
5	Chicago	50
6	The Four Seasons	48
7	Smokey Robinson & the Miracles	46
8 =	Four Tops	45
=	The Supremes	45
10	The Bee Gees	43

Source: *Music Information Database*

TOP 10 DUOS IN THE U.S.

	DUO	TOTAL CHART HITS
1	The Everly Brothers	38
2	Daryl Hall & John Oates	34
3	The Carpenters	28
4 =	Jan & Dean	24
=	Righteous Brothers	24
6	Ike & Tina Turner	20
7	Sonny & Cher	18
8	Simon & Garfunkel	17
9	Peaches & Herb	16
10 =	Eurythmics	14
=	Peter & Gordon	14

Source: *Music Information Database*

▼ **Supreme achievement**
The Supremes' unbeatable lead among female groups began in 1964 with US No. 1 "Where Did Our Love Go," and continued for a quarter of a century.

Singles of Each Year 1992–2003

TOP 10 SINGLES IN THE U.S., 1992

	SINGLE	ARTIST OR GROUP
1	I Will Always Love You	Whitney Houston
2	Baby Got Back	Sir Mix-A-Lot
3	End of the Road	Boyz II Men
4	Jump	Kris Kross
5	Achy Breaky Heart	Billy Ray Cyrus
6	Rump Shaker	Wreckx-N-Effect
7	Tears in Heaven	Eric Clapton
8	I'm Too Sexy	Right Said Fred
9	Smells Like Teen Spirit	Nirvana
10	Under the Bridge	Red Hot Chili Peppers

Source: *Soundscan*

Well on its way to becoming one of the bestselling singles in American chart history, the Dolly Parton–penned "I Will Always Love You" sold an incredible 4 million copies in only nine weeks in the US and continued amassing similar numbers well into 1993. Rap accounted for three entries in the top six: Nos 2, 4, and 6.

TOP 10 SINGLES IN THE U.S., 1993

	SINGLE	ARTIST OR GROUP
1	Whoomp! (There It Is)	Tag Team
2	I'd Do Anything for Love (But I Won't Do That)	Meat Loaf
3	I Will Always Love You	Whitney Houston
4	Freak Me	Silk
5	Informer	Snow
6	Can't Help Falling in Love	UB40
7	Nuthin' But a "G" Thang	Dr. Dre
8	All That She Wants	Ace of Base
9	Dazzey Duks	Duice
10	That's the Way Love Goes	Janet Jackson

Source: *Soundscan*

With the exception of Meat Loaf's rocking return at No. 2 and Whitney Houston's ballad at No. 3, all of these titles are either rap or R&B hits. All of the Top 10 singles achieved sales in excess of 1 million copies, with Tag Team selling twice as many as the No. 2 at 2.8 million.

TOP 10 SINGLES IN THE U.S., 1994

	SINGLE	ARTIST OR GROUP
1	I'll Make Love to You	Boyz II Men
2	I Swear	All-4-One
3	Bump 'N' Grind	R. Kelly
4	The Sign	Ace of Base
5	Tootsee Roll	69 Boyz
6	Fantastic Voyage	Coolio
7	Regulate	Warren G & Nate Dogg
8	The Power of Love	Celine Dion
9	Stay (I Missed You)	Lisa Loeb & Nine Stories
10	Here Comes the Hotstepper	Ini Kamoze

Source: *Soundscan*

The trend of rap/hip-hop/R&B continued, with seven of the Top 10 in that genre. "I'll Make Love to You" sold 1.6 million copies—one of seven singles to sell a million copies during the year.

TOP 10 SINGLES IN THE U.S., 1998

	SINGLE	ARTIST OR GROUP
1	The Boy Is Mine	Brandy & Monica
2	Too Close	Next
3	You're Still the One	Shania Twain
4	Nice & Slow	Usher
5	The First Night	Monica
6	My Way	Usher
7	My All	Mariah Carey
8	Body Bumpin' Yippie-Yi-Yo	Public Announcement
9	No, No, No Part 2	Destiny's Child (featuring Wyclef Jean)
10	Let's Ride	Montell Jordan featuring Master P & Silkk the Shocker

Source: *Soundscan*

A strong tune and a powerful bass line helped to make "The Boy is Mine" a huge summer hit—and the song went on to claim top spot in the annual list for Brandy & Monica.

TOP 10 SINGLES IN THE U.S., 1999

	SINGLE	ARTIST OR GROUP
1	Believe	Cher
2	Genie in a Bottle	Christina Aguilera
3	Heartbreak Hotel	Whitney Houston featuring Faith Evans & Kelly Price
4	Summer Girls	LFO
5	Smooth	Santana featuring Rob Thomas
6	If You Had My Love	Jennifer Lopez
7	Livin' La Vida Loca	Ricky Martin
8	Angel of Mine	Monica
9	Bills, Bills, Bills	Destiny's Child
10	All I Have to Give	Backstreet Boys

Source: *Soundscan*

Cher's worldwide dance smash "Believe"—distinguished by its catchy, vocoderized chorus—took the No. 1 spot in 1998 for an artist who has been at the top of her profession for more than three decades.

TOP 10 SINGLES IN THE U.S., 2000

	SINGLE	ARTIST OR GROUP
1	Maria Maria	Santana featuring the Product G&B
2	Music	Madonna
3	Incomplete	Sisqo
4	Breathe	Faith Hill
5	Get It on ... Tonite	Montell Jordan
6	From the Bottom of My Broken Heart	Britney Spears
7	Thank God I Found You	Mariah with Joe & 98°
8	Hot Boyz	Missy Elliott featuring Nas, Eve & Q-Tip
9	I Like It	Sammie
10	He Wasn't Man Enough	Toni Braxton

Source: *Soundscan*

All of the above sold in excess of 600,000 copies, with "Maria Maria" way out in front with sales of 1.3 million. "Music" and "Incomplete" both topped the million mark.

TOP 10 SINGLES IN THE U.S., 1995

	SINGLE	ARTIST OR GROUP
1	Gangsta's Paradise	Coolio featuring LV
2	Fantasy	Mariah Carey
3	One Sweet Day	Mariah Carey & Boyz II Men
4	Waterfalls	TLC
5	Boombastic/In the Summertime	Shaggy
6	Don't Take it Personal (Just One of Dem Days)	Monica
7	One More Chance/ Stay with Me	Notorious B.I.G.
8	Freak Like Me	Adina Howard
9	Exhale (Shoop Shoop)	Whitney Houston
10	This is How We Do It	Montell Jordan

Source: *Soundscan*

In a year dominated by rap, Coolio's "Gangsta's Paradise" achieved triple platinum status (for sales of 3 million), while even the No. 10, Montell Jordan's "This is How We Do It", made platinum within the year.

TOP 10 SINGLES IN THE U.S., 1996

	SINGLE	ARTIST OR GROUP
1	Macarena (Bayside Boys Mix)	Los Del Rio
2	How Do U Want It/ California Love	2Pac
3	Twisted	Keith Sweat
4	No Diggity	Blackstreet
5	You Makin' Me High/ Let It Flow	Toni Braxton
6	C'mon N' Ride It (The Train)	Quad City DJs
7	Because You Loved Me	Celine Dion
8	Loungin'	LL Cool J
9	Nobody Knows	Tony Rich Project
10	Unbreak My Heart	Toni Braxton

Source: *Soundscan*

Fronted by two middle-aged Spanish TV stars, Los Del Rio emerged as the surprise leaders in singles sales with their novelty dance hit "Macarena."

TOP 10 SINGLES IN THE U.S., 1997

	SINGLE	ARTIST OR GROUP
1	Candle in the Wind (1997)/ Something About the Way You Look Tonight	Elton John
2	I'll Be Missing You	Puff Daddy & Faith Evans featuring 112
3	Can't Nobody Hold Me Down	Puff Daddy featuring Mase
4	How Do I Live	LeAnn Rimes
5	You Make Me Wanna	Usher
6	Wannabe	The Spice Girls
7	MMMBop	Hanson
8	Return of the Mack	Mark Morrison
9	It's Your Love	Tim McGraw with Faith Hill
10	Mo Money Mo Problems	Notorious B.I.G. featuring Puff Daddy & Mase

Source: *Soundscan*

TOP 10 SINGLES IN THE U.S., 2001

	SINGLE	ARTIST OR GROUP
1	Loverboy	Mariah Carey
2	Stutter	Joe
3	Get Over Yourself	Eden's Crush
4	All for You	Janet Jackson
5	My Baby	Lil' Romeo
6	What Would You Do?	City High
7	Bizounce	Olivia
8	The Star Spangled Banner	Whitney Houston
9	Superwoman	Lil' Mo
10	Missing You	Case

Source: *Soundscan*

Maria Carey, whose albums had been a fixture among the annual bestsellers during the mid-1990s, took top place in the 2001 single charts with "Loverboy", a song from the soundtrack of the movie *Glitter*. Other established artists to score big hits during the year were Whitney Houston and Janet Jackson.

TOP 10 SINGLES IN THE U.S., 2002

	SINGLE	ARTIST OR GROUP
1	Before Your Love/ A Moment Like This	Kelly Clarkson
2	Uh Huh	B2K
3	Lights Camera Action!	Mr. Cheeks
4	Hush Lil' Lady	Corey
5	Girlfriend (remix)	*NSYNC featuring Nelly
6	A Thousand Miles	Vanessa Carlton
7	Die Another Day	Madonna
8	A Little Less Conversation	Elvis Presley Vs. JXL
9	Long Time Gone	Dixie Chicks
10	Can't Fight the Moonlight	LeAnn Rimes

Source: *Nielsen Soundscan*

Texas-born singer Kelly Clarkson scored the 2002 top selling hit after emerging from some 10,000 hopefuls to win the hugely popular TV talent show *American Idol*.

TOP 10 SINGLES IN THE U.S., 2003

	SINGLE	ARTIST OR GROUP
1	Bridge Over Troubled Water	Clay Aiken
2	Flying Without Wings	Ruben Studdard
3	Picture	Kid Rock featuring Allison Moorer
4	God Bless America	American Idol Finalists
5	So Yesterday	Hilary Duff
6	Did My Time	KoRn
7	Hole in the World	Eagles
8	Through the Rain	Mariah Carey
9	Miss You	Aaliyah
10	Intuition	Jewel

Source: *Nielsen SoundScan*

Aiken's single—the only platinum record listed—is the first to be the year's best-seller without ever making the *Billboard Hot 100*. Nos. 2, 3, and 4 are the only gold records, while Nos. 5, 6, 7, and 8 peaked at 42, 38, 69, and 81 respectively. Conversely, boy band Natural scored a gold award for "What If," but failed to crack the Top 10.

Albums of Each Year 1992-2003

TOP 10 | ALBUMS IN THE U.S., 1992

	ALBUM	ARTIST OR GROUP
1	Ropin' the Wind	Garth Brooks
2	Some Gave All	Billy Ray Cyrus
3	The Bodyguard (Original Soundtrack)	Whitney Houston
4	The Chase	Garth Brooks
5	Nevermind	Nirvana
6	Dangerous	Michael Jackson
7	No Fences	Garth Brooks
8	Metallica	Metallica
9	Achtung Baby	U2
10	Ten	Pearl Jam

Source: *Soundscan*

Virtually unknown outside the US, Nashville king Garth Brooks has been credited with turning country music into a nationwide mainstream phenomenon in the 1990s. At the year's end, the soundtrack to Whitney Houston's movie *The Bodyguard* was selling at the rate of 1 million copies a week.

TOP 10 | ALBUMS IN THE U.S., 1993

	ALBUM	ARTIST OR GROUP
1	The Bodyguard (Original Soundtrack)	Whitney Houston
2	Janet	Janet Jackson
3	VS	Pearl Jam
4	Breathless	Kenny G
5	Music Box	Mariah Carey
6	The Chronic	Dr. Dre
7	Unplugged	Eric Clapton
8	In Pieces	Garth Brooks
9	Core	Stone Temple Pilots
10	Bat Out of Hell II: Back into Hell	Meat Loaf

Source: *Soundscan*

Each of these albums sold over 2.5 million copies in the US during the year, with *The Bodyguard* adding over 5.5 million sales to its initial 1992 tally.

TOP 10 | ALBUMS IN THE U.S., 1994

	ALBUM	ARTIST OR GROUP
1	The Lion King (Original Soundtrack)	Various Artists
2	The Sign	Ace of Base
3	II	Boyz II Men
4	August and Everything After	Counting Crows
5	Dookie	Green Day
6	Not a Moment Too Soon	Tim McGraw
7	Purple	Stone Temple Pilots
8	Miracles: The Holiday Album	Kenny G
9	Smash	Offspring
10	Music Box	Mariah Carey

Source: *Soundscan*

Each of these albums sold over 2.5 million copies in the US during the year. A film soundtrack topped the list for the second year running, while second-place Ace of Base showed that saleable Swedish pop did not end with Abba.

TOP 10 | ALBUMS IN THE U.S., 1998

	ALBUM	ARTIST OR GROUP
1	Titanic (Original Soundtrack)	James Horner
2	Let's Talk About Love	Celine Dion
3	Backstreet Boys	Backstreet Boys
4	Come on Over	Shania Twain
5	*NSYNC	*NSYNC
6	City of Angels (Original Soundtrack)	Various Artists
7	Double Live	Garth Brooks
8	Big Willie Style	Will Smith
9	Savage Garden	Savage Garden
10	Armageddon (Original Soundtrack)	Various Artists

Source: *Soundscan*

Celine Dion not only claimed second place with *Let's Talk About Love*, making her third Top 10 appearance in as many years, but sang the title song for the only album to outsell it—the soundtrack to movie blockbuster *Titanic*.

TOP 10 | ALBUMS IN THE U.S., 1999

	ALBUM	ARTIST OR GROUP
1	Millennium	Backstreet Boys
2	...Baby One More Time	Britney Spears
3	Ricky Martin	Ricky Martin
4	Come on Over	Shania Twain
5	Significant Other	Limp Bizkit
6	Supernatural	Santana
7	Devil Without a Cause	Kid Rock
8	Fanmail	TLC
9	Christina Aguilera	Christina Aguilera
10	Wide Open Spaces	Dixie Chicks

Source: *Soundscan*

Shania Twain's *Come on Over* became her second album to feature in two consecutive annual countdowns, but newer faces—the Backstreet Boys, Britney Spears, and Ricky Martin—occupied the top three positions in this year's listing.

TOP 10 | ALBUMS IN THE U.S., 2000

	ALBUM	ARTIST OR GROUP
1	No Strings Attached	*NSYNC
2	The Marshall Mathers LP	Eminem
3	Oops! ... I Did It Again	Britney Spears
4	Human Clay	Creed
5	Supernatural	Santana
6	1	The Beatles
7	Country Grammar	Nelly
8	Black & Blue	Backstreet Boys
9	2001	Dr. Dre
10	The Writing's on the Wall	Destiny's Child

Source: *Soundscan*

Boy band *NSYNC, featuring Justin Timberlake, shot to the top of the list with *No Strings Attached*. Teen appeal was also the force that secured high positions for rapper Eminem and Britney Spears (for the second year running). Long-established artists to score well were Santana, and The Beatles, whose entry was a compilation of their No. 1 singles.

TOP 10 ALBUMS IN THE U.S., 1995

ALBUM	ARTIST OR GROUP
1 Cracked Rear View	Hootie & the Blowfish
2 Crazysexycool	TLC
3 Jagged Little Pill	Alanis Morissette
4 Daydream	Mariah Carey
5 The Hits	Garth Brooks
6 Throwing Copper	Live
7 II	Boyz II Men
8 Anthology 1	The Beatles
9 Hell Freezes Over	Eagles
10 The Woman in Me	Shania Twain

Source: *Soundscan*

Hootie & the Blowfish achieved one of the most impressive album debuts in US record history, with over 11 million copies of *Cracked Rear View* shipping during 1995. The Beatles and the Eagles were among the established artists to feature.

TOP 10 ALBUMS IN THE U.S., 1996

ALBUM	ARTIST OR GROUP
1 Jagged Little Pill	Alanis Morissette
2 Falling into You	Celine Dion
3 The Score	Fugees
4 Tragic Kingdom	No Doubt
5 Daydream	Mariah Carey
6 All Eyez on Me	2Pac
7 Load	Metallica
8 Secrets	Toni Braxton
9 The Woman in Me	Shania Twain
10 (What's the Story) Morning Glory?	Oasis

Source: *Soundscan*

Five of the year's Top 10 artists were female solo artists, and a further two entries (No Doubt and the Fugees) were acts fronted by women. Three of the solo artists (Alanis Morissette, Mariah Carey, and Shania Twain) were enjoying a second year of outstanding sales success with the same album.

TOP 10 ALBUMS IN THE U.S., 1997

ALBUM	ARTIST OR GROUP
1 Spice	The Spice Girls
2 Pieces of You	Jewel
3 No Way Out	Puff Daddy & the Family
4 Sevens	Garth Brooks
5 Middle of Nowhere	Hanson
6 Life After Death	Notorious B.I.G.
7 Bringing Down the Horse	The Wallflowers
8 Falling into You	Celine Dion
9 Space Jam (Original Soundtrack)	Various Artists
10 You Light Up My Life— Inspirational Songs	LeAnn Rimes

Source: *Soundscan*

The Spice Girls—the biggest UK music export in years—and Jewel kept female artists in the top chart positions for 1997. Tragically, the big album sales of rapper Notorious B.I.G. (a.k.a. Biggie Smalls) were—like those of 2Pac in 1996—registered posthumously.

TOP 10 ALBUMS IN THE U.S., 2001

ALBUM	ARTIST OR GROUP
1 Hybrid Theory	Linkin Park
2 Hotshot	Shaggy
3 Celebrity	*NSYNC
4 A Day Without Rain	Enya
5 Break the Cycle	Staind
6 Songs in A Minor	Alicia Keys
7 Survivor	Destiny's Child
8 Weathered	Creed
9 O Brother, Where Art Thou? (Original Soundtrack)	Various Artists
10 Now That's What I Call Music! 6	Various Artists

Source: *Soundscan*

LA band Linkin Park's album *Hybrid Theory* lived up to its name, fusing metal with rap to produce impressive sales that propelled this debut album all the way to the top of the year's best sellers.

TOP 10 ALBUMS IN THE U.S., 2002

ALBUM	ARTIST OR GROUP
1 The Eminem Show	Eminem
2 Nellyville	Nelly
3 Let Go	Avril Lavigne
4 Home	Dixie Chicks
5 8 Mile (Original Soundtrack)	Various Artists
6 M!ssundaztood	P!nk
7 Ashanti	Ashanti
8 Drive	Alan Jackson
9 Up	Shania Twain
10 O Brother, Where Art Thou?	Various Artists

Source: *Nielsen Soundscan*

Denied the top spot by *NSYNC two years previously, rapper Eminem (a.k.a. Slim Shady) claimed it with his "comeback" *The Eminem Show*. Shania Twain's *Up* is her fifth appearance on these pages, making her the most regularly featured artist.

TOP 10 ALBUMS IN THE U.S., 2003

ALBUM	ARTIST OR GROUP
1 Get Rich or Die Tryin'	50 Cent
2 Come Away with Me	Norah Jones
3 Meteora	Linkin Park
4 Fallen	Evanescence
5 Speakerboxxx/The Love Below	OutKast
6 Dangerously in Love	Beyoncé
7 Chocolate Factory	R. Kelly
8 Metamorphosis	Hilary Duff
9 Shock'n Y'all	Toby Keith
10 A Rush of Blood to the Head	Coldplay

Source: *Nielsen Soundscan*

Taking rap music's second consecutive No. 1 position was 50 Cent (real name Curtis Jackson). Texan-born Norah Jones, who scored second with her debut CD, is from the resurgent singer-songwriter tradition.

TOP 10 GROUPS WITH THE MOST GOLD ALBUM AWARDS IN THE U.S.

	GROUP	GOLD ALBUM AWARDS
1	The Beatles	42
2	The Rolling Stones	39
3	Kiss	25
4	= Aerosmith	23
	= Chicago	23
6	= Alabama	22
	= Rush	22
	= The Beach Boys	22
9	Jefferson Airplane/Starship	20
10	AC/DC	19

Source: *RIAA*

The Recording Industry Association of America's (RIAA) Gold Awards have been presented since 1958 to artists who have sold 500,000 units of a single, album, or multi-disc set. The first single to be so honored was Perry Como's *Catch a Falling Star*, and the first album the soundtrack of *Oklahoma!*.

TOP 10 MALE ARTISTS WITH THE MOST PLATINUM ALBUMS AWARDS IN THE U.S.

	ARTIST	PLATINUM ALBUM AWARDS
1	Garth Brooks	105
2	Elvis Presley	88
3	Billy Joel	76
4	Elton John	62
5	Bruce Springsteen	61
6	Michael Jackson	58
7	George Strait	52
8	Kenny G	46
9	Kenny Rogers	41*
10	Neil Diamond	37

* *Excluding one platinum album with Dottie West, one with Kim Carnes, Dottie West, and Sheena Easton, and a double platinum album with Dolly Parton*

Source: *RIAA*

Platinum singles and albums in the US are those that have achieved sales of one million units. The award has been made by the RIAA since 1976.

TOP 10 GROUPS WITH THE MOST PLATINUM ALBUM AWARDS IN THE U.S.

	GROUP	PLATINUM ALBUM AWARDS*
1	The Beatles	162
2	Led Zeppelin	107
3	Eagles	88
4	Pink Floyd	72
5	Aerosmith	61
6	AC/DC	60
7	= Metallica	57
	= The Rolling Stones	57
9	Van Halen	50
10	= Fleetwood Mac	46
	= U2	46

* *Double/triple albums counted once*

TOP 10 MALE ARTISTS WITH THE MOST GOLD ALBUM AWARDS IN THE U.S.

	ARTIST	GOLD ALBUM AWARDS
1	Elvis Presley	80
2	Neil Diamond	39
3	Elton John	35
4	Frank Sinatra	33
5	Bob Dylan	32*
6	George Strait	31
7	= Kenny Rogers	23#
	= Rod Stewart	23
	= Hank Williams Jr.	23
10	Eric Clapton	20[†]

* *Excluding one gold album with Grateful Dead*

\# *Excluding one gold album with Dolly Parton, two with Dottie West, and one with Kim Carnes, Dottie West, and Sheena Easton*

† *Excluding one gold album with B.B. King*

▶ **Platinum Blonde**
Mariah Carey had more No. 1 albums than any female artist in the 1990s, becoming the first female artist to have two albums selling over 10 million. She is the only female artist to have eight albums certified triple-platinum or better, with every one of her albums achieving multi-platinum status.

TOP 10 FEMALE ARTISTS WITH THE MOST GOLD ALBUM AWARDS IN THE U.S.

	ARTIST	GOLD ALBUM AWARDS
1	Barbra Streisand	43*
2	Reba McEntire	22
3	Linda Ronstadt	17#
4	Madonna	16
5	Anne Murray	14
6	Aretha Franklin	13
7 =	Amy Grant	12
=	Olivia Newton-John	12†
=	Tanya Tucker	12
10 =	Mariah Carey	11
=	Natalie Cole	11
=	Donna Summer	11

* Excluding one with Kris Kristofferson and the original cast/soundtrack recordings of Funny Girl, Funny Lady,, and The Mirror Has Two Faces

Excluding two with Dolly Parton and Emmylou Harris

† Excluding two with John Travolta and three with Electric Light Orchestra

TOP 10 FEMALE ARTISTS WITH THE MOST PLATINUM ALBUM AWARDS IN THE U.S.

	ARTIST	PLATINUM ALBUM AWARDS
1	Madonna	60
2	Barbra Streisand	55*
3 =	Mariah Carey	54
=	Whitney Houston	54
5	Celine Dion	45
6	Shania Twain	42
7	Reba McEntire	32
8	Linda Ronstadt	28#
9	Janet Jackson	24
10	Alanis Morissette	20

* Excluding four with Kris Kristofferson and two original cast/soundtrack recordings

Excluding one with Dolly Parton and Emmylou Harris

Music Awards

THE 10 | LATEST GRAMMY RECORDS OF THE YEAR

YEAR	RECORD	ARTIST
2003	Clocks	Coldplay
2002	Don't Know Why	Norah Jones
2001	Walk On	U2
2000	Beautiful Day	U2
1999	Smooth	Santana featuring Rob Thomas
1998	My Heart Will Go On	Celine Dion
1997	Sunny Came Home	Shawn Colvin
1996	Change the World	Eric Clapton
1995	Kiss From a Rose	Seal
1994	All I Wanna Do	Sheryl Crow

The Grammys are awarded retrospectively. Thus the 46th awards were presented in 2004 in recognition of musical accomplishment during 2003. Coldplay confirmed their place as the most successful British band in the US by winning the "Record of the Year" award. They had won two Grammys the previous year: "Best Rock Performance by a Duo or Group with a Vocal" for "In My Place" and "Best Alternative Album" with *A Rush of Blood to the Head*.

▶ **Hot Coldplay**
Led by guitarist Chris Martin, Coldplay has won fans and accolades worldwide, gaining Grammy awards in two consecutive years.

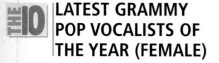

THE 10 LATEST GRAMMY POP VOCALISTS OF THE YEAR (FEMALE)

YEAR	VOCALIST	SONG
2003	Christina Aguilera	Beautiful
2002	Norah Jones	Don't Know Why
2001	Nelly Furtado	I'm Like a Bird
2000	Macy Gray	I Try
1999	Sarah McLachlan	I Will Remember You
1998	Celine Dion	My Heart Will Go On
1997	Sarah McLachlan	Building a Mystery
1996	Toni Braxon	Un-Break My Heart
1995	Annie Lennox	No More "I Love You's"
1994	Sheryl Crow	All I Wanna Do

The first-ever Grammy for a "Female Pop Vocal Performance" was won in 1959 by Ella Fitzgerald for *Ella Fitzgerald Sings the Irving Berlin Song Book*. She was to win again on three occasions, beaten only by Barbra Streisand with a tally of five wins.

THE 10 LATEST GRAMMY POP VOCALISTS OF THE YEAR (MALE)

YEAR	VOCALIST	SONG
2003	Justin Timberlake	Cry Me a River
2002	John Mayer	Your Body Is a Wonderland
2001	James Taylor	Don't Let Me Be Lonely Tonight
2000	Sting	She Walks This Earth (Soberana Rosa)
1999	Sting	Brand New Day
1998	Eric Clapton	My Father's Eyes
1997	Elton John	Candle in the Wind 1997
1996	Eric Clapton	Change the World
1995	Seal	Kiss From a Rose
1994	Elton John	Can You Feel the Love Tonight

The first Grammy Award in this category was presented in 1959 for Perry Como's record of the previous year, "Catch a Falling Star." Its subsequent recipients represent the cream of popular music and include multiple wins by the likes of Frank Sinatra, Stevie Wonder, and Eric Clapton.

THE 10 LATEST WINNERS OF THE ASCAP SONGWRITER OF THE YEAR (POP CATEGORY)

YEAR	SONGWRITER(S)
2003	= Nelly
	= Seven
2002	Beyoncé Knowles
2001	= Andreas Carlsson
	= Max Martin
2000	Max Martin
1999	= Max Martin
	= Diane Warren
1998	Diane Warren
1997	Glen Ballard
1996	= Melissa Etheridge
	= Hootie and the Blowfish (Darius Rucker, Jim Sonefeld, Dean Felber, and Mark Bryan)

Source: *American Society of Composers, Authors, and Publishers*

THE 10 LATEST GRAMMY ROCK VOCALISTS OF THE YEAR (FEMALE)

YEAR	VOCALIST	SONG
2003	Pink	Trouble
2002	Sheryl Crow	Steve McQueen
2001	Lucinda Williams	Get Right with God
2000	Sheryl Crow	There Goes the Neighborhood
1999	Sheryl Crow	Sweet Child of Mine
1998	Alanis Morissette	Uninvited
1997	Fiona Apple	Criminal
1996	Sheryl Crow	If It Makes You Happy
1995	Alanis Morissette	You Oughta Know
1994	Melissa Etheridge	Come to My Window

In the year that saw Pink (a.k.a. Alecia Moore) picking up her Grammy award, she also appeared in *Charlie's Angels: Full Throttle*, and, with Beyoncé Knowles and Britney Spears, as a gladiator in a Pepsi ad, emphasizing the crossover between music, movies, and merchandise.

THE 10 LATEST GRAMMY ROCK VOCALISTS OF THE YEAR (MALE)

YEAR	VOCALIST	SONG
2003	Dave Matthews	Gravedigger
2002	Bruce Springsteen	The Rising
2001	Lennie Kravitz	Dig In
2000	Lenny Kravitz	Again
1999	Lenny Kravitz	American Woman
1998	Lenny Kravitz	Fly Away
1997	Bob Dylan	Cold Irons Bound
1996	Beck	Where It's At
1995	Tom Petty	You Don't Know How It Feels
1994	Bruce Springsteen	Streets of Philadelphia

Grammy's Rock Vocalist category was first won by Bob Dylan in 1980 for "Gotta Serve Somebody." In 1988, 1992, and 1994, the award was not differentiated by gender, but Bonny Raitt's "Luck of the Draw" (1992) was the only instance of a female triumph against male competition.

THE 10 LATEST "BEST SONG" OSCAR WINNERS

YEAR	SONG	FILM
2003	Into the West	The Lord of the Rings: The Return of the King
2002	Lose Yourself	8 Mile
2001	If I Didn't Have You	Monsters, Inc.
2000	Things Have Changed	Wonder Boys
1999	You'll Be in My Heart	Tarzan
1998	When You Believe	The Prince of Egypt
1997	My Heart Will Go On	Titanic
1996	You Must Love Me	Evita
1995	Colors of the Wind	Pocahontas
1994	Can You Feel the Love Tonight	The Lion King

The first Oscars were presented during the last days of silent films, and the "Best Song" Oscar was not introduced until the 1934 Academy Awards ceremony. It was then won by "The Continental" from the film *The Gay Divorcee*.

Classical & Opera

TOP 10 CLASSICAL ALBUMS IN THE U.S.

	TITLE	PERFORMER(S)/ORCHESTRA	YEAR
1	The Three Tenors in Concert	José Carreras, Placido Domingo, Luciano Pavarotti	1990
2	Romanza	Andrea Bocelli	1997
3	Sogno	Andrea Bocelli	1999
4	Voice of an Angel	Charlotte Church	1999
5	Chant	Benedictine Monks of Santo Domingo De Silos	1994
6	The Three Tenors – in Concert 1994	José Carreras, Placido Domingo, Luciano Pavarotti	1994
7	Sacred Arias	Andrea Bocelli	1999
8	Tchaikovsky: Piano Concerto No. 1	Van Cliburn	1958
9	Fantasia (50th Anniversary Edition)	Philadelphia Orchestra	1990
10	Perhaps Love	Placido Domingo	1981

Source: *Music Information Database*

The Three Tenors' concert in Rome's Baths of Caracalla was held in July 1990 to mark the soccer World Cup. It reached 5 x platinum status in the US and sold more than 10 million worldwide, matching many mega-selling rock albums. With most of the albums in the Top 10 dating from the 1990s, Van Cliburn's 1958 recording is a surprise entry: it was, however, the first classical album to sell over a million copies and remained in the US charts for a total of almost 300 weeks.

TOP 10 OPERAS MOST FREQUENTLY PERFORMED AT THE METROPOLITAN OPERA HOUSE, NEW YORK

	OPERA	COMPOSER	PERFORMANCES*
1	La Bohème	Giacomo Puccini	1,140
2	Aïda	Giuseppi Verdi	1,066
3	Carmen	Georges Bizet	908
4	La Traviata	Giuseppi Verdi	897
5	Tosca	Giacomo Puccini	851
6	Madama Butterfly	Giacomo Puccini	780
7	Rigoletto	Giuseppi Verdi	769
8	Faust	Charles Gounod	713
9	Pagliacci	Ruggero Leoncavallo	688
10	Cavalleria Rusticana	Pietro Mascagni	648

* As at end of 2003–2004 season

Source: *Metropolitan Opera*

The Metropolitan Opera House opened on October 22, 1883, with a performance of Charles Gounod's *Faust*, which remains prominent in the repertoire. The most performed operas closely mirror those of its British counterpart, the Royal Opera House, whose Top 10 is also headed by *La Bohème*, while eight of the ROH's most popular works are also in the Met list.

► **From a land of song**
Welsh-born Charlotte Church was just 13 when her *Voice of an Angel* album was released, establishing her as the youngest-ever artist with a No. 1 in the US classical charts.

THE 10 | LATEST WINNERS OF THE "BEST OPERA RECORDING" GRAMMY AWARD

YEAR	TITLE/COMPOSER	PRINCIPAL SOLOISTS/ORCHESTRA
2003	**Jenufa,** Leos Janácek	Jerry Hadley, Karita Mattila, Eva Randová, Anja Silja, Jorma Silvasti, Orchestra of the Royal Opera House, Covent Garden
2002	**Tannhäuser,** Richard Wagner	Jane Eaglen, Peter Seiffert, Rene Pape, Thomas Hampson, Waltraud Meier, Staatskapelle Berlin
2001	**Les Troyens** Hector Belioz	Sir Colin Davis, Ben Heppner, Kenneth Tarver, Michelle De Young, Peter Mattei, Petra Lang, Sara Mingardo, Stephen Milling, London Symphony Orchestra
2000	**Doktor Faust,** Ferruccio Busoni	Kent Nagano, Kim Begley, Dietrich Fischer-Dieskau, Dietrich Henschel, Markus Hollop, Eva Jenis
1999	**The Rake's Progress,** Igor Stravinsky	Ian Bostridge, Bryn Terfel, Anne Sofie von Otter, Deborah York, Monteverdi Choir, London Symphony Orchestra
1998	**Bluebeard's Castle,** Béla Bartók	Jessye Norman, Laszlo Polgar, Karl-August Naegler, Chicago Symphony Orchestra
1997	**Die Meistersinger Von Nürnberg,** Richard Wagner	Ben Heppner, Herbert Lippert, Karita Mattila, Alan Opie, Rene Pape, Jose van Dam, Iris Vermillion, Chicago Symphony Chorus, Chicago Symphony Orchestra
1996	**Peter Grimes,** Benjamin Britten	Philip Langridge, Alan Opie, Janice Watson, Opera London, London Symphony Chorus, City of London Sinfonia
1995	**Les Troyens,** Hector Berlioz	Charles Dutoit, Orchestra Symphonie de Montreal
1994	**Susannah,** Carlisle Floyd	Jerry Hadley, Samuel Ramey, Cheryl Studer, Kenn Chester

Source: *NARAS*

THE 10 | LATEST WINNERS OF THE "BEST CLASSICAL ALBUM" GRAMMY AWARD

YEAR	TITLE/COMPOSER	CONDUCTOR/SOLOIST/ORCHESTRA
2003	**Symphony No. 3; Kindertotenlieder;** Gustav Mahler	Michael Tilson Thomas, Michelle DeYoung, San Francisco Symphony
2002	**A Sea Symphony (Symphony No. 1),** Vaughan Williams	Robert Spano, Norman Mackenzie, Brett Polegato, Christine Goerke, Atlanta Symphony Orchestra
2001	**Les Troyens,** Hector Belioz	Sir Colin Davis, Ben Heppner, Kenneth Tarver, Michelle De Young, Peter Mattei, Petra Lang, Sara Mingardo, Stephen Milling, London Symphony Orchestra
2000	**The String Quartets,** Dmitri Shostakovich	Emerson String Quartet
1999	**Firebird; The Right of Spring; Perséphone,** Igor Stravinsky	Michael Tilson Thomas, Stuart Neill, San Francisco Symphony Orchestra
1998	**Prayers of Kierkegaard,** Samuel Barber **Dona Nobis Pacem,** Ralph Vaughan Williams **Cantata Profana,** Béla Bartók	Robert Shaw, Richard Clement, Nathan Gunn, Atlanta Symphony Orchestra and chorus
1997	**Premieres – Cello Concertos,** Richard Danielpour, Leon Kirchner, Christopher Rouse	Yo-Yo Ma, David Zinman, Philadelphia Orchestra
1996	**Of Rage and Remembrance,** John Corigliano	Leonard Slatkin, National Symphony Orchestra
1995	**La Mer,** Claude Debussy	Pierre Boulez, Cleveland Orchestra
1994	**Concerto for Orchestra; Four Orchestral Pieces, Op. 12,** Béla Bartók	Pierre Boulez, Chicago Symphony Orchestra

Source: *NARAS*

STAGE & SCREEN

Stage World

THE 10 | LATEST NEW YORK DRAMA CRITICS CIRCLE AWARDS FOR BEST NEW PLAY*

YEAR	PLAY	PLAYWRIGHT
2003	Take Me Out	Richard Greenberg
2002	The Goat, or Who /is Sylvia	Edward Albee
2001	The Invention of Love	Tom Stoppard
2000	Jitney	August Wilson
1999	Wit	Margaret Edson
1998	Art	Yasmina Reza
1997	How I Learned to Drive	Paula Vogel
1996	Seven Guitars	August Wilson
1995	Arcadia	Tom Stoppard
1994	Three Tall Women	Edward Albee

* Award was for "Best Play" prior to 1996

The New York Drama Critics Circle was established in 1935 as a reaction against the decisions of the Pulitzer committee, which similarly presents awards for plays, rather than individual performances or directors. In contrast to the Tony Awards, they also recognize off-Broadway productions. If the winning play is American, a second award is presented for the Best Foreign Play, while if the winner is foreign, another award is presented for Best American Play. Musicals have been separately acknowledged since 1945.

TOP 10 | LONGEST-RUNNING THRILLERS ON BROADWAY

THRILLER/RUN	PERFORMANCES
1 Deathtrap, 1978–82	1,793
2 Arsenic and Old Lace, 1941–44	1,444
3 Angel Street, 1941–1944	1,295
4 Sleuth, 1970–73	1,222
5 Dracula, 1977–80	925
6 Witness for the Prosecution, 1954–56	645
7 Dial M for Murder, 1952–54	556
8 Sherlock Holmes, 1974–76	471
9 An Inspector Calls, 1994–95	454
10 Ten Little Indians, 1944–45	426

Source: The League of American Theaters and Producers

▶ **A Hit for Miss**

Composer Claude-Michel Schönberg and lyricist Alain Boublil—who were also responsible for the even longer-running *Les Misérables*—based their hugely successful musical *Miss Saigon* on the opera *Madam Butterfly*.

TOP 10 | LONGEST-RUNNING NON-MUSICALS ON BROADWAY

SHOW/RUN	PERFORMANCES
1 Oh! Calcutta!, 1976–89	5,959
2 Life with Father, 1939–47	3,224
3 Tobacco Road, 1933–41	3,182
4 Abie's Irish Rose, 1922–27	2,327
5 Gemini, 1977–81	1,819
6 Deathtrap, 1978–82	1,793
7 Harvey, 1944–49	1,775
8 Born Yesterday, 1946–49	1,642
9 Mary, Mary, 1961–64	1,572
10 The Voice of the Turtle, 1943–48	1,557

Source: The League of American Theaters and Producers

More than half the longest-running non-musical shows on Broadway began their runs before World War II; the others all date from the period up to the 1970s, before the long-running musical came to dominate the Broadway stage. Off Broadway, these records have all been broken by *The Drunkard*, which was performed at the Mart Theater, Los Angeles, from July 6, 1933 to September 6, 1953, and then reopened with a musical adapation until October 17, 1959— a grand total of 9,477 performances seen by some 3 million people.

TOP 10 | LONGEST-RUNNING MUSICALS ON BROADWAY

MUSICAL/RUN	PERFORMANCES
1 Cats, 1982–2000	7,485
2 The Phantom of the Opera, 1988–	6,710*
3 Les Misérables, 1987–2003	6,680
4 A Chorus Line, 1975–90	6,137
5 Miss Saigon, 1991–2001	4,092
6 Beauty and the Beast, 1994–	4,036*
7 42nd Street, 1980–89	3,486
8 Grease, 1972–80	3,388
9 Rent, 1996–	3,265*
10 Fiddler on the Roof, 1964–72	3,242

* Still running; total as of March 1, 2004

Source: The League of American Theaters and Producers

All the longest-running musicals date from the past 40 years. Prior to these record-breakers, the longest runner of the 1940s was *Oklahoma!*, which debuted in 1943 and ran for 2,212 performances, and from the 1950s *My Fair Lady*, which opened in 1956 and closed after 2,717 performances.

OLDEST AMERICAN THEATERS AND OPERA HOUSES

	THEATER OR OPERA HOUSE	LOCATION	BUILT*
1	The Walnut Street Theater	Philadelphia, PA	1809
2	The Woodward Opera House	Mount Vernon, OH	1851
3	The Fulton Opera House	Lancaster, PA	1852
4	Loring Hall	Hingham, MA	1852
5	Institute Hall	Natchez, MS	1853
6	The Majestic Theater	Chillicothe, OH	1853
7	Saco Town Hall	Saco, ME	1856
8	The Academy of Music	Philadelphia, PA	1857
9	Thespian Hall	Boonville, MO	1857
10	Thalian Hall	Wilmington, NC	1858

* Most have been remodeled inside and/or outside since

OLDEST BROADWAY THEATERS

	THEATER	OPENING SHOW	OPENED
1	New Victory Theatre (originally Theatre Republic)	Sag Harbor	Sept. 27, 1900
2	= Lyceum Theatre*	The Proud Prince	Nov. 2, 1903
	= New Amsterdam Theatre*	A Midsummer Night's Dream	Nov. 2, 1903
4	Belasco Theatre (originally Stuyvesant)	A Grand Army Man	Oct. 16, 1907
5	Lunt-Fontanne Theatre (originally Globe Theatre)	The Old Town	Jan. 10, 1910
6	Winter Garden Theatre	La Belle Paree	Mar. 20, 1911
7	Helen Hayes Theatre	The Pigeon	Mar. 12, 1912
8	Cort Theatre	Peg o' My Heart	Dec. 20, 1912
9	Palace Theatre	Miss Civilization	Apr., 1913
10	Longacre Theatre	Are You a Crook?	May 1, 1913

* Opened on the same day

The Film Business

TOP 10 MOVIE-GOING COUNTRIES (PER CAPITA)

COUNTRY	ATTENDANCE PER INHABITANT (2002)
1 US	6.09
2 Iceland	5.71
3 Australia	4.95
4 Singapore	4.91
5 New Zealand	4.73
6 Ireland	4.68
7 Canada	4.22
8 Spain	3.58
9 Luxembourg	3.30
10 France	3.14

Source: Screen Digest

In its relatively short history, cinema has become an important part of the culture of many countries, though one that is being increasingly challenged by television, video, and DVDs.

TOP 10 COUNTRIES SPENDING THE MOST ON MOVIE THEATER VISITS

COUNTRY	AVERAGE SPENDING ON THEATER VISITS PER CAPITA (2002) ($)
1 Iceland	41.51
2 US	33.84
3 Switzerland	23.30
4 Australia	23.07
5 Ireland	22.31
6 Norway	19.53
7 Singapore	18.88
8 UK	18.86
9 Canada	18.70
10 Denmark	17.43

Source: Screen Digest

This ranking is a factor of both the level of movie-going and the average price of tickets. The latter range from $7.62 in Iceland and $5.81 in the US to as little as 21 cents in India.

TOP 10 COUNTRIES WITH THE HIGHEST BOX OFFICE REVENUE

COUNTRY	BOX OFFICE REVENUE (2002) ($)
1 US	9,519,600,000
2 UK	1,134,400,000
3 France	971,800,000
4 Germany	908,000,000
5 Canada	602,100,000
6 Spain	591,700,000
7 Italy	496,300,000
8 Switzerland	168,300,000
9 Netherlands	147,500,000
10 Sweden	137,300,000

Source: Screen Digest

▶ **Bollywood blockbuster**
The Indian film industry leads the world in terms of output. Big-budget *Devdas* (2002), starring Madhuri Dixit, typifies the Indian take on the sumptuous Hollywood musical.

TOP 10 COUNTRIES WITH THE MOST MOVIE THEATERS

COUNTRY	SCREENS MOVIE (2002)
1 China	65,500
2 US	35,280
3 India	11,000
4 France	5,280
5 Germany	4,868
6 Spain	4,039
7 Italy	3,495
8 UK	3,402
9 Mexico	2,755
10 Canada	2,753

Source: Screen Digest

For propaganda purposes, the former Soviet Union once claimed to have 176,172 movie theaters— locations able to show 35 mm films, the format used for most feature films.

TOP 10 COUNTRIES WITH THE MOST MOVIE THEATRES PER MILLION PEOPLE

COUNTRY	CINEMA SCREENS PER MILLION PEOPLE (2002)
1 Iceland	166.6
2 Sweden	131.9
3 US	125.4
4 Australia	94.0
5 France	89.3
6 Norway	88.5
7 Canada	85.5
8 Ireland	85.2
9 New Zealand	82.1
10 Czech Republic	76.5
World average	26.4

Source: Screen Digest

COUNTRIES MAKING THE MOST FILMS PER MILLION PEOPLE

	COUNTRY	FILMS PRODUCED PER MILLION PEOPLE (2002)
1	Iceland	32.12
2	Hong Kong	14.00
3	Switzerland	5.16
4	Slovenia	4.53
5	Denmark	3.56
6	Spain	3.47
7	France	3.40
8	Hungary	3.29
9	Austria	3.21
10	Norway	3.13
	US	*1.98*

Source: Screen Digest

COUNTRIES SPENDING THE MOST ON FILM PRODUCTION

	COUNTRY	INVESTMENT (2002) ($)
1	US	14,661,000,000
2	Japan	1,292,130,000
3	UK	851,620,000
4	France	813,040,000
5	Germany	687,000,000
6	Spain	304,320,000
7	Italy	247,970,000
8	India	192,000,000
9	South Korea	133,830,000*
10	Canada	133,090,000

* 2001 figure

Source: Screen Digest

MOST PROLIFIC FILM-PRODUCING COUNTRIES

	COUNTRY	FILMS PRODUCED (2002)
1	India	1,200
2	US	543
3	Japan	293
4	France	200
5	Spain	137
6	Italy	130
7	Germany	116
8	China	100
9	Philippines	97
10	Hong Kong	92

Source: Screen Digest

Based on the number of full-length feature films produced, Hollywood's "golden age" was the 1920s and 1930s, with a peak of 854 films made in 1954, and its nadir 1978, with just 354.

Blockbusters

TOP 10 HIGHEST-GROSSING FILMS

	FILM	YEAR	GROSS INCOME ($) US	OVERSEAS	WORLD TOTAL
1	Titanic*	1997	600,788,188	1,234,600,000	1,835,388,188
2	The Lord of the Rings: The Return of the King	2003	372,008,809	679,442,744	1,051,431,553
3	Harry Potter and the Sorcerer's Stone	2001	317,575,550	649,423,059	966,998,609
4	Star Wars: Episode I—The Phantom Menace	1999	431,088,297	492,048,523	923,136,820
5	Jurassic Park	1993	357,067,947	563,000,000	920,067,947
6	The Lord of the Rings: The Two Towers	2002	339,687,608	579,024,667	918,712,285
7	Harry Potter and the Chamber of Secrets	2002	261,979,634	604,407,177	866,386,811
8	The Lord of the Rings: The Fellowship of the Ring	2001	314,776,170	547,198,215	861,974,385
9	Independence Day	1996	306,169,255	505,000,000	811,169,255
10	Spider-Man	2002	403,706,375	402,000,000	805,706,375

* *Winner of "Best Picture" Academy Award*

Prior to the release of *Star Wars* in 1977, no film had ever made more than $500 million worldwide. Since then, some 30 films have done so. *Titanic* remains the only film to have grossed more than this amount in the US alone, while eight of the films listed above have exceeded this total outside the US. To date, those in the Top 10 are the only films to have earned more than $800 million globally.

TOP 10 FILM BUDGETS

	FILM	YEAR	BUDGET ($)
1	= Spider-Man 2	2004	200,000,000
	= Titanic	1997	200,000,000
3	= Waterworld	1995	175,000,000
	= Wild, Wild West	1999	175,000,000
5	Terminator 3: Rise of the Machines	2003	170,000,000
6	= Master and Commander: The Far Side of the World	2003	150,000,000
	= The Polar Express*	2004	150,000,000
8	Tarzan*	1999	145,000,000
9	Die Another Day	2002	142,000,000
10	= Armageddon	1998	140,000,000
	= Lethal Weapon 4	1998	140,000,000
	= Men in Black II	2002	140,000,000
	= Treasure Planet*	2002	140,000,000

* *Animated*

TOP 10 FILMS WORLDWIDE, 2003

	FILM
1	Finding Nemo
2	The Matrix Reloaded
3	The Lord of the Rings: The Return of the King
4	Pirates of the Caribbean: The Curse of the Black Pearl
5	Bruce Almighty
6	Terminator 3: The Rise of the Machines
7	The Matrix Revolutions
8	X2: X-Men United
9	Bad Boys II
10	Charlie's Angels 2: Full Throttle

While these were the top earners during 2003, *The Lord of the Rings: The Return of the King* was not released until December, and even later in certain countries. If its post-2003 world box office income were taken into account, it would easily head this list, while *The Last Samurai*, another December release, would be in 6th place.

TOP 10 FILM TRILOGIES

FILMS	DATES
1 The Lord of the Rings	2001–03
2 Jurassic Park	1993–2002
3 The Matrix	1999–2003
4 Indiana Jones	1981–89
5 Terminator	1984–2003
6 Back to the Future	1985–90
7 The Silence of the Lambs	1991–2001
8 American Pie	1999–2003
9 Die Hard	1988–95
10 Austin Powers	1997–2002

This is based on the cumulative global earnings of all three parts. The first five trilogies in the list have each earned in excess of $1 billion worldwide—$2.5 billion in the case of the *Lord of the Rings* trilogy. *Home Alone* is excluded, since *Home Alone 3* was not presented as sequel to the first two parts, but if it were included, it would be in 7th place.

TOP 10 FILMS IN THE U.S., 2003

FILM
1 Finding Nemo
2 Pirates of the Caribbean: The Curse of the Black Pearl
3 The Lord of the Rings: The Return of the King
4 The Matrix Reloaded
5 Bruce Almighty
6 X2: X-Men United
7 Elf
8 Terminator 3: The Rise of the Machines
9 Bad Boys II
10 The Matrix Revolutions

◄ **Sword and sorcery**
The Lord of the Rings: The Return of the King outstripped even the colossal success of its predecessors, becoming only the second film ever to earn more than $1 billion.

Oscar-Winning Films

 "BEST PICTURE" OSCAR-WINNERS OF THE 1930s*

YEAR	FILM
1930	All Quiet on the Western Front#
1931	Cimarron
1932	Grand Hotel
1933	Cavalcade#
1934	It Happened One Night#
1935	Mutiny on the Bounty
1936	The Great Ziegfeld
1937	The Life of Emile Zola
1938	You Can't Take it With You#
1939	Gone with the Wind#

* "Oscar"® is a Registered Trade Mark

Winner of "Best Director" Academy Award

The first Academy Awards, popularly known as Oscars, were presented on May 16, 1929, and were for films released in 1927–28. *Wings*, the first film to be honored as "Best Picture," was silent. A second ceremony on October 31 of the same year was for films released in 1928–29, and was won by *Broadway Melody*, the first talkie and the first musical to win. *Gone with the Wind* was the first all-color winner.

"BEST PICTURE" OSCAR-WINNERS OF THE 1940s

YEAR	FILM
1940	Rebecca
1941	How Green Was My Valley*
1942	Mrs. Miniver*
1943	Casablanca*
1944	Going My Way*
1945	The Lost Weekend*
1946	The Best Years of Our Lives*
1947	Gentleman's Agreement*
1948	Hamlet
1949	All the King's Men

* Winner of "Best Director" Academy Award

Several of the "Best Picture" winners are now regarded as film classics, with many critics rating *Casablanca* among the greatest films of all time. *Mrs. Miniver* (which won a total of six Academy Awards) and *The Best Years of Our Lives* (seven Academy Awards) were both directed by William Wyler and reflected the concerns of wartime and postwar life, respectively. *How Green Was My Valley* and *Going My Way* each won five Academy Awards.

"BEST PICTURE" OSCAR-WINNERS OF THE 1950s

YEAR	FILM
1950	All About Eve*
1951	An American in Paris
1952	The Greatest Show on Earth
1953	From Here to Eternity*
1954	On the Waterfront*
1955	Marty*
1956	Around the World in 80 Days
1957	The Bridge on the River Kwai*
1958	Gigi*
1959	Ben-Hur*

* Winner of "Best Director" Academy Award

The first film of the 1950s, *All About Eve*, received the most nominations (14), while the last, *Ben-Hur*, won the most (11).

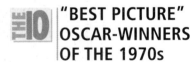 "BEST PICTURE" OSCAR-WINNERS OF THE 1970s

YEAR	FILM
1970	Patton*
1971	The French Connection*
1972	The Godfather
1973	The Sting*
1974	The Godfather, Part II*
1975	One Flew Over the Cuckoo's Nest*
1976	Rocky*
1977	Annie Hall*
1978	The Deer Hunter*
1979	Kramer vs. Kramer*

* Winner of "Best Director" Academy Award

"BEST PICTURE" OSCAR-WINNERS OF THE 1980s

YEAR	FILM
1980	Ordinary People*
1981	Chariots of Fire
1982	Gandhi*
1983	Terms of Endearment*
1984	Amadeus*
1985	Out of Africa*
1986	Platoon*
1987	The Last Emperor*
1988	Rain Man*
1989	Driving Miss Daisy

* Winner of "Best Director" Academy Award

"BEST PICTURE" OSCAR-WINNERS OF THE 1990s

YEAR	FILM
1990	Dances With Wolves*
1991	The Silence of the Lambs*
1992	Unforgiven*
1993	Schindler's List*
1994	Forrest Gump*
1995	Braveheart*
1996	The English Patient*
1997	Titanic*
1998	Shakespeare in Love
1999	American Beauty*

* Winner of "Best Director" Academy Award

THE 10 "BEST PICTURE" OSCAR-WINNERS OF THE 1960s

YEAR	FILM
1960	The Apartment*
1961	West Side Story*
1962	Lawrence of Arabia*
1963	Tom Jones*
1964	My Fair Lady*
1965	The Sound of Music*
1966	A Man for All Seasons*
1967	In the Heat of the Night
1968	Oliver!*
1969	Midnight Cowboy*

Winner of "Best Director" Academy Award

▶ **Epic achievement**
Peter O'Toole in the title role of *Lawrence of Arabia*. The film was nominated for 10 Oscars and won seven. Director David Lean's previous film, *The Bridge on the River Kwai*, had also won a "Best Picture" Oscar.

"BEST ACTOR" OSCAR-WINNERS OF THE 1930s

YEAR	ACTOR	FILM
1930	George Arliss	Disraeli
1931	Lionel Barrymore	A Free Soul
1932 =	Wallace Beery	The Champ
=	Fredric March	Dr. Jekyll and Mr. Hyde
1933	Charles Laughton	The Private Life of Henry VIII
1934	Clarke Gable	It Happened One Night*#
1935	Victor McLaglen	The Informer#
1936	Paul Muni	The Story of Louis Pasteur
1937	Spencer Tracy	Captains Courageous
1938	Spencer Tracy	Boys Town
1939	Robert Donat	Goodbye, Mr. Chips

* Winner of "Best Picture" Academy Award

Winner of "Best Director" Academy Award

"BEST ACTOR" OSCAR-WINNERS OF THE 1940s

YEAR	ACTOR	FILM
1940	James Stewart	The Philadelphia Story
1941	Gary Cooper	Sergeant York
1942	James Cagney	Yankee Doodle Dandy
1943	Paul Lukas	Watch on the Rhine
1944	Bing Crosby	Going My Way*#
1945	Ray Milland	The Lost Weekend*#
1946	Fredric March	The Best Years of Our Lives*#
1947	Ronald Colman	A Double Life
1948	Laurence Olivier	Hamlet*
1949	Broderick Crawford	All the King's Men*

* Winner of "Best Picture" Academy Award

Winner of "Best Director" Academy Award

"BEST ACTOR" OSCAR-WINNERS OF THE 1950s

YEAR	ACTOR	FILM
1950	Jose Ferrer	Cyrano de Bergerac
1951	Humphrey Bogart	The African Queen
1952	Gary Cooper	High Noon
1953	William Holden	Stalag 17
1954	Marlon Brando	On the Waterfront*#
1955	Ernest Borgnine	Marty*#
1956	Yul Brynner	The King and I
1957	Alec Guinness	The Bridge on the River Kwai*#
1958	David Niven	Separate Tables
1959	Charlton Heston	Ben Hur*#

* Winner of "Best Picture" Academy Award

Winner of "Best Director" Academy Award

▼ Out of Africa

Humphrey Bogart won his one and only Oscar for his role as Charlie Allnut in *The African Queen*, based on a novel by C.S. Forester. His co-star Katharine Hepburn was nominated as "Best Actress," but did not win.

"BEST ACTOR" OSCAR-WINNERS OF THE 1960s

YEAR	ACTOR	FILM
1960	Burt Lancaster	Elmer Gantry
1961	Maximilian Schell	Judgement at Nuremberg
1962	Gregory Peck	To Kill a Mockingbird
1963	Sidney Poitier	Lilies of the Field
1964	Rex Harrison	My Fair Lady*#
1965	Lee Marvin	Cat Ballou
1966	Paul Scofield	A Man for All Seasons*#
1967	Rod Steiger	In the Heat of the Night*
1968	Cliff Robertson	Charly
1969	John Wayne	True Grit

* *Winner of "Best Picture" Academy Award*

\# *Winner of "Best Director" Academy Award*

Sydney Poitier was the first black actor to win an Academy Award. He subsequently (2002) received an honorary Oscar for his life's work. These were the sole wins of the other recipients of "Best Actor" Oscars during the 1960s, despite being nominated on other occasions, with the exceptions of Lee Marvin and Cliff Robertson, whose wins were achieved as a result of these single nominations in their careers.

"BEST ACTOR" OSCAR-WINNERS OF THE 1970s

YEAR	ACTOR	FILM
1970	George C. Scott	Patton*#
1971	Gene Hackman	The French Connection*#
1972	Marlon Brando	The Godfather*
1973	Jack Lemmon	Save the Tiger
1974	Art Carney	Harry and Tonto
1975	Jack Nicholson	One Flew Over the Cuckoo's Nest*#
1976	Peter Finch	Network
1977	Richard Dreyfuss	The Goodbye Girl
1978	John Voight	Coming Home
1979	Dustin Hoffman	Kramer vs Kramer*#

* *Winner of "Best Picture" Academy Award*

\# *Winner of "Best Director" Academy Award*

Peter Finch was the first (and so far only) "Best Actor" to be honored posthumously: he died on January 14, 1977, and the award was announced at the 1976 ceremony held on March 28, 1977. He was not the first posthumous winner of any Academy Award, however: that distinction went to Sidney Howard for his screenplay for *Gone with the Wind*. Howard died on August 23, 1939, and at the award ceremony on February 29, 1940, the Nobel Prize–winning novelist Sinclair Lewis accepted the Oscar on his behalf.

"BEST ACTOR" OSCAR-WINNERS OF THE 1980s

YEAR	ACTOR	FILM
1980	Robert De Niro	Raging Bull
1981	Henry Fonda	On Golden Pond
1982	Ben Kingsley	Gandhi*#
1983	Robert Duvall	Tender Mercies
1984	F. Murray Abraham	Amadeus*#
1985	William Hurt	Kiss of the Spider Woman
1986	Paul Newman	The Color of Money
1987	Michael Douglas	Wall Street
1988	Dustin Hoffman	Rain Man*#
1989	Daniel Day-Lewis	My Left Foot

* *Winner of "Best Picture" Academy Award*

\# *Winner of "Best Director" Academy Award*

Although Michael Douglas gained his acting Oscar for *Wall Street*, he had previously won in his capacity as co-producer, with Saul Zaentz, of "Best Picture" *One Flew Over the Cuckoo's Nest* (1975)—a 100 percent success ratio from his only two nominations. Paul Newman's only Oscar came after being nominated in leading roles seven times from 1958 onward.

"BEST ACTOR" OSCAR-WINNERS OF THE 1990s

YEAR	ACTOR	FILM
1990	Jeremy Irons	Reversal of Fortune
1991	Anthony Hopkins	The Silence of the Lambs*#
1992	Al Pacino	Scent of a Woman
1993	Tom Hanks	Philadelphia
1994	Tom Hanks	Forrest Gump*#
1995	Nicolas Cage	Leaving Las Vegas
1996	Geoffrey Rush	Shine
1997	Jack Nicholson	As Good as It Gets#
1998	Roberto Benigni	Life Is Beautiful
1999	Kevin Spacey	American Beauty*#

* *Winner of "Best Picture" Academy Award*

\# *Winner of "Best Director" Academy Award*

Tom Hanks is only the second actor to win in consecutive years since Spencer Tracy (1937 and 1938). The "Best Actor" Oscar winners in the 21st century are: 2000, Russell Crowe for Gladiator; 2001, Denzel Washington for Training Day; 2002, Adrien Brody for The Pianist; and 2003, Sean Penn for Mystic River.

Oscar-Winning Actresses

"BEST ACTRESS" OSCAR-WINNERS OF THE 1930s

YEAR	ACTRESS	FILM
1930	Norma Shearer	The Divorcee
1931	Marie Dressler	Min and Bill
1932	Helen Hayes	The Sin of Madelon Claudet
1933	Katharine Hepburn	Morning Glory
1934	Claudette Colbert	It Happened One Night*#
1935	Bette Davis	Dangerous
1936	Luise Rainer	The Great Ziegfeld
1937	Luise Rainer	The Good Earth
1938	Bette Davis	Jezebel
1939	Vivien Leigh	Gone With the Wind*#

Winner of "Best Picture" Academy Award
 # Winner of "Best Director" Academy Award

The first winner of a "Best Actress" Oscar was Janet Gaynor for her roles in three films, *Seventh Heaven* (1927), *Sunrise* (1927), and *Street Angel* (1928), and the second was Mary Pickford for *Coquette* (1929).

"BEST ACTRESS" OSCAR-WINNERS OF THE 1940s

YEAR	ACTRESS	FILM
1940	Ginger Rogers	Kitty Foyle
1941	Joan Fontaine	Suspicion
1942	Greer Garson	Mrs. Miniver*#
1943	Jennifer Jones	The Song of Bernadette
1944	Ingrid Bergman	Gaslight
1945	Joan Crawford	Mildred Pierce
1946	Olivia de Havilland	To Each His Own
1947	Loretta Young	The Farmer's Daughter
1948	Jane Wyman	Johnny Belinda
1949	Olivia de Havilland	The Heiress

Winner of "Best Picture" Academy Award
 # Winner of "Best Director" Academy Award

Joan Fontaine and Olivia de Havilland are the only sisters to win "Best Actress" Oscars. Both also shared the unusual distinction of having been born in Tokyo, Japan, where their British parents had settled.

"BEST ACTRESS" OSCAR-WINNERS OF THE 1950s

YEAR	ACTRESS	FILM
1950	Judy Holiday	Born Yesterday
1951	Vivien Leigh	A Streetcar Named Desire
1952	Shirley Booth	Come Back, Little Sheba
1953	Audrey Hepburn	Roman Holiday
1954	Grace Kelly	The Country Girl
1955	Anna Magnani	The Rose Tattoo
1956	Ingrid Bergman	Anastasia
1957	Joanne Woodward	The Three Faces of Eve
1958	Susan Hayward	I Want to Live!
1959	Simone Signoret	Room at the Top

▶ **A fair cop**
Frances McDormand as police officer Marge Gunderson in black comedy *Fargo*, for which she won the 1996 "Best Actress" Oscar. The film also won an Oscar for "Best Screenplay."

"BEST ACTRESS" OSCAR-WINNERS OF THE 1960s

YEAR	ACTRESS	FILM
1960	Elizabeth Taylor	Butterfield 8
1961	Sophia Loren	Two Women
1962	Anne Bancroft	The Miracle Worker
1963	Patricia Neal	Hud
1964	Julie Andrews	Mary Poppins
1965	Julie Christie	Darling
1966	Elizabeth Taylor	Who's Afraid of Virginia Woolf?
1967	Katharine Hepburn	Guess Who's Coming to Dinner
1968 =	Katharine Hepburn*	The Lion in Winter
=	Barbra Streisand*	Funny Girl
1969	Maggie Smith	The Prime of Miss Jean Brodie

The only tie for "Best Actress"

Elizabeth Taylor had been nominated for leading-role Oscars in three consecutive years during the previous decade—for *Raintree County* (1957), *Cat on a Hot Tin Roof* (1958), and *Suddenly, Last Summer* (1959)—but without winning. None of the films listed above won in the "Best Picture" category.

"BEST ACTRESS" OSCAR-WINNERS OF THE 1970s

YEAR	ACTRESS	FILM
1970	Glenda Jackson	Women in Love
1971	Jane Fonda	Klute
1972	Liza Minnelli	Cabaret#
1973	Glenda Jackson	A Touch of Class
1974	Ellen Burstyn	Alice Doesn't Live Here Any More
1975	Louise Fletcher	One Flew over the Cuckoo's Nest*#
1976	Faye Dunaway	Network
1977	Diane Keaton	Annie Hall*#
1978	Jane Fonda	Coming Home
1979	Sally Field	Norma Rae

Winner of "Best Picture" Academy Award
 # Winner of "Best Director Academy Award

Glenda Jackson's two wins were garnered from a total of four nominations for leading-role Oscars during the decade: the other two were for *Sunday, Bloody Sunday* (1971) and *Hedda* (1975). Jane Fonda, the other double winner of the decade, was also nominated for her title role in *Julia* (1977).

THE 10 | "BEST ACTRESS" OSCAR-WINNERS OF THE 1980s

YEAR	ACTRESS	FILM
1980	Sissy Spacek	The Coal Miner's Daughter
1981	Katharine Hepburn	On Golden Pond
1982	Meryl Streep	Sophie's Choice
1983	Shirley MacLaine	Terms of Endearment*#
1984	Sally Field	Places in the Heart
1985	Geraldine Page	The Trip to Bountiful
1986	Marlee Matlin	Children of a Lesser God
1987	Cher	Moonstruck
1988	Jodie Foster	The Accused
1989	Jessica Tandy	Driving Miss Daisy*

* Winner of "Best Picture" Academy Award

Winner of "Best Director" Academy Award

As with the "Best Actor" award, only one actress has ever won in consecutive years—Katharine Hepburn in 1967 and 1968. A further 10 have won twice: Ingrid Bergman, Bette Davis, Olivia De Havilland, Sally Field, Jane Fonda, Jodie Foster, Glenda Jackson, Vivien Leigh, Luise Rainer, and Elizabeth Taylor.

THE 10 | "BEST ACTRESS" OSCAR-WINNERS OF THE 1990s

YEAR	ACTRESS	FILM
1990	Kathy Bates	Misery
1991	Jodie Foster	The Silence of the Lambs*#
1992	Emma Thompson	Howard's End
1993	Holly Hunter	The Piano
1994	Jessica Lange	Blue Sky
1995	Susan Sarandon	Dead Man Walking
1996	Frances McDormand	Fargo
1997	Helen Hunt	As Good As It Gets
1998	Gwyneth Paltrow	Shakespeare in Love*
1999	Hilary Swank	Boys Don't Cry

* Winner of "Best Picture" Academy Award

Winner of "Best Director" Academy Award

The "Best Actress" Oscar-winners in the 21st century are: 2000, Julia Roberts for *Erin Brockovich*; 2001, Halle Berry for *Monster's Ball*; 2002, Nicole Kidman for *The Hours*; and 2003, Charlize Theron for *Monster*.

Films of the Decades

TOP 10 | FILMS OF THE 1920s

	FILM	YEAR
1	The Big Parade	1925
2	The Four Horsemen of the Apocalypse	1921
3	Ben-Hur	1926
4	The Ten Commandments	1923
5	What Price Glory?	1926
6	The Covered Wagon	1923
7	Way Down East	1921
8	The Singing Fool	1928
9	Wings	1927
10	The Gold Rush	1925

Earnings data for early films is unreliable, but if this list were extended back to the first decade of the 20th century, *The Birth of a Nation* (1915) would be a contender as the highest-earning film of the silent era. It is also credited as the most successful film made before 1937, when *Snow White and the Seven Dwarfs* took the crown. All the films in this list were black and white, with the exception of *Ben-Hur*, which contains a color sequence.

TOP 10 | FILMS OF THE 1930s

	FILM	YEAR
1	Gone with the Wind*	1939
2	Snow White and the Seven Dwarfs	1937
3	The Wizard of Oz	1939
4	Frankenstein	1931
5	King Kong	1933
6	San Francisco	1936
7	= Hell's Angels	1930
	= Lost Horizon	1937
	= Mr. Smith Goes to Washington	1939
10	Maytime	1937

* *Winner of "Best Picture" Academy Award*

Gone with the Wind and *Snow White and the Seven Dwarfs* have generated more income than any other prewar film. However, if the income of *Gone with the Wind* is adjusted to allow for inflation in the period since its release, it could be regarded as the most successful film ever. Academy Award–winning *Cavalcade* (1932) is a potential contender for a place in this Top 10, but its earnings have been disputed.

TOP 10 | FILMS OF THE 1940s

	FILM	YEAR
1	Bambi*	1942
2	Pinocchio*	1940
3	Fantasia*	1940
4	Song of the South#	1946
5	Mom and Dad	1944
6	Samson and Delilah	1949
7	The Best Years of Our Lives†	1946
8	The Bells of St. Mary's	1945
9	Duel in the Sun	1946
10	This Is the Army	1943

* *Animated*

Part animated/part live-action

† *Winner of "Best Picture" Academy Award*

The top four films of the decade were classic Disney cartoons. Songs from two of them, "When You Wish Upon a Star" from *Pinocchio* and "Zip-A-Dee-Doo-Dah" from *Song of the South*, also won "Best Song" Oscars.

TOP 10 | FILMS OF THE 1950s

	FILM	YEAR
1	Lady and the Tramp*	1955
2	Peter Pan*	1953
3	Cinderella*	1950
4	The Ten Commandments	1956
5	Ben-Hur#	1959
6	Sleeping Beauty*	1959
7	Around the World in 80 Days#	1956
8	This Is Cinerama	1952
9	South Pacific	1958
10	The Robe	1953

* *Animated*

Winner of "Best Picture" Academy Award

While the popularity of animated films continued, the 1950s stood out as the decade of the "big" picture: many of the most successful films were enormous in terms of not only cast and scale but also the magnitude of the subjects they tackled: three of these were major biblical epics, with *The Robe* the first film to offer the wide screen of CinemaScope.

TOP 10 | FILMS OF THE 1960s

	FILM	YEAR
1	One Hundred and One Dalmatians*	1961
2	The Jungle Book*	1967
3	The Sound of Music#	1965
4	Thunderball	1965
5	Goldfinger	1964
6	Doctor Zhivago	1965
7	You Only Live Twice	1967
8	The Graduate	1968
9	Butch Cassidy and the Sundance Kid	1969
10	Mary Poppins	1964

* *Animated*

Winner of "Best Picture" Academy Award

For the first time ever, each of the Top 10 films of the decade earned more than $100 million globally. A high proportion of the top-earning films of the 1960s were musicals, with *The Sound of Music* producing the fastest-selling album ever, while *Mary Poppins* and those featuring the music from *The Jungle Book* and *Doctor Zhivago* were all No. 1 albums.

TOP 10 | FILMS OF THE 1970s

	FILM	YEAR
1	Star Wars*	1977
2	Jaws	1975
3	Grease	1978
4	Close Encounters of the Third Kind	1977
5	The Exorcist	1973
6	Superman	1978
7	Saturday Night Fever	1977
8	Jaws 2	1978
9	Moonraker	1979
10	The Spy Who Loved Me	1977

* *Later retitled* Star Wars: Episode IV—A New Hope

In the 1970s, the arrival of the two prodigies, Steven Spielberg and George Lucas, set the scene for the high adventure blockbusters, the domination of which has continued ever since. Lucas wrote and directed *Star Wars*, while Spielberg directed *Jaws* and wrote and directed *Close Encounters of the Third Kind*. *Grease* and *Saturday Night Fever* continued the musical trend that was established in the 1960s.

FILMS OF THE 1980s

FILM	YEAR
1 E.T. the Extra-Terrestrial	1982
2 Return of the Jedi*	1983
3 The Empire Strikes Back#	1980
4 Indiana Jones and the Last Crusade	1989
5 Rain Man†	1988
6 Raiders of the Lost Ark	1981
7 Batman	1989
8 Back to the Future	1985
9 Who Framed Roger Rabbit	1988
10 Top Gun	1986

* *Later retitled* Star Wars: Episode VI—Return of The Jedi

Later retitled Star Wars: Episode V—The Empire Strikes Back

† *Winner of "Best Picture" Academy Award*

▼ Glittering prize
Indiana Jones prepares to seize a priceless idol in the dramatic opening scene of *Raiders of the Lost Ark*—said to have been inspired by a 1959 Donald Duck comic strip, *The Prize of Pizarro.*

FILMS OF THE 1990s

FILM	YEAR
1 Titanic*	1997
2 Star Wars: Episode I—The Phantom Menace	1999
3 Jurassic Park	1993
4 Independence Day	1996
5 The Lion King#	1994
6 Forrest Gump*	1994
7 The Sixth Sense	1999
8 The Lost World: Jurassic Park	1997
9 Men in Black	1997
10 Armageddon	1998

* *Winner of "Best Picture" Academy Award*

Animated

Each of the Top 10 films of the 1990s has earned more than $550 million around the world, a total of more than $8.4 billion between them.

FILMS OF THE 2000s

FILM	YEAR
1 The Lord of the Rings: The Return of the King	2003
2 Harry Potter and the Sorcerer's Stone	2001
3 The Lord of the Rings: The Two Towers	2002
4 Harry Potter and the Chamber of Secrets	2002
5 The Lord of the Rings: The Fellowship of the Ring	2001
6 Finding Nemo	2003
7 Spider-Man	2002
8 The Matrix Reloaded	2003
9 Pirates of the Caribbean: The Curse of the Black Pearl	2003
10 Star Wars: Episode II—Attack of the Clones	2002

As at May 1, 2004

* *Animated*

Star Actors

TOP 10 TOM CRUISE FILMS

FILM	YEAR
1 Mission: Impossible II	2000
2 Mission: Impossible	1996
3 The Last Samurai	2003
4 Rain Man	1988
5 Top Gun	1986
6 Minority Report	2002
7 Jerry Maguire	1996
8 The Firm	1993
9 A Few Good Men	1992
10 Interview with the Vampire: The Vampire Chronicles	1994

Tom Cruise (real name Thomas Cruise Mapother IV) built his career on playing a combination of handsome all-American heroes, military and light comedy roles, but has shown himself equally at home with dramatic parts, for which he has been nominated for Oscars on three occasions. Few actors have matched his commercial success: each of his Top 10 films has earned more than $220 million worldwide, making a total of more than $3.3 billion. Cruise appeared as himself in *Austin Powers in Goldmember*, which has not been included, but if it were it would be ranked 7th.

TOP 10 KEANU REEVES FILMS

FILM	YEAR
1 The Matrix Reloaded	2003
2 The Matrix	1999
3 The Matrix Revolutions	2003
4 Speed	1994
5 Something's Gotta Give	2003
6 Bram Stoker's Dracula	1992
7 The Devil's Advocate	1997
8 Parenthood	1989
9 A Walk in the Clouds	1995
10 Chain Reaction	1996

The son of an English mother and a part-Hawaiian, part-Chinese father, Keanu Reeves first came to public attention in the late 1980s with films such as *Dangerous Liaisons* (1988) and *Bill & Ted's Excellent Adventure* (1989). The huge international success of *The Matrix*, which has made more than $450 million worldwide, meant that was able to command a reputed per-picture salary of $15 million for the two big-budget 2003 sequels.

▶ **Number one**
Keanu Reeves as Neo, "The One" (of which his name is an anagram), star of *The Matrix* trilogy that heads his personal Top 10.

TOP 10 RUSSELL CROWE FILMS

FILM	YEAR
1 Gladiator*	2000
2 A Beautiful Mind	2001
3 Master and Commander: The Far Side of the World	2003
4 L.A. Confidential	1997
5 The Insider	1999
6 The Quick and the Dead	1995
7 Proof of Life	2000
8 Virtuosity	1995
9 Mystery, Alaska	1999
10 The Sum of Us	1994

Won Academy Award for "Best Actor"

TOP 10 JACK NICHOLSON FILMS

FILM	YEAR
1 Batman	1989
2 As Good as It Gets*	1997
3 A Few Good Men	1992
4 Something's Gotta Give	2003
5 Anger Management	2003
6 Terms of Endearment	1983
7 Wolf	1994
8 One Flew Over the Cuckoo's Nest*	1975
9 Mars Attacks!	1996
10 About Schmidt	2002

Won Academy Award for "Best Actor"

TOP 10 JIM CARREY FILMS

FILM	YEAR
1 Bruce Almighty	2003
2 Dr. Seuss's How the Grinch Stole Christmas	2000
3 Batman Forever	1995
4 The Mask	1994
5 Liar Liar	1997
6 The Truman Show	1998
7 Dumb & Dumber	1994
8 Ace Ventura: When Nature Calls	1995
9 Me, Myself & Irene	2000
10 Ace Ventura: Pet Detective	1994

Jim Carrey is a member of an elite club of actors whose Top 10 films have each earned more than $100 million worldwide.

TOP 10 | ACTORS AT THE U.S. BOX OFFICE

	ACTOR	FILMS	TOTAL US BOX OFFICE ($)*
1	Harrison Ford	33	3,230,893,589
2	Samuel L. Jackson	59	2,941,724,894
3	Tom Hanks	29	2,803,217,369
4	Eddie Murphy	28	2,403,718,530
5	Robin Williams	39	2,174,174,824
6	Mel Gibson	33	2,157,971,535
7	Tom Cruise	24	2,146,781,940
8	Gene Hackman	76	2,121,529,692
9	Bruce Willis	38	2,094,706,324
10	Bill Paxton	45	2,039,209,824

As at September 20, 2003

TOP 10 | BRAD PITT FILMS

	FILM	YEAR
1	Ocean's Eleven	2001
2	Se7en	1995
3	Interview with the Vampire: The Vampire Chronicles	1994
4	Sleepers	1996
5	Twelve Monkeys	1995
6	Legends of the Fall	1994
7	The Mexican	2001
8	The Devil's Own	1997
9	Meet Joe Black	1998
10	Seven Years in Tibet	1997

Each of Brad (William Bradley) Pitt's 10 highest-earning films have made more than $130 million in total at the world box office.

TOP 10 | JOHNNY DEPP FILMS

	FILM	YEAR
1	Pirates of the Carribbean: The Curse of the Black Pearl	2003
2	Sleepy Hollow	1999
2	Platoon	1986
3	Chocolat	2000
4	Donnie Brasco	1997
5	Blow	2001
6	Edward Scissorhands	1990
7	Once Upon a Time in Mexico	2003
9	Don Juan DeMarco	1995
10	The Ninth Gate	1999

Johnny Depp's run of successes means that *Freddy's Dead: The Final Nightmare* (1991), in which his performance was credited as "Oprah Noodlemantra," has now been relegated from his Top 10.

Star Actresses

TOP 10 CAMERON DIAZ FILMS

FILM	YEAR
1 There's Something About Mary	1998
2 The Mask	1994
3 My Best Friend's Wedding	1997
4 Charlie's Angels	2000
5 Charlie's Angels: Full Throttle	2003
6 Vanilla Sky	2001
7 Gangs of New York	2002
8 Any Given Sunday	1999
9 The Sweetest Thing	2002
10 Being John Malkovich	1999

Cameron Diaz's Top 10 films include several that are among the highest-earning of recent years. She also provided the voice of Princess Fiona in *Shrek* (2001)—which has outearned all of them.

TOP 10 DREW BARRYMORE FILMS

FILM	YEAR
1 E.T.: the Extra-Terrestrial	1982
2 Batman Forever	1995
3 Charlie's Angels	2000
4 Charlie's Angels: Full Throttle	2003
5 Scream	1996
6 The Wedding Singer	1998
7 50 First Dates	2004
8 Ever After: A Cinderella Story	1998
9 Never Been Kissed	1999
10 Wayne's World 2	1993

Granddaughter of Hollywood legend John Barrymore, Drew Barrymore had her first film role in *Altered States*, when she was 5; by the time of her part in *E.T. the Extra-Terrestrial* she was aged 7. She commanded a reputed $14 million for her role in *Charlie's Angels: Full Throttle* (2003).

◀ **A fistful of dollars**
Cameron Diaz in *Charlie's Angels: Full Throttle*, one of six of her films that have each earned more than $200 million globally.

TOP 10 NICOLE KIDMAN FILMS

	FILM	YEAR
1	Batman Forever	1995
2	Moulin Rouge!	2001
3	The Others	2001
4	Days of Thunder	1990
5	Eyes Wide Shut	1999
6	Cold Mountain	2003
7	The Peacemaker	1997
8	Practical Magic	1998
9	Far and Away	1992
10	The Hours*	2002

* Won Academy Award for "Best Actress"

Honolulu-born Nicole Kidman was raised in Australia, where she acted on TV before her break into film, in which she has pursued a highly successful career: seven of her Top 10 films have earned over $100 million worldwide.

TOP 10 ACTRESSES AT THE U.S. BOX OFFICE

	ACTRESS	FILMS	TOTAL US BOX OFFICE ($)*
1	Julia Roberts	29	1,885,864,955
2	Carrie Fisher	25	1,546,860,122
3	Whoopi Goldberg	37	1,505,537,440
4	Kathy Bates	34	1,339,011,662
5	Drew Barrymore	34	1,287,426,803
6	Bonnie Hunt	16	1,271,323,335
7	Sally Field	27	1,199,668,305
8	Glenn Close	27	1,191,268,890
9	Meg Ryan	27	1,170,858,199
10	Michelle Pfeiffer	32	1,160,106,123

* As at June 2, 2003

Bonnie Hunt's inclusion, with relatively few but high-earning films, encompasses two animated blockbusters, *A Bug's Life* (1998) and *Monsters, Inc.* (2001), for which she provided voices.

TOP 10 UMA THURMAN FILMS

	FILM	YEAR
1	Batman & Robin	1997
2	Pulp Fiction	1994
3	Kill Bill: Vol. 1	2003
4	Paycheck	2003
5	The Truth About Cats and Dogs	1996
6	The Avengers	1998
7	Final Analysis	1992
8	Dangerous Liaisons	1988
9	Beautiful Girls	1996
10	Les Misérables	1998

Although featuring in her Top 10 by virtue of its global box office income, *The Avengers* did not earn back its substantial production budget, and may thus be regarded as a flop. Conversely, *Pulp Fiction* had a budget of some $8 million but made more than $200 million globally.

TOP 10 RENEE ZELLWEGER FILMS

	FILM	YEAR
1	Chicago	2002
2	Bridget Jones's Diary	2001
3	Jerry Maguire	1996
4	Me, Myself & Irene	2000
5	Cold Mountain	2003
6	Nurse Betty	2000
7	Down with Love	2003
8	The Bachelor	1999
9	One True Thing	1998
10	Reality Bites	1994

Since her early roles in films such as *The Return of the Texas Chainsaw Massacre* (1994), Renée Zellweger has followed an ever-upward trajectory in her film career, gaining consecutive "Best Actress" Oscar nominations for *Bridget Jones's Diary* (2001) and *Chicago* (2002), and winning "Best Actress in a Supporting Role" for *Cold Mountain* (2003).

TOP 10 CATHERINE ZETA-JONES FILMS

	FILM	YEAR
1	Chicago	2002
2	The Mask of Zorro	1998
3	Entrapment	1999
4	Traffic	2000
5	The Haunting	1999
6	America's Sweethearts	2001
7	Intolerable Cruelty	2003
8	High Fidelity	2000
9	The Phantom	1996
10	Christopher Columbus: The Discovery	1992

In little over 10 years, Catherine Zeta-Jones has graduated from stage musicals and TV series *The Darling Buds of May*, in which she appeared as Mariette Larkin, to starring roles in major Hollywood blockbusters, six of them earning more than $100 million worldwide. She won an Oscar for "Best Actress in a Supporting Role" for *Chicago* (2002).

TOP 10 JULIA ROBERTS FILMS

	FILM	YEAR
1	Pretty Woman	1990
2	Ocean's Eleven	2001
3	Notting Hill	1999
4	Runaway Bride	1999
5	Hook	1991
6	My Best Friend's Wedding	1997
7	Erin Brockovich*	2000
8	The Pelican Brief	1993
9	Sleeping with the Enemy	1991
10	Stepmom	1998

* Won Academy Award for "Best Actress"

Julia Roberts is in a league of her own: all of her Top 10 films earned more than $155 million worldwide, a cumulative total just short of $3 billion. In addition to these, she has made a further four $100 million-plus films— *Conspiracy Theory* (1997), *America's Sweethearts* (2001), *The Mexican* (2001), and *Mona Lisa Smile* (2003), a record unmatched by any other actress.

Animated Films

TOP 10 ## ANIMATED FILM BUDGETS

	FILM	YEAR	BUDGET ($)
1	The Polar Express	2004	150,000,000
2	Tarzan	1999	145,000,000
3	Treasure Planet	2002	140,000,000
4	Final Fantasy: The Spirits Within	2001	137,000,000
5	Dinosaur	2000	128,000,000
6	Monsters, Inc.	2001	115,000,000
7	Home on the Range	2004	110,000,000
8	The Emperor's New Groove	2000	100,000,000
9	The Road to El Dorado	2000	95,000,000
10	Finding Nemo	2003	94,000,000

Animated film budgets have come a long way since *Snow White and the Seven Dwarfs* (1937) established a then record of $1.49 million. The $2.6 million budget for *Pinocchio* (1940) and $2.28 million for the original *Fantasia* (1940) were the two biggest of the 1940s, while *Sleeping Beauty* (1959) at $6 million was the highest of the 1950s. *Robin Hood* (1973) had a budget of $15 million, a record that remained unbroken until 1985, when *The Black Cauldron* (1985) became the first to break the $25 million barrier. Since the 1990s, budgets of $50 million or more have become commonplace: *The Lion King* (1994) cost $79.3 million, while *Tarzan* became the first to break through the $100 million barrier.

▶ **Finders keepers**
With worldwide earnings of over $850 million and the "Best Animated Feature" Oscar to its credit, *Finding Nemo* has broken every record for an animated film.

NON-DISNEY ANIMATED FEATURE FILMS

	FILM	PRODUCTION COMPANY	YEAR	WORLDWIDE TOTAL GROSS ($)
1	Shrek	DreamWorks	2001	477,000,000
2	Ice Age	Fox Animation	2002	366,300,000
3	Casper*	Amblin Entertainment	1995	288,000,000
4	Space Jam*	Warner Bros.	1996	225,400,000
5	Chicken Run	DreamWorks	2000	224,900,000
6	The Prince of Egypt	DreamWorks	1998	218,300,000
7	Cats & Dogs*	Warner Bros.	2001	200,400,000
8	Antz	DreamWorks	1998	181,700,000
9	Monoke-hime (Princess Mononke)	Dentsu Inc.	1997	159,400,000
10	Pokémon: The First Movie	4 Kids Entertainment, etc.	1999	155,700,000

* Part animated, part live action

THE 10 | LATEST OSCAR-WINNING ANIMATED FILMS*

YEAR	FILM	DIRECTOR/COUNTRY
2003	Harvie Krumpet	Adam Elliot, Australia
2002	The ChubbChubbs!	Eric Armstrong, Canada
2001	For the Birds	Ralph Eggleston, US
2000	Father and Daughter	Michael Dudok de Wit, Netherlands
1999	The Old Man and the Sea	Aleksandr Petrov, US
1998	Bunny	Chris Wedge, US
1997	Geri's Game	Jan Pinkava, US
1996	Quest	Tyron Montgomery, UK
1995	Wallace & Gromit: A Close Shave	Nick Park, UK
1994	Bob's Birthday	David Fine and Alison Snowden, UK

* In the category "Short Films (Animated)"

Although Snow White and the Seven Dwarfs (1937) received an honorary Academy Award, animated feature films were not eligible for an Oscar until the 2001 ceremony, when the first animated winner was Shrek, followed by Spirited Away in 2002 and Finding Nemo in 2003.

THE 10 | FIRST OSCAR-WINNING ANIMATED FILMS*

	FILM	DIRECTOR#	YEAR
1	Flowers and Trees	Walt Disney	1931/32
2	The Three Little Pigs	Walt Disney	1932/33
3	The Tortoise and the Hare	Walt Disney	1934
4	Three Orphan Kittens	Walt Disney	1935
5	The Country Cousin	Walt Disney	1936
6	The Old Mill	Walt Disney	1937
7	Ferdinand the Bull	Walt Disney	1938
8	The Ugly Duckling	Walt Disney	1939
9	The Milky Way	Rudolf Ising	1940
10	Lend a Paw	Walt Disney	1941

* In the category "Short Subjects (Cartoons)"
# All US

With the exception of The Milky Way, which was directed by Rudolf Ising, all were directed by Walt Disney. Oscars were awarded in the category "Short Subjects (Cartoons)" until 1972, when it was altered to "Short Subjects (Animated Films)," and in 1976 to "Short Films(Animated)."

TOP 10 | WALT DISNEY ANIMATED FEATURE FILMS

	FILM	YEAR	WORLDWIDE TOTAL GROSS ($)
1	Finding Nemo	2003	797,700,000
2	The Lion King	1994	787,500,000
3	Monsters, Inc.	2001	529,000,000
4	Aladdin	1992	502,300,000
5	Toy Story 2	1999	485,700,000
6	Tarzan	1999	449,300,000
7	A Bug's Life	1998	363,300,000
8	Toy Story	1995	361,500,000
9	Dinosaur	2000	356,100,000
10	Beauty and the Beast	1991	352,900,000

Within just a month of its May 30, 2003 release, Finding Nemo had earned more than $256 million at the US box office, and has more than trebled that figure since its international release. Each film in this Top 10 has made in excess of $350 million worldwide, but even some of the studio's earlier productions, including Bambi (1942) and Snow White and the Seven Dwarfs (1937), are close runners-up.

TOP 10 | ANIMATED FILM OPENING WEEKENDS IN THE U.S.

	FILM	US RELEASE	OPENING WEEKEND GROSS ($)
1	Finding Nemo	May 30, 2003	70,251,710
2	Monsters, Inc.	Nov. 2, 2001	62,577,067
3	Toy Story 2*	Nov. 26, 1999	57,388,839
4	Ice Age	Mar. 15, 2002	46,312,454
5	Shrek	May 18, 2001	42,347,760
6	The Lion King	June 24, 1994	40,888,194
7	Dinosaur	May 19, 2000	38,854,851
8	Lilo & Stitch	June 21, 2002	35,260,212
9	Tarzan	June 18, 1999	34,221,968
10	A Bug's Life*	Nov. 28, 1998	33,258,052

* Second weekend; opening weekend release in limited number of cinemas only

Finding Nemo not only heads this list, but, exceptionally for an animated film, fails by only one place to be included among the Top 10 opening weekends of all time.

Film Genres

TOP 10 MUSICAL FILMS

	FILM	YEAR
1	Grease	1978
2	Chicago	2002
3	Saturday Night Fever	1977
4	8 Mile	2002
5	Moulin Rouge!	2001
6	The Sound of Music	1965
7	Evita	1996
8	The Rocky Horror Picture Show	1975
9	Staying Alive	1983
10	Mary Poppins	1964

Traditional musicals (films in which the cast actually sing) and films in which a musical soundtrack is a major component of the film are included here. The success of *Chicago* suggests that the age of the blockbuster musical film is not yet over, but in recent years films with an important musical content appear to have taken over from them – the film soundtrack album of *Titanic* is the bestselling ever, while animated films' *Beauty and the Beast*, *Aladdin*, *The Lion King*, *Pocahontas*, *The Prince of Egypt*, and *Tarzan* all won "Best Original Song" Oscars.

TOP 10 PIRATE FILMS

	FILM	YEAR
1	Pirates of the Caribbean: The Curse of the Black Pearl	2003
2	Hook	1991
3	Treasure Planet*	2002
4	Peter Pan*	1953
5	Peter Pan: Return to Never Land*	2002
6	The Goonies	1985
7	Muppet Treasure Island	1996
8	Swiss Family Robinson	1960
9	The Island	1980
10	Shipwrecked	1990

* Animated

After notable pirate film flops such as *Pirates* (1986) and *Cutthroat Island* (1995), it seemed that the genre was finished, but then along came *Pirates of the Caribbean: The Curse of the Black Pearl*, which has earned so much worldwide that it is ranked as one of the Top 20 films of all time.

TOP 10 VAMPIRE FILMS

	FILM	YEAR
1	Interview with the Vampire: The Vampire Chronicles	1994
2	Bram Stoker's Dracula	1992
3	Blade II	2002
4	Blade	1998
5	Underworld	2003
6	From Dusk Till Dawn	1996
7	Love at First Bite	1979
8	Wes Craven Presents Dracula 2000	2000
9	Queen of the Damned	2002
10	The Lost Boys	1987

Vampires have figured in films since the silent era. The German film *Nächte des Grauens* (1916) was the first to tackle the theme, *The Great London Mystery* (1920) the first to do so in English, and the Hungarian film *Drakula halála* (1921) the first adaptation of Bram Stoker's *Dracula*. Since then, there have been over 400 vampire films, with those in the Top 10 the highest earning worldwide.

▲ **Greased lightning**
With worldwide earnings topping $380 million, *Grease* was not only the blockbuster movie of 1978, but remains the biggest movie musical of all time.

TOP 10 JAMES BOND FILMS

FILM	BOND ACTOR	YEAR
1 Die Another Day	Pierce Brosnan	2002
2 The World is Not Enough	Pierce Brosnan	1999
3 GoldenEye	Pierce Brosnan	1995
4 Tomorrow Never Dies	Pierce Brosnan	1997
5 Moonraker	Roger Moore	1979
6 The Living Daylights	Timothy Dalton	1987
7 For Your Eyes Only	Roger Moore	1981
8 The Spy Who Loved Me	Roger Moore	1977
9 Octopussy	Roger Moore	1983
10 License to Kill	Timothy Dalton	1990

Ian Fleming wrote 12 James Bond novels, only two of which, *Moonraker* (1955) and *The Spy Who Loved Me* (1962), figure in this Top 10. After his death in 1964, *For Your Eyes Only*, *Octopussy*, *The Living Daylights*, and *GoldenEye* were developed by other writers from his short stories, while subsequent releases were written without reference to Fleming's writings. *Casino Royale* (book 1953, film 1967), featuring 56-year-old David Niven as the retired spy Sir James Bond, is an oddity in that it was presented as a comedy. This and *Never Say Never Again* (1983), effectively a remake of *Thunderball*, are not considered "official" Bond films, making the 2002 release *Die Another Day* the 20th in the canonical series.

TOP 10 DISASTER FILMS

FILM	YEAR	DISASTER
1 Titanic	1997	Shipwreck
2 Armageddon	1998	Asteroid impact
3 Twister	1996	Tornado
4 Die Hard: With a Vengeance	1995	Terrorist city bomber
5 Apollo 13	1995	Space capsule explosion
6 Deep Impact	1998	Comet impact
7 The Perfect Storm	2000	Storm at sea
8 Die Hard 2: Die Harder	1990	Terrorists at airport
9 Outbreak	1995	Epidemic
10 Dante's Peak	1997	Volcano

Excluding science-fiction subjects (alien attacks, rampaging dinosaurs, and other fantasy themes), disasters involving blazing buildings, natural disasters such as volcanoes, earthquakes, and tidal waves, train and air crashes, sinking ships, and terrorist attacks have long been a staple of Hollywood movies, while latterly asteroid impact, tornadoes, exploding space capsules, and killer viruses have been added to the genre. The list comprises films that have earned an average of almost $500 million worldwide. Since the real-life tragedy of 9/11, however, Hollywood studios have been understandably reluctant to make films in this genre.

TOP 10 SCIENCE-FICTION FILMS

FILM	YEAR
1 Star Wars: Episode I—The Phantom Menace	1999
2 Jurassic Park	1993
3 Independence Day	1996
4 Spider-Man	2002
5 Star Wars: Episode IV—A New Hope	1977
6 E.T. the Extra-Terrestrial	1982
7 The Matrix Reloaded	2003
8 Star Wars: Episode II—Attack of the Clones	2002
9 The Lost World: Jurassic Park	1997
10 Men in Black	1997

Science-fiction features more prominently than any other genre among the highest-earning films of all time—within the Top 10, the first five films are also in the all-time Top 10, and all 10 are among the 21 most successful films ever, having earned over $587 million each— a total of more than $7.6 billion at the worldwide box office. The *Star Wars* franchise represents a special achievement: as well as occupying three places in the list, the original film held its commanding place as the biggest money-making film worldwide from 1977 until 1993.

TOP 10 DOCUMENTARY FILMS

FILM	YEAR	SUBJECT
1 Everest	1998	Exploration
2 To Fly	1976	History of flying
3 Jackass: The Movie	2002	Comedy stunts
4 Mysteries of Egypt	1998	Historical
5 Space Station 3-D	2002	International Space Station
6 In Search of Noah's Ark	1977	Exploration
7 Grand Canyon: The Hidden Secrets	1984	Exploration
8 The Dream is Alive	1985	Space Shuttle
9 Across the Sea of Time	1995	Historical
10 Eddie Murphy Raw	1987	Comedy

Each of these has earned more than $50 million, with *Everest* making in excess of $100 million worldwide. A number of them are IMAX (large format) films, the earnings of which have accrued from releases over periods of several years, in contrast to the more limited runs of feature films.

Radio Active

TOP 10 RADIO-OWNING COUNTRIES

	COUNTRY	RADIOS PER 1,000 POPULATION (2001)
1	Norway	3,324
2	Sweden	2,811
3	US	2,117
4	Australia	1,999
5	Finland	1,624
6	UK	1,446
7	Denmark	1,400
8	Estonia	1,136
9	Canada	1,047
10	South Korea	1,034
	World average	*419*

Source: *World Bank*, World Development Indicators 2003

TOP 10 RADIO FORMATS IN THE U.S.

	FORMAT	NO. OF STATIONS
1	Country	2,056
2	News/talk	1,852
3	Oldies	838
4	Religious talk/teaching	832
5	Adult contemporary	712
6	Contemporary Christian	625
7	Spanish	613
8	CHR (Top 40)	534
9	Adult standards	483
10	Sports	456

Source: *M Street*

THE 10 LATEST N.A.B. NETWORK/SYNDICATED PERSONALITIES OF THE YEAR

YEAR	RECIPIENT
2003	**Sean Hannity,** ABC Radio Networks
2002	**Paul Harvey,** Paul Harvey News and Comment, ABC Radio Networks
2001	**Rick Dees,** Premiere Radio Networks
2000	**Rush Limbaugh,** The Rush Limbaugh Show, Premiere Radio Networks
1999	**Bob Kevoian and Tom Griswold,** The Bob & Tom Show, AMFM Radio Networks
1998	**Paul Harvey,** ABC Radio Networks
1997	**Dr. Laura Schlessinger,** Synergy Broadcasting
1996	**Paul Harvey,** ABC Radio Networks
1995	**Rush Limbaugh,** EFM Media Management
1994	**Don Imus,** Westwood One Radio Networks

TOP 10 U.S. RADIO STATIONS BY AUDIENCE SHARE

	STATION/CITY	FORMAT	PERCENTAGE SHARE
1	**WFRY-FM,** Watertown, NY	Country	29.3
2	**WTHI-FM,** Terre Haute, IN	Country	23.2
3	**KYKZ-FM,** Lake Charles, LA	Country	23.1
4	**WZID-FM,** Manchester, NH	AC	21.8
5	**WGSQ-FM,** Cookeville, TN	Country	21.7
6	**WJIZ-FM,** Albany, GA	Black/Urban	21.3
7	**WBKR-FM,** Owensboro, KY	Country	21.0
8	**WXBQ-FM,** Johnson City–Kingsport–Bristol, VA	Country	20.3
9	**WIVK-FM,** Knoxville, TN	Country	20.2
10	**WJLS-FM,** Beckley, WV	Country	20.1

Source: *Duncan's American Radio, Spring 2001 Arbitron data*

More US radio stations are dedicated to country music than any other format, and expressed as a percentage of the total potential market, country stations clearly have the biggest and most loyal audiences, with just one entry apiece for AC ("adult contemporary"), aimed at people age 30 and older, and black/urban.

THE 10 LATEST N.A.B. MARCONI LEGENDARY STATIONS OF THE YEAR

YEAR	STATION	LOCATION
2003	WABC	New York, NY
2002	WSB-AM	Atlanta, GA
2001	KNIX	Phoenix, AZ
2000	WEBN	Cincinnati, OH
1999	KOA	Denver, CO
1998	WCBS-FM	New York, NY
1997	KVIL-FM	Dallas, TX
1996	WJR-AM	Detroit, MI
1995	KGO-AM	San Francisco, CA
1994	KDKA-AM	Pittsburgh, PA

Unlike the National Association of Broadcasters' other awards (which are concerned with a station or personality's achievements during the preceding year), the "Legendary Station" award can be presented only once to a station. It recognizes overall excellence in radio, and considers the station's history and heritage. Established in 1989, it is named after Nobel Prize winner and "Father of Wireless Telegraphy" Guglielmo Marconi (1874–1937). Five finalists are selected, with the eventual winner being voted on by their peers.

THE 10 LATEST PEABODY AWARDS FOR BROADCASTING WON BY NATIONAL PUBLIC RADIO*

	PROGRAM	YEAR
1	The Yiddish Radio Project	2002
2	= Coverage of September 11, 2001	2001
	= Jazz Profiles	2001
4	The NPR 100	2000
5	= Lost & Found Sound	1999
	= Morning Edition with Bob Edwards	1999
7	= Coverage of Africa	1998
	= I Must Keep Fightin': The Art of Paul Robeson	1998
	= Performance Today	1998
10	Jazz from Lincoln Center	1997

* *Includes only programs made or co-produced by NPR*

Source: *George Foster Peabody Awards*

◀ **Listen and learn**
A century after its invention, radio maintains its value as a medium to educate, inform, and entertain.

TOP 10 LONGEST-RUNNING PROGRAMS ON NATIONAL PUBLIC RADIO

	PROGRAM	FIRST BROADCAST
1	All Things Considered*	1971
2	Weekend All Things Considered	1974
3	Fresh Air with Terry Gross	1977
4	Marian McPartland's Piano Jazz	1978
5	Morning Edition	1979
6	Weekend Edition/ Saturday with Scott Simon	1985
7	Performance Today	1987
8	Weekend Edition/ Sunday with Liane Hansen	1987
9	Car Talk	1987
10	Talk of the Nation	1991

Source: *National Public Radio*

* *The longest-running NPR program, first broadcast on May 3, 1971*

TALK RADIO PIONEER

THE WORLD'S FIRST professional radio announcer was Harold W. Arlin (1895–1986). He started work for Philadelphia radio station KDKA in January 1921. KDKA was the first station to be licensed in the United States— and at that time operated out of a tent! Arlin broadcast the first US presidential inauguration on March 4, 1921, reading Warren Harding's address on air as the new president read his script. He also provided the first-ever live commentary of a baseball game (Pirates vs. Phillies, August 5, 1921) and the first football match (Pitt College vs. University of West Virginia, October 8, 1921). Arlin's commentaries were broadcast abroad; *The Times* once described him as having "the best known American voice in Europe."

THE FIRST TO...

Top TV

TOP 10 PROGRAMS WITH THE HIGHEST TV AUDIENCE SHARE IN THE U.S.

	PROGRAM	DATE	VIEWERS TOTAL	%
1	M*A*S*H Special	Feb. 28, 1983	50,150,000	60.2
2	Dallas	Nov. 21, 1980	41,470,000	53.3
3	Roots Part 8	Jan. 30, 1977	36,380,000	51.1
4	Super Bowl XVI	Jan. 24, 1982	40,020,000	49.1
5	Super Bowl XVII	Jan. 30, 1983	40,480,000	48.6
6	XVII Winter Olympics	Feb. 23, 1994	45,690,000	48.5
7	Super Bowl XX	Jan. 26, 1986	41,490,000	48.3
8	Gone with the Wind Pt.1	Nov. 7, 1976	33,960,000	47.7
9	Gone with the Wind Pt.2	Nov. 8, 1976	33,750,000	47.4
10	Super Bowl XII	Jan. 15, 1978	34,410,000	47.2

Source: *Nielsen Media Research*

Historically, as more households acquired television sets (there are currently 108.4 million "TV households" in the US), audiences generally increased. However, the rise in channel choice and the use of VCRs has somewhat checked this trend. Listing the Top 10 according to percentage of households viewing provides a clearer picture of who watches what. *M*A*S*H*, which heads the list, aired from September 17, 1972 to February 28, 1983, with the final "Goodbye, Farewell, and Amen" episode seen by some 125 million Americans.

TOP 10 PRIMETIME PROGRAMS ON NETWORK TELEVISION, 2003

	PROGRAM TITLE*	DATE	AVERAGE VIEWERS %	TOTAL
1	Joe Millionaire	Feb. 17	21.8	23,244,000
2	American Idol	May 21	20.3	21,707,000
3	CSI: Miami	Nov. 6	18.1	19,579,000
4	Friends	Jan. 30	16.3	17,440,000
5	ER	Sept. 25	15.5	16,848,000
6	Primetime Thursday	Feb. 6	15.0	16,007,000
7	Everybody Loves Raymond	May 19	14.3	15,279,000
8	Will & Grace	Sept. 25	13.5	14,676,000
9	Law & Order	Sept. 24	13.4	14,519,000
10	Survivor: Amazon	Mar. 6	13.5	14,442,000

* *Excluding sport; highest ranked screening only listed*

Source: *Nielsen Media Research*

► **TV time**
In little over 50 years, television has become such an integral part of most people's lives that the pre-TV age is little more than a distant memory.

THE FIRST TO... TRANSMIT TV PICTURES

FOLLOWING EXPERIMENTAL low-definition broadcasts, the first daily high-definition TV service was inaugurated by the BBC in London at 3.00 pm on Monday, November 2, 1936. Up to the end of that year, only 280 sets had been sold, increasing to between 20,000 and 25,000 by September 1939, when the service was suspended at the outbreak of war. The first US public service began on April 30, 1939, when an outside broadcast showed President Roosevelt opening the New York World's Fair. He thereby became the first president of the TV era.

TOP 10 CABLE TELEVISION COUNTRIES

	COUNTRY	CABLE TV SUBSCRIBERS (2002) TOTAL	% OF TV HOMES
1	Bhutan	11,200	93.5
2	Netherlands	6,500,000	92.9
3	Belgium	3,880,300	90.5
4	Switzerland	2,739,000	90.4
5	Luxembourg	138,000	86.2
6	Malta	95,100	77.3
7	Israel	1,221,000	73.3
8	Taiwan	4,642,000	69.8
9	US	73,525,200	68.9
10	Canada	7,868,300	66.7
	World	*351,097,600*	*31.8*

Source: *International Telecommunication Union*, World Telecommunication Development Report, *2003*

THE 10 FIRST COUNTRIES TO HAVE TELEVISION*

	COUNTRY	YEAR
1	UK	1936
2	US	1939
3	USSR	1939
4	France	1948
5	Brazil	1950
6	Cuba	1950
7	Mexico	1950
8	Argentina	1951
9	Denmark	1951
10	Netherlands	1951

* *High-definition regular public broadcasting service*

After the pioneer countries listed above, Canada and Germany introduced TV in 1952. Belgium and Japan did the same in 1953 and were followed, ultimately, by almost every other country in the world.

TOP 10 TALK SHOWS ON U.S. TELEVISION, 2003

	TALK SHOW*	ORIGINATOR	AVERAGE AUDIENCE TOTAL
1	The Oprah Winfrey Show	Kingworld Media Sales	7,589,000
2	The Dr. Phil Show	Kingworld Media Sales	5,761,000
3	Live with Regis and Kelly	Buena Vista Television	4,183,000
4	Maury	Studios USA	3,328,000
5	The View	ABC	2,818,000
6	The Montel Williams Show	Paramount	2,755,000
7	Jerry Springer	Studios USA	2,653,000
8	The Ellen DeGeneres Show	Warner Bros. TV	1,886,000
9	The Sharon Osbourne Show	Warner Bros. TV	1,480,000
10	Ricki Lake	Sony Pictures Television	1,459,000

* Highest rated shows only—i.e. excludes alternative orginators

Source: Nielsen Media Research

TOP 10 DAYTIME DRAMAS ON U.S. TELEVISION, 2003

	DRAMA	NETWORK	AVERAGE VIEWERS %	TOTAL
1	The Young and the Restless	CBS	4.6	4,954,000
2	The Bold and the Beautiful	CBS	3.5	3,753,000
3	General Hospital	ABC	3.3	3,536,000
4	Days of Our Lives	NBC	3.2	3,519,000
5	As the World Turns	CBS	3.0	3,237,000
6	All My Children	ABC	3.1	3,229,000
7	One Life to Live	ABC	2.9	3,169,000
8	Guiding Light	CBS	2.5	2,741,000
9	Passions	NBC	2.1	2,253,000
10	Port Charles	ABC	1.3	1,401,000

* Excludes specials

Source: Nielsen Media Research

DVD & Video

TOP 10 VIDEOS IN THE U.S., 1994

FILM

1 Snow White and the Seven Dwarfs
2 Jurassic Park
3 The Fox and the Hound
4 Mrs. Doubtfire
5 The Return of Jafar
6 Aladdin
7 Barney (various)
8 Once Upon a Forest
9 Free Willy
10 The Fugitive

The success of Disney's program of re-releasing its classic animated features on video is exemplified by *Snow White and the Seven Dwarfs*, which became the year's top seller as the movie celebrated its 57th birthday. *The Return of Jafar* was a direct-to-video release designed to capitalize on 1993's chart-topper, *Aladdin*, which continued to sell well into 1994.

TOP 10 VIDEOS IN THE U.S., 1995

FILM

1 The Lion King
2 Forrest Gump
3 The Fox and the Hound
4 Cinderella
5 Snow White and the Seven Dwarfs
6 The Mask
7 Caspar
8 Angels in the Outfield
9 Speed
10 Batman Forever

The Lion King was to overtake *Aladdin* as the highest-earning animated film of all time—until eventually being beaten itself by *Finding Nemo*. The success of its 1995 video release established it as not only the top seller of the year, edging out "Best Picture" Oscar winner *Forrest Gump*, but the bestselling video of the 20th century.

TOP 10 VIDEOS IN THE U.S., 1996

FILM

1 Toy Story
2 Pocahontas
3 Babe
4 The Aristocats
5 Independence Day
6 Twister
7 Aladdin
8 Oliver & Company
9 Jumanji
10 Indian in the Cupboard

Disney's *Toy Story*, the first major computer generated movie and the biggest film at the 1995 US box office, became the top video seller of the year. The studio's other blockbuster, *Pocahontas*, ran a close second, along with the video release of *The Aristocats*, originally screened in 1970, and *Aladdin*, still selling strongly four years after its release.

TOP 10 VIDEOS IN THE U.S., 1997

FILM

1 Independence Day
2 Bambi
3 The Hunchback of Notre Dame
4 Space Jam
5 101 Dalmatians
6 Jerry Maguire
7 Sleeping Beauty
8 Men in Black
9 Jumanji
10 The Lost World: Jurassic Park

The video success of *Independence Day*, the top US movie of 1996 by a big margin, was inevitable, as was that of the latest of Disney's re-releases, the 55-year-old *Bambi* and 39-year-old *Sleeping Beauty*, together with its recent *The Hunchback of Notre Dame* and the live action *101 Dalmatians*.

TOP 10 VIDEOS IN THE U.S., 1998

FILM

1 Titanic
2 Hercules
3 The Little Mermaid
4 The Lion King II: Simba's Pride
5 Peter Pan
6 Lady and the Tramp
7 Flubber
8 Men in Black
9 Anastasia
10 Air Force One

Titanic added to its still unbroken record as the highest-earning film of all time by becoming the biggest video release of the year, while *Hercules*, Disney's animated smash hit of the previous year, ran a close second among the year's top video releases.

TOP 10 VIDEOS IN THE U.S., 1999

FILM

1 Mulan
2 A Bug's Life
3 Antz
4 Armageddon
5 Titanic
6 The Rugrats Movie
7 Mighty Joe Young
8 The Prince of Egypt
9 Dr. Doolittle
10 Saving Private Ryan

A mix of adventure and animated (especially insect-infested releases *A Bug's Life* and *Antz*) occupy this last Top 10 of the 20th century. As the new millennium dawned, DVD, introduced in the US in 1997, became the format of choice for increasing numbers of consumers, outselling and progressively replacing the 20-year-old VHS format.

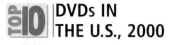 DVDs IN THE U.S., 2000
FILM

1 Gladiator
2 X-Men
3 The Sixth Sense
4 The Matrix
5 The Patriot
6 Mission: Impossible 2
7 The Green Mile
8 The Perfect Storm
9 Gone in 60 Seconds
10 Toy Story/Toy Story 2 box set

DVDs IN THE U.S., 2001
FILM

1 Shrek
2 Pearl Harbor
3 Dr. Seuss' How the Grinch Stole Christmas
4 Planet of the Apes
5 Cast Away
6 Star Wars: Episode 1— The Phantom Menace
7 The Godfather Collection
8 The Mummy Returns
9 Jurassic Park III
10 Snow White

DVDs IN THE U.S., 2002
FILM

1 The Lord of the Rings: The Fellowship of the Ring
2 Spider-Man
3 Monsters, Inc.
4 Harry Potter and the Sorcerers's Stone
5 Star Wars: Episode 2— Attack of the Clones
6 The Fast and the Furious
7 Ice Age
8 Lilo & Stitch
9 Austin Powers in Goldmember
10 Band of Brothers

DVD sales were up 25 percent in 2002, hitting $8.7 billion out of a DVD-and-VHS total of $12.1 billion. This upward trend saw certain DVD and video releases earning greater revenue than they had at the box office.

DVDs IN THE U.S., 2003
FILM

1 Finding Nemo
2 The Lord of the Rings: The Two Towers
3 Pirates of the Caribbean
4 Harry Potter and the Chamber of Secrets
5 The Indiana Jones Collection
6 The Matrix Reloaded
7 The Lion King Special Edition
8 My Big Fat Greek Wedding
9 Signs
10 Bruce Almighty

Sales of DVDs in the US in 2003 were thought to be worth $14.3 billion of a total spend (including VHS) of $22.5 billion, greatly aided by the release of recent movie blockbusters, with *Finding Nemo* becoming the highest-earning animated film and bestselling DVD of all time.

◀ **Video Pirate**
Despite its December release, *Pirates of the Caribbean* matched its earlier box office success with massive DVD sales in the last few weeks of 2003.

COMMERCIAL WORLD

Workers of the World

TOP 10 COUNTRIES WITH THE MOST WORKERS

	COUNTRY	WORKERS* (2000)
1	China	766,889,000
2	India	442,156,000
3	US	145,105,000
4	Indonesia	102,561,000
5	Brazil	79,247,000
6	Russia	78,041,000
7	Bangladesh	69,611,000
8	Japan	68,369,000
9	Pakistan	52,077,000
10	Nigeria	45,129,000
	Canada	*16,559,000*

Source: *Food and Agriculture Organization of the United Nations*

As defined by the International Labor Organization, the "labor force" includes people between the ages of 15 and 64 who are currently employed and those who are unemployed. It excludes unpaid groups, such as students, housewives, and retired people. In practice it is difficult to count those not employed accurately, especially in developing countries.

TOP 10 COUNTRIES WITH THE HIGHEST PROPORTION OF SERVICE INDUSTRY WORKERS

	COUNTRY	PERCENTAGE OF LABOR FORCE IN SERVICES* (1998–2001) (FEMALE)	(MALE)	COUNTRY	
1	Argentina	89	71	Hong Kong (China)	1
2 =	Hong Kong (China)	88	68	Columbia	2
=	Norway	88	67	Peru =	3
=	Panama	88	67	Singapore =	
5 =	Canada	87	65	Argentina	5
=	Sweden	87	64	United States	6
=	UK	87	63	Australia =	7
8 =	Australia	86	63	Canada =	
=	Belgium	86	63	Ecuador =	
=	France	86	63	France =	
=	Israel	86	63	Morocco =	
=	Peru	86	63	Netherlands =	
=	US	86	61	*UK*	

* *Service industries include wholesale and retail trade, restaurants and hotels; transportation, communications and storage; finance, insurance, real estate, and business services; and community, social, and personal services*

Source: *World Bank*, World Development Indicators 2003

TOP 10 TYPES OF JOBS IN THE U.S. 100 YEARS AGO

	JOB SECTOR	EMPLOYEES
1	Farmers and farm managers	5,763,000
2	Farm laborers and foremen	5,125,000
3	Operatives and kindred workers (miners, etc.)	3,720,000
4	Laborers (except farm and mine)	3,620,000
5	Craftsmen and foremen	3,062,000
6	Private household workers	1,579,000
7	Salesworkers	1,307,000
8	Professional and technical workers	1,234,000
9	Service workers (except private household)	1,047,000
10	Clerical workers	877,000
	Total labor force	*29,030,000*

Source: *US Bureau of the Census*

▶ **Screen trade**
In many countries, jobs in service industries— from online banking to call centers—have inexorably overtaken those in "traditional" manufacturing trades.

TOP 10 OCCUPATIONS IN THE U.S.

	OCCUPATION	EMPLOYEES (2002)
1	Retail salespersons	3,894,760
2	Cashiers	3,375,510
3	General office clerks	2,857,300
4	Registered nurses	2,239,530
5	Hand laborers and freight, stock and material movers	2,217,590
6	Waiters and waitresses	2,086,120
7	Janitors and cleaners (excludes maids and housekeeping cleaners)	2,052,090
8	Combined food preparation and serving workers (includes fast food)	2,000,070
9	General and operation managers	1,998,350
10	Customer services representatives	1,854,750

Source: *Bureau of Labor Statistics*

TOP 10 LABOR ORGANIZATIONS IN THE U.S.

	LABOR ORGANIZATION	MEMBERS
1	National Education Association	2,668,925
2	International Brotherhood of Teamsters	1,398,412
3	United Food and Commercial Workers' International Union	1,385,043
4	Service Employees International Union	1,376,292
5	American Federation of State, County and Municipal Employees	1,300,000
6	Laborers' International Union of North America	795,335
7	American Federation of Teachers	741,270
8	International Association of Machinists and Aerospace Workers	722,987
9	International Brotherhood of Electrical Workers	720,095
10	International Union, United Automobile, Aerospace, and Agricultural Implement Workers of America	701,818

The National Education Association is the oldest and largest public education organization in the US. Founded in Philadelphia in 1857, it has members who work at every level of education, from preschool to university graduate programs.

TOP 10 COUNTRIES WITH THE HIGHEST PROPORTION OF FEMALE WORKERS

	COUNTRY	LABOR FORCE PERCENTAGE*
1	Cambodia	51.6
2	Latvia	50.5
3	Ghana	50.4
4	Russia	49.2
5	= Estonia	49.0
	= Tanzania	49.0
	= Belarus	49.0
8	= Rwanda	48.8
	= Ukraine	48.8
	= Vietnam	48.8
	World	40.7
	US	46.1

* *Based on people aged 15–64 who are currently employed; unpaid groups are not included*

Source: *World Bank*, World Development Indicators 2003

Science & Invention

TOP 10 NOBEL PHYSICS PRIZE-WINNING COUNTRIES

	COUNTRY	PHYSICS PRIZES
1	US	75
2	UK	22
3	Germany	21
4	France	12
5	= Netherlands	8
	= USSR	8
7	= Japan	4
	= Sweden	4
9	= Austria	3
	= Denmark	3
	= Italy	3

TOP 10 U.S. PATENT-HOLDING COMPANIES

	COMPANY	PATENTS (2001)
1	International Business Machines Corp.	3,411
2	NEC Corporation	1,953
3	Canon Kabushiki Kaisha	1,877
4	Micron Technology, Inc.	1,643
5	Samsung Electronics Co., Ltd.	1,450
6	Matsushita Electric Industrial Co., Ltd.	1,440
7	Sony Corporation	1,363
8	Hitachi, Ltd.	1,271
9	Mitsubishi Denki Kabushiki Kaisha	1,184
10	Fujitsu Ltd.	1,166

Source: *US Patent and Trademark Office*

For the ninth consecutive year, IBM received more patents than any other organization, an increase of 18 per cent over the preceding year.

TOP 10 COUNTRIES WITH THE MOST INDUSTRIAL ROBOTS

	COUNTRY	NO. OF OPERATIONAL INDUSTRIAL ROBOTS (2002)
1	Japan	350,169
2	Germany	105,217
3	US	103,515
4	Italy	46,881
5	South Korea	44,265
6	France	24,277
7	Spain	18,352
8	UK	13,651
9	Taiwan	7,491
10	Sweden	6,846

Source: *United Nations Economic Commission for Europe*

▶ **Rise of the machines**
The number of robots used in motor manufacturing and other industries worldwide was put at 769,888 in 2002, with robot/industrial worker ratios highest in Japan at 308 per 10,000, compared with 58 per 10,0000 in the US.

TOP 10 CATEGORIES OF PATENTS IN THE U.S.

	CATEGORY/OFFICIAL CLASS NO.	PATENTS GRANTED (1977-2001)*
1	Drug (514)	76,846
2	Stock material and miscellaneous articles (428)	76,549
3	Chemical—molecular biology (435)	53,249
4	Measuring and testing (073)	47,208
5	Coating processes (427)	45,445
6	Plastic and nonmetallic shaping and treating processes (264)	43,763
7	Metalworking (029)	43,621
8	Drug (424)	43,150
9	Solid-state (transistor, etc.) devices (257)	42,453
10	Radiant energy (250)	40, 069
	Total (including categories not listed)	4,380,088

* Totals to Dec. 31, 2001

Source: *US Patent and Trademark Office*

The precise definition of patent categories and subcategories is essential to their protection under the law. Among thousands of such groups, two subtly different categories of pharmaceutical products (officially defined as "Drug, bio-affecting and body treating compositions") dominate the Top 10.

TOP 10 COUNTRIES REGISTERING THE MOST PATENTS

	COUNTRY	PATENTS REGISTERED (2001)
1	United States	166,038
2	Japan	121,742
3	Germany	48,207
4	France	42,963
5	UK	39,649
6	South Korea	34,675
7	Italy	25,130
8	Netherlands	20,624
9	Spain	19,709
10	China	16,296

Source: *World Intellectual Property Organization*

A patent is an exclusive license to manufacture and exploit a unique product or process for a fixed period. This list, based on data from the World Intellectual Property Organization, provides a yardstick of each nation's technological development. A further 34,704 patents were granted by the European Patent Office, which has no national affiliation. The figures refer to the number of patents actually *granted* during 2001: in most instances, this represents only a fraction of the patents applied for.

World Finance

TOP 10 RICHEST COUNTRIES

	COUNTRY	GDP* PER CAPITA (2001) ($)
1	Luxembourg	53,780
2	US	34,320
3	Ireland	32,410
4	Iceland	29,990
5	Norway	29,620
6	Denmark	29,000
7	Switzerland	28,100
8	Netherlands	27,190
9	Canada	27,130
10	Austria	26,730
	World average	7,376

* *Gross Domestic Product*

Source: *United Nations*, Human Development Indicators, 2003

THE 10 POOREST COUNTRIES

	COUNTRY	GDP* PER CAPITA (2001) ($)
1	Sierra Leone	470
2	Tanzania	520
3	Malawi	570
4	Dem. Rep. of Congo	680
5	Burundi	690
6	Zambia	780
7	Yemen	790
8	= Ethiopia	810
	= Mali	810
10	Madagascar	830

* *Gross Domestic Product*

Source: *United Nations*, Human Development Indicators, 2003

TOP 10 MOST EXPENSIVE COUNTRIES IN WHICH TO BUY A BIG MAC

	COUNTRY	COST OF A BIG MAC* ($)
1	Switzerland	5.11
2	Denmark	4.72
3	Sweden	4.15
4	Euro area	3.48
5	UK	3.45
6	Turkey	2.94
7	= South Korea	2.80
	= US	2.80
9	New Zealand	2.70
10	Peru	2.60

* *As of Jan. 14, 2004; of those countries surveyed*

Source: The Economist/McDonald's *price data*

The Big Mac index assesses the value of countries' currencies against the standard US price of a Big Mac, by assuming that an identical amount of goods and services should cost the same in all countries.

 **COUNTRIES MOST IN DEBT**

	COUNTRY	TOTAL EXTERNAL DEBT (2001) ($)
1	Brazil	226,362,000,000
2	China	170,110,000,000
3	Mexico	158,290,000,000
4	Russia	152,649,000,000
5	Argentina	136,709,000,000
6	Indonesia	135,704,000,000
7	Turkey	115,118,000,000
8	South Korea	110,109,000,000
9	India	97,071,000,000
10	Thailand	67,384,000,000

Source: *World Bank*, World Development Indicators 2003

▼ **Pillars of the establishment**
The skyscrapers that dominate Manhattan Island in New York house the financial institutions that control much of the western world's trade.

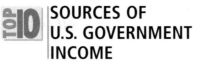 **SOURCES OF U.S. GOVERNMENT INCOME**

	SOURCE	ESTIMATED FEDERAL RECEIPTS (2002) ($)
1	Individual income tax	949,200,000,000
2	Old-age and survivors' insurance	442,100,000,000
3	Corporation income tax	201,400,000,000
4	Hospital insurance	151,700,000,000
5	Disability insurance	75,100,000,000
6	Highway trust funds	31,900,000,000
7	Unemployment insurance	30,300,000,000
8	Airport and airway trust funds	8,900,000,000
9	Tobacco excise duties	8,000,000,000
10	Alcohol excise duties	7,600,000,000

TOP 10 AREAS OF FEDERAL GOVERNMENT EXPENDITURE

	AREA OF EXPENDITURE	EXPENDITURE (2002) ($)
1	Social Security	459,700,000,000
2	National defense	348,000,000,000
3	Income security	310,700,000,000
4	Medicare	226,400,000,000
5	Health	195,200,000,000
6	Education, training, employment, and social services	71,700,000,000
7	Transportation	62,100,000,000
8	Administration of justice	34,400,000,000
9	Natural resources and environment	30,200,000,000
10	Agriculture	28,800,000,000

Source: *US Office of Management and Budget*, Budget of the United States Government, Historical Tables

Big Business

GLOBAL INDUSTRIAL COMPANIES

	COMPANY/COUNTRY	SECTOR	REVENUE (2002) ($)
1	**Wal-Mart Stores, Inc.,** US	Retailing	246,525,000,000
2	**General Motors Corp.,** US	Motor vehicles	186,753,000,000
3	**Exxon Mobil,** US	Oil, gas, fuel	182,466,000,000
4	**Royal Dutch/Shell Group,** Netherlands/UK	Oil, gas, chemicals	179,431,000,000
5	**BP plc,** UK	Oil, gas	178,721,000,000
6	**Ford Motor Co.,** US	Motor vehicles	163,871,000,000
7	**DaimlerChrysler AG,** Germany	Motor vehicles	141,421,100,000
8	**Toyota Motor,** Japan	Motor vehicles	131,754,200,000
9	**General Electric,** US	Electronics, electrical equipment	131,698,000,000
10	**Mitsubishi,** Japan,	Motor vehicles	109,386,100,000

Source: Fortune *magazine,* The 2003 Global 500, *July 21, 2003*

Sam Walton opened his first Wal-Mart store in Rogers, Arkansas, in 1962. Since then it has undergone phenomenal growth, becoming the world's No. 1 company. On the day after Thanksgiving, 2001, it achieved the largest single day's sales in retail history, taking $1.25 billion.

SPECIALTY RETAILERS

	COMPANY/COUNTRY	SPECIALTY	RETAIL SALES (2002*) ($)
1	**Home Depot, Inc.,** US	Home improvement supplies	57,247,000,000
2	**Lowe's Companies, Inc.,** US	Home improvement supplies	26,491,000,000
3	**Best Buy Co., Inc.,** US	Consumer electronics	20,946,000,000
4	**Kingsfisher plc,** UK	Home imporovement supplies	16,185,000,000
5	**The Gap, Inc.,** US	Clothing	14,455,000,000
6	**AutoNation, Inc.,** US	Car dealers	13,463,000,000
7	**TJX Companies, Inc.,** US	Clothing and accessories	11,981,000,000
8	**Toys "R" Us, Inc.,** US	Toys	11,305,000,000
9	**IKEA,** Sweden	Home furnishings	10,033,000,000
10	**Circuit City Stores, Inc.,** US	Consumer electronics	9,954,000,000

* Financial year

Source: *Stores Magazine Top 200 Global Retailers*

▼ Retail giant
The world's largest company Wal-Mart's total sales are almost as great as the Gross National Income of Russia. Five descendants of Sam Walton, the company's founder, are each worth $20.5 billion.

TOP 10 | OLDEST ESTABLISHED BUSINESSES IN THE U.S.

	BUSINESS*/LOCATION	BUSINESS	FOUNDED
1	**White Horse Tavern,** Newport, RI	Dining	1673
2	**J.E. Rhoads & Sons,** Branchburg, NJ	Conveyor belts	1702
3	**Wayside Inn,** Sudbury, MA	Inn	1716
4	**Elkridge Furnace Inn,** Elkridge, MD	Inn	1744
5	**Moravian Book Shop,** Bethlehem, PA	Retail, books	1745
6	**Pennsylvania Hospital,** Philadelphia, PA	Hospital	1751
7	**Philadelphia Contributorship,** Philadelphia, PA	Insurance	1752
8	**New Hampshire Gazette,** Portsmouth, NH	Newspaper	1756
9	**Hartford Courant,** Hartford, CT	Newspaper	1764
10	**Bachman Funeral Home,** Strasburg, PA	Funeral home	1769

* Excluding mergers and transplanted companies

Source: *Institute for Family Enterprise, Bryant College*

In addition to these businesses, there are a number of family farming concerns founded in the 17th century, among which the oldest are the Shirley Plantation, Charles City, VA, dating from 1638 and now a historical site, and Tuttle Market Gardens of Dover Point, NH, which dates from 1640. Older than any of these, but not founded in the US, is the Avedis Zildjian Company, a cymbal manufacturer established in Turkey in 1623 and transplanted to Norwell, MA, in 1929.

TOP 10 | GLOBAL RETAILERS

	COMPANY	COUNTRY	RETAIL SALES, (2002*) ($)
1	**Wal-Mart Stores, Inc.**	US	229,617,000,000
2	**Carrefour**	France	65,011,000,000
3	**Home Depot, Inc.**	US	58,247,000,000
4	**Kroger Co.**	US	51,760,000,000
5	**METRO AG**	Germany	48,349,000,000
6	**Target Corp.**	US	42,722,000,000
7	**Ahold**	Netherlands	40,755,000,000
8	**Tesco plc**	UK	40,071,000,000
9	**Costco Wholesale Corp.**	US	37,993,000,000
10	**Sears, Roebuck and Co.**	US	35,698,000,000

* Financial year

Source: *Stores* magazine Top 200 Global Retailers

Each of the world's top 200 retailers achieve sales of $2.4 billion or more. Of them, 42.5 percent are based in the US, but they are responsible for 50.6 per cent of these companies' sales. Total retail sales per capita are highest in Japan at $8,522 per annum, followed by the US at $8,347.

TOP 10 | PRIVATE COMPANIES IN THE U.S.

	COMPANY/LOCATION/SECTOR	REVENUE (2002*) ($)
1	**Cargill,** Minnesota, agricultural products	59,894,000,000
2	**Koch Industries,** Kansas, oil and gas operations	40,000,000,000
3	**Mars,** Virginia, food processing	16,800,000,000
4	**Publix Super Markets,** Florida, grocery retail	16,027,000,000
5	**PricewaterhouseCoopers,** New York, business services	15,900,000,000
6	**Ernst & Young,** New York, business services	13,100,000,000
7	**Bechtel,** California, construction services	11,600,000,000
8	**C&S Wholesale Grocers,** Vermont, grocery retail	11,300,000,000
9	**Meijer,** Michigan, grocery retail	10,900,000,000
10	**HE Butt Grocery,** Texas, grocery retail	10,700,000,000

* Financial years vary

Source: Forbes *magazine,* America's Largest Private Companies, *November 6, 2003*

Founded in Iowa in 1865 by William Wallace Cargill, the company that bears his name started as a grain warehousing business. Today it is involved in over 90 types of enterprise, employing almost 100,000 people in over 60 countries.

TOP 10 | MOST PROFITABLE BANKS

	BANK	COUNTRY	PROFITS ($)
1	**Citigroup**	US	15,276,000,000
2	**Bank of America**	US	9,249,200,000
3	**HSBC Holdings**	UK	6,239,700,000
4	**Wells Fargo**	US	5,434,300,000
5	**Royal Bank of Scotland**	UK	4,619,000,000
6	**Washington Mutual**	US	3,896,500,000
7	**Wachovia Corp.**	US	3,579,000,000
8	**Barclays**	UK	3,351,700,000
9	**Bank One Corp.**	US	3,295,000,000
10	**US Bancorp**	US	3,289,000,000

Source: Fortune *magazine,* The 2003 Global 500, *July 21, 2003*

The world's most profitable bank by a substantial margin, Citigroup began as the City Bank of New York, founded on June 16, 1812 with capital of $2 million. By 1894, it had grown to become the largest bank in the US, and in 1919 the first with assets of $1 billion. Following a series of acquisitions and mergers, it became Citigroup. Inc. in 1998, and today has some 200 million customers worldwide.

Richest by Year 1994–2003

TOP 10 | RICHEST PEOPLE, 1994*

	NAME/COUNTRY	SOURCE	NET WORTH ($)
1	**Bill Gates,** US	Microsoft	12,900,000,000
2	**Warren Buffett,** US	Berkshire Hathaway	10,700,000,000
3 =	**Hans Rausing,** Sweden	Packaging	9,000,000,000
=	**Yoshiaki Tsutsumi,** Japan	Property	9,000,000,000
5	**Paul Sacher,** Switzerland	Roche drug company	8,600,000,000
6	**Tsai Wan-lin family,** Taiwan	Insurance, financial services	8,500,000,000
7 =	**Lee Shau Kee,** Hong Kong	Property	6,500,000,000
=	**Kenneth T. Thomson,** Canada	Publishing	6,500,000,000
9	**Chung Ju-yung,** South Korea	Hyundai	6,200,000,000
10	**Li Ka-shing,** Hong Kong	Property, etc.	5,900,000,000

* Excluding royalty
Source: Forbes magazine, The World's Richest People, 1995

TOP 10 | RICHEST PEOPLE, 1995

	NAME/COUNTRY	SOURCE	NET WORTH ($)
1	**Bill Gates,** US	Microsoft	18,500,000,000
2	**Warren Buffett,** US	Berkshire Hathaway	15,000,000,000
3	**Paul Sacher, Oeri, and Hoffmann family,** Switzerland	Roche drug company	13,000,000,000
4	**Lee Shau Kee,** Hong Kong	Property	12,700,000,000
5	**Tsai Wan-lin family,** Taiwan	Insurance, financial services	12,200,000,000
6	**Kwok brothers,** Hong Kong	Property	11,200,000,000
7	**Li Ka-shing family,** Hong Kong	Property, etc.	10,600,000,000
8	**Yoshiaki Tsutsumi,** Japan	Property, transportation	9,200,000,000
9 =	**Karl and Theo Albrecht,** Germany	Retail	9,000,000,000
=	**Hans and Gad Rausing,** Sweden	Packaging	9,000,000,000

Source: Forbes magazine, The World's Richest People, 1996

TOP 10 | RICHEST PEOPLE, 1998

	NAME/COUNTRY	SOURCE	NET WORTH ($)
1	**Bill Gates,** US	Microsoft	90,000,000,000
2	**Warren Buffett,** US	Berkshire Hathaway	36,000,000,000
3	**Paul Allen,** US	Microsoft	30,000,000,000
4	**Steve Ballmer,** US	Microsoft	19,500,000,000
5	**Oeri, Hoffmann, and Sacher families**	Roche	17,000,000,000
6 =	**Philip F. Anschutz,** Switzerland	Qwest Communications	16,500,000,000
=	**Michael Dell,** US	Dell Computers	16,500,000,000
8	**S. Robson Walton,** US	Wal-Mart	15,800,000,000
9	**Prince Alwaleed Bin Talal Alsaud,** Saudi Arabia	Investments	15,000,000,000
10	**Liliane Bettencourt,** France	L'Oreal	13,900,000,000

Source: Forbes magazine, The World's Richest People, 1999

TOP 10 | RICHEST PEOPLE, 1999

	NAME/COUNTRY	SOURCE	NET WORTH ($)
1	**Bill Gates,** US	Microsoft	60,000,000,000
2	**Larry Ellison,** US	Oracle	47,000,000,000
3	**Paul Allen,** US	Microsoft	28,000,000,000
4	**Warren Buffett,** US	Berkshire Hathaway	25,600,000,000
5 =	**Karl and Theo Albrecht,** Germany	Retail	20,000,000,000
=	**Prince Alwaleed Bin Talal Alsaud,** Saudi Arabia	Investments	20,000,000,000
=	**S. Robson Walton,** US	Wal-Mart	20,000,000,000
8	**Masayoshi Son,** Japan	Softbank	19,400,000,000
9	**Michael Dell,** US	Dell Computers	19,100,000,000
10	**Kenneth T. Thomson,** Canada	Publishing	16,100,000,000

Source: Forbes magazine, The World's Richest People, 2000

◀ **Money, money, money**
Despite fluctuations, over the past decade the level of the wealth of the world's billionaires has increased so much that the total worth of today's Top 10 is four times that of their 1994 counterparts.

 **RICHEST PEOPLE, 1996**

	NAME/COUNTRY	SOURCE	NET WORTH ($)
1	Sultan Hassanal Bolkiah, Brunei	Investments	38,000,000,000
2	Bill Gates, US	Microsoft	36,400,000,000
3	Walton family, US	Walmart	27,600,000,000
4	Warren Buffett, US	Berkshire Hathaway	23,200,000,000
5	King Faud Bin Abdul Aziz Alsaud, Saudi Arabia	Investments	20,000,000,000
6	Suharto, Indonesia	Self-made	16,000,000,000
7	Paul Allen, US	Microsoft	15,314,000,000
8	Sheikh Jaber Al-ahmed Al-jaber Al-sabah, Kuwait	Investments	15,000,000,000
9	Lee Shau Kee, Hong Kong	Property	14,700,000,000
10	Oeri, Hoffmann, and Sacher families, Switzerland	Roche drug company	14,300,000,000

Source: Forbes *magazine*, The World's Richest People, 1997

RICHEST PEOPLE, 1997

	NAME/COUNTRY	SOURCE	NET WORTH ($)
1	Bill Gates, US	Microsoft	51,000,000,000
2	Walton family, US	Walmart	48,000,000,000
3	Sultan Hassanal Bolkiah, Brunei	Investments	36,000,000,000
4	Warren Buffett, US	Berkshire Hathaway	33,000,000,000
5	King Faud Bin Abdul Aziz Alsaud, Saudi Arabia	Investments	25,000,000,000
6	Paul Allen, US	Microsoft	21,000,000,000
7	= Sheikh Zayed Bin Sultan Al Nahyan, UAE	Investments	15,000,000,000
	= Sheikh Jaber Al-ahmed Al-jaber Al-sabah, Kuwait	Investments	15,000,000,000
9	Kenneth T. Thomson, Canada	Publishing	14,400,000,000
10	= Forest Edward Mars Sr. & family, US	Candy	13,500,000,000
	= Jay A. & Robert A. Pritzker, US	Industry	13,500,000,000

Source: Forbes *magazine*, The World's Richest People, 1998

RICHEST PEOPLE, 2000

	NAME/COUNTRY	SOURCE	NET WORTH ($)
1	Bill Gates, US	Microsoft	58,700,000,000
2	Warren Buffett, US	Berkshire Hathaway	32,300,000,000
3	Paul Allen, US	Microsoft	30,400,000,000
4	Larry Ellison, US	Oracle	26,000,000,000
5	Karl and Theo Albrecht, Germany	Retail	25,000,000,000
6	Prince Alwaleed Bin Talal Alsaud, Saudi Arabia	Investments	20,000,000,000
7	Jim C. Walton, US	Wal-Mart	18,800,000,000
8	John T. Walton, US	Wal-Mart	18,700,000,000
9	S. Robson Walton, US	Wal-Mart	18,600,000,000
10	= Alice L. Walton, US	Wal-Mart	18,500,000,000
	= Helen R. Walton, US	Wal-Mart	18,500,000,000

Source: Forbes *magazine*, The World's Richest People, 2001

RICHEST PEOPLE, 2001

	NAME/COUNTRY	SOURCE	NET WORTH ($)
1	Bill Gates, US	Microsoft	52,800,000,000
2	Warren Buffett, US	Berkshire Hathaway	35,000,000,000
3	Karl and Theo Albrecht, Germany	Retail	26,800,000,000
4	Paul Allen, US	Microsoft	25,200,000,000
5	Larry Ellison, US	Oracle	23,500,000,000
6	Jim C. Walton, US	Wal-Mart	20,800,000,000
7	John T. Walton, US	Wal-Mart	20,700,000,000
8	= Alice L. Walton, US	Wal-Mart	20,500,000,000
	= Helen R. Walton, US	Wal-Mart	20,500,000,000
10	S. Robson Walton, US	Wal-Mart	20,400,000,000

Source: Forbes *magazine*, The World's Richest People, 2002

RICHEST PEOPLE, 2002

	NAME/COUNTRY	SOURCE	NET WORTH ($)
1	Bill Gates, US	Microsoft	40,700,000,000
2	Warren Buffett, US	Berkshire Hathaway	30,500,000,000
3	Karl and Theo Albrecht, Germany	Retail	25,600,000,000
4	Paul Allen, US	Microsoft	20,100,000,000
5	Prince Alwaleed Bin Talal Alsaud, Saudi Arabia	Investments	17,700,000,000
6	Larry Ellison, US	Oracle	16,600,000,000
7	= Alice L. Walton, US	Wal-Mart	16,500,000,000
	= Helen R. Walton, US	Wal-Mart	16,500,000,000
	= Jim C. Walton, US	Wal-Mart	16,500,000,000
	= John T. Walton, US	Wal-Mart	16,500,000,000
	= S. Robson Walton, US	Wal-Mart	16,500,000,000

Source: Forbes *magazine*, The World's Richest People, 2003

RICHEST PEOPLE, 2003

	NAME/COUNTRY	SOURCE	NET WORTH ($)
1	Bill Gates, US	Microsoft	46,600,000,000
2	Warren Buffett, US	Berkshire Hathaway	42,900,000,000
3	Karl Albrecht, Germany	Retail	23,000,000,000
4	Prince Alwaleed Bin Talal Alsaud, Saudi Arabia	Investments	21,500,000,000
5	Paul Allen, US	Microsoft	21,000,000,000
6	= Alice L. Walton, US	Wal-Mart	20,000,000,000
	= Helen R. Walton, US	Wal-Mart	20,000,000,000
	= Jim C. Walton, US	Wal-Mart	20,000,000,000
	= John T. Walton, US	Wal-Mart	20,000,000,000
	= S. Robson Walton, US	Wal-Mart	20,000,000,000

Source: Forbes *magazine*, The World's Richest People, 2004

Diamonds & Gold

TOP 10 | LARGEST POLISHED GEM DIAMONDS

	DIAMOND/LAST KNOWN WHEREABOUTS OR OWNER	CARATS
1	**Golden Jubilee,** King of Thailand	545.67
2	**Great Star of Africa/Cullinan I,** British Crown Jewels	530.20
3	**Incomparable/Zale,** auctioned in New York, 1988	407.48
4	**Second Star of Africa/Cullinan II,** British Crown Jewels	317.40
5	**Centenary,** privately owned	273.85
6	**Jubilee,** Paul-Louis Weiller	245.35
7	**De Beers,** sold in Geneva, 1982	234.50
8	**Red Cross,** sold in Geneva, 1973	205.07
9	**De Beers Millennium Star,** De Beers	203.04
10	**Black Star of Africa,** unknown	202.00

Source: De Beers

The De Beers Millennium Star achieved unusual celebrity on November 7, 2000, when it was on display as part of a $500–million collection in the Millennium Dome, Greenwich, London, and armed raiders smashed their way in, intent on stealing it. They were caught by police and have since been jailed, but had they succeeded they would have been disappointed: following a tip-off, all the diamonds had been replaced by replicas.

▼ Diamonds are forever
The stuff of legends and a vital component of many world economies, diamonds have long been regarded as the ultimate symbol of durability and wealth.

TOP 10 | MOST EXPENSIVE SINGLE DIAMONDS SOLD AT AUCTION

	DIAMOND/SALE	PRICE ($)
1	**Star of the Season,** pear-shaped 100.10 carat D* IF[#] diamond Sotheby's, Geneva, May 17, 1995	16,548,750 (SF19,858,500)
2	**The Mouawad Splendor,** pear-shaped 101.84 carat D IF diamond Sotheby's, Geneva, Nov. 14, 1990	12,760,000 (SF15,950,000)
3	**Star of Happiness,** cut cornered rectangular-cut 36 carat D IF diamond Sotheby's, Geneva, Nov. 17, 1993	11,882,333 (SF17,823,500)
4	**Fancy blue emerald-cut** 20.17 carat diamond VS2[#] Sotheby's, New York, Oct. 18, 1994	9,902,500
5	**Eternal Light,** pear-shaped 85.91 carat D IF diamond Sotheby's, New York, Apr. 19, 1988	9,130,000
6	**Rectangular-cut fancy deep-blue** 13.49 carat IF diamond Christie's, New York, Apr. 13, 1995	7,482,500
7	**Rectangular-cut** 52.59 carat D IF diamond Christie's, New York, Apr. 20, 1988	7,480,000
8	**Fancy pink rectangular-cut** 19.66 carat diamond VVS2[#] Christie's, Geneva, Nov. 17, 1994	7,421,318 (SF9,573,500)
9	**The Jeddah Bride,** rectangular-cut 80.02 carat D IF diamond Sotheby's, New York, Oct. 24, 1991	7,150,000
10	**The Agra Diamond,** fancy light pink cushion-shaped 32.24 carat diamond VS1[#] Christie's, London, June 20, 1990	6,959,700 (£4,070,000)

* *A color grade given to a diamond for its whiteness, D being the highest grade*

\# *A clarity grade, which gives the relative position of a diamond on a flawless-to-imperfect scale. IF = internally flawless, VS = very slightly flawed, VVS = very, very slightly flawed. The numbers indicate the degree of the flaw*

Source: Christie's

TOP 10 | DIAMOND PRODUCERS— BY VALUE

	COUNTRY	VALUE (2003) ($)
1	**Botswana**	2,200,000,000
2	**Russia**	1,600,000,000
3	= **South Africa**	1,000,000,000
	= **Canada**	1,000,000,000
	= **Angola**	1,000,000,000
6	**Dem. Rep. of Congo**	600,000,000
7	**Namibia**	450,000,000
8	**Australia**	350,000,000
9	= **Guinea**	100,000,000
	= **Sierra Leone**	100,000,000

Source: De Beers

TOP 10 COUNTRIES MAKING GOLD JEWELRY

	COUNTRY	GOLD USED (2002) (TONS)
1	India	566.6
2	Italy	460.2
3	China	209.4
4	US	169.9
5	Turkey	161.4
6	Saudi Arabia and Yemen	133.4
7	Indonesia	109.5
8	Egypt	83.8
9	Malaysia	75.7
10	South Korea	75.1
	World total	2,964.22

Source: *Gold Fields Mineral Services Ltd, Gold Survey 2003*

TOP 10 GOLD-PRODUCING COUNTRIES

	COUNTRY	PRODUCTION (2002) (TONS)
1	South Africa	435.6
2	US	329.4
3	Australia	290.7
4	China	222.6
5	Russia	199.1
6	Indonesia	174.1
7	Peru	173.4
8	Canada	163.4
9	Uzbekistan	95.5
10	Ghana	77.5
	World total	2,587.0

Source: *Gold Fields Mineral Services Ltd, Gold Survey 2003*

Output by world-leading gold producer South Africa experienced a decline for the ninth consecutive year since its 1993 all-time high of 682.9 tons. Australia's output also fell, after having increased dramatically over recent years. Indonesia and Peru have each escalated production tenfold, while Papua New Guinea's production of 71.8 tons falls only just outside the Top 10.

TOP 10 COUNTRIES WITH THE MOST GOLD

	COUNTRY	GOLD RESERVES* (TROY OUNCES)	(METRIC TONS)
1	US	261,561,245	8,135.4
2	Germany	110,583,365	3,439.5
3	France	97,250,345	3,024.8
4	Italy	78,827,822	2,451.8
5	Switzerland	53,569,996	1,666.2
6	Netherlands	25,736,876	800.5
7	Japan	24,601,945	765.2
8	China	19,300,245	600.3
9	Spain	16,827,833	523.4
10	Portugal	16,628,497	517.2

* As at October 2003

Source: *World Gold Council*

Gold reserves are the government holdings of gold in each country. In the days of the "Gold Standard," this provided a tangible measure of a country's wealth, guaranteeing the convertibility of its currency, and determined such factors as exchange rates. Though less significant today, gold reserves remain a component in calculating a country's international reserves, alongside its holdings of foreign exchange and SDRs (Special Drawing Rights).

▲ **Glittering prize**
Discovered in Moliagul, Australia, in 1869, the almost pure gold 156-lb (70.92-kg) "Welcome Stranger" nugget was the largest ever found.

THE DEEPEST GOLDMINE

FOR THE PAST 30 YEARS, the Western Deep Levels goldmine, South Africa, has been the deepest in the world. It had reached 11,749 ft (3,581 m) by 1977 and is being extended to 12,600 ft (3,841 m) by the end of 2004, with an ultimate target depth of 13,450 ft (4,100 m). Such depths pose great engineering problems: they require very long elevator shafts, but the longer they are, the heavier the ropes required; they currently weigh 77 tons. The temperature this far below the earth's surface is 131°F (55°C), which means that the air has to be refrigerated to make it possible for miners to work there.

IT'S A FACT

Brands & Advertising

TOP 10 MOST VALUABLE GLOBAL BRANDS

	BRAND NAME*	INDUSTRY	BRAND VALUE (2003) ($)
1	Coca-Cola	Beverages	70,450,000,000
2	Microsoft	Technology	65,170,000,000
3	IBM	Technology	51,770,000,000
4	General Electric	Diversified	42,340,000,000
5	Intel	Technology	31,110,000,000
6	Nokia, Finland	Technology	29,440,000,000
7	Disney	Leisure	28,040,000,000
8	McDonald's	Food retail	24,700,000,000
9	Marlboro	Tobacco	22,180,000,000
10	Mercedes, Germany	Automobiles	21,370,000,000

* *US-owned unless otherwise stated*

Source: *Interbrand/BusinessWeek*

Brand consultants Interbrand use a method of estimating value that takes account of the profitability of individual brands within a business (rather than the companies that own them), as well as such factors as their potential for growth. Well over half of the 75 most valuable global brands surveyed by Interbrand are US-owned, with Europe accounting for another 30 percent.

▶ **Sign of the Times**
Formerly Longacre Square, New York's Times Square was renamed 100 years ago, becoming the hub of the city's nightlife and its most garish display of advertising.

TOP 10 CORPORATE ADVERTISERS IN THE U.S.

	COMPANY/HEADQUARTERS	ESTIMATED ADVERTISING SPENDING (2002) ($)
1	General Motors Corp., Detroit	3,652,200,000
2	AOL Time Warner, New York	2,922,800,000
3	Procter & Gamble Co., Cincinnati	2,673,400,000
4	Pfizer, New York	2,566,200,000
5	Ford Motor Co., Dearborn, Michigan	2,251,800.000
6	DaimlerChrysler, Auburn Hills, Michigan/Stuttgart, Germany	2,031,800,000
7	Walt Disney Co., Burbank, California	1,803,000,000
8	Johnson & Johnson, New Brunswick, New Jersey	1,799,000,000
9	Sear, Roebuck and Co., Hoffman Estates, Illinois	1,661,200,000
10	Unilever, London/Rotterdam	1,640,000,000

Source: *Crain Communications Inc./Advertising Age*

TOP 10 GLOBAL MARKETERS

	COMPANY/BASE	MEASURED MEDIA* SPENDING (2002) ($)
1	Procter & Gamble Co., US	4,479,000,000
2	Unilever, Netherlands/UK	3,315,000,000
3	General Motors Corp., US	3,218,000,000
4	Toyota Motor Corp., Japan	2,405,000,000
5	Ford Motor Co., US	2,387,000,000
6	Time Warner, US	2,349,000,000
7	DaimlerChrysler, Germany/US	1,800,000,000
8	L'Oréal, France	1,683,000,000
9	Nestlé, Switzerland	1,547,000,000
10	Sony Corp., Japan	1,513,000,000

* *Includes magazines, newspapers, outdoor, television, radio, Internet, and Yellow Pages*

Source: *Ad Age Global*

TOP 10 MOST TRUSTED BRANDS IN THE U.S.

	BRAND
1	Avis
2	Google.com
3	Sprint long distance
4	Verizon long distance
5	Miller genuine draft
6	Starbucks coffee and doughnuts
7	Samsung cellular telephone
8	Canon office copier
9	Keyspan energy
10	Motorola cellular telephone

Source: 2003 Brand Keys Customer Loyalty Leaders

Brand Keys uses a range of questionnaires and complex statistical methodology to determine loyalty rankings, with the Top 10 representing the leaders in a list of 182 well-known brands.

TOP 10 COUNTRIES IN WHICH COCA-COLA IS THE TOP COLA BRAND

	COUNTRY	PERCENTAGE OF TOTAL STANDARD COLA MARKET
1	Morocco	98.2
2	Indonesia	90.5
3	France	88.6
4	Australia	86.6
5	Chile	85.0
6	Greece	84.7
7	Bulgaria	84.0
8	Switzerland	83.5
9	= Brazil	83.2
	= South Africa	83.2
	US	47.1

Source: *Euromonitor*

TOP 10 COUNTRIES THAT SPEND THE MOST ON ADVERTISING

	COUNTRY	EST. ADVERTISING SPEND (2003) ($)
1	US	144,000,000,000
2	Japan	36,000,000,000
3	Germany	16,000,000,000
4	UK	15,000,000,000
5	China	10,000,000,000
6	France	9,000,000,000
7	Italy	7,000,000,000
8	South Korea	6,000,000,000
9	= Brazil	5,000,000,000
	= Canada	5,000,000,000

Source: *Zenith Optimedia*

Food Favorites

TOP 10 BREAD CONSUMERS

	COUNTRY	CONSUMPTION PER CAPITA (2003) (LB OZ)		(KG)
1	Turkey	393	7	178.6
2	Bulgaria	341	9	155.1
3	Egypt	322	1	146.1
4	Slovakia	320	1	145.2
5	Saudi Arabia	281	8	127.8
6	Romania	231	5	105.0
7	Norway	215	2	97.6
8	Chile	203	7	92.4
9	Poland	193	1	87.6
10	Belgium	183	4	83.2
	World	*39*	*5*	*17.9*
	US	*64*	*6*	*29.3*

Source: *Euromonitor*

◄ **Daily bread**
Mideastern and Eastern European countries lead the world in bread consumption, with the average Turkish citizen eating three times his own weight in bread every year.

TOP 10 RICE CONSUMERS

	COUNTRY	CONSUMPTION PER CAPITA* (2001) (LB OZ)		(KG)
1	Myanmar	651	3	295.4
2	Laos	570	5	258.7
3	Vietnam	552	7	250.6
4	Bangladesh	513	3	232.8
5	Cambodia	491	10	223.0
6	Indonesia	491	6	222.9
7	Thailand	360	0	163.3
8	Guinea-Bissau	345	14	156.9
9	Philippines	336	10	152.7
10	Nepal	330	0	149.7
	World average	*186*	*15*	*84.8*
	US	*30*	*6*	*13.8*

* *Paddy equivalent*

Source: *Food and Agricultural Organization of the United Nations*

TOP 10 FISH CONSUMERS

	COUNTRY	CONSUMPTION PER CAPITA*(2001) (LB OZ)		(KG)
1	Maldives	437	9	198.5
2	Iceland	198	10	90.1
3	Portugal	167	12	76.1
4	Kiribati	166	3	75.4
5	Japan	140	10	63.8
6	Guyana	126	5	57.3
7	= Malaysia	125	3	56.8
	= Seychelles	125	3	56.8
9	Antigua and Barbuda	121	0	54.9
10	= Norway	112	6	51.0
	= South Korea	112	6	51.0
	World average	*34*	*13*	*15.8*
	US	*46*	*11*	*21.2*

* *Marine only*

Source: *Food and Agriculture Organization of the United Nations*

The majority of the fish consumed in the world comes from the sea. The average annual consumption of freshwater fish is 9 lb 11 oz (4.4 kg).

TOP 10 MEAT CONSUMERS

	COUNTRY	CONSUMPTION PER CAPITA (2001) (LB OZ)		(KG)
1	US	267	13	121.5
2	Spain	260	5	118.1
3	Denmark	257	7	116.8
4	= Australia	242	11	110.1
	= Austria	242	11	110.1
6	= Bahamas	229	4	104.0
	= Cyprus	229	4	104.0
8	New Zealand	229	0	103.9
9	France	225	12	102.4
10	Canada	220	0	99.8
	World average	*83*	*15*	*38.1*

Source: *Food and Agriculture Organization of the United Nations*

FOOD ITEMS CONSUMED IN THE U.S.

	ITEM	CONSUMPTION PER CAPITA (2001) (LB OZ)		(KG)
1	Dairy products	587	2	266.3
2	Processed vegetables	216	3	98.1
3	Fresh vegetables	196	6	89.2
4	Flour and cereal products	195	7	88.7
5	Processed fruit	150	0	68.0
6	Caloric sweeteners	147	1	66.7
7	Fresh fruit	125	8	57.1
8	Red meat	111	3	50.5
9	Corn sweeteners	81	4	36.9
10	Fats and oils*	77	0	34.9

Figures for 2000

Source: *US Department of Agriculture, Economic Research Service*

While health concerns have led to a reduction in red meat and whole milk consumption, and an increase in fruit and vegetable intake, overall consumption of dairy products and fats and oils has actually increased.

BAKED BEAN CONSUMERS

	COUNTRY	EST. CONSUMPTION PER CAPITA (2004) (LB OZ)		(KG)
1	Ireland	12	5	5.6
2	UK	10	9	4.8
3	New Zealand	5	1	2.3
4	United States	4	6	2.0
5	Australia	4	3	1.9
6	= France	3	8	1.6
	= Saudi Arabia	3	8	1.6
8	Switzerland	3	5	1.5
9	Ukraine	2	13	1.3
10	= Canada	2	10	1.2
	= Mexico	2	10	1.2

Source: *Euromonitor*

Originating among American colonists, baked beans have become a popular and easy meal the world over, with Ireland and the UK the foremost consumers.

VEGETABLE CONSUMERS

	COUNTRY	CONSUMPTION PER CAPITA (2001) (LB OZ)		(KG)
1	Greece	599	6	271.9
2	United Arab Emirates	566	9	257.0
3	Lebanon	529	5	240.1
4	China	527	12	239.4
5	Libya	523	9	237.5
6	South Korea	505	15	229.5
7	Turkey	504	10	228.9
8	Israel	487	7	221.1
9	Albania	477	11	216.7
10	Kuwait	475	1	215.5
	World average	246	0	111.6
	US	274	7	124.5

Source: *Food and Agricultural Organization of the United Nations*

▶ Fruit and veggies
Year-round availability, rising prosperity, and the recommendation that we should eat five portions of fruit or vegetables per day have resulted in their increased consumption.

Sweet Success

TOP 10 SUGAR CONSUMERS

	COUNTRY	CONSUMPTION PER CAPITA* (2000) (LB OZ)		(KG)
1	United Arab Emirates	553	1	250.87
2	St. Kitts and Nevis	390	2	176.97
3	Israel	353	15	160.56
4	Swaziland	293	15	133.35
5	St. Vincent and the Grenadines	129	0	58.54
6	Cuba	128	2	58.13
7	Trinidad and Tobago	125	8	56.93
8	Austria	121	15	55.32
9	New Zealand	121	4	55.01
10	Barbados	120	14	54.84
	US	66	7	30.15

Refined equivalent

Source: *Food and Agriculture Organization of the United Nations*

TOP 10 CHOCOLATE CONFECTIONERY CONSUMERS

	COUNTRY	CONSUMPTION PER CAPITA (2003*) (LB OZ)		(KG)
1	Switzerland	25	0	11.4
2	UK	20	15	9.5
3	= Belgium	19	2	8.7
	= Germany	19	2	8.7
5	Ireland	17	13	8.1
6	Denmark	17	6	7.9
7	US	13	14	6.3
8	Norway	13	7	6.1
9	Austria	12	6	5.6
10	Poland	11	14	5.4

Source: *Euromonitor*

TOP 10 SUGAR CONFECTIONERY CONSUMERS

	COUNTRY	CONSUMPTION PER CAPITA (2003*) (LB OZ)		(KG)
1	Denmark	19	9	8.9
2	= Finland	14	2	6.4
	= Netherlands	14	2	6.4
4	Sweden	13	4	6.0
5	= Norway	11	7	5.2
	= Russia	11	7	5.2
7	= UK	9	7	4.3
	= Ukraine	9	7	4.3
9	Germany	9	0	4.1
10	US	8	13	4.0

Figures are provisional

Source: *Euromonitor*

TOP 10 CONFECTIONERY BRANDS IN THE U.S.

	BRAND	PERCENTAGE OF MARKET SHARE (2002)
1	M&M's	6.1
2	Reeses	4.7
3	Snickers	4.4
4	Y&S Twizzler	2.2
5	KitKat	2.0
6	Life Savers	1.9
7	= Wrigley's Extra	1.5
	= Hershey's Kisses	1.5
9	= Brach's	1.4
	= Russell Stover	1.4
	= Starburst	1.4

Source: *Euromonitor*

M&M's original Chocolate Candies were launched in 1941. They are said to owe their origin to a visit by Forrest Mars Sr. to Spain, where he saw Spanish Civil War soldiers eating chocolate coated in sugar to prevent it from melting. The product became America's favorite candy brand and was taken into space by NASA astronauts.

THE 10 FIRST MARS PRODUCTS

	PRODUCT	YEAR INTRODUCED
1	= Milky Way bar	1923
	= Snickers bar (non-chocolate)	1923
3	Snickers bar (chocolate)	1930
4	3 Musketeers bar	1932
5	Maltesers	1937
6	Kitekat (cat food; now Whiskas)	1939
7	Mars almond bar	1940
8	M&M's plain chocolate candies	1941
9	Uncle Ben's converted rice	1942
10	= M&M's peanut chocolate candies	1954
	= Pal (dog food)	1954

American candy manufacturer Franklin C. Mars established his first business in Tacoma, WA, in 1911, and formed the Mar-O-Bar company in Minneapolis in 1922 (later moving it to Chicago), with the first of its internationally known products, the Milky Way bar. The founder's son Forrest E. Mars set up in the UK in 1932, merging the firm with its American counterpart in 1964. Confusingly, outside the US, the Milky Way bar is known as a Mars Bar, while in the UK, a Milky Way is a different product.

TOP 10 CANDY MANUFACTURERS IN THE U.S.

	MANUFACTURER	PERCENTAGE OF MARKET SHARE (2002)*
1	Hershey Foods Corp.	23.3
2	Mars, Inc.	18.7
3	William Wrigley Jr. Co.	4.9
4	Nestlé USA, Inc.	4.7
5	= Kraft Foods, Inc.	2.6
	= Warner-Lambert Co.	2.6
7	Russell Stover Candies	2.0
8	Brach & Brock Confections, Inc.	1.8
9	General Mills, Inc.	1.6
10	Tootsie Roll Industries, Inc.	1.5

Based on dollar sales volume

Source: *Euromonitor*

TOP 10 ICE CREAM CONSUMERS

	COUNTRY	CONSUMPTION PER CAPITA (2003)	
		PINTS	LITERS
1	Australia	44.2	20.9
2	New Zealand	33.4	15.8
3	US	33.0	15.6
4	Sweden	28.5	13.5
5	Canada	26.6	12.6
6	Ireland	24.7	11.7
7	Norway	24.3	11.5
8	Finland	23.2	11.0
9	Denmark	20.3	9.6
10	Germany	20.1	9.5

Source: *Euromonitor*

◀ **Sundae best**
Total global sales of ice cream in 2003 were estimated at 32,374,504,440 pints (15,318,682,900 liters), equal to an average of 5 pints (2.4 liters) for everyone on the planet.

CONE CONTROVERSY!

THE IDENTITY OF THE INVENTOR of the ice-cream cone is disputed. Cones were sold at the St. Louis World's Fair in 1904. There, Ernest A. Hamwi, a Syrian pastry maker, was selling a waffle called a zalabia. When a nearby ice-cream vendor, Charles Menches, ran out of bowls, he used Hamwi's zalabia to serve his product. However, New York ice-cream maker Italo Marchiony, who was also at the Fair, had been granted a patent for a mold to make cones the previous year, and claimed to have been selling ice-cream cones since 1896.

THE FIRST TO...

Beverage Report

▼ A heady brew

With the honorable exception of Australia, the world's top beer-drinkers are all Europeans with a long tradition of brewing.

TOP 10 BEER DRINKERS

	COUNTRY	CONSUMPTION PER CAPITA (2001) (GALLONS)	(LITERS)
1	Czech Republic	41.8	158.1
2	Ireland	39.8	150.8
3	Germany	32.5	123.1
4	Austria	28.2	106.9
5	Luxembourg	26.7	100.9
6	Denmark	26.0	98.6
7	Belgium	25.9	98.0
8	UK	25.7	97.1
9	Australia	24.6	93.0
10	Slovak Republic	22.8	86.4*

* Estimated from beer production data due to lack of consumption data

Source: *Commission for Distilled Spirits*

Despite being the world's leading beer producer, the US is ranked 11th in terms of consumption. While no African countries appear above, many Africans do drink beer—usually brews that are made and sold locally, and hence excluded from national statistics.

TOP 10 TEA DRINKERS

	COUNTRY	ANNUAL CONSUMPTION PER CAPITA* (LB OZ)		(KG)	(CUPS#)
1	Iraq	6	2	2.77	1,219
2	Ireland	6	1	2.76	1,214
3	Libya	5	7	2.61	1,148
4	Qatar	5	1	2.29	1,008
5	UK	4	15	2.26	994
6	Turkey	4	7	2.01	884
7	Kuwait	4	5	1.97	867
8	Iran	3	4	1.48	651
9	= Afghanistan	3	1	1.39	612
	= Morocco	3	1	1.39	612
	US	0	11	0.33	145

* 2000–2002

 # Based on 440 cups per kilogram (2 lb 3 oz)

Source: *International Tea Committee Ltd., London*

Despite the UK's traditional passion for tea, over recent years its consumption has consistently lagged behind that of Ireland.

TOP 10 CHAMPAGNE IMPORTERS

	COUNTRY	BOTTLES IMPORTED (2003)
1	UK	34,465,159
2	US	18,957,031
3	Germany	12,053,665
4	Belgium	9,143,810
5	Italy	8,506,287
6	Switzerland	5,596,549
7	Japan	5,013,705
8	Netherlands	2,575,838
9	Spain	2,158,056
10	Australia	1,659,441

Source: *Comité Interprofessionnel du Vin de Champagne (CIVC)*

TOP 10 COFFEE DRINKERS

	COUNTRY	CONSUMPTION PER CAPITA (2002) (LB OZ)		(KG)	(CUPS*)
1	Finland	24	12	11.24	1,686
2	Denmark	20	3	9.16	1,374
3	Norway	20	2	9.15	1,372
4	Belgium and Luxembourg	19	14	9.03	1,354
5	Sweden	18	6	8.33	1,249
6	Austria	15	10	7.10	1,065
7	Switzerland	14	15	6.78	1,017
8	Germany	14	8	6.59	988
9	Netherlands	13	7	6.10	915
10	France	12	3	5.54	831
	US	8	10	3.94	591

* Based on 150 cups per kilogram (2 lb 3 oz)

Source: *International Coffee Organization*

 BOTTLED WATER DRINKERS

COUNTRY	CONSUMPTION PER CAPITA (2003) (GALLONS)	(LITERS)
1 Italy	46.8	177.1
2 Spain	41.4	156.7
3 France	40.3	152.5
4 Mexico	40.2	152.1
5 Belgium	34.7	130.1
6 Germany	31.3	118.6
7 Switzerland	29.6	112.0
8 Austria	25.9	98.0
9 Portugal	25.6	96.8
10 Argentina	21.5	81.4
World average	6.0	22.9
US	18.9	71.6

Source: *Euromonitor*

Worldwide consumption of bottled mineral water has more than doubled in the past decade, hitting a 2003 total of 38 billion gallons.

 CARBONATED SOFT DRINK CONSUMERS

COUNTRY	CONSUMPTION PER CAPITA (2003) (GALLONS)	(LITERS)
1 US	51.7	195.8
2 Mexico	33.3	126.0
3 Norway	32.2	122.0
4 Ireland	32.0	121.4
5 Canada	30.9	117.1
6 Belgium	28.9	109.3
7 Australia	27.3	103.2
8 Netherlands	26.4	99.8
9 Chile	26.3	99.7
10 Spain	26.0	98.3
World average	7.5	28.5

Source: *Euromonitor*

In 2003, the worldwide consumption of soft drinks was 47.4 billion gallons—equivalent to almost 60,000 Olympic swimming pools!

▼ **Soft sell**
Invented over 200 years ago, carbonated drinks became a major global industry in the 20th century, now worth over $200 billion a year.

TOP 10 WINE PRODUCERS

COUNTRY	PRODUCTION (1999) GALLONS	LITERS
1 France	1,609,732,000	6,093,500,000
2 Italy	1,535,104,000	5,811,000,000
3 Spain	972,206,000	3,680,200,000
4 US	546,598,000	2,069,100,000
5 Argentina	419,717,000	1,588,800,000
6 Germany	323,452,000	1,224,400,000
7 Australia	224,837,000	851,100,000
8 South Africa	210,492,000	796,800,000
9 Portugal	206,213,000	780,600,000
10 Romania	17,1816,000	650,400,000

Source: *Commission for Distilled Spirits*

The rise of New World and Southern Hemisphere wine-producing countries is the most notable development in recent years, ending the centuries-old domination of the winemaking industry by the vineyards of France, Italy, and Spain.

Mail & Phone

COUNTRIES RECEIVING THE MOST LETTERS FROM ABROAD

	COUNTRY	ITEMS OF MAIL RECEIVED (2002)*
1	US	541,200,000
2	France	468,300,000
3	UK	388,717,500
4	India	346,800,000
5	Netherlands	294,000,000
6	Saudi Arabia	269,568,000
7	Japan	262,264,000
8	Italy	218,826,373
9	Mexico	187,542,803
10	Australia	148,377,000

* Or latest year for which data available

Source: Universal Postal Union

LETTER-MAILING COUNTRIES

	COUNTRY	AVERAGE NO. OF LETTER POST ITEMS MAILED PER INHABITANT (2002*)
1	Vatican City	7,200.00
2	US	659.99
3	Norway	546.85
4	Liechtenstein	473.07
5	France	447.57
6	Luxembourg	428.57
7	Finland	371.99
8	UK	354.27
9	Slovenia	305.94
10	Iceland	239.20

* In those countries for which data available

Or latest year for which data available,

Source: Universal Postal Union

▼ **Mail drop**
Since the introduction of email, traditional "snail mail" has steadily declined, but the world still sends over 424 billion domestic and 6.7 billion international letters a year.

OLDEST POST OFFICES IN THE U.S.

	CITY	POST OFFICE ADDRESS	OPENED
1	Galena, IL	110 Green Street	Nov. 1, 1858
2	Memphis, TN	1 N. Front Street	June 1, 1887
3	Brooklyn, NY	271 Cadman Plaza East	Feb. 1, 1892
4	Hoboken, NJ	89 River Street	Jan. 1, 1893
5	Port Townsend, WA	1322 Washington Street	June 1, 1893
6	Atchison, KS	621 Kansas Avenue	June 1, 1894
7	Mankato, MN	401 S. Second Street	June 1, 1895
8	Pueblo, CO	421 N. Main Street	Jan. 1, 1898
9	Omaha, NE	4730 S. 24th Street	June 1, 1898
10	Carrollton, KY	520 Highland Avenue	June 1, 1901

Source: *United States Postal Service*

Galena Post Office and Customs House, which was founded by Galena Congressman Elihu B. Washburne, was the first to be named by the Smithsonian Institution as a "Great American Post Office." It is an unspoiled example of a mid-19th-century post office, replete with elegant mahogany counters and marble flooring. While it is identified by the US Postal Service as its oldest, offices in Castine, Maine, and Windsor, Vermont, claim even earlier foundation dates.

COUNTRIES WITH THE HIGHEST RATIO OF CELL PHONE USERS

	COUNTRY	SUBSCRIBERS (2002)	CELL PHONES PER 100 INHABITANTS (2002)
1	Luxembourg	473,000	106.50
2	Taiwan	23,905,000	106.15
3	Israel	6,334,000	95.45
4	Hong Kong	6,396,000	94.25
5	Italy	53,003,000	93.87
6	Iceland	261,000	90.60
7	Sweden	7,949,999	88.89
8	Finland	4,517,000	86.74
9	Greece	9,314,000	84.54
10	Norway	3,840,000	84.36
	US	140,767,000	48.81

Source: *International Telecommunication Union*, World Telecommunication Development Report, *2003*

The past 20 years has seen a revolution in the use of cell phones around the world, of which these countries are the leaders—with some having more subscribers than inhabitants. Relatively large numbers are also encountered as a proportion of total subscribers in certain developing countries, where cell phones are preferred over often antiquated and unreliable wireline networks.

COUNTRIES WITH THE MOST TELEPHONES

	COUNTRY	TELEPHONE LINES (2002)
1	China	214,420,000
2	US	186,232,300
3	Japan	71,149,000
4	Germany	53,720,000
5	India	41,420,000
6	Brazil	38,810,000
7	Russia	35,500,000
8	UK	34,898,000
9	France	33,928,700
10	Italy	27,142,000

Source: *International Telecommunication Union*, World Telecommunication Development Report, *2003*

It is estimated that there are some 1,091,575,700 telephone lines in use in the world, of which 329,462,500 are in Europe, 293,448,800 in North and South America, 433,647,800 in Asia, 22,356,500 in Africa, and 12,660,100 in Oceania.

COUNTRIES WITH THE MOST PUBLIC TELEPHONES

	COUNTRY	PUBLIC TELEPHONES PER 1,000 PEOPLE (2002*)
1	South Korea	10.83
2	United Arab Emirates	8.11
3	Brazil	7.87
4	China	7.67
5	Mexico	7.05
6	Malaysia	6.84
7	Taiwan	5.99
8	Greece	5.72
9	Argentina	5.64
10	Japan	5.63
	US	4.86

* Or latest year for which data available

Source: *International Telecommunication Union*, World Telecommunication Development Report, *2003*

World Wide Web

TOP 10 ONLINE LANGUAGES

	LANGUAGE	INTERNET ACCESS*
1	English	280,000,000
2	Chinese	170,000,000
3	Japanese	88,000,000
4	Spanish	70,000,000
5	German	62,000,000
6	Korean	43,000,000
7	French	41,000,000
8	Portuguese	32,000,000
9	Italian	30,000,000
10	Russian	23,000,000
	World total	940,000,000

* Online population estimate for 2004

Source: Global Reach

TOP 10 MOST SEARCHED TERMS OF ALL TIME ON LYCOS

	TERM	WEEKS ON LIST*
1	= Britney Spears	235
	= Dragonball	235
	= Jennifer Lopez	235
	= Las Vegas	235
	= Pamela Anderson	235
	= WWF	235
7	= Final Fantasy	232
	= The Bible	232
9	Tattoos	199
10	Harry Potter	188

* Continuous runs only; as of Feb. 14, 2004

Source: Lycos 50

TOP 10 COUNTRIES WITH THE MOST INTERNET USERS

	COUNTRY	ESTIMATED NO. OF INTERNET USERS (2002)
1	US	182,130,000
2	Japan	56,000,000
3	China	45,800,000
4	Germany	44,130,000
5	UK	34,300,000
6	South Korea	25,600,000
7	France	21,760,000
8	Italy	19,250,000
9	Russia	18,000,000
10	Canada	16,840,000
	World total	580,000,000

Source: CyberAtlas/Nielsen/NetRatings/CIA World Factbook

TOP 10 MOST POPULAR SEARCH ENGINES

	SEARCH ENGINE	PERCENTAGE OF VISITS*
1	Google	13.0
2	Yahoo! Search	10.1
3	MSN Search	7.4
4	Excite	1.3
5	Netscape	1.2
6	iWon	1.1
7	= Ask Jeeves	1.0
	= Google Image Search	0.7
9	Yahoo! Directory	0.6
10	Netscape White Pages	0.5

* Share of visits to both search and portal websties during September 2003; US traffic only

Source: *Hitwise.com/SearchEngineWatch.com*

◄ **Cyber café**
The arrival of Internet cafés in 1994 heralded a new era of communications and information gathering for people on the move, those lacking personal Internet access, or as a social activity.

THE WEB INVENTOR

WHEN OXFORD GRADUATE Tim Berners-Lee was working for CERN (the European Particle Physics Laboratory) in 1980, he investigated ways of accessing information on other computers, developing a pioneering program called "Enquire." However, "browsing" was almost impossible until 1989, when Berners-Lee devised the World Wide Web. This was so named after other names, such as "The Information Mine" (TIM), were rejected. CERN made the Internet available for public use and, rather than earn a potential fortune by patenting his invention, Berners-Lee made it freely available.

IT'S A FACT

TOP 10 INTERNET FRAUDS

	CATEGORY	PERCENTAGE OF ALL COMPLAINTS (2003)
1	Online auctions	89
2	General merchandise	5
3	Nigerian money offers	2
4	= Information/adult services	1
	Internet access services	1
6	= Computer equipment/software	0.2
	= Fake checks	0.2
	= Lotteries	0.2
	= Work-at-home plans	0.2
10	Advance-fee loans	0.1

Source: *National Fraud Information Center, National Consumers League*

The average loss in the USA to Internet fraud in 2003 per victim was $527. The Nigerian money offer, also known as "Advance fee fraud" or "4-1-9" (after the section of the Nigerian penal code that addresses it), has spread internationally and become so serious that the United States Secret Service devotes considerable resources to combating it – see: http://www.secretservice.gov/alert419.shtml

TOP 10 PARENT COMPANIES FOR U.S. WEB ACCESS

	PARENT COMPANY	EST. UNIQUE AUDIENCE*
1	Microsoft	93,672,000
2	Time Warner	82,530,000
3	Yahoo!	79,603,000
4	Google	47,427,000
5	eBay	45,698,000
6	United States Government	36,364,000
7	RealNetworks	26,125,000
8	Amazon	24,417,000
9	InterActiveCorp	22,870,000
10	Terra Lycos	22,113,000

* February 2004; home users only

Source: *Nielsen/NetRatings*

This list ranks the number of home users according to their unique (i.e., unduplicated) visits to at least one of the Internet sites owned by each parent company (defined as "a consolidation of multiple domains and URLs owned by a single entity") during a single month. Users spent an average of anything from 1 hr 32 min 48 sec (Microsoft) down to 9 min 10 sec (Terra Lycos) at one or more of the sites within the ownership of the company.

TOP 10 INTERNET-USING COUNTRIES

	COUNTRIES	USERS	USERS PER 100 INHABITANTS (2002)
1	Iceland	187,000	64.79
2	Sweden	5,125,000	57.31
3	South Korea	8,590,000	55.19
4	US	159,000,000	55.14
5	= Canada	16,110,000	51.28
	= Denmark	2,756,000	51.28
7	Finland	2,650,000	50.89
8	Netherlands	8,200,000	50.63
9	Singapore	2,100,000	50.44
10	Norway	2,288,000	50.26
	World average	*623,023,000*	*10.22*

Source: *International Telecommunication Union*, World Telecommunication Development Report, 2003

Energy Levels

TOP 10 | ENERGY-CONSUMING COUNTRIES

| COUNTRY | ENERGY CONSUMPTION (2002)* | | | | | |
	OIL	GAS	COAL	NUCLEAR	HEP[#]	TOTAL
1 **US**	894.3	600.7	553.8	185.8	58.2	2,293.0
2 **China**	245.7	27.0	663.4	5.9	55.8	997.8
3 **Russia**	122.9	349.6	98.5	32.0	37.2	640.2
4 **Japan**	242.6	69.7	105.3	71.3	20.5	509.4
5 **Germany**	127.2	74.3	84.6	37.3	5.9	329.4
6 **India**	97.7	25.4	180.8	4.4	16.9	325.1
7 **Canada**	89.7	72.6	30.7	17.0	78.6	288.7
8 **France**	92.8	38.5	12.7	98.9	15.0	258.0
9 **UK**	77.2	85.1	36.5	19.9	1.7	220.3
10 **South Korea**	105.0	23.6	49.1	27.0	1.2	205.8
World total	3,522.5	2,282.0	2,397.9	610.6	592.1	9,405.0

* *Millions of metric tons of oil equivalent*

[#] *Hydroelectric power*

Source: BP Statistical Review of World Energy 2003

▼ **Oil and water**
As land sites are exhausted and the demand for oil continues to escalate, increasing numbers of offshore oil rigs have been brought into use.

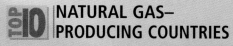

NATURAL GAS–PRODUCING COUNTRIES

COUNTRY	PRODUCTION (2002) (METRIC TONS OF OIL EQUIVALENT)
1 Russia	554,900,000
2 US	547,700,000
3 Canada	183,500,000
4 UK	103,100,000
5 Algeria	80,400,000
6 Indonesia	70,600,000
7 Norway	65,400,000
8 Iran	64,500,000
9 Netherlands	59,900,000
10 Saudi Arabia	56,400,000
World total	2,527,600,000

Source: BP Statistical Review of World Energy 2003

Russia saw its first increase in natural gas production for several years in 2002 as the huge Zapolyarnoye field was brought online. Norwegian output expanded by 21.4 percent as production in the UK and the Netherlands declined.

COUNTRIES WITH THE MOST NUCLEAR REACTORS

COUNTRY	REACTORS
1 US	104
2 France	59
3 Japan	54
4 Russia	30
5 UK	27
6 Germany	19
7 South Korea	18
8 Canada	16
9 India	14
10 Ukraine	13

Source: *International Atomic Energy Agency*

There are some 440 nuclear power stations in operation in a total of 32 countries around the world, with a further 32 under construction.

OIL-PRODUCING COUNTRIES

COUNTRY	PRODUCTION (2002) (METRIC TONS)
1 Saudi Arabia	418,100,000
2 Russia	379,600,000
3 United States	350,400,000
4 Mexico	178,400,000
5 China	168,900,000
6 Iran	166,800,000
7 Norway	157,400,000
8 Venezuela	151,400,000
9 Canada	135,600,000
10 UK	115,900,000
World total	3,556,800,000

Source: BP Statistical Review of World Energy 2003

Restrictions on output by Iraq and a reduction in production by OPEC member countries were countered in 2002 by substantial increases by Canada—up by 170,000 barrels a day—and by oil producers falling outside the Top 10, such as Angola and Brazil.

NATURAL GAS–CONSUMING COUNTRIES

COUNTRY	CONSUMPTION (2002) (METRIC TONS OF OIL EQUIVALENT)
1 United States	600,700,000
2 Russia	349,600,000
3 UK	85,100,000
4 Germany	74,300,000
5 Canada	72,600,000
6 Japan	69,700,000
7 Ukraine	62,800,000
8 Iran	61,100,000
9 Italy	57,200,000
10 Saudi Arabia	50,800,000
World total	2,282,000,000

Source:BP Statistical Review of World Energy 2003

World consumption of natural gas grew by 2.8 percent in 2002, with a figure of 3.9 percent in the US. Even higher increases of up to 7 percent were experienced in the non-OECD Asian Pacific region.

COAL-CONSUMING COUNTRIES

COUNTRY	CONSUMPTION (2002) (METRIC TONS OF OIL EQUIVALENT)
1 China	663,400,000
2 United States	553,800,000
3 India	180,800,000
4 Japan	105,300,000
5 Russia	98,500,000
6 Germany	84,600,000
7 South Africa	81,800,000
8 Poland	56,400,000
9 Australia	49,500,000
10 South Korea	49,100,000
World total	2,397,900,000

Source: BP Statistical Review of World Energy 2003

The rapid expansion of China's economy and industrial output meant that in 2002 the country's coal consumption increased by a remarkable 27.9 percent, thereby escalating the overall world figure by 6.9 percent.

OIL-CONSUMING COUNTRIES

COUNTRY	CONSUMPTION (2002) (METRIC TONS)
1 US	894,300,000
2 China	245,700,000
3 Japan	242,600,000
4 Germany	127,200,000
5 Russia	122,900,000
6 South Korea	105,000,000
7 India	97,700,000
8 Italy	92,900,000
9 France	92,800,000
10 Canada	89,700,000
World total	3,522,500,000

Source: BP Statistical Review of World Energy 2003

Environmental Issues

WIND-POWER GENERATING COUNTRIES

	COUNTRY	CAPACITY (MEGAWATTS) (2003*)
1	Germany	12,836
2	Spain	5,060
3	US	4,685
4	Denmark	2,916
5	India	1,702
6	Netherlands	803
7	Italy	800
8	UK	586
9	China	468
10	Japan	415

* 2002 data for non-European countries

Source: *American Wind Energy Association/European Wind Energy Association*

▼ Catching the sun
Technological advances and price drops are starting to make solar panels viable as an alternative and environmentally friendly source of renewable energy.

ALTERNATIVE POWER–CONSUMING COUNTRIES

	COUNTRY	CONSUMPTION* KW/HR (2001)
1	US	84,800,000,000
2	Germany	22,600,000,000
3	Japan	19,100,000,000
4	Brazil	14,800,000,000
5	Philippines	12,200,000,000
6	Spain	9,200,000,000
7	Finland	8,400,000,000
8	= Italy	7,800,000,000
	= Luxembourg	7,800,000,000
10	Canada	7,200,000,000
	World total	251,100,000,000

* Includes geothermal, solar, wind, wood, and waste electric power

Source: *Energy Information Administration*

PAPER-RECYCLING COUNTRIES (PER CAPITA)

	COUNTRY	PRODUCTION PER 1,000 PEOPLE 2002 (TONS)
1	Sweden	185.28
2	Switzerland	178.25
3	Austria	168.44
4	Belgium	168.31
5	Netherlands	163.52
6	Germany	161.84
7	US	158.92
8	Finland	149.52
9	South Korea	139.54
10	Japan	128.28
	World average	22.65

Source: *Food and Agriculture Organization of the United Nations*

With paper comprising up to 40 percent of municipal waste, recycling preserves trees and reduces not only energy and water consumption, but also the pollution caused by creating new paper.

TOP 10 CARBON DIOXIDE–EMITTING COUNTRIES

COUNTRY	EMISSIONS PER CAPITA, 2001 (METRIC TONS OF CARBON)
1 Qatar	13.66
2 United Arab Emirates	13.31
3 Bahrain	9.47
4 Kuwait	8.32
5 Singapore	7.57
6 Trinidad and Tobago	6.25
7 Luxembourg	5.61
8 US	5.51
9 Canada	5.22
10 Guam	5.18
World average	1.07

Source: *Energy Information Administration*

Carbon dioxide emissions derive from three principal sources— fossil fuel burning, cement manufacturing, and gas flaring. Since World War II, increasing industrialization in many countries has resulted in huge increases in carbon output, a trend that most countries are now actively attempting to reverse.

TOP 10 FRESH-WATER CONSUMING COUNTRIES

COUNTRY	ANNUAL FRESH-WATER WITHDRAWALS (CUBIC METERS)*
1 China	525,500,000,000
2 India	500,000,000,000
3 US	467,300,000,000
4 Pakistan	155,600,000,000
5 Japan	91,400,000,000
6 Mexico	77,800,000,000
7 Russia	77,100,000,000
8 Indonesia	74,300,000,000
9 Iran	70,000,000,000
10 Egypt	66,000,000,000

* In latest year for which data available

Source: *World Bank,* World Development Indicators 2003

Water is used for agricultural, as well as for industrial and domestic purposes. In the cases of China, India, and the US, agriculture consumes 78, 92, and 42 percent of the total, respectively.

TOP 10 GARBAGE PRODUCING COUNTRIES

COUNTRY*	DOMESTIC WASTE PER HEAD (2000#) (LB)	(KG)
1 Denmark	1,278	580
2 Netherlands	1,168	530
3 Luxembourg	1,124	510
4 UK	1,058	480
5 US	1,014	460
6 = Belgium	992	450
= Switzerland	992	450
8 Germany	879	430
9 Australia	881	400
10 = Austria	837	380
= New Zealand	837	380

* In those countries for which data available

Or latest year for which data available

Source: *Organisation for Economic Co-Operation and Development*

THE 10 COUNTRIES PRODUCING THE MOST ELECTRICITY FROM NUCLEAR SOURCES

COUNTRY	NUCLEAR POWER STATIONS IN OPERATION	NUCLEAR AS % OF TOTAL	OUTPUT (MEGAWATT-HOURS)
1 US	104	20.3	98,230
2 France	59	78.0	63,073
3 Japan	54	36.1	44,287
4 Germany	19	29.9	21,283
5 Russia	30	16.0	20,793
6 South Korea	18	38.6	14,890
7 UK	27	22.4	12,052
8 Canada	16	12.3	11,323
9 Ukraine	13	45.7	11,207
10 Sweden	11	45.7	9,432
World total	440	100.0	360,431

Source: *International Atomic Energy Agency*

If ranked according to reliance on nuclear power, Lithuania would head the list, with 80.1 percent of its electricity derived from nuclear sources, with France at 78.0 percent and the UK and US at a lowly 22.4 and 20.3 percent, respectively.

Hazards at Work

THE 10 MOST DANGEROUS OCCUPATIONS IN THE U.S.

OCCUPATION	FATALITIES PER 100,000 EMPLOYEES (2002)*
1 Timber cutters	117.8
2 Fishers	71.1
3 Pilots and navigators	69.8
4 Structural metal workers	58.2
5 Drivers—sales workers	37.9
6 Roofers	37.0
7 Electrical power installers	32.5
8 Farm occupations	28.0
9 Construction laborers	27.7
10 Truck drivers	25.0

* Occupations with a minimum of 30 fatalities and 45,000 workers

Source: Bureau of Labor Statistics

THE 10 MOST COMMON CAUSES OF WORK INJURIES IN THE U.S.

EVENT/EXPOSURE	NONFATAL CASES (2001)* TOTAL	RATE PER 10,000 EMPLOYEES
1 Overexertion in lifting	227,300	25.0
2 Struck by object	199,900	22.0
3 Fall on same level	182,600	20.1
4 Overexertion (except lifting)	181,700	20.0
5 Struck against object	101,200	11.1
6 Fall to lower level	96,400	10.6
7 Exposure to harmful substances	68,300	7.5
8 = Caught in equipment or object	67,300	7.4
= Transportation accidents	66,800	7.4
10 Repetitive motion	65,200	7.2

* Requiring days away from work

Source: Bureau of Labor Statistics

◀ **Danger on deck**
Deep sea fishing is ranked among the most hazardous of all jobs. Although relatively small numbers are involved in the industry, fishing boats are vulnerable to storms—and workers to such risks as being swept overboard.

THE 10 | WORST INDUSTRIAL DISASTERS*

LOCATION/DATE/INCIDENT	FATALITIES
1 Bhopal, India, Dec. 3, 1984 Methyl isocyanate gas escape at Union Carbide plant	3,849
2 Jesse, Nigeria, Oct. 17, 1998 Oil pipeline explosion	more than 700
3 Oppau, Germany, Sept.21, 1921 Chemical plant explosion	561
4 San Juanico, Mexico, Nov. 19, 1984 Explosion at a PEMEX liquified petroleum gas plant	540
5 Cubatão, Brazil, Feb. 25, 1984 Oil pipeline explosion	508
6 Durunkah, Egypt, Nov. 2, 1994 Fuel storage depot fire	more than 500
7 Novosibirsk, USSR, Apr. 1979 (precise date unknown) Anthrax infection following an accident at a biological and chemical warfare plant	up to 300
8 Adeje, Nigeria, July 10, 2000 Oil pipeline explosion	more than 250
9 Guadalajara, Mexico, Apr. 22, 1992 Explosions caused by a gas leak into sewers	230
10 Ludwigshafen, Germany, July 28, 1948 Dimethyl ether explosion in a lacquer plant	184

* *Including industrial sites, factories, and fuel depots and pipelines; excluding military, munitions, bombs, mining, marine and other transportation disasters, dam failures, and mass poisonings*

Officially, the meltdown of the nuclear reactor in Chernobyl, Ukraine, on April 26, 1986 caused the immediate death of 31 people, but it has been suggested that by 1992 some 6,000 to 8,000 people had died as a result of radioactive contamination, a toll that will continue to rise for many years. Extending the parameters of "industrial" to include construction work, as many as 25,000 workers may have died during the building of the Panama Canal in the period 1881–1914, largely as a result of diseases such as yellow fever, malaria, and cholera, while the building of the Madeira-Mamore railroads in Brazil (1870–1912) resulted in over 6,000 deaths from disease, poison arrow attacks, and snakebites. The boring of the Gauley Bridge Water Tunnel in West Virginia killed some 476 workers in 1935 as a result of inhalation of silica dust, with perhaps 1,500 becoming disabled.

THE 10 | WORST MINING DISASTERS

	LOCATION/DATE	FATALITIES
1	**Honkeiko,** China, Apr. 26, 1942	1,549
2	**Courrières,** France, Mar. 10, 1906	1,060
3	**Omuta,** Japan, Nov. 9, 1963	447
4	**Senghenydd,** UK, Oct.14, 1913	439
5	**= Coalbrook,** South Africa, Jan. 21, 1960	437
	= Hokkaido, Japan, Dec. 1, 1914	437
7	**Wankie,** Rhodesia, June 6, 1972	427
8	**Tsinan,** China, May 13, 1935	400
9	**Dhanbad,** India, May 28, 1965	375
10	**Chasnala,** India, Dec. 27, 1975	372

A mine disaster at the Fushun mines, Manchuria, on February 12, 1931 may have resulted in up to 3,000 deaths, but information was suppressed by the Chinese government. Soviet security was responsible for obscuring details of an explosion at the East German Johanngeorgendstadt uranium mine, November 29, 1949, when as many as 3,700 may have died. The two worst disasters both resulted from underground explosions: a large numbers of the deaths among mine workers have resulted from that cause, and from asphyxiation by poisonous gases.

THE 10 | MOST COMMON CAUSES OF DEATH AT WORK IN THE U.S.

INJURY EVENT/EXPOSURE	FATALITIES (2002)
1 Highway transportation: collision between moving vehicles	635
2 Fall to lower level	634
3 Homicide (includes 469 shootings)	609
4 Worker struck by a vehicle	356
5 Highway: vehicle struck stationary object or equipment	326
6 Transportation on farm/industrial premises	322
7 Highway transportation: jackknifed or overturned (no collision)	312
8 Struck by falling object	303
9 Contact with electric current	289
10 Caught in or compressed by equipment or machinery	231
Total fatalities in 2002	5,524

Source: *Bureau of Labor Statistics*, National Census of Fatal Occupational Injuries, 2002

TRANSPORTATION & TOURISM

On the Road

TOP 10 MOTOR VEHICLE MANUFACTURERS

	MANUFACTURER	MOTOR VEHICLE PRODUCTION* (2002)
1	General Motors	8,325,835
2	Ford	6,729,499
3	Toyota–Daihatsu–Hino	6,626,387
4	Volkswagen Group	5,017,438
5	DaimlerChrysler	4,456,325
6	PSA Peugeot Citroën	3,262,146
7	Honda	2,988,427
8	Nissan–Nissan Diesel	2,718,828
9	Hyundai–Kia	2,641,825
10	Renault–Dacia–Samsung	2,328,508

* Includes cars, light trucks, heavy trucks, and buses
Source: *OICA Correspondents Survey*

Overall world production in 2002 was estimated at 58,954,220 vehicles, with the top three manufacturers making 36.8 percent of the world total. US car companies were responsible for 12,279,582 vehicles, compared with Europe's 19,929,073 and Asia/Oceania's 20,015,264.

TOP 10 OFF-ROAD VEHICLES IN THE U.S.

	VEHICLE	SALES (2003)
1	Explorer	268,644
2	Grand Cherokee	207,479
3	Tahoe	199,065
4	Expedition	181,547
5	TrailBlazer	175,093
6	Escape	167,678
7	Liberty	162,987
8	CR-V	143,909
9	Chevy Suburban	135,222
10	Highlander	120,174

Source: *J.D. Power and Associates*

In recent years, mid- and full-size SUVs have figured increasingly among Americans' favorite vehicles, with sales of many models rivaling those of conventional cars—despite their reputation as "gas-guzzlers" and the irony that, although designed to do so, few ever exploit their off-road capabilities.

TOP 10 CARS IN THE U.S.

	CAR	SALES (2003)
1	Honda Accord	397,750
2	Toyota Camry	369,562
3	Ford Taurus	300,496
4	Honda Civic	299,672
5	Chevrolet Impala	267,882
6	Chevrolet Cavalier	256,550
7	Toyota Corolla	237,597
8	Ford Focus	229,353
9	Nissan Altima—New	201,240
10	Chevrolet Malibu	173,263

Source: *J.D. Power and Associates*

▶ Wheels over water
Recent shifts in the pattern of the world auto industry mean that many cars are imported; even those produced locally are often built by foreign-owned companies.

TOP 10 COUNTRIES WITH THE LONGEST ROAD NETWORKS

	COUNTRY	LENGTH (MILES)	(KM)
1	US	3,936,298	6,334,859
2	India	2,062,731	3,319,644
3	Brazil	1,071,821	1,724,929
4	Canada	874,891	1,408,000
5	China	871,596	1,402,698
6	Japan	721,967	1,161,894
7	France	555,506	894,000
8	Australia	504,307	811,603
9	Spain	412,463	663,795
10	Russia	330,814	532,393

Source: *Central Intelligence Agency*

The CIA's assessment of road lengths includes both paved (mostly asphalt-surfaced) and unpaved highways (gravel and earth-surfaced).

TOP 10 MOTOR VEHICLE MANUFACTUERS IN THE U.S.

	MANUFACTURER	MOTOR VEHICLE PRODUCTION* (2002)
1	General Motors	3,890,239
2	Ford	3,118,524
3	Chrysler Corp.	1,726,004
4	Honda	845,313
5	Toyota	727,369
6	Nissan	522,271
7	NUMMI	395,083
8	Mitsubishi	173,699
9	BMW	166,090
10	Subaru	122,232

* Includes cars, light trucks, lorries, buses, and coaches
Source: *WardsAuto.com*

MOST EXPENSIVE CAR

ONLY SIX EXAMPLES of the Bugatti Royale were ever produced. One of the largest vehicles of all time, it was 22 ft (6.7 m) long and had a 12.7-liter engine originally designed for aircraft, and sold for $42,000. On November 19, 1987 an example of this rare vehicle—a 1931 Bugatti Type 41 Royale Sports Coupe—established a new world record price for a production car when it was sold at auction in London for £5.5 million ($9,735,000). On April 12, 1990, the same car broke its own record when it was sold privately for $15 million. Rare examples of the Ferrari 250 GTO, fewer than 40 of which were built between 1962 and 1964, have changed hands for prices close to this.

IT'S A FACT

Track Records

Like a bullet
The Japanese Shinkhasen "bullet trains" were introduced in 1964 and have been constantly improved since: the Nozomi 500 is capable of 186 mph (300 km/h)

TOP 10 | FASTEST RAIL TRIPS*

TRIP/COUNTRY	TRAIN	DISTANCE (MILES)	(KM)	SPEED (MPH)	(KM/H)
1 Hiroshima to Kokura, Japan	15 Nozomi	119.3	192.0	162.7	261.8
2 Valence TGV to Avignon TGV, France	TGV 5102	80.6	129.7	161.2	259.4
3 Brussels Midi to Valence TGV, International	ThalysSoleil	516.5	831.3	150.4	242.1
4 Frankfurt Flughafen (airport) to Siegburg/Bonn, Germany	19 ICE	89.0	143.3	144.4	232.4
5 Madrid Atocha to Sevilla (Seville), Spain	2 AVE	292.4	470.5	129.9	209.1
6 Alvesta to Hassleholm, Sweden	X2000 541	61.0	98.0	111.0	178.2
7 Darlington to York, UK	6 Voyager	44.1	71.0	110.3	177.5
8 Roma (Rome) Termini to Firenze (Florence) SMN, Italy	Eurostar 9458	162.2	261.0	103.5	166.6
9 Wilmington, DE to Baltimore, MD	Acela Express	68.4	110.1	102.6	165.1
10 Salo to Karjaa, Finland	2 Pendolinos	33.0	53.1	94.3	151.7

* Fastest trip for each country; all those in the Top 10 have other similarly or equally fast services

Source: Railway Gazette International

Falling just outside the Top 10, China's Fex T806 between Shenzhen and Guangzhou Dong achieves a speed of 94.2 mph (151.6 km/h), while on the Dorval-to-Guildwood leg of the Montreal–Toronto journey, Canada's Sunday-only Train 67 averages 92.9 mph (149.5 km/h).

TOP 10 | LONGEST RAIL NETWORKS

LOCATION	TOTAL RAIL LENGTH (MILES)	(KM)
1 US	121,000	194,731
2 Russia	54,157	87,157
3 China	44,490	71,600
4 India	39,468	63,518
5 Canada	30,709	49,422
6 Germany	28,281	45,514
7 Australia	25,842	41,588
8 Argentina	21,414	34,463
9 France	20,308	32,682
10 Brazil	19,600	31,543

Source: Central Intelligence Agency

The length of the world's rail network is thought to be 697,582 miles (1,122,650 km). Some 118,060 to 121,165 miles (190,000 to 195,000 km) is electrified, and 148,775 miles (239,430 km) is narrow-gauge. In Europe, 91,814 miles (147,760 km) is electrified, compared with 15,229 miles (24,509 km) in the Far East, 6,866 miles (11,050 km) in Africa, 2,624 miles (4,223 km) in South America, and 2,585 miles (4,160 km) in North America.

TOP 10 OLDEST UNDERGROUND RAIL SYSTEMS

	CITY	OPENED
1	**London,** UK	1863
2	**Budapest,** Hungary	1896
3	**Glasgow,** UK	1896
4	**Boston,** MA	1897
5	**Paris,** France	1900
6	**Berlin,** Germany	1902
7	**New York,** NY	1904
8	**Philadelphia,** PA	1907
9	**Hamburg,** Germany	1912
10	**Buenos Aires,** Argentina	1913

Source: *Tony Pattison, Centre for Environmental Initiatives Researcher*

The world's first underground system, a section of the Metropolitan Railway from Paddington to Farringdon Street in London, with specially adapted steam trains, was opened on January 10, 1863. The second opened in Budapest in 1896 to celebrate the 1,000th anniversary of the state of Hungary.

THE 10 FIRST COUNTRIES WITH RAILROADS

	COUNTRY	FIRST RAILROAD ESTABLISHED
1	**UK**	Sept. 27, 1825
2	**France**	Nov. 7, 1829
3	**United States**	May 24, 1830
4	**Ireland**	Dec. 17, 1834
5	**Belgium**	May 5, 1835
6	**Germany**	Dec. 7, 1835
7	**Canada**	July 21, 1836
8	**Russia**	Oct. 30, 1837
9	**Austria**	Jan. 6, 1838
10	**Netherlands**	Sept. 24, 1839

Although there were earlier horse-drawn railroads, the UK's Stockton & Darlington Railway was the world's first steam service. Some of those listed here offered only limited services, but their opening dates mark the generally accepted beginning of each country's steam railroad system. By 1850, there were railroads in other countries, including Italy (1839), Hungary (1846), Denmark (1847), and Spain (1848).

TOP 10 BUSIEST AMTRAK RAIL STATIONS IN THE U.S.

	STATION	BOARDINGS (2003*)
1	**New York–Penn.,** NY	4,262,741
2	**Philadelphia 30th St.,** PA	1,796,583
3	**Washington–Union,** DC	1,794,435
4	**Chicago,** IL	1,093,887
5	**Newark City,** NJ	672,291
6	**Los Angeles–Union,** CA	611,979
7	**Trenton,** NJ	495,593
8	**Boston–South,** MA	473,311
9	**Princeton Junction,** NJ	436,898
10	**Sacramento,** CA	431,891

* *Fiscal year*

Source: *Amtrak*

Amtrak—run as a private company, the National Railroad Passenger Corporation, but one whose stock is entirely owned by the federal government—was launched on May 1, 1971 to counter the years of US railroad decline in the face of competition with automobile and air transportation. It operates in 46 of the 50 states with a focus on intercity traffic.

TOP 10 LONGEST UNDERGROUND RAIL NETWORKS

	CITY	OPENED	STATIONS	TOTAL TRACK LENGTH (MILES)	(KM)
1	**London,** UK	1863	267	244	392
2	**New York,** NY	1904	468	231	371
3	**Moscow,** Russia	1935	160	163	262
4	**Tokyo,** Japan*	1927	241	160	256
5	**Paris,** France#	1900	297	126	202
6	**Mexico City,** Mexico	1969	175	125	201
7	**San Francisco,** CA	1972	42	124	200
8	**Chicago,** IL	1943	140	107	173
9	**Madrid,** Spain	1919	201	107	171
10	**Washington,** DC	1976	83	166	166

* *Includes Toei, Eidan lines*

Metro and RER

Source: *Tony Pattison, Centre for Environmental Initiatives Researcher*

▼ **Underground first**
London's Baker Street was one of the stations on the world's first-ever underground rail system.

BAKER STREET

Water Ways

LONGEST
SHIP CANALS

	CANAL/COUNTRY	DATE	LENGTH (MILES)	(KM)
1	**Grand Canal,** China	283*	1,114	1,795
2	**Erie Canal,** US	1825	363	584
3	**Göta Canal,** Sweden	1832	240	386
4	**St. Lawrence Seaway,** Canada/US	1959	180	290
5	**Canal du Midi,** France	1692	149	240
6	**Main-Danube,** Germany	1992	106	171
7	**Suez,** Egypt	1869	101	162
8	= **Albert,** Belgium	1939	80	129
	= **Moscow-Volga,** Russia	1937	80	129
10	**Kiel,** Germany	1895	62	99

* Extended from 605–10 and rebuilt between 1958–72

Connecting Hang Zhou in the south to Beijing in the north, China's Grand Canal was largely built by manual labor, long before the invention of the mechanized techniques used in the construction of the other waterways listed above.

LARGEST
CRUISE SHIPS

	SHIP	YEAR BUILT	COUNTRY BUILT	PASSENGER CAPACITY	GROSS TONNAGE
1	**Queen Mary 2**	2003	France	2,800	142,200
2	**Navigator of the Seas**	2002	Finland	3,807	138,279
3	**Explorer of the Seas**	2000	Finland	3,840	137,308
4	= **Adventure of the Seas**	2001	Finland	3,840	137,276
	= **Mariner of the Seas**	2003	Finland	3,840	137,276
	= **Voyager of the Seas**	1999	Finland	3,840	137,276
7	**Caribbean Princess**	2004	Italy	3,100	115,000
8	= **Diamond Princess**	2004	Japan	2,600	113,000
	= **Sapphire Princess**	2004	Japan	3,100	113,000
10	**Carnival Conquest**	2002	Italy	3,783	110,239

Source: Lloyd's Register-Fairplay Ltd. www.lrfairplay.com

TOP 10 LONGEST CRUISE SHIPS

	SHIP	YEAR BUILT	COUNTRY BUILT	LENGTH (FT)	(IN)	(M)
1	Queen Mary 2	2003	France	1,131	9	345.03
2	Norway (former France)	1961	France	1,035	2	315.53
3 =	Adventure of the Seas	2001	Finland	1,020	7	311.12
=	Mariner of the Seas	2003	Finland	1,020	7	311.12
=	Navigator of the Seas	2002	Finland	1,020	7	311.12
6 =	Explorer of the Seas	2000	Finland	1,020	3	311.00
=	Voyager of the Seas	1999	Finland	1,020	3	311.00
8	United States	1952	US	990	0	301.75
9 =	Norwegian Dawn	2002	Germany	965	0	294.13
=	Norwegian Star	2001	Germany	965	0	294.13

Source: *Lloyd's Register-Fairplay Ltd. www.lrfairplay.com*

For comparison, the *Great Eastern* (launched 1858) measured 692 ft (211 m), while the *Titanic*, which sank dramatically on its maiden voyage in 1912, was 882 ft (269 m) long. Former entrant in this list the *Queen Mary* (1,019 ft/311 m) is now a floating museum in Long Beach, CA, while the *Queen Elizabeth* (1,031 ft/314 m) was taken out of service and destroyed by fire in 1972.

TOP 10 LARGEST OIL TANKERS*

	TANKER	YEAR BUILT	COUNTRY BUILT	GROSS TONNAGE#	DEADWEIGHT TONNAGE†
1	Jahre Viking	1976	Japan	260,851	564,763
2 =	Hellespont Alhambra	2002	South Korea	234,006	441,893
=	Hellespont Metropolis	2002	South Korea	234,006	441,893
=	Hellespont Tara	2002	South Korea	234,006	441,893
5	Hellespont Fairfax	2002	South Korea	234,006	441,585
6	Empress des Mers	1976	Japan	203,110	423,677
7	Hellespont Embassy	1976	Japan	199,210	413,015
8	Marine Pacific	1979	US	192,707	404,536
9	Marine Atlantic	1979	US	192,707	404,531
10 =	Berge Enterprise	1981	Japan	188,728	360,700
=	Berge Pioneer	1980	Japan	188,728	360,700

* As of October 2003

The weight of the ship when empty

† The total weight of the vessel, including its cargo, crew, passengers, and supplies

Source: *Lloyd's Register-Fairplay Ltd. www.lrfairplay.com*

TOP 10 BUSIEST PORTS

	PORT/COUNTRY	CONTAINER TRAFFIC (2000) (TEUS*)
1	Hong Kong, China	18,098,000
2	Singapore, Singapore	17,090,000
3	Pusan, South Korea	7,540,387
4	Kaohsiung, Taiwan	7,425,832
5	Rotterdam, Netherlands	6,274,000
6	Los Angeles, CA, US	4,879,429
7	Long Beach, CA, US	4,600,787
8	Hamburg, Germany	4,248,247
9	Antwerp, Belgium	4,082,334
10	Tanjung Priok, Indonesia	3,368,629

* Twenty-Foot Equivalent Units

Source: *American Association of Port Authorities*

◀ **Med to Red**
Connecting the Mediterranean and Red Sea, the Suez Canal, seen here from space, dramatically reduced the time and cost of transportation from Europe to Asia.

TOP 10 COUNTRIES WITH THE LONGEST INLAND WATERWAY NETWORKS*

	COUNTRY	LENGTH (MILES)	(KM)
1	China	68,351	110,000
2	Russia	59,589	95,900
3	Brazil	31,069	50,000
4	US#	25,482	41,009
5	Indonesia	13,409	21,579
6	Colombia	11,272	18,140
7	Vietnam	11,000	17,702
8	India	10,054	16,180
9	Dem. Rep. of Congo	9,321	15,000
10	France	9,278	14,932

* Canals and navigable rivers

Excluding Great Lakes

Source: *Central Intelligence Agency*

TOP 10 MERCHANT SHIPPING FLEETS (OWNERSHIP)

	COUNTRY OF OWNERSHIP	SHIPS IN FLEET*
1	Japan	3,942
2	Greece	3,039
3	Germany	2,446
4	China	2,089
5	US	2,015
6	Russia	1,858
7	Norway	1,441
8	Singapore	1,112
9	Netherlands	1,010
10	UK	952
	All countries	35,590

* Ships over 1,000 DWT (deadweight tonnage— total weight of the vessel, including its cargo, crew, passengers, and supplies) in service in October 2003

Source: *Lloyd's Register-Fairplay Ltd. www.lrfairplay.com*

This Top 10 ranks merchant fleets according to the country of ownership, which is not necessarily where the ships are registered. Among the vessels included in a country's merchant fleet are tankers, container ships, passenger ships, and refrigerated cargo ships.

Air Lines

TOP 10 AIRLINES WITH THE MOST PASSENGER TRAFFIC

	AIRLINE/COUNTRY	PASSENGER MILES FLOWN (2001)*
1	United Airlines, US	116,643,800,000
2	American Airlines, US	108,359,679,000
3	Delta Airlines, US	101,758,853,000
4	Northwest Airlines, US	73,155,895,000
5	British Airways, UK	66,033,117,000
6	Continental Airlines, US	61,126,149,000
7	Air France, France	58,923,387,000
8	Lufthansa German Airlines, Germany	53,869,776,000
9	Japan Airlines, Japan	49,313,882,000
10	US Airways, US	45,997,624,000

* Total distance traveled by aircraft of these airlines multiplied by number of passengers carried

Source: Airline Business/*Air Transport Intelligence* at *www.rati.com*

TOP 10 COUNTRIES WITH THE MOST AIRPORTS

	COUNTRY	AIRPORTS
1	US	14,801
2	Brazil	3,590
3	Russia	2,743
4	Mexico	1,823
5	Canada	1,389
6	Argentina	1,342
7	Bolivia	1,081
8	Colombia	1,050
9	Paraguay	879
10	Ukraine	790

Source: *Central Intelligence Agency*

TOP 10 AIRLINERS IN SERVICE

	AIRCRAFT MODEL	NO. IN SERVICE
1	Boeing B-737-300	985
2	Airbus A-320-200	960
3	Boeing B-757-200	813
4	Boeing B-737-200 Advanced	479
5	Boeing B-737-400	464
6	Boeing B-767-300ER	422
7	Boeing B-747-400	405
8	McDonnell Douglas DC-9-30	308
9	Raytheon Beech 1900D	278
10	Boeing B-727-200 Advanced	270

Source: *Air Transport Intelligence at www.rati.com*

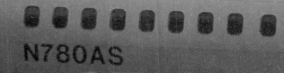

TOP 10 BUSIEST AIRPORTS IN THE U.S.

	AIRPORT	LOCATION	TOTAL PASSENGERS (2002)*
1	Atlanta Hartsfield International	Atlanta, GA	76,876,128
2	Chicago O'Hare International	Chicago, IL	66,565,952
3	Los Angeles International	Los Angeles, CA	56,198,447
4	Dallas/Fort Worth International	Irving, TX	52,836,304
5	Denver International	Denver, CO	35,651,098
6	Phoenix Sky Harbor International	Phoenix, AZ	35,547,167
7	McCarran International	Las Vegas, NV	35,009,011
8	George Bush Intercontinental	Houston, TX	34,000,000
9	Minneapolis/St. Paul International	St. Paul, MN	32,630,177
10	Detroit Metropolitan Wayne County	Detroit, MI	32,436,999

Includes international, domestic, and in transit

Source: *Air Transport Intelligence at www.rati.com*

TOP 10 BUSIEST INTERNATIONAL AIRPORTS

	AIRPORT	LOCATION	INTERNATIONAL PASSENGERS (2001)
1	London Heathrow	London, UK	53,796,000
2	Charles de Gaulle	Paris, France	43,352,000
3	Frankfurt	Frankfurt, Germany	40,283,000*
4	Schiphol	Amsterdam, Netherlands	39,167,000
5	Hong Kong	Hong Kong, China	32,027,000
6	London Gatwick	Gatwick, UK	28,114,000
7	Singapore Changi	Singapore	26,542,000
8	Narita International	Tokyo, Japan	22,241,000
9	Bangkok International	Bangkok, Thailand	21,394,000
10	Kloten	Zurich, Switzerland	19,698,000

* 2002 data

Source: *Air Transport Intelligence at www.rati.com*

World's leading international airport London Heathrow was created 60 years ago when the privately-owned Great Western Aerodrome, requisitioned for use as an RAF airfield during wartime, was acquired for civilian use.

TOP 10 AIRLINES WITH THE MOST AIRCRAFT

	AIRLINE/COUNTRY*	FLEET SIZE (2001)
1	American Airlines	834
2	United Airlines	554
3	Delta Airlines	551
4	Northwest Airlines	437
5	Continental Airlines	370
6	Southwest Airlines	367
7	US Airways	295
8	Air France, France	247
9	British Airways, UK	236
10	Air Canada, Canada	224

All from the US unless otherwise stated

Source: *Airline Business/Air Transport Intelligence at www.rati.com*

◀ Come fly with me
The world's airlines carry over 1.6 billion passengers annually, flying a total of some 2 trillion passenger miles.

Transportation Disasters

 ## WORST MARINE DISASTERS

LOCATION/DATE/INCIDENT	NO. KILLED
1 Off Gdansk, Poland, January 30, 1945	up to 7,800
The German liner *Wilhelm Gustloff*, laden with refugees, was torpedoed by a Soviet submarine, *S-13*. The precise death toll remains uncertain, but is in the range of 5,348 to 7,800.	
2 Off Cape Rixhöft (Rozeewie), Poland, April 16, 1945	6,800
A German ship, *Goya*, carrying evacuees from Gdansk, was torpedoed in the Baltic.	
3 Off Yingkow, China, December 3, 1948	over 6,000
The boilers of an unidentified Chinese troop ship carrying Nationalist soldiers from Manchuria exploded, detonating ammunition.	
4 Lübeck, Germany, May 3, 1945	5,000
The German ship *Cap Arcona*, carrying concentration-camp survivors, was bombed and sunk by British Typhoon fighter-bombers.	
5 Off Stolpmünde (Ustka), Poland, February 10, 1945	3,500
German war wounded and refugees were lost when the *General Steuben* was torpedoed by the same Russian submarine that had sunk the *Wilhelm Gustloff* ten days earlier.	
6 Off St. Nazaire, France, June 17, 1940	3,050
The British troop ship *Lancastria* sank.	
7 Tabias Strait, Philippines, December 20, 1987	up to 3,000
The ferry *Dona Paz* was struck by oil tanker *MV Victor*.	
8 Woosung, China, December 3, 1948	over 2,750
The overloaded steamship *Kiangya*, carrying refugees, struck a Japanese mine.	
9 Lübeck, Germany, May 3, 1945	2,750
The refugee ship *Thielbeck* sank along with the *Cap Arcona* during the British bombardment of Lübeck harbor in the closing weeks of World War II.	
10 South Atlantic, September 12, 1942	2,279
The British passenger vessel *Laconia*, carrying Italian prisoners of war, was sunk by German U-boat *U-156*.	

Recent reassessments of the death tolls in some of World War II's marine disasters means that the most famous marine disaster of all, the *Titanic*, the British liner that struck an iceberg in the North Atlantic and sank on April 15, 1912, with the loss of 1,517 lives, no longer ranks in the Top 10. However, the *Titanic* tragedy remains one of the worst-ever peacetime disasters, along with such notable incidents as that involving the *General Slocum*, an excursion liner that caught fire in the port of New York on June 15, 1904 with the loss of 1,021. Among other disasters occurring during wartime and resulting in losses of more than 1,000 are the explosion of *Mont Blanc*, a French ammunition ship, following its collision with a Belgian steamer *Imo* off Halifax, Nova Scotia, on December 6, 1917, with 1,635 lost; the sinking of the British cruiser *HMS Hood* by the German battleship *Bismarck* in the Denmark Strait on May 24, 1941, with 1,418 killed; the torpedoing by German submarine *U-20* of the *Lusitania*, a British passenger liner, off the Irish coast on May 7, 1915, with the loss of 1,198 civilians; and the accidental sinking by a US submarine of *Rakuyo Maru*, a Japanese troop ship carrying Allied prisoners of war, on September 12, 1944, killing some 1,350.

 ## WORST AIR DISASTERS

LOCATION/DATE/INCIDENT	NO. KILLED
1 New York City, September 11, 2001	c. 1,622
Following a hijacking by terrorists, an American Airlines Boeing 767 was deliberately flown into the North Tower of the World Trade Center, killing all 81 passengers and 11 crew on board and an estimated 1,530 in and around the building, both as a direct result of the crash and in the subsequent fire and collapse of the building.	
2 New York City, September 11, 2001	c. 677
As part of the coordinated attack, hijackers commandeered a second Boeing 767 and crashed it into the South Tower, killing all 56 passengers and 9 crew on board and approximately 612 in and around the building.	
3 Tenerife, Canary Islands, March 27, 1977	583
Two Boeing 747s (PanAm and KLM, carrying 380 passengers and 16 crew and 234 passengers and 14 crew, respectively) collided and caught fire on the runway of Los Rodeos airport after the pilots received incorrect instructions from air traffic control. A total of 61 escaped.	
4 Mt. Ogura, Japan, August 12, 1985	520
A JAL Boeing 747 on an internal flight from Tokyo to Osaka crashed, killing all but four of the 509 passengers and all 15 crew on board.	
5 Charkhi Dadri, India, November 12, 1996	349
Soon after taking off from New Delhi's Indira Gandhi International Airport, a Saudi Airways Boeing 747 collided with a Kazakh Airlines Ilyushin IL-76 cargo aircraft on its descent and exploded, killing all 312 (289 passengers and 23 crew) on the Boeing and all 37 (27 passengers and 10 crew) on the Ilyushin in the world's worst midair crash.	
6 Paris, France, March 3, 1974	346
Immediately after takeoff for London, a Turkish Airlines DC-10 crashed in Ermenonville, north of Paris, killing all 335 passengers and 11 crew.	
7 Off the Irish coast, June 23, 1985	329
An Air India Boeing 747 on a flight from Vancouver to Delhi exploded in midair, probably as a result of a terrorist bomb, killing all 307 passengers and 22 crew.	
8 Riyadh, Saudi Arabia, August 19, 1980	301
A Saudia (Saudi Arabian) Airlines Lockheed TriStar caught fire during an emergency landing, killing all 287 passengers and 14 crew.	
9 Off the Iranian coast, July 3, 1988	290
An Iran Air A300 Airbus was shot down in error by a missile fired by the *USS Vincennes*, with 274 passengers and 16 crew killed.	
10 Chicago, May 25, 1979	273
An engine fell off an American Airlines DC-10 as it took off from Chicago O'Hare airport, and the plane plunged out of control, killing all 258 passengers and 13 crew and two people on the ground.	

THE 10 WORST RAIL DISASTERS

LOCATION/DATE/INCIDENT	NO. KILLED
1 Bagmati River, India, June 6, 1981	*c.* 800
The cars of a train traveling from Samastipur to Banmukhi in Bihar plunged off a bridge over the Bagmati River near Mansi when the engineer braked, apparently to avoid hitting a sacred cow. Although the official death toll was said to have been 268, many authorities have claimed that the train was so massively overcrowded that the actual figure was in excess of 800, making it probably the worst rail disaster of all time.	
2 Chelyabinsk, Russia, June 3, 1989	up to 800
Two passenger trains, laden with vacationers heading to and from Black Sea resorts, were destroyed when liquid gas from a nearby pipeline exploded.	
3 Guadalajara, Mexico, January 18, 1915	over 600
A train derailed on a steep incline, but political strife in the country meant that full details of the disaster were suppressed.	
4 Modane, France, December 12, 1917	573
A troop train ran out of control and derailed. It has been claimed that the train was overloaded and that as many as 1,000 may have died.	
5 Balvano, Italy, March 2, 1944	521
A heavily laden train stalled in the Armi Tunnel, and many passengers were asphyxiated. Like the disaster in Torre (No. 6), wartime secrecy prevented full details from being published.	
6 Torre, Spain, January 3, 1944	over 500
A double collision and fire in a tunnel resulted in many deaths— some have put the total as high as 800.	
7 Awash, Ethiopia, January 13, 1985	428
A derailment hurled a train laden with some 1,000 passengers into a ravine.	
8 Cireau, Romania, January 7, 1917	374
An overcrowded passenger train crashed into a military train and derailed.	
9 Reqa al-Gharbiya, Egypt, February 20, 2002	372
A fire on the Cairo–Luxor train engulfed the cars. The engineer was unaware of the fire and continued driving while passengers burned or leaped from the train to their deaths.	
10 Quipungo, Angola, May 31, 1993	355
A trail was derailed by UNITA guerrilla action.	

Casualty figures for rail accidents are often extremely imprecise, especially during wartime—and no fewer than half of the 10 worst disasters occurred during the two World Wars. Other, poorly documented incidents, such as one in Kalish, Poland, in December 1914, with "400 dead," one in November 1918 in Norrköpping, Sweden, alleged to have killed 300, and certain other similarly uncertain cases, have been omitted.

▲ **Casualty of war**
Background picture: designed to carry some 1,500, the *Wilhelm Gustloff* may have had nearly 8,000 on board when it was torpedoed in 1945—the worst ever loss of life at sea.

THE 10 WORST MOTOR VEHICLE AND ROAD DISASTERS

LOCATION/DATE/INCIDENT	NO. KILLED
1 Afghanistan, November 3, 1982	over 2,000
Following a collision with a Soviet army truck, a gasoline tanker exploded in the 1.7-mile (2.7-km) Salang Tunnel. Some authorities have put the death toll from the explosion, fire, and fumes as high as 3,000.	
2 Colombia, August 7, 1956	1,200
Seven army ammunition trucks exploded at night in the center of Cali, destroying eight city blocks, including a barracks where 500 soldiers were sleeping.	
3 Spain, July 11, 1978	217
A liquid gas tanker exploded in Los Alfaques, a campsite in San Carlos de la Rapita.	
4 Thailand, February 15, 1991	171
A dynamite truck exploded in Phang Nga.	
5 Nigeria, November 4, 2000	150
A gasoline tanker collided with a line of stationary cars on the Ile-Ife-Ibadan Expressway, exploding and burning many people to death. Some 96 bodies were recovered, but some estimates put the final toll as high as 200.	
6 Nepal, November 23, 1974	148
Hindu pilgrims were killed when a suspension bridge over the Mahahali River collapsed.	
7 Egypt, August 9, 1973	127
A bus drove into an irrigation canal.	
8 Togo, December 6, 1965	over 125
Two trucks collided with dancers during a festival in Sotouboua.	
9 South Korea, April 28, 1995	110
An underground explosion destroyed vehicles and caused about 100 cars and buses to plunge into the pit it created.	
10 Kenya, early December 1992	106
A bus carrying 112 skidded, hit a bridge, and plunged into a river.	

The worst-ever auto racing accident occurred on June 13, 1955, in Le Mans, France, when French driver Pierre Levegh's Mercedes-Benz 300 SLR went out of control, hit a wall, and exploded in midair, showering wreckage into the crowd and killing a total of 82 people. It is believed that the worst-ever accident involving a single car occurred on December 17, 1956, when eight adults and four children were killed when the overcrowded car in which they were traveling was hit by a train near Phoenix, Arizona. Although she was injured, 20-month-old Crucita Alires survived after being hurled into a tree by the impact. The worst single US highway disaster occurred on December 15, 1967, when the Silver Bridge, spanning the Ohio River from Kanauga, Ohio, to Point Pleasant, West Virginia, collapsed during heavy pre-Christmas afternoon rush hour traffic, plunging some 60 vehicles into the river, resulting in 46 deaths and many injuries.

World Tourism

COUNTRIES OF ORIGIN OF OVERSEAS VISITORS TO THE U.S.

	COUNTRY	OVERSEAS VISITORS TO THE US (2002)	(2003*)
1	UK	3,816,736	3,936,112
2	Japan	3,627,264	3,169,682
3	Germany	1,189,856	1,180,212
4	France	734,260	688,887
5	South Korea	638,697	617,573
6	Italy	406,160	408,633
7	Australia	407,130	405,698
8	Netherlands	384,367	373,690
9	Brazil	405,094	348,945
10	Venezuela	395,913	284,423

* Provisional figures

Source: *US Department of Commerce, International Trade Administration, Office of Travel and Tourism Industries*

Fears of global terrorism, as well as economic and other factors, have adversely affected US tourist visitor numbers. The total declined from 41,891,707 in 2002 to 40,356,213 in 2003, and is more than 10 million lower than the peak year of 2000.

TOURIST DESTINATIONS

	COUNTRY	INTERNATIONAL VISITORS (2002)
1	France	77,000,000
2	Spain	51,700,000
3	US	41,900,000
4	Italy	39,800,000
5	China	36,800,000
6	UK	24,200,000
7	Canada	20,100,000
8	Mexico	19,700,000
9	Austria	18,600,000
10	Germany	18,000,000

Source: *World Tourism Organization*

After a 0.5 percent decrease in 2001, tourist numbers grew globally by 2.7 percent in 2002, with the US and Mexico the only countries in the Top 10 to show a decline. Worldwide, international (cross-border) tourism was worth a total of some $474 billion, compared with a 1990 figure of $264 billion.

TOURIST EARNING COUNTRIES

	COUNTRY	INTERNATIONAL TOURISM RECEIPTS (2002) ($)
1	US	66,500,000,000
2	Spain	33,600,000,000
3	France	32,300,000,000
4	Italy	26,900,000,000
5	China	20,400,000,000
6	Germany	19,200,000,000
7	UK	17,800,000,000
8	Austria	11,200,000,000
9	Hong Kong	10,100,000,000
10	Greece	9,700,000,000

Source: *World Tourism Organization*

DESTINATIONS FOR U.S. TOURISTS

	DESTINATION COUNTRY	U.S. VISITORS (2002)
1	Mexico	16,810,000
2	Canada	16,161,000
3	UK	3,229,000
4	France	2,223,000
5	Germany	1,661,000
6	Italy	1,591,000
7	Japan	1,287,000
8	Dominican Republic	1,100,000
9	Jamaica	983,000
10 =	Netherlands	866,000
=	Spain	866,000

Source: *Tourism Industries/International Trade Administration, Department of Commerce*

▼ **French leave**
The cultural and other attractions of Paris and the rest of France have long made the country the world's foremost magnet for tourists.

TOP 10 WORLDWIDE AMUSEMENT AND THEME PARKS

PARK/LOCATION	ATTENDANCE (2003)
1 **The Magic Kingdom at Walt Disney World,** Lake Buena Vista, Florida	14,044,000
2 **Tokyo Disneyland,** Tokyo, Japan	13,188,000
3 **Disneyland,** Anaheim, California	12,720,000
4 **Disneysea,** Tokyo, Japan	12,174,000
5 **Disneyland Paris,** Marne-La-Vallée, France	10,230,000
6 **Universal Studios Japan,** Osaka, Japan	8,811,000
7 **Everland,** Kyonggi-Do, South Korea	8,800,000
8 **Epcot at Walt Disney World,** Lake Buena Vista, Florida	8,620,768
9 **Lotte World,** Seoul, South Korea	8,500,000
10 **Disney-MGM Studios at Walt Disney World,** Lake Buena Vista, Florida	7,870,733

Source: Amusement Business

Most amusement and theme parks have experienced flat or declining entrance numbers in recent years, while the introduction of South Korea's Everland (1976) and Lotte World (1989) and new parks in Japan, such as Tokyo's Disneysea and Universal Studios and Osaka's Universal Studios, which all opened in 2001, has shifted the global balance away from the US.

TOP 10 MOST VISITED NATIONAL PARKS IN THE U.S.

PARK/LOCATION	RECREATION VISITS (2003)
1 **Great Smoky Mountains National Park,** North Carolina/Tennessee	9,366,845
2 **Grand Canyon National Park,** Arizona	4,124,900
3 **Olympic National Park,** Washington	3,691,310
4 **Yosemite National Park,** California	3,225,327
5 **Rocky Mountain National Park,** Colorado	3,067,256
6 **Yellowstone National Park,** Wyoming	3,019,375
7 **Cuyahoga Valley National Park,** near Cleveland and Akron, Ohio	2,879,591
8 **Zion National Park,** Utah	2,458,792
9 **Grand Teton National Park,** Wyoming	2,431,062
10 **Acadia National Park,** Maine	2,355,693

The total number of recreation visits to the US National Park System in 2003 was 266,099,641—more than the population of the United States. This includes visitors to National Recreation Areas, National Monuments, and other areas under the management of the National Park Service not included in this list, which is exclusively of National Parks.

SPORT &
LEISURE

Olympic Feats

TOP 10 WINTER OLYMPICS MEDAL-WINNERS

	MEDALIST/COUNTRY	SPORT	YEARS	GOLD	SILVER	BRONZE	TOTAL
1	**Bjørn Dählie**, Norway	Nordic skiing	1992–98	8	4	0	12
2	**Raisa Smetanina**, USSR	Nordic skiing	1976–92	4	5	1	10
3 =	**Stefania Belmondo**, Italy	Nordic skiing	1992–2002	2	3	4	9
=	**Sixten Jernberg**, Sweden	Nordic skiing	1956–64	4	3	2	9
=	**Lyubov Egorova**, EUN#/Russia	Nordic skiing	1992–94	6	3	0	9
=	**Larisa Lazutina**, EUN#/Russia	Nordic skiing	1992–2002	5	3	1	9
7 =	**Karin Kania** (née Enke), East Germany	Speed skating	1980–88	3	4	1	8
=	**Galina Kulakova**, USSR	Nordic skiing	1968–80	4	2	2	8
=	**Gunda Neimann-Stirnemann** East Germany/Germany	Speed skating	1992–98	3	4	1	8
10 =	**Kjetil Andre Aamoldt**, Norway	Alpine skiing	1992–2002	3	2	2	7
=	**Peter Angerer**, West Germany/Germany	Biathlon	1984–94	3	2	2	7
=	**Ivar Ballangrud**, Norway	Speed skating	1928–36	4	2	1	7
=	**Andrea Ehrig** (née Mitscherlich; formerly Schöne), East Germany	Speed skating	1976–88	1	5	1	7
=	**Rico Gross**, Germany	Biathlon	1992–2002	3	2	2	7
=	**Veikko Hakulinen**, Finland	Nordic skiing	1952–60	3	3	1	7
=	**Marja-Liisa Kirvesniemi** (née Hämäläinen), Finland	Nordic skiing	1980–98	3	0	4	7
=	**Eero Mäntyranta**, Finland	Nordic skiing	1960–68	3	2	2	7
=	**Bogdan Musiol**, East Germany/Germany	Bobsledding	1986–92	1	5	1	7
=	**Claudia Pechstein**, Germany	Speed skating	1992–2002	4	1	2	7
=	**Clas Thunberg**, Norway	Speed skating	1924–28	5	1	1	7
=	**Elena Valbe**, EUN#/Russia	Nordic skiing	1992–98	3	0	4	7

Medals column spans GOLD, SILVER, BRONZE marked MEDALS*

* All events up to and including the 2002 Salt Lake City Games

EUN = Unified Team (Commonwealth of Independent States 1992)

The only person to win gold medals at both the Summer and Winter Games is Eddie Eagan of the United States. After winning the 1920 light-heavyweight boxing title, he then went on to win a gold medal as a member of the US four-man bobsled team in 1932.

▶ **A Bjørn winner**
Known as the "Nannestad Express," after his home town in Norway, Bjørn Dählie is the most successful winter Olympic medalist of all time, winning four medals in each of three consecutive Games.

TOP 10 SUMMER OLYMPICS MEDAL-WINNERS (WOMEN)

	MEDALIST/COUNTRY	SPORT	YEARS	GOLD	MEDALS* SILVER	BRONZE	TOTAL
1	**Larissa Latynina**, USSR	Gymnastics	1956–64	9	5	4	18
2	**Vera Cáslavská**, Czechoslovakia	Gymnastics	1960–68	7	4	0	11
3	= **Polina Astakhova**, USSR	Gymnastics	1956–64	5	2	3	10
	= **Birgit Fischer-Schmidt** East Germany/Germany	Canoeing	1980–2000	7	3	0	10
	= **Agnes Keleti**, Hungary	Gymnastics	1952–56	5	3	2	10
	= **Jenny Thompson**, US	Swimming	1992–2000	8	1	1	10
7	= **Nadia Comaneci**, Romania	Gymnastics	1976–80	5	3	1	9
	= **Dara Torres**, US	Swimming	1984–2000	4	1	4	9
	= **Lyudmila Turishcheva**, USSR	Gymnastics	1968–76	4	3	2	9
10	= **Shirley Babashoff**, US	Swimming	1972–76	2	6	0	8
	= **Kornelia Ender**, East Germany	Swimming	1972–76	4	4	0	8
	= **Dawn Fraser**, Australia	Swimming	1956–64	4	4	0	8
	= **Sofia Muratova**, USSR	Gymnastics	1956–60	2	2	4	8

* 1896–2000 inclusive

Larissa Latynina holds the record for total medals won by any athlete in any sport in Olympic history. Vera Cáslavská (1968) and Daniela Silivas of Romania (1988) are the only gymnasts to earn medals in all six events at one Olympics. Canoeist Birgit Fischer-Schmidt holds the most Olympic canoeing medals ever.

TOP 10 SUMMER OLYMPICS MEDAL-WINNERS (MEN)

	MEDALIST/COUNTRY	SPORT	YEARS	GOLD	MEDALS* SILVER	BRONZE	TOTAL
1	**Nikolai Andrianov**, USSR	Gymnastics	1972–80	7	5	3	15
2	= **Edoardo Mangiarotti**, Italy	Fencing	1936–60	6	5	2	13
	= **Takashi Ono**, Japan	Gymnastics	1952–64	5	4	4	13
	= **Boris Shakhlin**, USSR	Gymnastics	1956–64	7	4	2	13
5	= **Sawao Kato**, Japan	Gymnastics	1968–76	8	3	1	12
	= **Alexei Nemov**, Russia	Gymnastics	1996–2000	4	2	6	12
	= **Paavo Nurmi**, Finland	Track & field	1920–28	9	3	0	12
8	= **Matt Biondi**, US	Swimming	1984–92	8	2	1	11
	= **Viktor Chukarin**, USSR	Gymnastics	1952–56	7	3	1	11
	= **Carl Osburn**, US	Shooting	1912–24	5	4	2	11
	= **Mark Spitz**, US	Swimming	1968–72	9	1	1	11

* 1896–2000 inclusive

Nikolai Andrianov is married to Olympic gymnast Lyubov Burda, who herself won two Olympic gold medals. Fencer Edoardo Mangiarotti won his first gold at the age of 17, making him the youngest male medalist at the 1936 Berlin Games. Although his overall total relegates him to the bottom of this list, Mark Spitz has the distinction of winning the most gold medals at a single Olympics, with seven in 1972.

TOP 10 SUMMER OLYMPICS MEDAL-WINNING COUNTRIES

	COUNTRY	GOLD	MEDALS* SILVER	BRONZE	TOTAL
1	US	872	658	586	2,116
2	USSR/Unified Team/Russia	498	409	371	1,278
3	Germany/ West Germany	214	242	280	736
4	Great Britain	180	233	225	638
5	France	188	193	217	598
6	Italy	179	143	157	479
7	Sweden	136	156	177	469
8	East Germany	159	150	136	445
9	Hungary	150	135	158	443
10	Australia	102	110	138	350

* 1896–2000 inclusive

There have been 24 Summer Olympics since the 1896 Games in Athens (including the 1906 Intercalated Games, also in Athens). The USSR first entered the Olympics in 1952, but boycotted the 1984 Games. The US boycotted the 1980 Games.

TOP 10 WINTER OLYMPICS MEDAL-WINNING COUNTRIES

	COUNTRY	GOLD	MEDALS* SILVER	BRONZE	TOTAL
1	USSR/Unified Team/Russia	113	82	78	273
2	Norway	94	93	73	260
3	US	70	70	51	191
4	Germany/ West Germany	68	67	52	187
5	Austria	41	57	65	163
6	Finland	41	51	49	141
7	East Germany	39	37	35	111
8	Sweden	36	28	38	102
9	Switzerland	32	33	36	101
10	Canada	30	28	37	95

* Up to and including the 2002 Lake Placid Games; includes medals won in figure skating and hockey, which were included in the Summer Games prior to the launch of the Winter Olympics in 1924

Winter Sports

TOP 10 | SKIERS WITH THE MOST ALPINE SKIING WORLD CUP TITLES (FEMALE)

	SKIIER/COUNTRY	YEARS	OA	S	GS	SG	DH	C*	TOTAL
1	**Annemarie Moser–Pröll**, Austria	1971–79	6	–	3	–	7	1	16
2	**Vreni Schneider**, Switzerland	1986–95	3	6	5	–	–	–	14
3	**Katia Seizinger**, Germany	1992–98	2	–	–	5	4	–	11
4	**Erika Hess**, Switzerland	1981–84	2	5	1	–	–	1	8
5	= **Hanni Wenzel**, Liechenstein	1974–80	2	1	2	–	–	3	8
	= **Renate Goetschl**, Germany	1997–2000	–	–	1	1	4	2	8
7	**Michela Figini**, Switzerland	1985–89	2	–	–	1	4	–	7
8	= **Lise–Marie Morerod**, Switzerland	1975–78	1	2	3	–	–	–	6
	= **Maria Walliser**, Switzerland	1986–87	2	–	–	1	2	1	6
	= **Janica Kostelic**, Croatia	2001–03	2	2	–	–	–	2	6
	= **Anita Wachter**, Austria	1990–92	3	1	–	–	–	3	6

* OA = Overall; S = Slalom; GS = Giant slalom; SG = Super-giant slalom; DH = Downhill; C= Combined

The Alpine Skiing World Cup was launched as an annual event in 1967, with the addition of the super–giant slalom in 1986. Points are awarded for performances over a series of selected races during the winter months at meetings worldwide. As well as her 17 titles, Annemarie Moser-Pröll won a record 62 individual events in the period 1970–79, and went on to win gold for the Downhill event in the 1980 Olympic Games, when she achieved a record speed of 99.598 kmph (61.887 mph).

TOP 10 | SKIERS IN THE 2003/04 ALPINE WORLD CUP (FEMALE)

	SKIIER/COUNTRY	OVERALL POINTS*
1	**Anja Paerson**, Sweden	1,561
2	**Renate Goetschl**, Austria	1,344
3	**Maria Reisch**, Germany	977
4	**Hilde Gerg**, Germany	962
5	**Carole Montillet**, France	957
6	**Michaela Dorfmeister**, Austria	943
7	**Martina Ertl**, Germany	770
8	**Alexandra Meissnitzer**, Austria	734
9	**Tania Poutiainen**, Finland	669
10	**Elizabeth Georgl**, Austria	654

* Awarded for performances in slalom, giant slalom, super giant, downhill, and combination disciplines

Source: International Ski Federation

▶ **Downhill racer**
The first Croatian to win an Olympic medal, Janica Kostelic, who won three golds at the 2002 Olympics, has gained more World Cup titles in the 21st century than any other skier.

TOP 10 | SKIERS WITH THE MOST ALPINE SKIING WORLD CUP TITLES (MALE)

	SKIIER/COUNTRY	YEARS	OA	S	GS	SG	DH	C*	TOTAL
1	**Ingemar Stenmark**, Sweden	1976–84	3	8	7	–	–	–	18
2	= **Marc Girardelli**, Luxembourg	1984–94	5	3	1	–	2	4	15
	= **Pirmin Zurbriggen**, Switzerland	1984–90	4	–	3	4	2	2	15
4	**Hermann Maier**, Austria	1998–2001	4	–	2	5	2	–	13
5	= **Phil Mahre**, US	1981–83	3	1	2	–	–	3	9
	= **Gustavo Thoeni**, Italy	1971–74	4	2	3	–	–	–	9
	= **Alberto Tomba**, Italy	1988–95	1	4	4	–	–	–	9
8	= **Stephan Eberharter**, Austria	2002–03	2	–	–	2	3	–	7
9	**Jean–Claude Killy**, France	1967–68	2	1	2	–	1	–	6
10	= **Luc Alphand**, France	1997	1	–	–	1	3	–	5
	= **Franz Klammer**, Austria	1975–83	–	–	–	–	5	–	5
	= **Karl Schranz**, Austria	1969–70	2	–	2	–	1	–	5
	= **Andreas Wenzel**, Liechtentein	1979–85	1	–	–	–	–	4	5

* OA = Overall; S = Slalom; GS = Giant slalom; SG = Super-giant slalom; DH = Downhill

TOP 10 | SKIERS IN THE 2003/04 ALPINE WORLD CUP (MALE)

	SKIER/COUNTRY	OVERALL POINTS*
1	**Hermann Maier**, Austria	1,265
2	**Stephan Eberharter**, Austria	1,223
3	**Benjamin Raich**, Austria	1,139
4	**Bode Miller**, US	1,134
5	**Daron Rahlves**, US	1,004
6	**Kalle Palander**, Finland	944
7	**Michael Walchhofer**, Austria	828
8	= **Ivica Kostelic**, Croatia	796
	= **Hans Knauss**, Austria	796
10	**Rainer Shoenfelder**, Austria	727

* Awarded for performances in slalom, giant slalom, super giant, downhill, and combination disciplines

Source: International Ski Federation

TOP 10 | OLYMPIC FIGURE-SKATING COUNTRIES

	COUNTRY	GOLD	MEDALS SILVER	BRONZE	TOTAL
1	US	13	13	16	42
2	USSR*	13	10	6	29
3	Austria	7	9	4	20
4	Canada	3	7	9	19
5	Russia	9	7	0	16
6	UK	5	3	7	15
7	France	3	2	7	12
8	Germany/West Germany	4	4	13	11
9	= East Germany	3	3	4	10
	= Sweden	5	3	2	10

Includes United Team of 1992; excludes Russia since

 # Not including West Germany or East Germany 1968–88

Figure skating was part of the Summer Olympics in 1908 and 1920, becoming part of the Winter program in 1924.

Track & Field

OLYMPIC TRACK AND FIELD GOLD MEDAL-WINNING COUNTRIES, 1896–2000 (MEN)

	COUNTRY	GOLD MEDALS
1	US	268
2	Finland	48
3	UK	45
4	USSR*	37
5	Sweden	18
6	Kenya	15
7	East Germany	14
8	= Germany/West Germany	13
	= Italy	13
	= Poland	13

Includes Unified Team of 1992; does not include Russia since then

The first American Olympic champion was James Connolly, in the Hop, Step and Jump. An undergraduate at Harvard, his dean refused him permission to travel to Athens in 1896, so he dropped out of university in order to compete.

TOP 10 OLYMPIC TRACK AND FIELD GOLD MEDAL-WINNING COUNTRIES, 1896–2000 (WOMEN)

	COUNTRY	GOLD MEDALS
1	US	44
2	USSR*	34
3	East Germany	24
4	= Australia	18
	= Germany/West Germany	18
6	Romania	10
7	Poland	7
8	= France	6
	= Netherlands	6
	= UK	6

Includes Unified Team of 1992; does not include Russia since then

TOP 10 FASTEST MILES EVER RUN

	ATHLETE/COUNTRY	YEAR	TIME (MIN:SEC)
1	Hicham El Guerrouj, Morocco	1999	3:43.13
2	Noah Ngeny, Kenya	1999	3:43.40
3	Noureddine Morceli, Algeria	1993	3:44.39
4	Hicham El Guerrouj	1998	3:44.60
5	Hicham El Guerrouj	1997	3:44.90
6	Hicham El Guerrouj	2001	3:44.95
7	Noureddine Morceli	1995	3:45.19
8	Hicham El Guerrouj	1997	3:45.64
9	Hicham El Guerrouj	2000	3:45.96
10	Hicham El Guerrouj	2000	3:46.24

World record-holder Hicham El Guerrouj was inspired by his countryman Said Aouita, the 1984 Olympic 5,000-meters champion. Opting instead for the shorter distance, El Guerroj set the current world record in Rome in July 1999. As of March 23, 2004, he holds three world records.

TOP 10 HIGHEST HIGH JUMPS

	ATHLETE/COUNTRY	YEAR	HEIGHT* (M)
1	Javier Sotomayor, Cuba	1993	2.45
2	= Patrik Sjöberg, Sweden	1987	2.42
	= Carlo Thränhardt, West Germany#	1988	2.42
4	Igor Paklin, USSR	1985	2.41
5	= Charles Austin, US	1991	2.40
	= Hollis Conway, US#	1991	2.40
	= Sorin Matei, Romania	1990	2.40
	= Rudolf Povarnitsyn, USSR	1985	2.40
	= Vyochaslav Voronin, Russia	2000	2.40
10	= Dietmar Mögenburg, West Germany#	1985	2.39
	= Ralph Sonn, Germany#	1991	2.39
	= Jianhua Zhu, China	1984	2.39

Highest by each athlete only; as of January 1, 2004

Indoor

Javier Sotomayor followed up his Olympic gold in 1992 by winning the 1993 World Indoor title; he then set the world record in Salamanca, followed by gold in the World Championships in Stuttgart.

TOP 10 LONGEST LONG JUMPS

	ATHLETE/COUNTRY	YEAR	DISTANCE* (M)
1	Mike Powell, US	1991	8.95
2	Bob Beamon, US	1968	8.90
3	Carl Lewis, US	1991	8.87
4	Robert Emmiyan, USSR	1987	8.86
5	= Larry Myricks, US	1988	8.74
	= Erick Walder, US	1994	8.74
7	Iván Pedroso, Cuba	1995	8.71
8	Kareem Streete-Thompson, US	1994	8.63
9	James Beckford, Jamaica	1997	8.62
10	Miguel Pate, US#	2002	8.59

Longest by each athlete only; as of January 1, 2004

Indoor

The long jump world record has been broken by just four men since 1935 when Jesse Owens set a new world record mark of 8.13 meters. Ralph Boston broke it six times and the Russian Igor Ter-Ovanesyan twice. Their joint record of 8.35 meters was destroyed in Mexico City, when Bob Beamon leapt 8.90 meters. Beamon's record stood for 23 years until it was beaten by Mike Powell.

TOP 10 FASTEST WOMEN EVER*

	ATHLETE/COUNTRY	YEAR	TIME
1	**Florence Griffith Joyner**, US	1988	10.49
2	**Marion Jones**, US	1998	10.65
3	**Christine Arron**, France	1998	10.73
4	**Merlene Ottey**, Jamaica	1996	10.74
5	**Evelyn Ashford**, US	1984	10.76
6	**Irina Privalova**, Russia	1994	10.77
7	**Dawn Sowell**, US	1989	10.78
8	= **Inger Miller**, US	1999	10.79
	= **Xuemei Li**, China	1997	10.79
10	**Marlies Oelsner-Göhr**, East Germany	1983	10.81

* Based on fastest time for the 100 meters; as of January 1, 2004

◄ **Tim's time**
The world's fastest man, Tim Montgomery of the United States, who set a new world record mark of 9.78 seconds for the 100 meters in Paris on September 14, 2002.

TOP 10 FASTEST MEN EVER*

	ATHLETE/COUNTRY	YEAR	TIME
1	**Tim Montgomery**, US	2002	9.78
2	**Maurice Greene**, US	1999	9.79
3	= **Donovan Bailey**, Canada	1996	9.84
	= **Bruny Surin**, Canada	1999	9.84
5	**Leroy Burrell**, US	1994	9.85
6	= **Ato Boldon**, Trinidad	1998	9.86
	= **Frank Fredericks**, Namibia	1996	9.86
	= **Carl Lewis**, US	1991	9.86
9	= **Dwain Chambers**, UK	2002	9.87
	= **Linford Christie**, UK	1993	9.87
	= **Obadele Thompson**, Barbados	1998	9.87

* Based on fastest time for the 100 meters; as of January 1, 2004

Some would argue that Michael Johnson (US) should be in this category with his remarkable 200-meter record of 19.32 seconds in 1996 (equivalent to a 100-meter time of 9.66 seconds), but his best 100-meter time is only 10.09 seconds.

Football Facts

▼ **A Cowboy catch**
The Dallas Cowboys, winners of a joint record five Super Bowls, have appeared in eight finals—an outright record.

TOP 10 | BIGGEST WINNING MARGINS IN THE SUPER BOWL

	WINNERS	RUNNERS-UP	YEAR	SCORE	MARGIN
1	San Francisco 49ers	Denver Broncos	1990	55–10	45
2	Chicago Bears	New England Patriots	1986	46–10	36
3	Dallas Cowboys	Buffalo Bills	1993	52–17	35
4	Washington Redskins	Denver Broncos	1988	42–10	32
5	Los Angeles Raiders	Washington Redskins	1984	38–9	29
6 =	Baltimore Ravens	New York Giants	2001	34–7	27
=	Tampa Bay Buccaneers	Oakland Raiders	2003	48–21	27
8	Green Bay Packers	Kansas City Chiefs	1967	35–10	25
9	San Francisco 49ers	San Diego Chargers	1995	49–26	23
10	San Francisco 49ers	Miami Dolphins	1985	38–16	22

Source: *National Football League*

The closest Super Bowl was in 1991, when the New York Giants beat the Buffalo Bills 20–19. Scott Norwood missed a 47-yard field goal eight seconds from the end, depriving the Bills of their first-ever Super Bowl win.

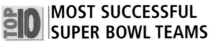

MOST SUCCESSFUL SUPER BOWL TEAMS

	TEAM	WINS	RUNNERS-UP	POINTS*
1	Dallas Cowboys	5	3	13
2 =	Pittsburgh Steelers	4	1	10
=	San Francisco 49ers	5	0	10
4 =	Denver Broncos	2	4	8
=	Oakland/Los Angeles Raiders	3	2	8
=	Washington Redskins	3	2	8
7 =	Green Bay Packers	3	1	7
=	Miami Dolphins	2	3	7
9	New England Patriots	2	2	6
10	New York Giants	2	1	5

SUPER BOWL GAMES

* Based on two points for a Super Bowl win, and one for runner-up; wins take precedence over runners-up in determining ranking

Source: *National Football League*

POINTS-SCORERS IN AN NFL SEASON

	PLAYER	TEAM	YEAR	POINTS
1	Paul Hornung	Green Bay Packers	1960	176
2	Gary Anderson	Minnesota Vikings	1998	164
3	Jeff Wilkins	St. Louis Rams	2003	163
4	Priest Holmes	Kansas City Chiefs	2003	162
5	Mark Moseley	Washington Redskins	1983	161
6	Marshall Faulk	St. Louis Rams	2000	160
7	Mike Vanderjagt	Indianapolis Colts	1999	157
8	Gino Cappelletti	Boston Patriots	1964	155*
9	Emmitt Smith	Dallas Cowboys	1995	150
10	Chip Lohmiller	Washington Redskins	1991	149

* Including a two-point conversion

Source: *National Football League*

A former Heisman Trophy winner, Paul Hornung played for the crack Green Bay team in the 1960s. He led the NFL three times in scoring, and was voted MVP (Most Valuable Player) in 1960 and 1961.

PLAYERS WITH THE MOST CAREER POINTS

	PLAYER	POINTS
1	Gary Anderson*	2,346
2	Morten Andersen*	2,259
3	George Blanda	2,002
4	Norm Johnson	1,736
5	Nick Lowery	1,711
6	Jan Stenerud	1,699
7	Eddie Murray	1,594
8	Al Del Greco	1,584
9	Pat Leahy	1,470
10	Jim Turner	1,439

* Still active at end of 2003 season

Source: *National Football League*

Born in 1959, Gary Anderson started his career with the Steelers in 1982 before two seasons with Philadelphia in 1995–96. He had a year with the 49ers in 1997, moving on to the Minnesota Vikings in 1998 and then to the Tennessee Titans in 2003. He broke George Blanda's points record in 2000.

PLAYERS WITH THE MOST CAREER TOUCHDOWNS

	PLAYER	TOUCHDOWNS
1	Jerry Rice*	205
2	Emmitt Smith*	166
3	Marcus Allen	145
4 =	Cris Carter	131
=	Marshall Faulk*	131
6	Jim Brown	126
7	Walter Payton	125
8	John Riggins	116
9	Lenny Moore	113
10	Barry Sanders	109

* Still active at end of 2003 season

Source: *National Football League*

A wide receiver, Jerry Rice holds Super Bowl records in touchdowns, receptions, and receiving yards, winning three Super Bowls with the San Francisco 49ers (1989, 1990, 1995). He topped the NFL scoring list in 1987 with 130 points.

PLAYERS WITH THE MOST PASSING YARDS IN AN NFL CAREER

	PLAYER	PASSING YARDS
1	Dan Marino	61,361
2	John Elway	51,475
3	Warren Moon	49,325
4	Fran Tarkenton	47,003
5	Brett Favre*	45,646
6	Dan Fouts	43,040
7	Vinny Testaverde*	40,943
8	Joe Montana	40,551
9	Johnny Unitas	40,239
10	Dave Krieg	38,147

* Still active at end of 2003 season

Source: *National Football League*

After 17 consecutive seasons with the Dolphins, Dan Marino quit the game in 1999, but left with 20 NFL records to his credit. At the time of his retirement, he led the NFL in touchdown passes, yards passing, pass attempts, and completions.

Basketball Bests

TOP 10 TEAMS WITH THE MOST NBA TITLES

	TEAM*	TITLES
1	Boston Celtics	16
2	Minneapolis/Los Angeles Lakers	15
3	Chicago Bulls	6
4	= Philadelphia/Golden State Warriors	3
	= Syracuse Nationals/Philadelphia 76ers	3
6	= Baltimore/Washington Bullets	2
	= Detroit Pistons	2
	= Houston Rockets	2
	= New York Knicks	2
	= San Antonio Spurs	2

Teams separated by / have changed franchise and won the championship under both names

Source: *National Basketball Association*

Professional basketball in the United States dates to 1898, but the National Basketball Association (NBA) was not formed until 1949, when the National Basketball League and Basketball Association of America merged. The NBA consists of 27 teams split into Eastern and Western Conferences. At the end of an 82-game regular season, the top eight teams in each Conference play off, and the two Conference champions meet in a best-of-seven final.

TOP 10 PLAYERS TO HAVE PLAYED MOST GAMES IN THE NBA AND ABA

	PLAYER	GAMES PLAYED*
1	Robert Parish	1,611
2	Kareem Abdul-Jabbar	1,560
3	John Stockton	1,504
4	Karl Malone#	1,476
5	Moses Malone	1,455
6	Kevin Willis#	1,390
7	Buck Williams	1,348
8	Artis Gilmore	1,329
9	Reggie Miller#	1,323
10	Elvin Hayes	1,303

Regular season games only; up to end of 2003–04 season

Still active in the 2003-04 season

Source: *National Basketball Association*

The American Basketball Association (ABA) was established as a rival to the National Basketball Association (NBA) in 1968 and ran until 1976. As many of the sport's top players "defected," its figures are still included above. Robert Parish moved to the top of this list on April 6, 1996, playing his 1,561st game at the Gateway Arena in Cleveland, between the Charlotte Hornets and the Cleveland Cavaliers.

TOP 10 POINT-SCORERS IN AN NBA CAREER

	PLAYER	TOTAL POINTS*
1	Kareem Abdul-Jabbar	38,387
2	Karl Malone#	36,928
3	Michael Jordan	32,292
4	Wilt Chamberlain	31,419
5	Moses Malone	27,409
6	Elvin Hayes	27,313
7	Hakeem Olajuwon	26,946
8	Oscar Robertson	26,710
9	Dominique Wilkins	26,668
10	John Havlicek	26,395

Regular season games only; up to end of 2003–04 season

Still active in the 2003-04 season

Source: *National Basketball Association*

If points from the ABA were also considered, then Abdul-Jabbar would still be No. 1. Born Lew Alcindor, he took a new name when he converted to the Islamic faith in 1969. The following year he turned professional, playing for Milwaukee until he retired in 1989. Despite holding the NBA record, he never scored 100 points in a game, a feat achieved by Wilt Chamberlain for Philadelphia against New York at Hershey, Pennsylvania, on March 2, 1962.

TOP 10 COACHES WITH THE MOST WINS IN THE NBA

	COACH	YEARS	REGULAR SEASON WINS	PLAY-OFF WINS	TOTAL WINS
1	Lenny Wilkens*	30	1,292	80	1,372
2	Pat Riley*	21	1,110	155	1,265
3	Don Nelson*	25	1,096	69	1,165
4	Red Auerbach	20	938	99	1,037
5	Bill Fitch	25	944	55	999
6	Dick Motta	25	935	56	991
7	Jerry Sloan*	18	875	78	953
8	Larry Brown*	20	879	69	948
9	Phil Jackson*	12	776	162	938
10	Jack Ramsay	21	864	44	908

Still active in the 2002–03 season

Source: *National Basketball Association*

Pat Riley, coach of the LA Lakers, the New York Knicks, and the Miami Heat, has the best percentage record of those listed above, with 1,110 wins from 1,679 games, representing a 0.608 percent success rate.

TOP 10 HIGHEST SCORES IN THE NBA

	MATCH	DATE	SCORE*
1	Detroit Pistons vs. Denver Nuggets	13 Dec 1983	186(3)
2	Denver Nuggets vs. Detroit Pistons	13 Dec 1983	184(3)
3	= Boston Celtics vs. Minneapolis Lakers	27 Feb 1959	173
	= Phoenix Suns vs. Denver Nuggets	10 Nov 1990	173(3)
5	San Antonio Spurs vs. Milwaukee Bucks	6 Mar 1982	171(3)
6	Philadelphia 76ers vs. New York Knicks#	2 Mar 1962	169
7	Milwaukee Bucks vs. San Antonio Spurs	6 Mar 1982	166(3)
8	Cincinatti Royals vs. San Diego Clippers	12 Mar 1970	165
9	= Denver Nuggets v San Antonio Spurs	11 Jan 1984	163
	= Philadelphia 76ers v San Francisco Warriors	10 Mar 1963	163
	= San Antonio Spurs v San Diego Clippers	8 Nov 1978	163

Figures in brackets indicate periods of overtime played

Game played at Hershey, Pennsylvania

The Denver—Detroit match on December 13, 1983 is the highest-scoring game on aggregate, with a total of 370 points scored. The score stood at 145-all at the end of normal play, with Detroit eventually winning after three extra periods of play.

TOP 10 PLAYERS WITH THE HIGHEST POINTS AVERAGE

	PLAYER	GAMES PLAYED	POINTS SCORED	POINTS AVERAGE*
1	= Wilt Chamberlain	1,045	31,419	30.1
	= Michael Jordan	1,072	32,292	30.1
3	Elgin Baylor	846	23,149	27.4
4	Shaquille O'Neal#	809	21,916	27.1
5	= Allen Iverson#	535	14,436	27.0
	= Jerry West	932	25,192	27.0
7	Bob Pettit	792	20,880	26.4
8	George Gervin	791	20,708	26.2
9	Oscar Robertson	1,040	26,710	25.7
10	Karl Malone#	1,476	36,928	25.0

* Regular season games only; up to end of 2003–04 season

\# Still active in the 2003–04 season

Source: National Basketball Association

▶ **West Coast winners**
Along with the Boston Celtics, the Lakers are the most successful team in NBA history. They have won one less title than the Celtics but have appeared in nine more finals than their rivals.

TOP 10 POINT-SCORERS IN THE 2003–04 SEASON

	PLAYER/TEAM	GAMES	FIELD GOALS	FREE THROWS	TOTAL
1	**Kevin Garnett,** Minnesota Timberwolves	82	804	368	1,987
2	**Predrag Stojakovic,** Sacramento Kings	81	665	394	1,964
3	**Tracy McGrady,** Orlando Magic	67	653	398	1,878
4	**Paul Pierce,** Boston Celtics	80	602	517	1,836
5	**Michael Redd,** Milwaukee Bucks	82	633	383	1,776
6	**Carmelo Anthony,** Denver Nuggets	82	624	408	1,725
7	**Dirk Nowitksi,** Dallas Mavericks	77	605	371	1,680
8	**LeBron James,** Cleveland Cavaliers	79	622	347	1,654
9	**Vince Carter,** Toronto Raptors	73	608	336	1,645
10	**Stephon Marbury,** New Orleans Hornets	81	598	356	1,639

Source: National Basketball Association

Baseball Teams

TOP 10 BASEBALL TEAMS WITH THE MOST MAJOR LEAGUE WINS

	TEAM	GAMES WON*
1	New York Yankees	8,996
2	San Francisco Giants	8,597
3	Los Angeles Dodgers	8,328
4	St. Louis Cardinals	8,231
5	Pittsburgh Pirates	8,204
6	Boston Red Sox	8,165
7	Cleveland Indians	8,129
8	Detroit Tigers	8,078
9	Chicago Cubs	8,046
10	Cincinnati Reds	8,031

* Regular season games up to and including 2003

The Yankees made their American League debut as the Baltimore Orioles in 1901, and the following season they finished at the bottom of the League. It was then that they moved to New York and became the Highlanders. They changed their name to the Yankees in 1913.

TOP 10 TEAMS WINNING THE MOST AMERICAN LEAGUE SEASON AND DIVISION TITLES

	TEAM	FIRST TITLE	LAST TITLE	TOTAL
1	New York Yankees	1921	2003	39
2	Oakland Athletics	1902	1990	15
3 =	Boston Red Sox	1903	1986	10
=	Detroit Tigers	1907	1984	9
5	Baltimore Orioles	1944	1983	7
6	Minnesota Twins	1924	1991	6
7	Cleveland Indians	1920	1997	5
8	Chicago White Sox	1906	1959	4
9 =	Kansas City Royals	1980	1985	2
=	Toronto Blue Jays	1992	1993	2

The Yankees won their first title in 1921, when they won the League from Cleveland with a 98–55 record and a .641 percentage. The Seattle Mariners, the Tampa Bay Devil Rays, and the Texas Rangers are the only three American League teams never to have won a title.

TOP 10 LATEST WINNERS OF THE WORLD SERIES

YEAR	WINNER/LEAGUE	LOSER/LEAGUE	SCORE
2003	Florida Marlins (N)	New York Yankees (A)	4-2
2002	Anaheim Angels (A)	San Francisco Giants (N)	4-3
2001	Arizona Diamondbacks (N)	New York Yankees (A)	4-3
2000	New York Yankees (A)	New York Mets (N)	4-1
1999	New York Yankees (A)	Atlanta Braves (N)	4-0
1998	New York Yankees (A)	San Diego Padres (N)	4-0
1997	Florida Marlins (N)	Cleveland Indians (A)	4-3
1996	New York Yankees (A)	Atlanta Braves (N)	4-2
1995	Atlanta Braves (N)	Cleveland Indians (A)	4-2
1993	Toronto Blue Jays (A)	Philadelphia Phillies (N)	4-2*

* The 1994 event was canceled due to a players' strike

A = American League

N = National League

Source: *Major League Baseball*

TOP 10 BASEBALL TEAMS PLAYING THE MOST GAMES IN MAJOR LEAGUE BASEBALL

	TEAM	GAMES PLAYED*
1	Atlanta Braves	16,042
2	Detroit Tigers	16,040
3	Cincinnati Reds	16,037
4	St. Louis Cardinals	16,035
5	San Francisco Giants	16,024
6 =	Los Angeles Dodgers	16,023
=	Pittsburgh Pirates	16,023
8	Minnesota Twins	16,021
9	Cleveland Indians	16,015
10	Baltimore Orioles	16,014

* Regular season games up to and including 2003

Originally based in Boston, the Braves played their first National League game at Philadelphia in front of 3,000 fans on April 22, 1876. Thanks to two runs in the ninth, the Braves ran out 6-5 winners.

TEAMS WITH THE BEST BATTING AVERAGE, 2003

	TEAM	AVERAGE*
1	Boston Red Sox	.289
2	Atlanta Braves	.284
3	= St. Louis Cardinals	.279
	= Toronto Blue Jays	.279
5	Minnesota Twins	.277
6	Kansas City Royals	.274
7	= New York Yankees	.271
	= Seattle Mariners	.271
9	= Anaheim Angels	.268
	= Baltimore Orioles	.268

* Regular season

Source: *Major League Baseball*

Despite having the best batting average in the American League, the Red Sox still finished second to the Yankees. The Yankees also beat them in the American League Championship game, winning the 7th and last game 6–5.

BIGGEST SINGLE-GAME WINS IN THE WORLD SERIES

	TEAMS*/GAME	DATE	SCORE
1	New York Yankees vs. New York Giants (Game 2)	Oct. 2, 1936	18–4
2	New York Yankees vs. Pittsburgh Pirates (Game 2)	Oct. 6, 1960	16–3
	= Arizona Diamondbacks vs. New York Yankees (Game 6)	Nov. 3, 2001	15–2
4	= New York Yankees vs. New York Giants (Game 5)	Oct. 9, 1951	13–1
	= New York Yankees vs. Pittsburgh Pirates (Game 6)	Oct. 12, 1960	12–0
	= Detroit Tigers vs. St. Louis Cardinals (Game 6)	Oct. 9, 1968	13–1
	= New York Yankees vs. Milwaukee Brewers (Game 6)	Oct. 19, 1982	13–1
	= San Francisco Giants vs. Anaheim Angels (Game 5)	Oct. 24, 2002	16–4
9	= New York Yankees vs. Philadelphia Athletics (Game 6)	Oct. 26, 1911	13–2
	= St. Louis Cardinals vs. Detroit Tigers (Game 7)	Oct. 9, 1934	11–0
	= Chicago White Sox vs. Los Angeles Dodgers (Game 1)	Oct. 1, 1959	11–0
	= Kansas City Royals vs. St. Louis Cardinals (Game 7)	Oct. 27, 1985	11–0
	= Atlanta Braves vs. New York Yankees (Game 1)	Oct. 20, 1996	12–1

* Winners listed first

Source: *Major League Baseball*

TEAMS WINNING THE MOST NATIONAL LEAGUE SEASON AND DIVISION TITLES

	TEAM	FIRST TITLE	LAST TITLE	TOTAL*
1	Los Angeles Dodgers	1890	1988	21
2	San Francisco Giants	1888	1989	20
3	St. Louis Cardinals	1926	1987	15
4	Chicago Cubs	1876	1945	16
5	= Atlanta Braves	1877	1999	17
	= Cincinnati Reds	1919	1990	9
7	Pittsburgh Pirates	1901	1979	9
8	Philadelphia Phillies	1915	1993	5
9	New York Mets	1969	2000	4
10	= Florida Marlins	1997	2003	2
	= San Diego Padres	1984	1998	2

The Dodgers won their first title in their inaugural season in the National League. They were known as the Brooklyn Dodgers at the time they won the title from Chicago, and went on to meet Louisville in the "World Championship" game. The Colorado Rockies, the Houston Astros, and the Montreal Expos are the only National League teams never to have won a title.

TEAMS WITH THE MOST WORLD SERIES WINS

	TEAM*	WINS
1	New York Yankees	26
2	= Philadelphia/Kansas City/Oakland Athletics	9
	= St. Louis Cardinals	9
4	Brooklyn/Los Angeles Dodgers	6
5	= Boston Red Sox	5
	= Cincinnati Reds	5
	= New York/San Francisco Giants	5
	= Pittsburgh Pirates	5
9	Detroit Tigers	4
10	= Boston/Milwaukee/Atlanta Braves	3
	= St. Louis/Baltimore Orioles	3
	= Washington Senators/Minnesota Twins	3

* Teams separated by / indicate changes of franchise and are regarded as the same team for Major League record purposes

Source: *Major League Baseball*

The World Series has been held every year since 1905, except in 1994, when a players' strike curtailed the season. It has been a best-of-seven games series since 1905, with the exception of 1919–21, when it was to a nine-game series.

Baseball Stars

TOP 10 | PLAYERS WITH THE MOST RUNS IN A CAREER

	PLAYER	YEARS	RUNS*
1	Rickey Henderson	1979–2003	2,295
2	Ty Cobb	1905–28	2,245
3	= Hank Aaron	1954–76	2,174
	= Babe Ruth	1914–35	2,174
5	Pete Rose	1963–86	2,165
6	Willie Mays	1951–73	2,062
7	Cap Anson	1871–97	1,996
8	Stan Musial	1941–63	1,949
9	Barry Bonds	1986–2003	1,941
10	Lou Gehrig	1923–39	1,888

* Regular season only up to and including 2003

Source: Major League Baseball

Ty Cobb's 73-year old record of 2,245 runs was eventually beaten by the San Diego Padres' Rickey Henderson against the Dodgers in October 2001. Even though he had hit a home run, Henderson still slid in to home base as he promised he would if he broke the record.

TOP 10 | PLAYERS WITH THE HIGHEST CAREER BATTING AVERAGES

	PLAYER	AT BAT	HITS	AVERAGE*
1	Ty Cobb	11,434	4,189	.366
2	Rogers Hornsby	8,173	2,930	.358
3	Joe Jackson	4,981	1,772	.356
4	Ed Delahanty	7,505	2,596	.346
5	Tris Speaker	10,195	3,514	.345
6	= Billy Hamilton	6,269	2,159	.344
	= Ted Williams	7,706	2,654	.344
8	= Dan Brouthers	6,711	2,296	.342
	= Harry Heilmann	7,787	2,660	.342
	= Babe Ruth	8,399	2,873	.342

* Calculated by dividing the number of hits by the number of times a batter was at bat; up to and including 2003 season

Source: Major League Baseball

Second only to the legendary Ty Cobb, Rogers Hornsby stands as the best-hitting second-baseman of all time, with an average of over .400 in a five-year period. Baseball's greatest right-handed hitter, slugging 20-plus homers on seven occasions, he achieved a career average of .358.

TOP 10 | PITCHERS WITH THE MOST CAREER WINS

	PITCHER	YEARS	WINS
1	Cy Young	1890–1911	511
2	Walter Johnson	1907–27	417
3	= Grover Alexander	1911–30	373
	= Christy Mathewson	1900–16	373
5	Jim Galvin	1875–92	365
6	Warren Spahn	1942–65	363
7	Kid Nichols	1890–1906	361
8	Tim Keefe	1880–93	342
9	Steve Carlton	1965–88	329
10	John Clarkson	1882–94	328

* Regular season only up to and including 2003

Source: Major League Baseball

Denton True 'Cy' Young won almost 100 games more than any other pitcher. In a 22-year career he played for nine different teams, but enjoyed his best spell with the Red Sox. He won two games for them in the first World Series in 1903, which they won. In 1904 he pitched the first perfect game in the American League.

TOP 10 | PLAYERS WITH THE MOST HOME RUNS IN A CAREER

	PLAYER	YEARS	HOME RUNS*
1	Hank Aaron	1954–76	755
2	Babe Ruth	1914–35	714
3	Willie Mays	1951–73	660
4	Barry Bonds	1986–2003	658
5	Frank Robinson	1956–76	586
6	Mark McGwire	1986–2001	583
7	Harmon Killebrew	1954–75	573
8	Reggie Jackson	1967–87	563
9	Mike Schmidt	1972–89	548
10	Sammy Sosa	1989–2003	539

* Regular season only up to and including 2003

Source: Major League Baseball

George Herman "Babe" Ruth set a home run record in 1919 by hitting 29, breaking it the next season by hitting 54. His career (1914–35) total of 714 came from 8,399 at-bats, which represents an average of 8.5 percent—considerably better than his nearest rival, Harmon Killebrew, who averaged 7.0 percent.

TOP 10 PLAYERS WHO PLAYED THE MOST GAMES IN A CAREER

	PLAYER	YEARS	GAMES*
1	Pete Rose	1963–86	3,562
2	Carl Yastrzemski	1961–83	3,308
3	Hank Aaron	1954–76	3,298
4	Rickey Henderson	1979–2003	3,081
5	Ty Cobb	1905–28	3,035
6	= Eddie Murray	1977–97	3,026
	= Stan Musial	1941–63	3,026
8	Cal Ripken Jr.	1981–2001	3,001
9	Willie Mays	1951–73	2,992
10	Dave Winfield	1973–95	2,973

Regular season only up to and including 2003

Source: *Major League Baseball*

The top run maker in baseball history, Chicago-born Rickey Henderson started his Major League career with the Oakland Athletics in 1979. Since then he has played with nine different teams in a 25-year career. Known as "The Man of Steal," Henderson was the 1990 American League MVP.

TOP 10 LOWEST EARNED RUN AVERAGES IN A CAREER

	PLAYER	YEARS	ERA
1	Ed Walsh	1904–17	1.82
2	Addie Joss	1902–10	1.89
3	Al Spalding	1871–78	2.04
4	Mordecai Brown	1903–16	2.06
5	John Ward	1878–94	2.10
6	Christy Mathewson	1900–16	2.13
7	Tommy Bond	1874–84	2.14
8	Rube Waddell	1897–10	2.16
9	Walter Johnson	1907–27	2.17
10	= Ed Reulbach	1905–17	2.28
	= Will White	1877–86	2.28

Regular season only up to and including 2003

Source: *Major League Baseball*

Ed Walsh spent 13 seasons playing with the White Sox between 1904 and 1916 before ending his career with the Boston Braves. Between 1906 and 1912 he averaged 24 wins a season, and when he retired he had a 195–126 career record. Walsh was indcted into the Hall of Fame in 1946 and died at age 78 in 1959.

TOP 10 PLAYERS WITH THE MOST HOME RUNS IN A SEASON

	PLAYER	TEAM	YEAR	RUNS
1	Barry Bonds	San Francisco Giants	2001	73
2	Mark McGwire	St. Louis Cardinals	1998	70
3	Sammy Sosa	Chicago Cubs	1998	66
4	Mark McGuire	St. Louis Cardinals	1999	65
5	Sammy Sosa	Chicago Cubs	2001	64
6	Sammy Sosa	Chicago Cubs	1999	63
7	Roger Maris	New York Yankees	1961	61
8	Babe Ruth	New York Yankees	1927	60
9	Babe Ruth	New York Yankees	1921	59
10	= Jimmie Foxx	Philadelphia Phillies	1932	58
	= Hank Greenberg	Detroit Tigers	1938	58
	= Mark McGuire	St. Louis Cardinals	1997	58

Regular season only up to and including 2003

Source: *Major League Baseball*

TOP 10 PITCHERS WITH THE MOST CAREER STRIKEOUTS

	PITCHER	YEARS	STRIKEOUTS*
1	Nolan Ryan	1966–93	5,714
2	Steve Carlton	1965–88	4,136
3	Roger Clemens	1983–2003	4,099
4	Randy Johnson	1985–2003	3,871
5	Bert Blyleven	1970–92	3,701
6	Tom Seaver	1967–86	3,640
7	Don Sutton	1966–88	3,574
8	Gaylord Perry	1962–83	3,534
9	Walter Johnson	1907–27	3,508
10	Phil Niekro	1964–87	3,342

Regular season only up to and including 2003

Source: *Major League Baseball*

Nolan Ryan was known as the "Babe Ruth of strikeout pitchers," pitching faster (a record 101 mph/162.5 km/h) and longer (27 seasons—1966 and 1968–93) than any previous player. As well as his 5,714 strikeouts, including 383 in one season, he walked 2,795 batters and allowed the fewest hits (6.55) per nine innings.

International Soccer

MOST-CAPPED INTERNATIONAL PLAYERS

	PLAYER	COUNTRY	YEARS	CAPS*
1	Claudio Suarez#	Mexico	1992–2003	171
2	Mohamed Al-Deayea#	Saudi Arabia	1990–2004	166
3	Adnan Kh. Al-Talyania	United Arab Republic	1984–1997	164
4	= Hossam Hassan#	Egypt	1985–2004	160
	= Cobi Jones#	US	1992–2003	160
6	Lothar Matthäus	West Germany/Germany	1980–2000	150
7	= Mohammed Al-Khilaiwi#	Saudi Arabia	1992–2002	143
	= Thomas Ravelli	Sweden	1981–1997	143
9	Majed Abdullah	Saudi Arabia	1978–1994	140
10	Marko Kristal#	Estonia	1992–2004	138

* As of March 8, 2004

Still active in 2004

Source: Roberto Mamrud, Karel Stokkermans, and RSSSF 1998/2004

Caps are awarded when players appear in a senior international match against another country. Some countries award caps for every individual appearance while others will issue only one cap per tournament, as long as they play at some point.

HIGHEST-EARNING FOOTBALLERS

	PLAYER/CLUB	ANNUAL INCOME* ($)
1	David Beckham (Real Madrid#)	16,941,000
2	Zinedine Zidane (Real Madrid)	15,812,000
3	Ronaldo (Real Madrid)	13,214,000
4	Rio Ferdinand (Manchester United)	10,865,000
5	Alessandro Del Piero (Juventus)	10,786,000
6	Hidetoshi Nakata (Bologna†)	10,571,000
7	Raul (Real Madrid)	10,503,000
8	Christian Vieri (Inter Milan)	10,481,000
9	Michael Owen (Liverpool)	10,052,000
10	Roy Keane (Manchester United)	9,769,000

* As at May 6, 2003

Formerly Manchester United

† Formerly Parma

Source: France Football, as of May 6, 2003

▶ **ZZ Top**

Marseille-born Zinedine Zidane is not only the most expensive footballer ever, but probably the greatest player in the world today as well. When he joined Real Madrid from Juventus in 2001, he cost more than $67 million.

TOP 10 TRANSFERS IN INTERNATIONAL SOCCER

	PLAYER/COUNTRY	FROM	TO	YEAR	FEE ($)*
1	Zinedine Zidane, France	Juventus, Italy	Real Madrid, Spain	2001	67,300,000
2	Luis Figo, Portugal	Barcelona, Spain	Real Madrid, Spain	2000	56,800,000
3	Hernan Crespo, Argentina	Parma, Italy	Lazio, Italy	2000	54,100,000
4	Rio Ferdinand, UK	Leeds United, England	Manchester United, England	2002	47,300,000
5	Gianluigi Buffon, Italy	Parma, Italy	Juventus, Italy	2001	46,200,000
6	Gaizka Mendieta, Spain	Valencia, Spain	Lazio, Italy	2001	41,300,000
7	Rui Costa, Portugal	Fiorentina, Italy	AC Milan, Italy	2001	39,700,000
8	Juan Sebastian Veron, Argentina	Lazio, Italy	Manchester United, England	2001	39,600,000
9	Christian Vieri, Italy	Lazio, Italy	Inter Milan, Italy	1999	38,500,000#
10	Nicolas Anelka, France	Arsenal, England	Real Madrid, Spain	1999	38,000,000

* Figures vary slightly from source to source, depending on whether local taxes, agents' fees, and player's commission are included

Vieri's transfer was part of a package deal with Nicola Ventola, who was valued at $11.2 million. Vieri was valued at $38.5 million

The £17 million ($28 million) transfer of David Beckham from Manchester United (England) to Real Madrid (Spain) in 2003 does not make this list, but the England captain has eclipsed his costlier team-mates Zinadine Zidane (France), Luis Figo (Portugal), and Ronaldo (Brazil) to become the world's highest-earning footballer.

TOP 10 RICHEST FOOTBALL CLUBS

	CLUB	COUNTRY	TURNOVER (2002/3) ($)
1	Manchester United	England	263,995,140
2	Juventus	Italy	229,236,830
3	AC Milan	Italy	210,230,020
4	Real Madrid	Spain	202,249,260
5	Bayern Munich	Germany	170,851,270
6	Inter Milan	Italy	170,536,240
7	Arsenal	England	157,094,960
8	Liverpool	England	156,884,940
9	Newcastle United	England	145,858,890
10	Chelsea	England	140,503,380

Source: Sport Business Group at Deloitte

In August 1989, the sale of Manchester United for £20 million ($33 million) to UK businessman Michael Knighton was agreed, but the deal fell through after his backers pulled out and, he duly bought Carlisle United instead. Two years later Manchester United was floated on the Stock Exchange, when it was valued at £18 million ($30 million), and the club is now valued at over £160 million ($250 million).

TOP 10 BIGGEST WINS IN MAJOR INTERNATIONAL TOURNAMENTS

	WINNER/LOSER	TOURNAMENT	SCORE
1	Australia vs. American Samoa	2002 World Cup Qualifier	31–0
2	Australia vs. Tonga	2002 World Cup Qualifier	22–0
3	Kuwait vs. Bhutan	2000 Asian Championship Qualifier	20–0
4 =	China vs. Guam	2000 Asian Championship Qualifier	19–0
=	Iran vs. Guam	2002 World Cup Qualifier	19–0
6	Tahiti vs. American Samoa	2000 Oceanian Championship Qualifier	18–0
7 =	Australia vs. Cook Islands	2000 Oceanian Championship	17–0
=	China vs. Maldives	1992 Olympic Games Qualifier	17–0
=	Iran vs. Maldives	1998 World Cup Qualifier	17–0
10 =	Australia vs. Cook Islands	1998 Oceanian Championship	16–0
=	Denmark vs. France	1908 Olympic Games	17–1
=	South Korea vs. Nepal	2004 Asian Championship	16–0
=	Tajikistan vs. Guam	2002 World Cup Qualifier	16–0

The record wins for other major tournaments are: Copa America: Argentina vs. Ecuador, 1942, 12–0; European Championship: Spain vs. Malta, 1984, 12–1; British Championship: England vs. Ireland, 1899, 13–2.

TOP 10 GOAL-SCORERS IN INTERNATIONAL SOCCER

	PLAYER	COUNTRY	YEARS	GOALS*
1	Ali Daei#	Iran	1993–2004	87
2	Ferenc Puskás	Hungary/Spain	1945–56	84
3	Pelé	Brazil	1957–71	77
4	Sándor Kocsis	Hungary	1948–56	75
5	Gerd Müller	West Germany	1966–74	68
6	Majed Abdullah	Saudi Arabia	1978–94	67
7	Jassem Al-Houwaidi#	Kuwait	1992–2004	63
8	Kiatisuk Senamuang#	Thailand	1993–2004	62
9	Hossam Hassan#	Egypt	1985–2004	61
10	Imre Schlosser	Hungary	1906–27	60

* As of March 8, 2004

Still active in 2004

Source: Roberto Mamrud, Karel Stokkermans, and RSSSF 1998/2004

If amateur appearances were included, Vivian Woodward (England) would figure on the list at No. 5 because he scored 73 goals for both the full and amateur England sides between 1903–14.

Hockey Highlights

TOP 10 GOAL-SCORERS IN AN NHL CAREER

	PLAYER	SEASONS	GOALS*
1	Wayne Gretzky	20	894
2	Gordie Howe	26	801
3	Brett Hull#	19	741
4	Marcel Dionne	18	731
5	Phil Esposito	18	717
6	Mike Gartner	19	708
7	Mark Messier#	25	694
8	Mario Lemieux#	16	683
9	Steve Yzerman#	21	678
10	Luc Robitaille#	18	653

* Regular season only

Active during 2004–04 season

Source: *National Hockey League*

Wayne Gretzky's first goal in the NHL was against Vancouver on October 14, 1979. The goalie who had the distinction of letting in that first goal was Glen Hanlon. Gretzky's best season was 1981–82, when he scored 92 goals in 80 games with the Edmonton Oilers.

TOP 10 GOALIES IN AN NHL CAREER

	GOALTENDER	SEASONS	GAMES WON*
1	Patrick Roy	19	551
2	Terry Sawchuk	21	447
3	= Ed Belfour#	16	435
	= Jacques Plante	18	435
5	Tony Esposito	16	423
6	Glenn Hall	18	407
7	= Martin Brodeur	12	403
	= Grant Fuhr	19	403
9	Curtis Joseph#	15	396
10	Mike Vernon	19	385

* Regular season only

Active during 2004–04 season

Source: *National Hockey League*

In 1959, Jacques Plante became the first goaltender to wear a mask regularly, after being hit in the face by a backhander from Andy Bathgate, an injury that required seven stitches.

TOP 10 PLAYERS WITH THE MOST ASSISTS IN AN NHL CAREER

	PLAYER	SEASONS	ASSISTS*
1	Wayne Gretzky	20	1,963
2	Ron Francis#	23	1,249
3	Mark Messier#	25	1,193
4	Ray Bourque	22	1,169
5	Paul Coffey	21	1,135
6	Adam Oates#	21	1,079
7	Gordie Howe	26	1,049
8	Steve Yzerman#	21	1,043
9	Marcel Dionne	18	1,040
10	Mario Lemieux#	16	1,018

* Regular season only

Active during 2003–04 season

Source: *National Hockey League/Hockey Database*

Not only does Wayne Gretzky top the career assists list, but he dominates the "most assists in a season" list, occupying all Top 10 positions. His best season was in 1985–86 with 163 assists in 80 games with the Oilers. With the Kings, his best season was 122 assists in 78 games in 1990–91.

TOP 10 PLAYERS WITH THE MOST GAMES IN AN NHL CAREER

	PLAYER	YEARS	GAMES
1	Gordie Howe	1946–80	1,767
2	Mark Messier*	1979–2004	1,756
3	Ron Francis*	1981–2004	1,731
4	Scott Stevens*	1982–2004	1,635
5	Larry Murphy	1980–2001	1,615
6	Ray Bourque	1979–2001	1,612
7	Dave Andreychuk	1982–2004	1,597
8	Alex Delvecchio	1950–74	1,549
9	John Buyck	1955–78	1,540
10	Phil Housley	1982–2003	1,495

* Active during 2004–04 season

Gordie Howe, who holds the record for the most seasons (26) and games played (1,767) in the NHL, retired in 1971 but then returned to play alongside his sons Mark and Marty for Houston in the newly-formed World Hockey Association. He finally retired in 1980 with 801 goals and 1,049 assists to his credit.

THE 10 LATEST STANLEY CUP WINNERS

YEAR	WINNING TEAM	LOSING TEAM	SCORE
2003	New Jersey Devils	Mighty Ducks of Anheim	4–3
2002	Detroit Red Wings	Carolina Hurricanes	4–1
2001	Colorado Avalanche	New Jersey Devils	4–3
2000	New Jersey Devils	Dallas Stars	4–2
1999	Dallas Stars	Buffalo Sabres	4–2
1998	Detroit Red Wings	Washington Capitals	4–0
1997	Detroit Red Wings	Philadelphia Flyers	4–0
1996	Colorado Avalanche	Florida Panthers	4–0
1995	New Jersey Devils	Detroit Red Wings	4–0
1994	New York Rangers	Vancouver Canucks	4–3

Source: *National Hockey League*

The Stanley Cup was originally a challenge trophy—any amateur team in Canada could challenge for it over a single game, or later, in a best-of-three series. . Following the formation of a new league, the Pacific Coast Hockey Association (PCHA) in 1912–13, there began the first end-of-season series of games between the champions of the respective leagues. After the arrival of Portland, Oregon, in the PCHA in 1914, it was decided to let teams from the United States challenge for the Stanley Cup, and in 1917 the Seattle Metropolitans became the first US team to win it. The National Hockey League (NHL) succeeded the NHA in 1917–18, and that season saw the abolition of the challenge system. The NHL has had total control over the Stanley Cup since 1926.

TOP 10 POINT-SCORERS IN THE STANLEY CUP

	PLAYER	GAMES	GOALS	ASSISTS	POINTS*
1	Wayne Gretzky	208	122	260	382
2	Mark Messier#	236	109	186	295
3	Jari Kurri	200	106	127	233
4	Glenn Anderson	225	93	121	214
5	Paul Coffey	194	59	137	196
6	Doug Gilmore#	182	60	128	188
7	Brett Hull#	190	100	85	185
8	Bryan Trottier	221	71	113	184
9	Ray Bourque	214	41	139	180
10 =	Jean Beliveau	162	79	97	176
=	Steve Yzerman	181	67	109	176

* *Up to and including the 2002–03 season*

Active during 2002-03 season

Wayne Gretzky was wearing ice skates from the age of 2. He turned to professional hockey with the Indianapolis Racers in the WHA at 17, but after just eight games he was traded to the Edmonton Oilers. He went on to break 60 NHL records, including the most goals, assists, and points in the Stanley Cup.

TOP 10 NHL GAMES TO PRODUCE THE MOST GOALS

	TEAMS	SCORE	DATE	TOTAL GOALS*
1 =	Montreal Canadiens vs. Toronto St. Patricks	14–7	Jan. 10, 1920	21
=	Edmonton Oilers vs. Chicago Blackhawks	12–9	Dec. 11, 1985	21
3 =	Edmonton Oilers vs. Minnesota North Stars	12–8	Jan. 4, 1984	20
=	Toronto Maple Leafs vs. Edmonton Oilers	11–9	Jan. 8, 1986	20
5 =	Boston Bruins vs. New York Rangers	10–9	Mar. 4, 1944	19
=	Boston Bruins vs. Detroit Red Wings	10–9	Mar. 16, 1944	19
=	Montreal Wanderers vs. Toronto Arenas	10–9	Dec. 19, 1917	19
=	Montreal Canadiens vs. Quebec Bulldogs	16–3	Mar. 3, 1920	19
=	Montreal Canadiens vs. Hamilton Tigers	13–3	Feb. 26, 1921	19
=	Vancouver Canucks vs. Minnesota North Stars	10–9	Oct. 7, 1983	19

* *Up to and including the 2003-04 season*

TOP 10 TEAMS WINNING THE MOST STANLEY CUP TITLES

	TEAM	YEARS	WINS*
1	Montreal Canadiens	1916–93	24
2	Toronto Maple Leafs	1918–67	13
3	Detroit Red Wings	1936–2002	10
4 =	Boston Bruins	1929–72	5
=	Edmonton Oilers	1984–90	5
6 =	New York Islanders	1980–83	4
=	New York Rangers	1933–94	4
=	Ottawa Senators	1920–27	4
9 =	Chicago Black Hawks	1934–1961	3
=	New Jersey Devils	1995–2003	3

* *Since 1918 after the abolition of the challenge match format, up to and including 2003*

The Montreal Canadiens' first Stanley Cup win was in 1916, when they beat Portland 3–2 in the best-of-five series. They have enjoyed two great periods of Stanley Cup success. The first was 1956–60, when they won the trophy five years in succession under coach Hector "Toe" Blake, and the second was in the 1970s, when they won four consecutive titles during 1976–79 under Scotty Bowman.

Tennis Aces

TOP 10 CAREER MONEY WINNERS (WOMEN)

PLAYER/COUNTRY	WINNINGS ($)*
1 Steffi Graf, West Germany/Germany	21,895,277
2 Martina Navratilova, Czechoslovakia/US	20,942,793
3 Martina Hingis, Switzerland	18,344,660
4 Arantxa Sanchez Vicario, Spain	16,917,312
5 Lindsay Davenport, US	16,474,970
6 Monica Seles, Yugoslavia/US	14,891,762
7 Venus Williams, US	13,029,463
8 Serena Williams, US	12,546,863
9 Jana Novotna, Czechoslovakia	11,249,284
10 Conchita Martinez, Spain	10,613,659

* As at end 2003 season

TOP 10 CAREER MONEY WINNERS (MEN)

PLAYER/COUNTRY	WINNINGS ($)*
1 Pete Sampras, US	43,280,489
2 Andre Agassi, US	28,189,425
3 Boris Becker, West Germany/Germany	25,080,956
4 Yevgeny Kafelnikov, Russia	23,883,797
5 Ivan Lendl, Czechoslovakia/US	21,262,417
6 Stefan Edberg, Sweden	20,630,941
7 Goran Ivanisevic, Croatia	19,769,363
8 Michael Chang, US	19,145,632
9 Gustavo Kuerten, Brazil	14,224,746
10 Jim Courier, US	14,033,132

* As at end 2003 season

◀ **Volleying to victory**
Germany's Steffi Graf eventually ended Martina Navratilova's five-year reign as the world number one in 1986, going on to win 22 Grand Slam singles titles.

TOP 10 WINNERS OF MEN'S GRAND SLAM TENNIS SINGLES TITLES

	PLAYER/COUNTRY	A	F	W	US	TOTAL*
1	Pete Sampras, US	2	0	7	5	14
2	Roy Emerson, Australia	6	2	2	2	12
3	= Björn Borg, Sweden	0	6	5	0	11
	= Rod Laver, Australia	3	2	4	2	11
5	Bill Tilden, US	0	0	3	7	10
6	= Jimmy Connors, US	1	0	2	5	8
	= Ivan Lendl, Czechoslovakia/US	2	3	0	3	8
	= Fred Perry, Great Britain	1	1	3	3	8
	= Ken Rosewall, Australia	4	2	0	2	8
	= Andre Agassi, US	4	1	1	2	8

Up to and including the 2003 events

A – Australian Open; F – French Open; W – Wimbledon; US – US Open

Australia's Roy Emerson had held the record for the most Grand Slam singles titles since 1968, but Pete Sampras equaled his record of 12 wins when he won Wimbledon in 1999 and the following year. When he beat Pat Rafter to retain his title, it was his 13th—and record-breaking—title.

TOP 10 COUNTRIES WITH THE MOST WIMBLEDON SINGLES TITLES

	COUNTRY	SINGLES TITLES WOMEN'S	MEN'S	TOTAL
1	US	47	33	80
2	UK	36	35	71
3	Australia		22	22
4	France	6	7	13
5	Germany	8	4	12
6	Sweden	-	7	7
7	Czechoslovakia/Czech Republic	3	2	5
8	New Zealand	-	4	4
9	Brazil	3	-	3
10	Spain	1	1	2

The first of the United States' 80 Wimbledon singles champions was May Sutton, who beat Britain's Dorothea Douglass 6–3 6–4 to win the ladies' title in 1905. The first American to win the men's title was "Big" Bill Tilden, who beat Gerald Patterson of Australia 2–6, 6–2, 6–3, 6–4 to win the first of his three titles in 1920. Tilden was the first American to win back-to-back singles.

TOP 10 PLAYERS WITH THE MOST APPEARANCES IN THE DAVIS CUP

	PLAYER	COUNTRY	TIES PLAYED*
1	Nicola Pietrangeli	Italy	66
2	Ilie Nastase	Romania	52
3	= Manuel Santana	Spain	46
	= Orlando Sirola	Italy	46
5	Tomas Koch	Brazil	44
6	= Wilhelm Bungert	Germany	43
	= Ramanathan Krishnan	India	43
	= José-Edison Mandarino	Brazil	43
	= Jaidip Mukerjea	India	43
	= Ion Tiriac	Romania	43

Number of ties played for one country

Despite playing in a record 66 Davis Cup ties between 1954 and 1972, "Nicky" Pietrangeli was never on the winning team, losing in two finals (1960 and 1961). However, he was the non-playing captain of the 1976 winning Italian side. Born in Tunis, Pietrangeli won the singles title at the 1960 and 1961 French Open. He also won doubles and mixed doubles titles at the French Open. The most ties played for the United States is 30 by John McEnroe.

TOP 10 WINNERS OF WOMEN'S GRAND SLAM SINGLES TITLES

	PLAYER/COUNTRY	A	F	W	US	TOTAL
1	Margaret Court (née Smith), Australia	11	5	3	5	24
2	Steffi Graf, West Germany/Germany	4	6	7	5	22
3	Helen Wills-Moody, US	0	4	8	7	19
4	= Chris Evert, US	2	7	3	6	18
	= Martina Navratilova, Czechoslovakia/US	3	2	9	4	18
6	Billie Jean King (née Moffitt), US	1	1	6	4	12
7	= Maureen Connolly, US	1	2	3	3	9
	= Monica Seles, Yugoslavia/US	4	3	0	2	9
9	= Suzanne Lenglen, France	0	2	6	0	8
	= Molla Mallory (née Bjurstedt), US	0	0	0	8	8

A – Australian Open; F – French Open; W – Wimbledon; US – US Open

Margaret Court's first Grand Slam singles title was achieved on home soil when she won the 1960 Australian Open. Ten years later she became only the second woman after Maureen Connolly to win all four Grand Slam events in one year. The 1973 US Open was her final Grand Slam singles title.

Golfing Greats

TOP 10 MONEY-WINNING GOLFERS

	GOLFER/COUNTRY*	CAREER WINNINGS# ($)
1	Tiger Woods	41,707,315
2	Vijay Singh, Fiji	28,304,789
3	Davis Love III	28,110,850
4	Phil Mickelson	27,261,706
5	Ernie Els, South Africa	20,381,567
6	Nick Price, Zimbabwe	19,278,428
7	Jim Furyk	19,179,707
8	Scott Hoch	17,456,762
9	David Toms	16,815,009
10	Justin Leonard	16,529,546

* All US unless otherwise stated

\# As of April 14, 2004

TOP 10 MONEY-WINNING GOLFERS ON THE PGA U.S. TOUR, 2003

	GOLFER/COUNTRY*	WINNINGS# ($)
1	Vijay Singh, Fiji	7,573,907
2	Tiger Woods	6,673,413
3	Davis Love III	6,081,896
4	Jim Furyk	5,182,865
5	Mike Weir	4,918,910
6	Kenny Perry	4,400,122
7	Chad Campbell	3,912,064
8	David Toms	3,710,905
9	Ernie Els, South Africa	3,371,237
10	Retief Goosen, South Africa	3,166,373

* All US unless otherwise stated

\# As of January 1, 2004

TOP 10 MONEY-WINNING GOLFERS ON THE PGA EUROPEAN TOUR, 2003

	GOLFER/COUNTRY	WINNINGS* ($)
1	Ernie Els, South Africa	2,975,374
2	Darren Clarke, N. Ireland	2,210,051
3	Padraig Harrington, Ireland	1,555,623
4	Fredrik Jacobsen, Sweden	1,521,303
5	Ian Poulter, England	1,500,855
6	Paul Caey, England	1,360,456
7	Lee Westwood, England	1,330,713
8	Thomas Björn, Denmark	1,327,148
9	Brian Davis, England	1,245,513
10	Phillip Price, Wales	1,234,018

* As of January 1, 2004

TOP 10 WINNERS OF WOMEN'S MAJORS

	GOLFER/COUNTRY*	TITLES#
1	Patty Berg	16
2 =	Louise Suggs	13
=	Mickey Wright	13
4	Babe Zaharias	12
5	Julie Inkster	11
6	Betsy Rawls	8
7	JoAnne Carner	7
8 =	Pat Bradley	6
=	Glenna Collett Vare	6
=	Betsy King	6
=	Patty Sheehan	6
=	Annika Sörenstam, Sweden	6
=	Karrie Webb, Australia	6
=	Kathy Whitworth	6

* All US unless otherwise stated

\# As of April 14, 2004

The present-day Majors are: the US Open, LPGA Championship, Nabisco Championship, British Open, and the amateur championships of both the US and the UK. Also taken into account in this Top 10 are wins in the former Majors: the Western Open (1937–67), Titleholders Championship (1930–72), and the du Maurier Classic (1977–2000).

▶ **First lady**
Louise Suggs turned professional in 1948 and went on to win 50 LPGA events. She was the first woman elected to the LPGA Hall of Fame.

TOP 10 GOLFERS TO WIN THE MOST MAJORS

	GOLFER/COUNTRY*	BRITISH OPEN	US OPEN	US MASTERS	US PGA	TOTAL#
1	Jack Nicklaus	3	4	6	5	18
2	Walter Hagen	4	2	0	5	11
3 =	Ben Hogan	1	4	2	2	9
=	Gary Player, South Africa	3	1	3	2	9
5 =	Tom Watson	5	1	2	0	8
=	Tiger Woods	1	2	3	2	8
7 =	Bobby Jones	3	4	0	0	7
=	Arnold Palmer	2	1	4	0	7
=	Gene Sarazen	1	2	1	3	7
=	Sam Snead	1	0	3	3	7
=	Harry Vardon, Great Britain	6	1	0	0	7

* All US unless otherwise indicated

As of April 14, 2004

The four majors are the British Open, the US Open, the US Masters, and the US PGA. No man has won all four Majors in one year. Ben Hogan, in 1953, won three of the four, but did not compete in the PGA Championship. Bobby Jones achieved a unique Grand Slam in 1930 by winning the British Open and US Open, as well as winning the amateur titles in both countries.

TOP 10 LOWEST FOUR-ROUND TOTALS IN MAJOR CHAMPIONSHIPS

	GOLFER/COUNTRY	VENUE	YEAR	TOTAL
1	David Toms, US	Atlanta, GA*	2001	265
2	Phil Mickelson, US	Atlanta, GA*	2001	266
3 =	Greg Norman, Australia	Royal St. George's, Sandwich#	1993	267
=	Steve Elkington, Australia	Riviera, CA*	1995	267
=	Colin Montgomerie, UK	Riviera, CA*	1995	267
6 =	Tom Watson, US	Turnberry#	1977	268
=	Nick Price, Zimbabwe	Turnberry#	1994	268
=	Steve Lowery, US	Atlanta, GA*	2001	268
9 =	Jack Nicklaus, US	Turnberry#	1977	269
=	Nick Faldo, UK	Royal St. George's, Sandwich#	1993	269
=	Jesper Parnevik, Sweden	Turnberry#	1994	269
=	Nick Price, Zimbabwe	Southern Hills, OK*	1994	269
=	Davis Love III, US	Winged Foot, NY*	1997	269
=	Tiger Woods, US	St. Andrews#	2000	269

* US PGA Championship

British Open Championship

▼ In the swing
Phil Mickelson eventually lost his "best golfer never to win a Major" tag when he won the Masters at Augusta in 2004.

Water Sports

TOP 10 | OLYMPIC CANOEING COUNTRIES

	COUNTRY	GOLD	MEDALS SILVER	BRONZE	TOTAL
1	Hungary	14	25	21	60
2 =	Germany*	22	16	15	53
=	Soviet Union#	30	14	9	53
4	Romania	10	10	14	34
5	East Germany	14	7	9	30
6	Sweden	14	11	4	29
7	France	3	7	16	26
8	Bulgaria	4	5	8	17
9	Canada	3	8	5	16
10 =	Poland	0	5	10	15
=	US	5	4	6	15

* Not including West/East Germany 1968–88

\# Includes Unified Team of 1992; excludes Russia since then

Canoeing has been an official Olympic sport since 1936, although it was first seen as a demonstration sport at the 1924 Paris Olympics.

TOP 10 | OLYMPIC SWIMMING COUNTRIES

	COUNTRY	GOLD	MEDALS* SILVER	BRONZE	TOTAL
1	US	192	138	104	434
2	Australia	45	46	51	142
3	East Germany	38	32	22	92
4	Soviet Union#	18	24	27	69
5	Germany†	12	23	30	65
6	Great Britain	14	22	26	62
7	Hungary	24	20	16	60
8	Japan	15	20	14	49
9	Holland	14	14	16	44
10	Canada	7	13	19	39

* Excluding diving, water polo, and synchronized swimming

\# Includes Unified Team of 1992; excludes Russia since then

† Not including West/East Germany 1968–88

TOP 10 | SWIMMERS WITH THE MOST OLYMPIC GOLD MEDALS

	SWIMMER/COUNTRY	YEARS	GOLD MEDALS
1	Mark Spitz, US	1968–72	9
2 =	Matt Biondi, US	1984–92	8
=	Jenny Thompson, US	1992–2000	8
4 =	Kristin Otto, East Germany	1988	6
=	Amy Van Dyken, US	1996–2000	6
6 =	Charles Daniels, US	1904–08	5
=	Krisztina Egerszegi, Hungary	1988–96	5
=	Don Schollander, US	1964–68	5
=	Johnny Weissmuller, US	1924–28	5
10 =	Tamus Darnyi, Hungary	1988–92	4
=	Kornelia Ender, East Germany	1976	4
=	Dawn Fraser, Australia	1956v64	4
=	Gary Hall Jr., US	1996–2000	4
=	Roland Matthes, East Germany	1968–72	4
=	John Naber, US	1976	4
=	Alexander Popov, EUN*/Russia	1992–1996	4
=	Murray Rose, Australia	1956–60	4
=	Vladimir Salnikov, Soviet Union	1980–88	4
=	Henry Taylor, Great Britain	1906–08	4
=	Dara Torres, US	1984–2000	4

* Unified Team representing the Commonwealth of Independent States (former Soviet republics)

Mark Spitz holds the record for winning the most gold medals at one Games—seven in 1972, which is the most by any competitor in any sport. His overall tally of golds is nine, but it should have been much more. He went into the 1968 Mexico Olympics as the holder of several world records and was expecting to win six gold medals, but came away with just two, and they were in relay events. His gold medals haul at the 1972 Munich Games came in the following events and, remarkably, all were won in world record-breaking times:

EVENT	TIME (MIN:SEC)	EVENT	TIME (MIN:SEC)
100-meter freestyle	0:51.22	4 x 100-meter freestyle relay	3:26.42
200-meter freestyle	1:52.78	4 x 200-meter freestyle relay	7:35.78
100-meter butterfly	0:54.27	4 x 100-meter medley relay	3:48.16
200-meter butterfly	2:00.70		

▼ A team player
All of Jenny Thompson's gold medals came in relay events. She won an individual silver in 1992 and a bronze in 2000, when she tied with Dara Torres (also from the USA) for third place.

TOP 10 MOST OLYMPIC SAILING* MEDALS

	COUNTRY	MEDALS GOLD	SILVER	BRONZE	TOTAL
1	United States	17	21	16	54
2	Great Britain	18	12	8	38
3	Sweden	9	12	10	31
4	Norway	16	11	3	30
5	France	11	7	9	27
6	Denmark	11	8	4	23
7	Germany/ West Germany	5	6	7	18
8	= Australia	5	3	8	16
	= Holland	4	5	7	16
10	New Zealand	6	4	5	15

* *Previously named Olympic yachting*

THE 10 LATEST WINNERS OF THE AMERICA'S CUP

	WINNING BOAT/SKIPPER/COUNTRY	CHALLENGER/COUNTRY	SCORE
2003	**Alinghi,** Russell Coutts, Switzerland	Team New Zealand, New Zealand	5–0
2000	**Black Magic,** Russell Coutts, New Zealand	Prada Luna Rossa, Italy	5–0
1995	**Black Magic,** Russell Coutts, New Zealand	Young America, US	5–0
1992	**America3,** Bill Koch, US	Il Moro di Venezia, Italy	4–1
1988	**Stars and Stripes,** Dennis Conner, US	New Zealand, New Zealand	2–0
1987	**Stars and Stripes,** Dennis Conner, US	Kookaburra III, Australia	4–0
1983	**Australia II,** John Bertrand, Australia	Liberty, US	4–3
1980	**Freedom,** Dennis Conner, US	Australia, Australia	4–1
1977	**Courageous,** Ted Turner, US	Australia, Australia	4–0
1974	**Courageous,** Ted Hood, US	Southern Cross, Australia	4–0

The America's Cup was first contested as the One Hundred Guinea Cup in 1851 and was renamed after the first winner, the 101-foot schooner *America*. The cup was available to challengers thereafter but remained on American soil for 132 years until 1983, when *Australia II* won the trophy.

LATEST WINNERS OF THE WORLD'S STRONGEST MAN CONTEST

YEAR	STRONGMAN	COUNTRY
2003	Mariusz Pudzianowski	Poland
2002	Mariusz Pudzianowski	Poland
2001	Svend Karlsen	Norway
2000	Janne Virtanen	Finland
1999	Jouko Ahola	Finland
1998	Magnus Samuelsson	Sweden
1997	Jouko Ahola	Finland
1996	Magnus Ver Magnusson	Iceland
1995	Magnus Ver Magnusson	Iceland
1994	Magnus Ver Magnusson	Iceland

Mariusz Pudzianowski won his second world title in 2003. He was the joint top-scorer with Svend Karlsen of Norway after the opening round, but in the final, Pudzianowski destroyed all opposition to win by 20 points over Zydrunas Savickas of Lithuania.

LATEST UNDISPUTED WORLD HEAVYWEIGHT BOXING CHAMPIONS

	BOXER/COUNTRY*	YEAR
1	Lennox Lewis, UK	1999
2	Riddick Bowe	1992
3	Evander Holyfield	1990
4	James Buster Douglas	1990
5	Mike Tyson	1987
6	Leon Spinks	1978
7	Muhammad Ali	1974
8	George Foreman	1973
9	Joe Frazier	1970
10	Muhammad Ali	1967

*All US unless otherwise stated

"Undisputed" champions are those who are recognized by the main governing bodies at the time of winning their world title. The current main governing bodies are: the World Boxing Council (WBC), World Boxing Association (WBA), International Boxing Federation (IBF), and World Boxing Organization (WBO).

TOP 10 OLYMPIC JUDO COUNTRIES

	COUNTRY	GOLD	MEDALS SILVER	BRONZE	TOTAL
1	Japan	23	12	13	48
2	France	10	5	17	32
3	South Korea	7	10	13	30
4	USSR*	7	5	15	27
5	Cuba	5	7	8	20
6	Germany/ West Germany	2	5	10	17
7	Great Britain	–	7	9	16
8	Netherlands	4	–	7	11
9	= Brazil	2	3	5	10
	= China	4	1	5	10
	= Italy	2	3	5	10
	US	–	3	5	8

* Includes Unified Team of 1992; excludes Russia since then

Judo made its debut at the 1964 Tokyo Olympics, but for men only, and was not included in the 1968 Mexico City Games. Women's judo was not introduced until the 1992 Barcelona Games. ,

BOX WITH GLOVES

ALTHOUGH ANCIENT GREEK BOXERS used leather hand coverings, bareknuckle fighting was popular for centuries, and serious injuries and even death were common. Gloves known as "mufflers" had been invented in 1743, but were used only for sparring until the Marquess of Queensberry drew up his rules, under which gloves became mandatory. The first world heavyweight contest under the new rules was fought on August 29, 1885 in Cincinnati, Ohio, between bareknuckle champion John L. Sullivan and Dominick McCaffrey.

THE FIRST TO...

LENNOX

FASTEST WINNING TIMES FOR THE HAWAII IRONMAN

	WINNER/COUNTRY	YEAR	TIME (HR:MIN:SEC)
1	Luc Van Lierde, Belgium	1996	8:04:08
2	Mark Allen, US	1993	8:07:45
3	Mark Allen	1992	8:09:08
4	Mark Allen	1989	8:09:16
5	Luc Van Lierde	1999	8:17:17
6	Mark Allen	1991	8:18:32
7	Greg Welch, Australia	1994	8:20:27
8	Mark Allen	1995	8:20:34
9	Peter Reid, Canada	2000	8:21:01
10	Peter Reid	2003	8:22:05

This is perhaps one of the most grueling of all sporting contests, in which competitors engage in a 2.4-mile (3.86-km) swim, followed by a 112-mile (180-km) cycle race, ending with a full marathon (26 miles 385 yards/42.195 km). The first Hawaii Ironman was held at Waikiki Beach in 1978, but since 1981 the event's home has been at Kailua-Kona. Dave Scott and Mark Allen have dominated the race, each winning on a total of six occasions. The fastest woman is Paula Newby-Fraser of Zimbabwe, who has won eight times, in 1992 with a women's record time of 8 hours 55 minutes 28 seconds.

◄ A heavyweight punch
Lennox Lewis first hit the headlines when he won the Olympic Super-Heavyweight title in 1988, representing Canada. In his first pro bout in June 1989, he beat Al Malcolm with a second-round knockout.

LONGEST-REIGNING BOXING WORLD CHAMPIONS*

	BOXER/COUNTRY	WEIGHT	YEARS	REIGN[#] (YRS)	(MTHS)
1	Joe Louis, US	Heavyweight	1937–49	11	7
2	Johnny Kilbane, US	Featherweight	1912–23	11	4
3	Ricardo Lopez, Mexico	Strawweight	1990–2000	9	8
4	Archie Moore, US	Light-heavyweight	1952–62	9	2
5	Bernard Hopkins, US	Middleweight	1995–2004	8	11
6	Felix Trinidad, Puerto Rico	Welterweight	1993–99	8	5
7	Benny Leonard, US	Lightweight	1917–25	7	8
8	Jimmy Wilde, UK	Flyweight	1916–23	7	4
9	Flash Elorde, Philippines	Junior-lightweight	1960–67	7	3
10	Kaosai Galaxy, Thailand	Junior-bantamweight	1984–91	7	1

* Based on longest uninterrupted reign in each weight division
# As of April 14, 2004

Boxing history was made on May 9, 1988, when Kaokar Galaxy won the WBA bantamweight title, while his twin brother Kaosai was the holder of the WBA junior-Bantamweight title at the time—the first time twins had held world titles.

OLYMPIC FREESTYLE WRESTLING COUNTRIES

	COUNTRY	MEDALS GOLD	TOTAL
1	US	44	103
2	USSR*	31	63
3	= Bulgaria	7	33
	= Japan	16	33
	= Turkey	16	33
6	= Iran	5	26
	= Sweden	8	26
8	Finland	8	25
9	South Korea	4	19
10	Great Britain	3	17

* Includes Unified Team of 1992; excludes Russia since then

Horses for Courses

MONEY-WINNING NORTH AMERICAN JOCKEYS

	JOCKEY	WINNINGS* ($)
1	Pat Day	285,701,353
2	Jerry Bailey	264,982,137
3	Chris McCarron	264,700,863
4	Laffit Pincay Jr.	237,507,671
5	Gary Stevens	211,949,124
6	Eddie Delahoussaye	196,114,964
7	Alexis Solis	170,500,372
8	Jose Santos	166,824,842
9	Kent Desormeaux	166,103,162
10	Angel Cordero Jr.	164,561,227

* As at the end of the 2003 season

Source: *National Thoroughbred Racing Association (NTRA) Communications*

MONEY-WINNING DRIVERS

	DRIVER	WINNINGS ($)*
1	John D. Campbell	219,777,637
2	Michel Lachance	155,704,981
3	William A. O'Donnell	94,993,088
4	Catello R. Manzi	93,967,536
5	Jack G. Moiseyev	93,463,006
6	Luc R. Ouellette	87,271,199
7	Herve Filion	86,855,644
8	Doug S. Brown	82,074,668
9	Ronald D. Pierce	79,558,055
10	Stephen P. Condren	79,222,829

* As of January 1, 2004

Source: *US Trotting Association*

MONEY-WINNING HORSES

	HORSE	WINS	WINNINGS ($)*
1	Cigar	19	9,999,815
2	Skip Away	18	9,616,360
3	Fantastic Light	12	8,486,957
4	Silver Charm	12	6,944,369
5	Captain Steve	9	6,828,356
6	Alysheba	11	6,679,242
7	John Henry	39	6,591,869
8	Tiznow	8	6,427,830
9	Singspiel	9	5,952,825
10	Best Pal	18	5,668,245

* As of January 1, 2004

Source: *National Thoroughbred Racing Association (NTRA) Communications*

List-leading horse *Cigar* achieved a total of 19 wins out of 33 starts—two in 1993 and 1994, 10 in 1995, and five in 1996—to gain his all-time North American record money total. Bred and owned by Allen Paulson, he retired as a 6-year-old on October 31, 1996 at the end of a 16-race winning streak, tying a record set 46 years earlier by racing legend *Citation*. In 2002, he was elected to the Racing Hall of Fame.

▼ **Success breeds success**
The leading day in US thoroughbred racing, the Breeders' Cup is an end-of-season gathering of the top horses racing in eight featured races. The first Breeders' Cup was held at Hollywood Park, California in 1984.

TOP 10 JOCKEYS IN THE U.S. TRIPLE CROWN RACES

	JOCKEY	KENTUCKY	PREAKNESS	BELMONT	TOTAL
1	Eddie Arcaro	5	6	6	17
2	Bill Shoemaker	4	2	5	11
3	= Pat Day	1	5	3	9
	= Bill Hartack	5	3	1	9
	= Earle Sande	3	1	5	9
6	= Jimmy McLaughlin	1	1	6	8
	= Gary Stevens	3	2	3	8
8	= Jerry Bailey	2	2	2	6
	= Angel Cordero Jr.	3	2	1	6
	= Chas Kurtsinger	2	2	2	6
	= Ron Turcotte	2	2	2	6

The US Triple Crown consists of the Kentucky Derby, Preakness Stakes (held in Pimlico, Maryland, since 1873), and Belmont Stakes (in Belmont, New York, since 1867). The only jockey to complete the Triple Crown twice is Eddie Arcaro, on *Whirlaway* in 1941 and on *Citation* in 1948.

THE RICHEST RACES

IT'S A FACT

Having been established in 1984, the US Breeders' Cup World Thoroughbred Championship is a relative newcomer to horse racing, but it is the most valuable. Each one of a series of races, culminating with the Breeders' Cup Event Day in November, has a purse of $1 million or more—$4 for the Classic—and a total prize fund of $14 million. On the 20th anniversary of the event in 2003, Julie Krone on *Halfbridled* became the first woman to win a Breeder's Cup race. The same year saw the event's first dead heat, between *High Chaparral* and *Johar*.

TOP 10 JOCKEYS IN THE BREEDERS' CUP

	JOCKEY	YEARS	WINS
1	Jerry Bailey	1991–2003	14
2	Pat Day	1984–2001	12
3	Mike Smith	1992–2002	10
4	Chris McCarron	1985–2001	9
5	Gary Stevens	1990–2000	8
6	= Eddie Delahoussaye	1984–93	7
	= Laffit Pincay Jr.	1985–93	7
	= Jose Santos	1986–2002	7
	= Pat Valenzuela	1986–2003	7
10	Corey Nakatani	1996–99	5

Source: *The Breeders' Cup*

Held at a different venue each year, the Breeders' Cup is an end-of-season gathering, culminating in seven races run over one day, with the season's best thoroughbreds competing in each category. Staged in October or November, there is $10 million prize money with $3 million going to the winner of the day's senior race, the Classic. Churchill Downs is the most-used venue, with five Breeders' Cups since the first in 1984. List leader Jerry Bailey, who was born in Dallas, Texas in 1957, had his first Breeders' Cup success in 1991 when he rode *Black Tie* to victory in the Classic. He has since won the Classic three times more, including in 1995, when his ride was *Cigar*.

TOP 10 OLYMPIC EQUESTRIAN COUNTRIES

	COUNTRY	MEDALS			TOTAL
		GOLD	SILVER	BRONZE	
1	Germany*	22	13	12	47
2	US	9	17	15	41
3	Sweden	17	8	14	39
4	France	11	12	11	34
5	West Germany	11	5	9	25
6	Italy	6	10	7	23
7	Great Britain	5	8	9	22
8	Switzerland	4	10	7	21
9	Netherlands	8	9	2	19
10	USSR#	6	5	4	15

* Not including West Germany or East Germany 1968–88

Includes United Team of 1992; excludes Russia since then

Germany has an outstanding record in all three Olympic equestrian disciplines: Three-Day Eventing, Dressage, and Show Jumping. In Hans-Günter Winkler and Alwin Schockemöhle, they have produced not only Olympic gold medalists but two of the greatest show jumpers of all time. In Dressage, Nicole Uphoff, Dr. Reiner Klimke (winner of eight medals), and Liselott Linsenhoff have been great German Olympic champions.

On Two Wheels

TOP 10 FASTEST WINNING SPEEDS OF THE DAYTONA 200

	RIDER/COUNTRY*	BIKE	YEAR	AVERAGE SPEED MPH	KM/H
1	**Mat Mladin,** Australia	Suzuki	2004	113.94	183.33
2	**Miguel Duhamel,** Canada	Honda	2003	113.83	183.20
3	**Mat Mladin,** Australia	Suzuki	2000	113.63	182.87
4	**Miguel Duhamel,** Canada	Honda	1999	113.47	182.61
5	**Kenny Roberts**	Yamaha	1984	113.14	182.08
6	**Scott Russell**	Yamaha	1998	111.78	179.89
7	**Kenny Roberts**	Yamaha	1983	110.93	178.52
8	**Scott Russell**	Kawasaki	1992	110.67	178.11
9	**Graeme Crosby,** New Zealand	Yamaha	1982	109.10	175.58
10	**Steve Baker**	Yamaha	1977	108.85	175.18

* From the US unless otherwise stated

Source: *American Motorcyclist Association*

The Daytona 200, which was first held in 1937, forms a round in the AMA (American Motorcyclist Association) Grand National Dirt Track series. It is raced over 57 laps of the 3.56-mile (5.73-km) Daytona International Speedway. In addition to those riders named above, the only other non-US winners have been: Billy Matthews (Canada) 1941, 1950; Jarno Saarinen (Finland) 1973; Giacomo Agostini (Italy) 1974; and Patrick Pons (France) 1980.

TOP 10 RIDERS WITH THE MOST MOTORCYCLE WORLD CHAMPIONSHIP WINS

	RIDER/COUNTRY	CLASSES (CC)	WINS
1	**Giacomo Agostini,** Italy	350, 500	15
2	**Angel Nieto,** Spain	50, 125	13
3	= **Mike Hailwood,** Great Britain	250, 350, 500	9
	= **Carlo Ubbiali,** Italy	125, 250	9
5	= **Phil Read,** Great Britain	125, 250, 500	7
	= **John Surtees,** Great Britain	350, 500	7
7	= **Geoff Duke,** Great Britain	350, 500	6
	= **Jim Redman,** Rhodesia	250, 350	6
9	= **Mick Doohan,** Australia	500	5
	= **Anton Mang,** Germany	250, 350	5
	= **Valentino Rossi,** Italy	125, 250, GP	5

The motorcycle World Championship had its inaugural season in 1949, when it was won by British rider Leslie Graham on an AJS. British riders dominated the event during the 1950s and 1960s, when Italian motorcycles won every Championship, a role consistently overtaken since the mid-1970s by Japanese models. In the 1980s, the title was won on six occasions by two US riders, Freddie Spencer and Eddie Lawson, while Australia's Mick Doohan rode Hondas to win the five races from 1994 to 1998. The 500cc class is now known as the GP class.

▶ **Valentino's victories**
The most successful rider of the modern era, Valentino Rossi won his first world title (125cc) in 1997, aged 18, and has since won the 250cc and MXGP (formerly 500cc) titles.

TOP 10 MANUFACTURERS WITH THE MOST MOTORCYCLE GRAND PRIX WINS

	MANUFACTURER	FIRST WIN	WINS*
1	Honda	1961	570
2	Yamaha	1963	401
3	MV Agusta	1952	275
4	Aprilia	1987	167
5	Suzuki	1962	153
6	Kawasaki	1969	87
7	Derbi	1970	81
8	Kreidler	1962	65
9	Garelli	1982	51
10	Gilera	1949	47

* As at end of 2003 season

If Superbike wins were also included, then Ducati would be No. 4 on the list with a total of 222 Grand Prix and Superbike wins. Japanese manufacturer Yamaha was originally a musical instrument maker, and did not make its first motorcycle—a single-cylinder 125cc two-stroke—until 1954. Their first Grand Prix win was at the 1963 Belgian GP at Spa.

TOP 10 MOTOCROSS COUNTRIES

	COUNTRY	WORLD CHAMPIONSHIP WINS* 125CC	250CC	500CC	TOTAL
1	**Belgium**	10	14	23	47
2	**Sweden**	0	6	8	14
3	**France**	3	5	0	8
4	= **Great Britain**	0	1	6	7
	= **Italy**	5	1	1	7
	= **US**	3	3	1	7
7	**Finland**	1	1	3	5
8	= **Netherlands**	3	1	0	4
	= **Russia**	0	4	0	4
	= **South Africa**	2	2	0	4

* As at end of 2003 season

World Moto Cross Championships have been held since 1947, when the five-man Moto Cross des Nations team championship was launched. The first individual championship was in 1957, when the 500cc class was launched; since then, 250cc (1962), 125cc (1975), and sidecar (1980) have been introduced. From the 2003 season the 250cc was replaced with a new 650 class and the 500cc became the MXGP.

RACE MOTORCYCLES

THE FIRST TO…

RACES ON THREE-WHEELED VEHICLES had taken place in France the previous year, but on November 29, 1897, Charles Jarrott organized the first-ever race for two-wheelers at Sheen House, Richmond, England, as part of an event to celebrate the first anniversary of the "Emancipation Act" that permitted motorists to drive on public roads without being preceded by a man waving a red flag. Jarrott himself won the race on a Fournier motorcycle on a 1-mile oval track in 2 minutes 8 seconds, an average speed of 28 mph (45 km/h).

TOP 10 | RIDERS WITH THE MOST GRAND PRIX RACE WINS

	RIDER/COUNTRY	YEARS	RACE WINS*
1	**Giacomo Agostini,** Italy	1965–76	122
2	**Angel Nieto,** Spain	1969–85	90
3	**Mike Hailwood,** Great Britain	1959–67	76
4	**Valentino Rossi,** Italy	1996–2003	59
5	**Rolf Biland,** Switzerland	1975–90	56
6	**Mick Doohan,** Australia	1990–98	54
7	**Phil Read,** Great Britain	1961–75	52
8	**Jim Redman,** Southern Rhodesia	1961–66	45
9	**Anton Mang,** West Germany	1976–88	42
10	**Max Biaggi,** Italy	1992–2003	41

* As at end of 2003 season

All except Rolf Biland were solo machine riders. Great Britain's Barry Sheene won 23 races during his career and despite not making the Top 10, is the only man to win Grands Prix at 750 and 500cc.

TOP 10 | FASTEST AVERAGE WINNING SPEEDS IN THE TOUR DE FRANCE

	WINNER/COUNTRY	YEAR	AVERAGE SPEED (MPH)	(KM/H)
1	**Lance Armstrong,** US	2003	25.448	40.956
2	**Lance Armstrong**	1999	25.026	40.276
3	**Lance Armstrong**	2001	24.898	40.070
4	**Marco Pantani,** Italy	1998	24.844	39.983
5	**Lance Armstrong**	2002	24.804	39.919
6	**Lance Armstrong**	2000	24.587	39.570
7	**Miguel Indurain,** Spain	1992	24.546	39.504
8	**Jan Ullrich,** Germany	1997	24.380	39.237
9	**Bjarne Rijs,** Denmark	1996	24.374	39.227
10	**Miguel Indurain,** Spain	1995	24.353	39.193

The first Tour de France, held in 1903, was won by Maurice Garin of France at an average speed of 15.956 mph (25.679 km/h). The race was over 1,509 miles (2,428 km) and consisted of just six stages.

Auto Racing

TOP 10 | DRIVERS WITH THE MOST FORMULA ONE WORLD TITLES

	DRIVER/COUNTRY	WORLD TITLES YEARS	RACES WON	WORLD TITLES
1	Michael Schumacher (Germany)	1994–2003	70	6
2	Juan Manuel Fangio (Argentina)	1951–57	24	5
3	Alain Prost (France)	1985–93	51	4
4	= Jack Brabbham (Australia)	1959–60	14	3
	= Niki Lauda (Austria)	1975–84	25	3
	= Nelson Piquet (Brazil)	1981–87	23	3
	= Ayrton Senna (Brazil)	1988–91	41	3
	= Jackie Stewart (UK)	1969–71	27	3
9	= Alberto Ascari (Italy)	1952–53	13	2
	= Jim Clark (UK)	1963–65	25	2
	= Emerson Fittipaldi (Brazil)	1972–74	14	2
	= Graham Hill (UK)	1962–68	14	2

TOP 10 | FORMULA ONE DRIVERS WITH THE MOST GRAND PRIX WINS

	DRIVER/COUNTRY	CAREER	WINS*
1	Michael Schumacher (Germany)	1991–2003	70
2	Alain Prost (France)	1980–93	51
3	Ayrton Senna (Brazil)	1984–94	41
4	Nigel Mansell (UK)	1980–95	31
5	Jackie Stewart (UK)	1965–73	27
6	= Jim Clark (UK)	1960–68	25
	= Niki Lauda (Austria)	1971–85	25
8	Juan Manuel Fangio (Argentina)	1950–58	24
9	Nelson Piquet (Brazil)	1978–91	23
10	Damon Hill (UK)	1992–99	22

As of end of 2003 season

Michael Schumacher's first Formula One drive was for Jordan in the 1991 Belgian Grand Prix. His first win was in Belgium too, a year later with Benetton. It was also in Belgium, in a Ferrari, that he beat Alain Prost's record of 51 wins in 2001.

TOP 10 | FASTEST WINNING SPEEDS OF THE INDIANAPOLIS 500

	DRIVER/COUNTRY	CAR	YEAR	SPEED (MPH)	(KM/H)
1	Arie Luyendyk (Netherlands)	Lola-Chevrolet	1990	185.981	299.307
2	Rick Mears (US)	Chevrolet-Lumina	1991	176.457	283.980
3	Bobby Rahal (US)	March-Cosworth	1986	170.722	274.750
4	Juan Pablo Montoya (Colombia)	G Force–Aurora	2000	167.607	269.730
5	Emerson Fittipaldi (Brazil)	Penske-Chevrolet	1989	167.581	269.695
6	Helio Castroneves (Brazil)	Dallara-Chevrolet	2002	166.499	267.954
7	Rick Mears (US)	March-Cosworth	1984	163.612	263.308
8	Mark Donohue (US)	McLaren-Offenhauser	1972	162.962	262.619
9	Al Unser (US)	March-Cosworth	1987	162.175	260.995
10	Tom Sneva (US)	March-Cosworth	1983	162.117	260.902

American drivers start on the run and race round oval circuits, and so consistently higher average lap speeds are achieved than in Formula One. Car racing in the United States on purpose-built circuits dates back to 1909, when Indianapolis Speedway opened. CART (Championship Auto Racing Teams, Inc.) was formed in 1978, and in 1996 the Indy Racing League was established in response to disputes over regulations governing the Indy 500. Indy 500 races have counted for CART points in 1979, 1980, and 1983–95.

TOP 10 | CART DRIVERS WITH THE MOST RACE WINS

	DRIVER	CAREER	WINS
1	A.J. Foyt Jr.	1960–81	67
2	Mario Andretti	1965–93	52
3	Michael Andretti	1986–2001	41
4	Al Unser	1965–87	39
5	Bobby Unser	1966–81	35
6	Al Unser Jr.	1984–95	31
7	Rick Mears	1978–91	29
8	Johnny Rutherford	1965–86	27
9	Rodger Ward	1953–66	26
10	Gordon Johncock	1965–83	25

Source: *Championship Auto Racing Teams*

Two generations of the Unser family dominate the CART scene: Al and Bobby, both of whom figure in this list, are brothers, while Al's son, Al Jr., also makes a showing here and as all-time money winner. In 1998, after pursuing other auto sports, Bobby's son Robby also entered Indy car racing. Michael Andretti, who started his CART career in 1983, is the only current driver in this list. Youngest-ever champion and 2000 Indianapolis 500 winner Juan Montoya also seemed destined for inclusion, but has since transferred to Formula One.

TOP 10 | NASCAR DRIVERS WITH THE MOST RACE WINS

	DRIVER*	CAREER	WINS#
1	Richard Petty	1958–92	200
2	David Pearson	1960–86	105
3 =	Bobby Allison	1975–88	84
=	Darrell Waltrip	1975–92	84
5	Cale Yarborough	1957–88	83
6	Dale Earnhardt	1979–2000	76
7	Jeff Gordon	1994–2003	64
8 =	Lee Petty	1949–64	54
=	Rusty Wallace	1986–2001	54
10 =	Ned Jarrett	1953–66	50
=	Junior Johnson	1953–66	50

* All from the US

\# As of March 15, 2004

◄ Six up for Schumacher
When Michael Schumacher won his fourth consecutive world title in 2003, it was his record-breaking sixth title—one more than the great Juan-Manuel Fangio of Argentina.

TOP 10 | MONEY-WINNERS IN THE WINSTON CUP, 2003

	DRIVER*	WINNINGS ($)
1	Jimmie Johnson	5,517,850
2	Tony Stewart	5,227,503
3	Jeff Gordon	5,107,762
4	Kurt Busch	5,020,485
5	Kevin Harvick	4,994,249
6	Dale Earnhardt Jr.	4,923,497
7	Ryan Newman	4,827,377
8	Bobby Labonte	4,745,258
9	Michael Waltrip	4,463,845
10	Bill Elliott	4,321,185

* All from the US

The Winston Cup changed its name to the Nextel Cup for the 2004 season.

Sports Media & Miscellany

TOP 10 LARGEST SPORTS STADIUMS

	STADIUM*	LOCATION	CURRENT CAPACITY#
1	Strahov Stadium	Prague, Czech Republic	250,000
2	Beaver Stadium	Pennsylvania, US	197,282
3	May Day Stadium	Pyŏngyang, North Korea	150,000
4	Yuba Bharati Krirangan	Kolkata, India	120,000
5	Estadio Azteca	Mexico City	114,465
6	Michigan Stadium	Ann Arbor, US	107,501
7	Neyland Stadium	Tennessee, US	104,079
8	Jornalista Mário Filho	Rio de Janeiro, Brazil	103,045
9	Ohio Stadium	Columbus, US	101,568
10 =	Azadi Stadium	Tehran, Iran	100,000
=	Kim Il-Sung Stadium	Pyŏngyang, North Korea	100,000
=	National Stadium Bukit Jal	Kuala Lumpur, Malaysia	100,000
=	Utama Senayan	Jakarta, Indonesia	100,000

* *Excluding speedway and motor racing circuits, and horse race tracks*

\# *For safety reasons, the capacity of many stadiums has been significantly reduced in recent years*

▶ Stadium of dreams
Brazil's Estádio Jornalista Mário Filho (formerly Maracaña Stadium) hosted a record crowd of over 200,000 for the 1950 soccer World Cup final.

TOP 10 SPORT FILMS

	FILM	YEAR	SPORT
1	Rocky IV	1985	Boxing
2	Space Jam	1996	Basketball
3	The Waterboy	1998	Football
4	Days of Thunder	1990	Stock car racing
5	Cool Runnings	1993	Bobsleighing
6	A League of Their Own	1992	Baseball
7	Remember the Titans	2000	Football
8	Rocky III	1982	Boxing
9	Rocky V	1990	Boxing
10	Rocky	1976	Boxing

TOP 10 COLLEGE SPORTS IN THE U.S.*

	SPORT	PARTICIPANTS (2001–02)		
		WOMEN	MEN	TOTAL
1	Football	–	58,090	58,090
2	Outdoor track	18,433	20,382	38,815
3	Soccer	19,467	18,559	38,026
4	Indoor track	16,334	17,483	33,817
5	Basketball	14,524	15,883	30,407
6	Baseball	–	26,343	26,343
7	Cross-country	12,008	10,840	22,848
8	Swimming/diving	10,279	7,307	17,586
9	Tennis	8,378	7,441	15,819
10	Softball	15,514	–	15,514

* *Based on participation in National Collegiate Athletic Association (NCAA) sports*

Source: *NCAA*

In the period surveyed by the NCAA (2001–02), a total of 155,513 women and 212,140 men (367,653 overall) participated in college sports. These figures include "emerging," or non-championship, sports such as squash and women's ice hockey.

TOP 10 SPORTING EVENTS WITH THE LARGEST TV AUDIENCES IN THE U.S.

	EVENT	DATE	RATING
1	Super Bowl XVI	Jan. 24, 1982	49.1
2	Super Bowl XVII	Jan. 30, 1983	48.6
3	XVII Winter Olympics	Feb. 23, 1994	48.5
4	Super Bowl XX	Jan. 26, 1986	48.3
5	Super Bowl XII	Jan. 15, 1978	47.2
6	Super Bowl XIII	Jan. 21, 1979	47.1
7	= Super Bowl XVIII	Jan. 22, 1984	46.4
	= Super Bowl XIX	Jan. 20, 1985	46.4
9	Super Bowl XIV	Jan. 20, 1980	46.3
10	Super Bowl XXX	Jan. 28, 1996	46.0

Source: *Nielsen Media Research*

Those listed here, along with ten further Super Bowls, back to VI in 1972, are among the Top 50 networked programs of all time in the US. In this extended list, the XVII Lillehammer, Norway, Winter Olympics makes two showings, on February 23 and February 25, 1994 (the latter achieving a rating of 44.2). Despite the national enthusiasm (fuelled by media interest in figure skater Nancy Kerrigan) the US finished a disappointing 5th in the overall medals table.

THE 10 LATEST WINNERS OF THE SPORTS ILLUSTRATED SPORTSMAN/SPORTSWOMAN OF THE YEAR AWARD

YEAR	WINNER(S)	SPORT
2003	Tim Duncan and David Robinson	Basketball
2002	Lance Armstrong	Cycling
2001	Curt Schilling and Randy Johnson	Baseball
2000	Tiger Woods	Golf
1999	US Women's World Cup Squad	Soccer
1998	Mark McGwire and Sammy Sosa	Baseball
1997	Dean Smith	Basketball coach
1996	Tiger Woods	Golf
1995	Cal Ripken Jr.	Baseball
1994	Johan Olav Koss and Bonnie Blair	Ice skating

First presented in 1954, when it was won by British athlete Roger Bannister, this annual award honors the sportsman or sportswoman who, in that year, in the opinion of the editors of *Sports Illustrated*, most "symbolizes in character and performance the ideals of sportsmanship." An analysis of the sports most honored (including ties) reveals that baseball heads the list with 12 winners, followed by basketball, football, and track with eight each, golf seven, and boxing, hockey, and tennis three wins each. Cycling and speed skating have each won twice, and auto racing, gymnastics, and horse racing have just one win each. Tiger Woods made history in 2000, when he became the first to be honored with this award twice.

TOP 10 THEMES OF SPORT FILMS

	SPORT	FILMS
1	Boxing	204
2	Horse racing	139
3	Football	123
4	= Baseball	85
	= Auto racing	85
6	Basketball	41
7	Athletics	33
8	Golf	24
9	Wrestling	20
10	Motorcycle racing	15

A survey of feature films with competitive sports as their principal themes produced in Hollywood from 1910 to 2000 identified a total of 891 films, with boxing accounting for 22.9 percent of the total.

Leisure Pursuits

TOP 10 ITEMS OF RECREATION SPENDING IN THE U.S.

	CATEGORY	TOTAL EXPENDITURE (2001) ($)
1	Video and audio goods, including musical instruments	66,700,000,000
2	Commercial participant amusements*	63,000,000,000
3	Nondurable toys and sports supplies	60,400,000,000
4	Wheel goods, sports and photographic equipment, boats and pleasure aircraft	50,400,000,000
5	Magazines, newspapers, and sheet music	32,500,000,000
6	Computers, peripherals, and software	31,400,000,000
7	Books and maps	30,800,000,000
8	Spectator amusements#	25,000,000,000
9	Flowers, seeds, and potted plants	16,700,000,000
10	Clubs and fraternal organizations	15,900,000,000

* Category includes amusement parks, billiards, bowling, dancing, casino gambling, golf, riding, shooting, sightseeing, skating, swimming, etc.

Category includes motion picture theaters, theaters, opera, nonprofit entertainments, spectator sports

Source: US Bureau of Economic Analysis, Survey of Current Business (April 2003)

TOP 10 PARTICIPATION ACTIVITIES IN THE U.S.

	ACTIVITY	PERCENTAGE CHANGE SINCE 2001	PARTICIPANTS (2002)*
1	Exercise walking	5.0	82,200,000
2	Camping (vacation/overnight)	13.8	55,400,000
3	Swimming	−0.2	54,700,000
4	Exercising with equipment	14.4	50,200,000
5	Fishing	−0.5	44,200,000
6	Bowling	4.8	43,900,000
7	Bicycle riding	6.1	41,400,000
8	Billiards/pool	7.8	35,300,000
9	Hiking	17.0	30,500,000
10	Aerobic exercising	10.4	29,000,000

* Seven years of age and older, who participated more than once during the year

Source: National Sporting Goods Association

▼ In the swim
Regarded as one of the most effective activities in promoting all-around fitness, swimming consistently ranks prominently in US surveys of the most popular activities.

COUNTRIES SPENDING THE MOST ON CONSOLE AND COMPUTER GAMES

	COUNTRY	SALES (2003) PER CAPITA	TOTAL ($)
1	US	37.4	10,866,000,000
2	Japan	33.5	4,267,250,000
3	UK	57.1	3,432,020,000
4	Germany	31.4	2,584,430,000
5	France	22.7	1,365,870,000
6	South Korea	26.3	1,269,850,000
7	Spain	23.9	960,880,000
8	Canada	22.2	713,650,000
9	Australia	34.8	687,550,000
10	Italy	11.3	653,660,000

Source: *Euromonitor*

INTERACTIVE ENTERTAINMENT SOFTWARE TITLES IN THE U.S.*

	GAME	PUBLISHER
1	Madden NFL 2004	Electronic Arts
2	Pokémon Ruby	Nintendo of America
3	Pokémon Sapphire	Nintendo of America
4	Need for Speed—Underground	Electronic Arts
5	Zelda—The Wind Waker	Nintendo of America
6	Grand Theft Auto—Vice City	Rockstar Games
7	Mario Kart—Double Dash!!	Nintendo of America
8	Tony Hawk's Underground	Activision
9	Enter the Matrix	Atari
10	Medal of Honor: Rising Sun	Electronic Arts

* Ranked by units sold in 2003

Source: *NPD TRSTS Toys Tracking Service*

MONOPOLY®MAN

MONOPOLY WAS DEVISED in Philadelphia in 1934 by Charles Darrow and patented on February 7, 1936. Darrow's streets were those of the New Jersey resort of Atlantic City—it is said because he dreamed of going there but, being unemployed during the Depression, could not afford the fare. Building on earlier property games, Monopoly, with its subtle balance of skill and luck, enjoyed rapidly growing sales. It was the bestselling board game in the US in 1935—and national versions were introduced worldwide. Darrow became a millionaire, devoting the rest of his life to travel and the cultivation of rare orchids.

IT'S A FACT

INCREASINGLY POPULAR PARTICIPATION ACTIVITIES IN THE U.S.

	ACTIVITY	PARTICIPANTS* (2002)	% CHANGE (2001-2)
1	Paintball games	6,900,000	24.4
2	Water skiing	6,900,000	18.4
3	Weight-lifing	28,100,000	17.4
4	Hiking	30,500,000	17.0
5	Exercising with equipment	50,200,000	14.4
6	Camping	55,400,000	13.8
7	Off–road mountain biking	7,800,000	12.6
8	Canoeing	7,600,000	11.5
9	Motor/power boating	26,600,000	11.4
10	Muzzleloading	3,600,000	11.0

* Seven years of age and older, participating more than once during the year

Source: *National Sporting Goods Association*

MOST POPULAR TYPES OF TOYS

	TYPE OF TOY	MARKET SHARE PERCENTAGE (2002)
1	Video games	27.7
2	Infant/preschool toys	12.0
3	Activity toys	11.4
4	Dolls	10.5
5	Other toys	9.8
6	Games/puzzles	9.6
7	Toy vehicles	8.6
8	Plush toys	4.2
9	Action figures	3.4
10	Ride-on toys	2.8

Source: *Eurotoys/The NPD Group Worldwide*

This list is based on a survey of toy consumption in the European Union, and can be taken as a reliable guide to the most popular types of toys in the developed world. Taken as a whole, a worldwide survey conducted in 2000 valued video game sales at $14.752 billion compared with a cumulative total for "traditional" toy sales of $54.742 billion.

TOY-BUYING COUNTRIES

	COUNTRY	SALES (2003) PER CAPITA	TOTAL($)
1	US	120.9	35,115,300,000
2	Japan	69.3	8,811,570,000
3	UK	112.5	6,758,620,000
4	Germany	63.3	5,213,810,000
5	France	70.8	4,259,480,000
6	Italy	46.8	2,714,230,000
7	China	1.9	2,384,270,000
8	Spain	48.7	1,957,960,000
9	Canada	54.1	1,743,950,000
10	Mexico	16.4	1,704,260,000

Source: *Euromonitor*

As the 21st century dawned, world toy industry sales were reported to have totaled $69.493 billion. This is equivalent to $11 for every person on the planet. Taking age into account, this figure represents an average of $32 for every child, and reflects an average expenditure of $328 in North America and $100 in Europe, but just $2 in Africa.

Further Information

THE UNIVERSE & THE EARTH

Encyclopedia Astronautica
www.astronautix.com/
Spaceflight news and reference

NASA
www.nasa.gov/
The principal website for the US space program

National Climactic Data Center
www.ncdc.noaa.gov/
Weather data, with an emphasis on the US

The Nine Planets
www.nineplanets.org/
A multimedia tour of the solar system

Peaklist
www.highalpex.com/Peaklist/peaklist.html
Lists of the world's tallest mountains

Space.com
www.space.com/
Reports on events in space exploration

United Nations Atlas of the Oceans
www.oceansatlas.org/index.jsp
An information resource on oceanographic issues

Volcano Live
www.volcanolive.com/
World volcano news and information

WebElements
www.webelements.com/
A guide to all the elements in the periodic table

World Space Flight
www.worldspaceflight.com/
Astronaut biographies and other data on human spaceflight

LIFE ON EARTH

Animal Diversity Web
http://animaldiversity.ummz.umich.edu/site/index.html
Animal data from the University of Michigan

Convention on International Trade in Endangered Species of Wild Fauna and Flora (CITES)
www.cites.org/
Lists endangered species of flora and fauna

The Electronic Zoo
http://netvet.wustl.edu/e-zoo.htm
Links to sites devoted to animals

FishBase
www.fishbase.org/home.htm
Global information on fish

Food and Agriculture Organization of the United Nations
www.fao.org/
FAO statistics on agriculture, fisheries, and forestry

Ichthyology at the Florida Museum of Natural History
www.flmnh.ufl.edu/fish/default.htm
Fish and shark data

International Union for the Conservation of Nature
http://iucn.org/
The leading nature conservation site

PetForum
http://petsforum.com/
Information about cats, dogs, and other pets

United Nations Environment Program
www.unep.ch/
Includes the UN's System-Wide Earthwatch and its Global Resource Information Database

University of Florida Book of Insect Records
http://ufbir.ifas.ufl.edu/
Insect champions in many categories

THE HUMAN WORLD

Amnesty International
www.amnesty.org/
The foremost human rights organization

Death Penalty Information Center
www.deathpenaltyinfo.org/
US-specific data on the death penalty

Federal Bureau of Prisons
www.bop.gov/
Public information on all aspects of the US prison system

Inter-Parliamentary Union
www.ipu.org/
Including data on women in parliaments

Interpol
www.interpol.int/
Worldwide crime statistics

National Center for Health Statistics
www.cdc.gov/nchs/
Information and links on health for US citizens

Popular Baby Names
www.ssa.gov/OACT/babynames/index.html
Most common names from the Social Security Administration

Rulers
http://rulers.org/
Database of the world's rulers and political leaders

United Nations
www.un.org/
The launch site for the UN's many bodies

World Health Organization
www.who.int/en/
World health information and advice

TOWN & COUNTRY

CIA World Factbook
www.odci.gov/cia/publications/factbook/
Detailed country-by-country data and rankings

Population Reference Bureau
www.prb.org/
US and international population issues

Skyscrapers.com
www.skyscrapers.com/re/en/
Searchable guide to the world's tallest buildings

United Nations City Data
www.photius.com/wfb1999/rankings/cities.html
City information for capitals and those with 100,000-plus populations

United Nations Population Division
www.un.org/esa/population/unpop.htm
Worldwide data on population issues

US Census Bureau
www.census.gov/
US and international population statistics

US Geological Survey
www.usgs.gov/
US national and regional geographical information

World Bank
www.worldbank.org/
Development and other statistics from around the world

World's Largest Bridges
www.struct.kth.se/research/bridges/Bridges.htm
The world's longest bridges listed by type

The World's Longest Tunnel Page
http://home.no.net/lotsberg/
A database of the longest rail, road, and canal tunnels

CULTURE & LEARNING

American Library Association
www.ala.org/
US library information and book awards

The Art Newspaper
www.theartnewspaper.com/
News and views on the art world

Dorling Kindersley
http://us.dk.com/
The website of the publishers of this book

Global Reach
http://global-reach.biz/globstats/index.php3
Facts and figures on online languages

The Library of Congress
www.loc.gov/
An online gateway to one of the world's greatest collections of words and pictures

National Center for Education Statistics
www.nces.ed.gov/
The home of federal education data

Nobel Prizes
www.nobel.se/
A searchable database of all Nobel Prize winners

Publishers Weekly
http://publishersweekly.reviewsnews.com/
The trade journal of US publishers

The Pulitzer Prize
www.pulitzer.org/
A guide to the prestigious US literary prize

United Nations Educational, Scientific and Cultural Organization (UNESCO)
www.unesco.org
Comparative international statistics on all aspects of education and culture

MUSIC & MUSICIANS

All Music Guide
www.allmusic.com/
A comprehensive guide to all genres of music

American Society of Composers, Authors and Publishers
www.ascap.com/
ASCAP songwriter and other awards

Billboard
www.billboard.com/
US music news and charts data

ClassicalUSA.com
http://classicalusa.com/
An online guide to classical music in the US

Grammy Awards
www.naras.org/
The official site for the famous US music awards

Mobile Beat **Magazine**
www.mobilebeat.com/
DJ song requests

MTV
www.mtv.com/
The online site for the TV music channel

Recording Industry Association of America
www.riaa.com/
Searchable data on gold and platinum disk award winners

Rock and Roll Hall of Fame
www.rockhall.com/
The museum of the history of rock

Rolling Stone **magazine**
www.rollingstone.com/
Features on popular music since 1967

STAGE & SCREEN

Academy of Motion Picture Arts and Sciences
www.oscars.org/
The official "Oscars" website

Emmy Awards
www.emmyonline.org/
Emmy TV awards from the National Television Academy site

Hollywood.com
www.hollywood.com/
Movie site with details on all the new releases

Golden Globe Awards
http://hfpa.org/html/
Hollywood Foreign Press Association's Golden Globes site

Internet Movie Database
www.imdb.com/
The best of the publicly accessible film websites; IMDbPro is available to subscribers

Internet Theatre Database
www.theatredb.com/
A Broadway-focused searchable stage site

Tony Awards
www.tonyawards.com/en_US/index.html
Official website of the American Theatre Wing's Tonys

Variety
www.variety.com/
Extensive entertainment information (extra features available to subscribers

Yahoo! Movies
http://movies.yahoo.com/
Charts, plus features, trailers, and links to the latest film releases

COMMERCIAL WORLD

Bureau of Labor Statistics
www.bis.gov/
US Department of Labor figures

Forbes **magazine**
www.forbes.com/
"Rich lists" and other business information

Fortune **magazine**
www.fortune.com/fortune/
Information on US and global companies

International Currency Converter
www.oanda.com/convert/
Daily exchange rates for 164 currencies, 1990–the present

International Labor Organization
www.ilo.org/
Facts and figures on the world's workers

International Telecommunications Union
www.itu.int/
Worldwide telecommunications statistics

Organisation for Economic Co-operation and Development
www.oecd.org/
World economic and social statistics

United Nations Development Programme
www.undp.org/
Country GDPs and other development data

Universal Postal Union
www.upu.int/
Information and statistics on the world's postal systems

The World Bank
www.worldbank.org/
World development and labor statistics

TRANSPORTATION & TOURISM

Aerofiles
www.aerofiles.com/
Information on a century of American aviation

AirDisaster.com
www.airdisaster.com/
Reports on aviation disasters

International Registry of Sunken Ships
http://users.accesscomm.ca/shipwreck/
A database of the world's wrecked and lost ships

International Road Federation
www.irfnet.org/
Facts and figures on the world's roads

Light Rail Transit Association
www.lrta.org/world/worldind.html
A guide to the world's light railroads and tram systems

National Park Service
www.nps.gov/
The official site of the US national park system

Railway Gazette International
www.railwaygazette.com/
The world's railroad business in depth

Tourism Offices Worldwide Directory
www.towd.com/
Contact details for tourism offices for US states and for countries around the world

Travel Industry Association of America
www.tia.org/
Statistics on travel to and within the US

World Tourism Organisation
www.world-tourism.org/
The world's principal travel and tourism organization

SPORTS & LEISURE

International Association of Athletics Foundations
www.iaaf.org/
The statistics and rankings of the world's top athletes

International Olympic Committee
www.olympic.org/
The official website of the Olympic movement, with a searchable database

Major League Baseball
www.mlb.com/
The official website of Major League Baseball

National Football League
www.nfl.com/
The official website of the NFL

National Hockey League
www.nhl.com/
The official website of the NHL.

Professional Golfers' Association (PGA) Tour
www.pgatour.com/

Sports Illustrated
http://sportsillustrated.cnn.com/
Sport's Illustrated's comprehensive coverage of all major sports

Sportscribe
www.sportscribe.com/cal.html
For details of forthcoming sporting events

Yahoo Sport
http://dir.yahoo.com/Recreation/Sports/
The directory of sports entries at Yahoo covering all minor as well as major sports

Index

Index

Index

Acknowledgments

Special US research: Dafydd Rees
Sports consultant: Ian Morrison

Alexander Ash; Caroline Ash; Nicholas Ash; David B. Barrett; Emma Beatty; Peter Bond; Richard Braddish; Thomas Brinkoff; Richard Chapman; Pete Compton; Dr. Chris Corrigan; Kaylee Coxall; Luke Crampton; David Crystal; Sidney S. Culbert; Philip Eden; Bonnie Fantasia; Christopher Forbes; Cullen Geiselman; Russell E. Gough; Monica Grady; Stan Greenberg; Brad Hackley; Duncan Hislop; Andreas Hörstemeier; Murray Hughes; Richard Hurley; Alan Jeffreys; Todd M. Johnson; Larry Kilman; Robert Lamb; Jo LaVerde; Dr. Benjamin Lucas; Roberto Mamrud; Chris Mead; Dr. William T. O'Hara; Roberto Ortiz de Zarate; Jim Osborne; Matthew Paton; Tony Pattison; Gillian Payne; Christiaan Rees; Linda Rees; Adrian Room; Robert Senior; Karel Stockkermans; Victor L. Streib; Mitchell Symons; Thomas Tranter; Robert Van Pelt; Lucy T. Verma

Absolut Elephant; Academy of Motion Picture Arts and Sciences (AMPAS) – Oscar ; statuette is the registered trademark and copyrighted ; property of the Academy of Motion Picture Arts and Sciences; *Ad Age Global*; Advertising Age; Air Transport Intelligence; *Airline Business*; Allergy Clinic, Guy's Hospital, London; American Association of Port Authorities; American Forests; American Kennel Club; American Library Association (ALA); American Motorcyclist Association (AMA); American Pet Classics; American Religious Identity Survey (ARIS); American Society of Composers, Authors, and Publishers (ASCAP); American Wind Energy Association; Amnesty International; Amtrak; *Amusement Business*; Arbitron; The Ark Trust; *The Art Newspaper*; Art Sales Index; Atlantic Oceanographic and Meteorological Laboratory/National ; Oceanic and Atmospheric Administration; *Billboard*; *BP Statistical Review of World Energy 2003*; Brand Keys; The Breeders' Cup; British Library; British Museum; British Phonographic Industry (BPI); *Business Week*; Cat Fanciers' Association; Center for Disease Control (CDC); Central Intelligence Agency (CIA); Centre for Environmental Initiatives, UK; Championship Auto Racing Teams (CART); Channel Swimming Association; Christie's;

Comité Interprofessionel du Vin de Champagne (CIVC); Commission for Distilled Spirits; Crain Communications Inc; CRC Handbook of Chemistry and Physics; Cremation Society; Death Penalty Information Center; De Beers; Department of Justice; Duncan's American Radio; *The Economist*; *Editor & Publisher Yearbook*; EM-DAT, CRED, University of Louvain, Belgium; Energy Information Administration (EIA); Euromonitor; European Wind Energy Association; Eurotoys; *FBI Uniform Crime Reports*; Federal Bureau of Prisons; Fédération Internationale de Football Association (FIFA); Food and Agriculture Organization of the United Nations (FAO); *Forbes*; *Fortune*; *France Football*; Gallup Organization; Gemstone Publishing Inc; Global Reach; Gold Fields Mineral Services Ltd; Hitwise.com; Hockey Database; Hollywood Foreign Press Association (Golden Globe Awards); Home Accident Surveillance System (HASS); Home Office, UK; Imperial War Museum, UK; Institute for Family Enterprise, Bryant College; Interbrand; International Atomic Energy Agency; International Bulletin of Missionary Research; International Coffee Organisation ; International Olympic Committee (IOC); International Shark Attack File/American Elasmobranch; Society/Florida Museum of Natural History; International Ski Federation (FIS); International Tea Committee Ltd; International Telecommunication Union (ITU); International Trade Administration (ITA); International Union for the Conservation of Nature (IUCN); Interpol; J.D. Power and Associates; Joint United Nations Programme on HIV/AIDS (UNAIDS); League of American Theaters and Producers; Library of Congress; Lloyds Register-Fairplay Ltd; Lycos; Magazine Publishers of America; Major League Baseball; Mars; McDonald's; Metropolitan Museum of Art; Metropolitan Opera; *Modern Bride*; MRIB; M Street; Music Information Database; NAACP Legal Defense Fund; National Academy of Recording Arts and Sciences (NARAS) (Grammy ; Awards); National Aeronautics and Space Administration (NASA); National Association of Broadcasters (NAB); National Basketball Association (NBA); National Center for Education Statistics (NCES); National Center for Health Statistics (NCHS); National Center for Injury Prevention and Control; National Climatic Data Center

(NCDC); National Collegiate Athletic Association (NCAA); National Football League (NFL); National Fraud Information Center, National Consumers League; National Hockey League (NHL); National Park Service; National Phobics Society; National Public Radio (NPR); National Sporting Goods Association; National Thoroughbred Racing Association (NTRA); New York Drama Critics Circle; Niagara Falls Museum; Nielsen; Nielsen Media Research; Nielsen/NetRatings; Nielsen Soundscan; The NPD Group Worldwide; Office of Travel and Tourism Industries; Organisation for Economic Co-operation and Development (OECD); Organisation Internationale des Constructeurs d'Automobiles ; (OICA); *The Overstreet Comic Book Price Guide*; Peabody Awards; Professional Golfers' Association (PGA); Public Library Association ; *Publishers Weekly*; *Railway Gazette International*; Recording Industry Association of America (RIAA); Relate National Marriage Guidance; RSSSF; *Screen Digest*; SearchEngineWatch.com; Sotheby's; Sport Business Group at Deloitte; *Statistical Abstract of the United States*; Statistics Canada; *Stores*; Swiss Re; Tour de France; Tourism Industries, International Trade Administration; UK Home Office; United Nations (UN); United Nations Children's Fund (UNICEF); United Nations Economic Commission for Europe; United Nations Educational, Scientific and Cultural ; Organization (UNESCO); United Nations Population Division (UNPD); Universal Postal Union; US Bureau of Economic Analysis; US Bureau of Labor Statistics; US Census Bureau ; US Consumer Product Safety Commission; US Department of Agriculture; US Department of Commerce; US Department of Education; US Department of Justice; US Department of Labor; US Geological Survey; US Office of Management and Budget; US Patent and Trademark Office; US Postal Service; US Trotting Association; *Variety*; *Video Business*; VSDA VidTrac; Ward's AutoInfoBank; WebElements; World Association of Newspapers (WAN); World Bank; *World Christian Database*; World Christian Encyclopedia; World Gold Council; World Health Organization (WHO); *World of Learning*; World Tourism Organization (WTO); World's Strongest Man Contest; Zenith Optimedia

Acknowledgments

Publisher's acknowledgments
Dorling Kindersley would like to thank the following for their contributions: Editorial Sharon Lucas; Design Marianne Markham; Picture Library Hayley Smith, Richard Dabb, Claire Bowers.

Index
Patricia Coward

Packager's acknowledgments
The Bridgewater Book Company would like to thank Alison Bolus, Julia Greenwood, Nicky Gyopari, Tom Kitch, Philippa Smith and Hazel Songhurst for editorial assistance, and Richard Constable, Chris Morris and Roger Wheeler for their design work.

Picture Credits

The publisher would like to thank the following for their kind permission to reproduce their photographs:
(Abbreviations key: t = top, b = bottom, r = right, l = left, c = centre)

1: Science Photo Library/David Nunuk (t); Science Photo Library/Alexis Rosenfeld (b); **2-3**: Corbis/Mark A Johnson (t); Alamy/Redferns Music Picture Library (b); **4**: Empics (bc); **5**: Rex/ Everett (tl); Corbis/Galen Rowell (b); **6-7**: Corbis/Bill Ross; **7**: Corbis/Jerry Cooke (bc); **8-9**: Science Photo Library/Alexis Rosenfeld (t); **11**: Robert Gendler/NASA (b); **13**: NASA (b); **15**: Galaxy Picture Library/NASA (l); **16**: Corbis/Ralph A Clevenger (b); **17**: Corbis 1996/Original image courtesy of NASA/Corbis (tr); **18-19**: Corbis/Galen Rowell (b); **21**: Naturepl.com/Hanne & Jens Eriksen (b); **22**: Corbis/James Marshall; **24**: Corbis/Paul Hardy (b); **26-27**: Rex/Sipa (bc); **28-29**: Naturepl.com/Anup Shah (t); **32**: Alamy/Stefan Binkert (bl); **33**: Naturepl.com/Jeff Rotman & Avi Klapfer (t); **42-43**: Corbis/Macduff Everton (b); **44-45**: Corbis/Bill Ross; **46-47**: Corbis/Erik Svensson (t); **48**: Getty Images/Sally Ullman (tr); **50**: Rex/Sipa (b); **52**: Corbis SABA/ Louise Gubb (r); **54-55**: Getty Images/Mark Douet (c); **56**: Corbis/Lynsey Addario (b); **58-59**: Corbis/Larry Williams (b); **61**: *Louis XIV (1638-1715)*, (oil on canvas) by Hyacinthe Rigaud (1659-1743): Bridgeman Art Library, London/New York, Museu do Caramulo, Portugal/ www.bridgeman.co.uk (l); **64-65**: Getty Images/Keystone (bc); **70**: Getty Images/Paul Buck/AFP (b); **72-73**: Getty Images/Hulton Archive (b); **74-75**: Corbis Sygma/China Features (t); **78-79**: Mark A Johnson/Corbis (t); **82-83**: Corbis/Brian A Vikander (b); **86-87**: Corbis SABA/David Butow (b); **88**: Panos Pictures (r); **92-93**: Axiom/Jim Homes (bc); **94-95**: Alamy/Oxford Picture Library (t); **96**: Getty Images/China Tourism Press (b);

99: Corbis/ Lindsay Hebberd (b); **100**: TopFoto (t); **102-103**: Corbis/Barry Lewis (b); **105**: Alamy/Leslie Garland Picture Library (r); **106**: *The Massacre of the Innocents* (1609-1611) by Sir Peter Paul Rubens (1577-1640): PA Photos, Sotheby's, London (b); **108-109**: Anatomical studies by Leonardo da Vinci (1452-1519): Bridgeman Art Library, London/New York, Galleria dell' Accademia, Venice, Italy/www.bridgeman.co.uk (c); **111**: *Noir et Blanche* (1926) by Man Ray (1890-1976): Corbis/Christie's Images/© Man Ray Trust/ADAGP, Paris and DACS, London 2004 (b); **112-113**: Alamy/Redferns Music Picture Library (t); **115**: Rex/Terry O' Neill (b); **116**: Rex/Crollalanza (b); **118**: Rex/Kern Mackay (r); **120-121**: Rex/Hoffman (b); **127**: PA Photos (l); **128**: Retna/Kelly A Swift (r); **130-131**: Redferns/Hayley Madden (c); **132-133**: Getty Images/Phil Hunt (t); **135**: ArenaPAL/Michael Le Poer Trench/ Cameron Mackintosh Ltd. (b); **136-137**: The Kobal Collection (b); **138-139**: TopFoto/New Line Productions (c); **141**: Corbis/ Underwood & Underwood; **142**: Getty Images/Variety (b); **145**: Getty Images/Variety (t); **147**: Rex/Lucas Films, Everett (b); **148-149**: TopFoto/Warner Bros (t); **150**: The Kobal Collection/ Columbia/Darren Michaels (l); **152-153**: Rex/Everett (b); **154**: The Kobal Collection/Paramount 1978 (b); **156**: Getty Images/Don Smetzer (b); **159**: Corbis/Jose Luis Pelaez, Inc. (t); **161**: The Kobal Collection/Touchstone (b); **162-163**: Alamy/Mark Lewis (t); **164-165**: Getty Images/Yellow Dog Productions (b); **167**: Rex/Cameron; **168-169**: Corbis/Alan Schein Photography (b); **170**: Corbis SABA/Keith Dannemiller (b); **175**: The Australian Museum (tr); **176-177**: Alamy/Chuck Pefley (t); **183**: Alamy (r); **184**: Corbis/ Owaki-Kulla (b); **186**: Rex/Nils Jorgsen (b); **188**: Alamy/Leslie Garland Picture Library (b); **190-191**: Alamy/Joe Sohm (b); **192**: Robert Harding Picture Library (t); **194-195**: Science Photo Library/David Nunuk (t); **197**: Alamy/Chuck Pefley; **198**: PA Photos (t); **200**: Corbis (b); **202-203**: Rex/Jian Chen (b); **204-205**: akg-images; **208-209**: Empics (t); **210**: Getty Images (r); **213**: Corbis/Reuters; **215**: Empics (l); **216**: Empics; **219**: Empics (r); **224**: Empics (r); **228**: Empics (l); **230**: Corbis/Bettmann (bl); **231**: Alamy/Popperfoto (r); **233**: Empics (t); **234-235**: Empics (bc); **236**: Corbis/Jerry Cooke (b); **239**: Empics (t); **241**: Empics (l); **242-243**: Empics (bc); **256**: Galaxy Picture Library/NASA (bc).

All other images © Dorling Kindersley. Additional Photography by Geoff Dann, Frank Greenaway, Dave King, Steve Shott, Max Alexander, Matthew Ward, Demetrio Carrasco, Alan Keohane, Peter Wilson, Karl Shone, Harry Taylor, Ian O'Leary, Andrew Whittuck, Nick Wright, Reuben Paris.

For further information see:
www.dkimages.com